The Last Option

'If I told you all I knew,' said
the Prophet, 'you would flog me
without pity.'

Old Arab proverb

David Kimche

THE LAST OPTION

After Nasser, Arafat & Saddam Hussein

The Quest for Peace in the Middle East

CHARLES SCRIBNER'S SONS
New York

MAXWELL MACMILLAN INTERNATIONAL
New York Oxford Singapore Sydney

Charles Scribner's Sons
Macmillan Publishing Company
866 Third Avenue
New York, NY 10022

Macmillan Publishing Company is part of the Maxwell Communication
Group of Companies.

Library of Congress Cataloging-in-Publication Data

Kimche, David.
    The last option: after Nasser, Arafat, & Saddam Hussein: the quest
for peace in the Middle East/David Kimche.
        p.   cm.
    Includes index.
    ISBN 0-684-19422-8
    1. Jewish-Arab relations—1967–1973.   2. Jewish-Arab relations—
1973–   3. Israel-Arab conflicts.   4. Munazzamat al-Taḥrīr al-
Filasṭīnīyah.   I. Title.
DS119.7.K49256   1992   91–37775   CIP
956.04—dc20

Contents

CONTENTS

Maps

Introduction

WHEN I MOVED INTO the Israeli Foreign Ministry as its Director-General in July 1980, seven years after the outbreak of the Yom Kippur War, Menachem Begin was head of the Government and Yitzhak Shamir was his Foreign Minister. In Cairo, President Sadat ruled supreme and was seen to be the power in the land by most of the world, even by those Arab leaders who had denounced the peace he had concluded with Israel in 1979. In Washington, Ronald Reagan was about to be elected by an unprecedented voters' landslide bringing new and unfamiliar – and often, in Israeli eyes, suspect – names into the administration. The Carter team which had been central to the negotiations at Camp David and the conclusion of the Peace Treaty with Egypt had been sunk, virtually without a trace. As far as we were concerned, the new Reagan team was one large question-mark at a time when we could ill afford uncertainty in Washington.

The Palestine Liberation Organization (PLO) was riding high. It had received a great boost a month earlier, in June, when the European Community virtually endorsed its position in a resolution passed at its Venice summit conference; the PLO had, moreover, effectively established itself (without protest from any quarter) as a state within a state in the Lebanon by means of a mixture of blackmail and terror. It held to ransom the legitimate government in Beirut; it controlled large areas of the capital and of southern Lebanon; it dominated the Shia communities and harassed them and the Christian Maronites; and it launched frequent attacks across the border into northern Israel. The PLO had become a constant worry to the Arab world and a serious challenge to the peaceful life of northern Israel and to the Government of Israel.

A decade had passed since the death of President Nasser and a new Middle Eastern landscape was emerging. The Arab world had become – so it seemed at the time – the top-ranking financial power in the world: the rich industrial countries of the western world, hungry for OPEC oil, were at the Arabs' mercy and sought economic favours at almost any political price. Oil revenue for the Arab Gulf countries and Libya amounted to some $200 billion that year, and there seemed to be no limit to Arab oil power

I

as the price of oil zoomed to dizzy heights. OPEC leaders were talking of the new norm of at least $40 for a barrel of crude oil, which cost them barely 50 cents a barrel to produce.

But that autumn there was also a darker side to Arab power, which was frequently overlooked or overshadowed by the glamour of oil. For at the same time, the Arab world was in a state of disarray and disorder such as it had rarely experienced. Iraq had just invaded Iran with her long-prepared main thrust aimed at the rich oilfields of Khuzistan. The Iraqi rulers anticipated that the Khomeini regime in Tehran would be overthrown within days, but it was Arab domestic relations that suffered most from the immediate political aftermath of the Iraqi attack on Iran. The Arab summit called by the Arab League to meet in Amman on 27 November 1980 was boycotted by Syria, Libya, Algeria, the Yemen, Lebanon and the PLO; Egypt, the most important Arab country, was still a pariah in the Arab world and was not invited. The Conference of Islamic Foreign Ministers, which had met in Fez during September, had decided to bring about the expulsion of Israel from the United Nations and had agreed on a plan for a Holy War against Israel so as to secure the future of Jerusalem for Islam.

In this kaleidoscope of ever-changing Arab alliances and estrangements, the one overriding consideration for me at this initial public induction into Israeli foreign policy – after having served twenty-seven years as a civil servant far from the public eye, albeit in one of the most central and sensitive offices under the direct authority of the Prime Minister – was our relationship with the volatile Arab people who were our neighbours. We wanted to consolidate the peace with Egypt, barely a year old, and use it as a springboard to reach out to other Arab countries in the hope that they would follow in the wake of Sadat. We were impatient to erase the scars left by thirty years of enmity and war. Looking back on those first weeks in the Foreign Ministry in 1980, I realize now that, despite all our understanding of the Middle East, we were still insufficiently knowledgeable of all the forces at work in the making and remaking of the Middle Eastern scene.

This became increasingly evident to me with every visit to Egypt (and to Lebanon). Egypt had been our enemy, and we had fought war after war with her. She had been the prime target of our intelligence services, and we thought that we knew everything there was to know about her. Yet every encounter with her – and there were very many – revealed new aspects of Egyptian society and politics. Intelligence reports usually draw clear, concise, black-and-white pictures. They do not easily capture the bewildering profusion of elements that together, often in Byzantine fashion, make up the real Egypt.

Similarly, the history of events in the Middle East over the past twenty years were much more complex than we had been taught. It was the realization of this which was impressed on me most forcefully during the more than six years I served as Director-General of Israel's Foreign

Ministry. It provided the stimulus for my decision to write this book, after my retirement from the Foreign Ministry in 1987.

David Kimche
March 1991

PART 1
Israel and Egypt

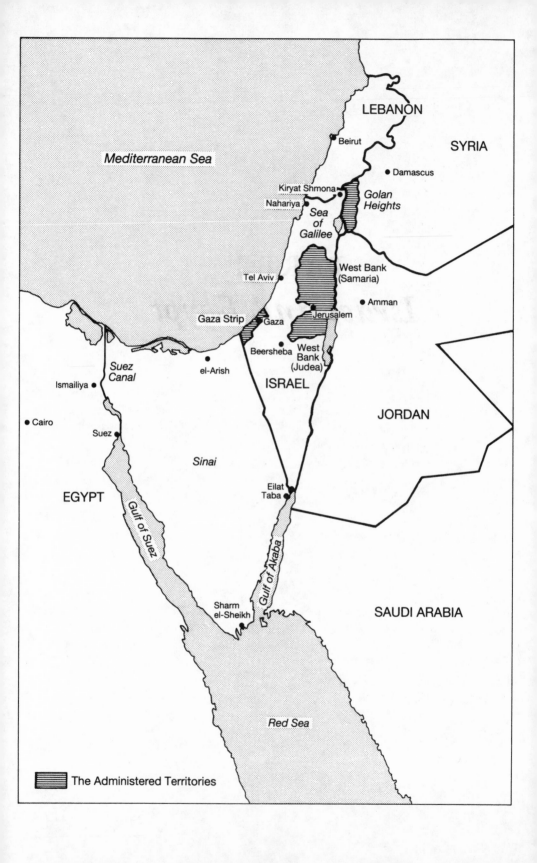

LEBANON

SYRIA

Mediterranean Sea

• Beirut

• Damascus

Kiryat Shmona
Nahariya •

*Golan
Heights*

*Sea
of
Galilee*

West Bank
(Samaria)

Tel Aviv •

• Amman

Gaza Strip
• Gaza

• Jerusalem

Beersheba •

West
Bank
(Judea)

*Suez
Canal*

• el-Arish

ISRAEL

Ismailiya •

JORDAN

• Cairo

Suez •

Sinai

Eilat
Taba •

EGYPT

Gulf of Suez

Gulf of Akaba

SAUDI ARABIA

Sharm
el-Sheikh •

Red Sea

The Administered Territories

1

Prelude: Brezhnev's War

1967–73

IT HAS TAKEN the best part of twenty years to understand fully what has been happening in our region during these two decades; to see the events of 1967 and 1973, in particular, in their actual context; and to strip away the layers upon layers of myth, disinformation and deception that have come to be accepted as authentic history, which left us with a corpus of conventional 'truths' that have covered up the essential realities of these years with set-piece conclusions about the Arab-Israeli wars of 1967, 1973 and 1982 and of the events which caused them.

Something of this sort had been suspected, but the evidence, the proof that would cast convincing doubt on the principal witnesses who have become the source for most of the accepted history of this period, was lacking. However, new evidence has become available which has made it possible to reassess the familiar versions which have been presented by Sadat and Hassanein Heikal, by the Israelis, and by American, Arab and Soviet writers and politicians.

The result was startling. The need for this revision was all the more necessary since it became evident that the mistake we all made was almost as serious as the misreading by Israeli intelligence of Sadat's intention on the eve of the Yom Kippur War in 1973, or of Nasser's misinterpretation of Israeli plans in 1967. What we all missed at the time was the extent to which Nasser in 1967 and Sadat in 1973 (and both during the intervening years), and the Israelis for good measure, had been manipulated by the Soviet leader, Leonid Brezhnev.

This is, I know, a disconcerting claim which will be documented as we move along Brezhnev's Six Year War against Israel from 1967 until 16 October 1973. On that day, he had the stature to recognize the defeat of his Egyptian proxy and of his policy since 1967, and to abandon military for political measures against Israel. With his military advisers, he also demonstrated his political acumen when he decided at that time to hand over responsibility for Sadat's Egypt to the United States without the American leaders being fully aware of what he was doing. In Brezhnev's opinion, Egypt was no longer an asset in the Middle East power-play; she had become a military and financial liability with which he would gladly burden the Americans. It was, on the face of it, a shrewd move; but, like all of us, Brezhnev failed to understand the convoluted thinking of Anwar el-Sadat.

It will thus be seen that what we need now is not another history of our times in the Middle East drawn from all the familiar sources, but rather a reassessment of the turning-points that mattered during these twenty years. We need to reconsider much more closely the personality and actions of Sadat, an extraordinary man by all accounts, whether you admire or detest him; for he was that rare creature, the individual who could shape history, even if it was not the history which he had himself depicted. We also need to look closely again at the role played by the PLO in Sadat's decision to go it alone: it was to become one of the seminal events in modern Arab history and in shaping the future of the Palestinian question.

But, when all this has been said, what we found in our reassessment is that the central figure during these years until 1973 was not Sadat, not President Assad of Syria, and not Henry Kissinger, but Brezhnev. He had manipulated Sadat and Assad, and had been a major influence on the unfolding crises from 1967 to the war of 1973. His decisions – and Soviet supplies – had controlled the build-up and timing for the Yom Kippur War, as has been shown in considerable detail in the notes taken by the then Egyptian Foreign Minister, Mahmoud Riad, in the diary of the then Egyptian Chief of the General Staff, General Saad ash-Shazli, by the archival researches of Commodore Mohrez Mahmoud el-Hussini, head of Egypt's Department of Naval History, and in conversations with Russian historians and former officials. According to the plans inspired by Moscow and made in Cairo and Damascus, Yom Kippur – the Day of Atonement, 1973 – should have been and could have been a day of unmitigated disaster for Israel. For Prime Minister Golda Meir, supported by Israel's political and military leaders, had refused to heed the information brought to them by Mossad, our foreign intelligence service, of Egyptian and Syrian preparations for war and of their intention to launch a war against Israel.

It must be said that in retrospect it seems incredible that they remained unconvinced by Mossad's repeated warnings that war was inevitable considering the manifold and impeccable sources of Mossad's very precise information. However, in the fateful summer of 1973, Israel's Government and military preferred to listen to the Israel Defence Force's expert intelligence 'evaluators', who, under General Eli Zeira, Chief of Military Intelligence, had reviewed Mossad's warnings and concluded reassuringly that, given all the circumstances and according to their own criteria, the probability of war in 1973 was minimal because the Egyptians knew that they had no chance of winning such a war.

Mossad's reports did not fit into the preconceived 'concept' that Egypt would not start a war she knew from the outset she could not win. Israel's military intelligence did not accept the possibility that Egypt might begin a war in order to gain political movement. The reports were therefore ignored. As a result, Sadat and Assad, backed by Brezhnev, almost succeeded – but not quite. Their failure, however, opened the way for Kissinger's intervention, which was to transform the aftermath of the war in a manner that would lead, despite many obstacles, to Sadat's peace with Israel.

This was the major turning-point in the Middle East of our time. But there were also others: the Palestinians, the fall of the Shah, the Gulf War and Israel's war in Lebanon. Central to all was the impact on Israel and on her neighbours of Brezhnev's aggressive Middle East policy and the Six Year War he waged against Israel. Brezhnev, despite the maladies and the senility which overtook him in the last years of his rule, was during this period the most powerful man in the Soviet Union. We should not minimize his importance because he has been discredited in the Gorbachev years largely for internal political reasons, for in the six years from the Six Day War to the Yom Kippur War he was the most powerful single factor opposed to Israel.

For Egypt's President Nasser, the Six Day War had become a national disaster which had to be overcome; for Brezhnev, it was a personal humiliation which had to be avenged. The Middle East lived in the shadow of these twin emotions for over twenty years until Sadat and Gorbachev, each in his own way, overcame the past for the sake of a new future.

We now have evidence showing to what extent Brezhnev had influenced and, in effect, provoked the war of 1967 – and how it had gone horribly wrong.* At the height of the crisis, Brezhnev was sure that his Arab allies were on the brink of a great political, if not a military, victory: Egypt and Syria were geared for action against Israel; so was King Hussein of Jordan. As if to flaunt his unconcern that nothing untoward could happen, Brezhnev, together with his Prime Minister, Alexei Kosygin, and his powerful Defence Minister, Marshal Andrei Grechko, demonstratively left Moscow on 31 May 1967 for the distant Soviet north on a four-day tour of inspection of the Fleet in the Arctic Sea, far from the troubled Mediterranean.

Barely a week after Brezhnev and his companions – the three most forceful men in the Soviet Union – had returned to Moscow, his expectations and his allies were in shambles. Israel, which had been the target of an orchestrated Soviet propaganda offensive, had never been more popular among the Soviet people than on the morrow of her victory over the Soviet Union's Arab allies – Egypt, Syria and Jordan – and on the day when the Soviet Union broke off diplomatic relations with her. Brezhnev, in his first public speech after the war to graduating military cadets, could not hide his state of shock: he denounced the Israelis as 'Nazis' in the pay of American and British imperialists.

Yet it was in the Soviet Union that admiration for Israel's military prowess and pleasure at Brezhnev's discomfiture were most pronounced. There were current jokes about the poor showing of the Arabs that were

* An excellent account of Soviet involvement in the Six Day War can be found in Joseph Govrin's *Six Day War in the Mirror of Soviet–Israel Relations April–June 1967*, written for the Soviet and East European Research Centre of the Hebrew University, Jerusalem, 1985.

targeted more at the Soviet leaders, especially Brezhnev, than at the failed Egyptians and Syrians.

The poet Semyon Lipkin, a translator of Islamic classics, published a poem in the monthly magazine *Moskva* which reflected this mood:

> I am told that overseas in Asia
> There is a people by the name of 'I' ...
> The breadth and joy and sadness
> Of all our human race
> Are condensed and powerfully united
> In this small tribe of 'I'.

Respect for Israel had never been greater among the people of the world than in the aftermath of the Six Day War, when, according to the always so well-informed diplomats and media correspondents, she was said to be most isolated.

But the official mood was very different. Brezhnev had set his stamp on the new Soviet policy towards Israel, a policy of total confrontation. It found instant expression in a speech by Prime Minister Kosygin to the special emergency session of the UN General Assembly on 19 June 1967, barely a week after the end of the war. This called for urgent steps to be taken to 'eliminate the consequence of Israel's aggression'. It was a Brezhnev phrase that could mean many things and was to become the flagship of Israel's unrelenting Arab and international opponents.

When the UN debated the possibility of an Israeli withdrawal to her pre-war positions in return for an end to the state of war, the Soviet Central Committee addressed an urgent warning to President Nasser in which it stressed that

such a move on the part of the UN should not involve a request for any political concessions from the Arab countries to Israel ... It should not be linked to an obligation on the part of the Arab countries to recognize or negotiate with Israel. The discussions should deal only with the ending of the state of war, and with nothing more and nothing less.

The Soviet message was clear and to the point. The Six Day War must not be allowed to lessen in any way the degree of hostility existing between the Arab world and Israel. There must be no negotiations and no recognition.

This theme was confirmed and expanded by the fourth Arab summit, which met in Khartoum in September 1967 under Nasser's chairmanship. It reiterated Kosygin's call for Israel's withdrawal from *all* territories occupied in 1967. In the words of the Arab summit conference decision:

This will be done within the framework of the main principles to which the Arab states adhere: no peace with Israel, no recognition of Israel, no negotiations with it, and the restoration of the rights of the Palestinian people in their country.

The Soviet leaders – political and military – and particularly Brezhnev considered this declaration by the Khartoum summit of Arab leaders as no more than a self-indulgent catechism, a declaration of faith which would not restore one centimetre of lost Arab territory or Soviet influence. Brezhnev, Kosygin and Grechko decided, therefore, after some considerable initial differences between the ruling civilian and military politicians, to present Nasser with the wherewithal for a realistic policy aimed at regaining the lost Arab territories.

It was a far-reaching, almost adventurist decision, advocated by both Brezhnev and Grechko. Neither man was reputed to be long on idealistic and disinterested policies conducted simply for the love of Egypt and out of admiration for Nasser's charisma: their primary concern was to advance the Soviet interest in the Mediterranean. Brezhnev lost no time in adjusting Soviet policy to the new conditions in Egypt. Like the professional gambler on a losing streak, he increased the Soviet stake and, unashamedly, displayed the Soviet hand.

On 18 June 1967, barely a week after Egypt's defeat, a Soviet delegation composed of admirals of the Soviet navy – according to the Egyptian Admiral Fahmy – arrived in Alexandria and presented their agenda to Nasser. They explained that 'in order to be able to defend Egypt effectively', the Soviet Union would need certain facilities. The Soviet admirals had a ready-made schedule, which they handed to the Egyptians. The Soviet Union would require permanent storage for fuel and 'spare parts' in Alexandria and Port Said. Soviet ships would need regular and unhindered access to Egyptian ports: an eight-day visit every month was considered an essential requirement. Repair facilities were to be available at all times for refitting or maintaining Soviet 'units'. There was to be a regular air shuttle between Egypt and the USSR. Soviet naval support ships would be stationed permanently in Alexandria. In future, Soviet ships would be required to give only twenty-four hours' notice before entering Egyptian ports.

Egypt would facilitate the establishment of an advance-warning system and forward reconnaissance, as required by the Soviet Union. Basic to this was to be a system to maintain effective surveillance of the US Sixth Fleet in the Mediterranean. The Soviet admirals were particularly concerned that Egypt should appreciate the vital importance of reliable warning systems on her western border with Libya and on her eastern front with Israel. These systems would be linked to Soviet maritime aircraft on reconnaissance over the Mediterranean. The whole of this warning system, including the aircraft involved, would function under absolute Soviet command.

Finally – and pointedly – the Soviet delegation stressed that the number of Soviet instructors and technicians already in Egypt would be greatly increased. This was a precondition for the supply of sophisticated new military equipment. Before the 1967 war, the Soviet admirals noted, there had been about a thousand Soviet instructors and technicians in Egypt, whose sole function was to give advice when asked. In future, there would be new arrangements. The status of the Soviet personnel would be different and they would have greater authority and responsibilities. The Soviet advisers would be attached to the Egyptian armed forces at all levels down to brigade level.

According to Admiral Fahmy, one of the principal Egyptians involved in the negotiations, Nasser accepted Brezhnev's conditions: the Soviet advisers would be authorized to impose their recommendations and would have overriding authority when dealing with their Egyptian colleagues.

Brezhnev wasted no time in implementing the new arrangement; both he and Nasser were beset by an overriding sense of urgency, an almost unreasoning expectation of what Israel might do next. Three days after the Soviet admirals came the Soviet generals: ninety-one senior officers with Soviet President Podgorny and Chief of Staff Marshal Zakharov at their head to emphasize their status. It was no accident that the admirals came first to obtain Nasser's agreement in principle, for in Soviet eyes it was the Mediterranean and the domination of the US Sixth Fleet that were of prime concern.

Egypt's plight offered an unforeseen opportunity for the establishment of a powerful Soviet naval presence in the Mediterranean with a suitable land-based back-up centred on Egypt. Speed was of the essence – and secrecy. The Soviet presence had to be implemented before the Americans – or, for that matter, the Egyptians – became fully aware of the extent of the Soviet military colonization of Egypt. The Podgorny–Zakharov mission arrived on 21 June. Zakharov and his team of senior officers assessed the state of Egypt's officer corps and of her military needs. After ten days, on 1 July, Zakharov returned to Moscow with twenty-four of his generals; the other sixty-seven senior officers remained in Egypt to supervise the reorganization of Egypt's armed forces.

While the Soviet military delegation was in Egypt, Nasser departed for Moscow to meet Brezhnev. The Soviet leader questioned Nasser at length on Egypt's intentions: was he proposing to settle the crisis with Israel by peace or war? Nasser replied that there would be no peaceful settlement until Egypt had the power to impose her terms of settlement on Israel.

On 10 July, less than a month after the cease-fire and Israel's occupation of the Sinai Peninsula, the West Bank, the Golan Heights and East Jerusalem, fourteen ships of the Soviet Mediterranean Fleet anchored in Egyptian waters, eight at Port Said and six at Alexandria. Their purpose was described by their commander, Rear Admiral Igor Molotov. These ships, he said in Alexandria, 'are ready to co-operate with the Egyptian armed forces in repelling any aggression'. An Egyptian naval historian with access to the contemporary documentation later described this Soviet statement as undoubtedly marking 'the dawn of Soviet coercive diplomacy in the Third World'. It was evidence of the degree of nervousness in Moscow and in Cairo that the Soviet precautions were put into effect without waiting for the conclusion of a formal agreement granting the Soviet Union extraordinary privileges in Egypt. This was not signed by Nasser until March 1968. On its anniversary, eight years later, President Sadat described its terms as so sweeping that they ensured 'Soviet dominance affecting Egypt's independence and sovereignty'.

Egyptian naval historians have emphasized that the Soviet leaders' main concern was to ensure the Soviet presence in the Mediterranean as a counter to the US Sixth Fleet, and that to this end Egypt's Mediterranean ports were turned into advanced Soviet bases flying the Egyptian flag. However, this satisfied only one strand of Soviet policy: Grechko's preoccupation with superpower parity in the Mediterranean. It left unassuaged Brezhnev's all-pervading urge to wrest from the Israelis the territories they had occupied in June 1967, in order to restore Egypt's pre-eminence in the Arab world and, with it, Soviet influence and his own reputation, which had suffered grievously as a result of the Egyptian and Syrian defeats.

It was left to Brezhnev to co-ordinate the Mediterranean policy of the Soviet admirals with the Middle Eastern policy of the army, which wanted strategic bases and Egyptian intransigence towards Israel. According to Soviet historians with whom I was able to discuss this Brezhnev period, the army increasingly took charge of Soviet foreign policy in the Middle East after 1967. Defence Minister Grechko, reputedly the recipient of fabulous presents from Arab rulers, and fully supported by Brezhnev, conducted the politico-military policy which was to cut Israel down to size – to a very small size. Moreover, this policy was admirably suited in Soviet eyes to complement prevailing attitudes in Moscow, where the Jews were rated as the single, most potent, destabilizing influence in Soviet domestic affairs. By the same token, Israel was also tarred with the same brush and identified as a negative influence on the Jews of the Soviet Union. After having thus demonstrated their importance to Egypt by the speedy re-equipment of her armed forces, Brezhnev and Grechko were able to address Nasser from positions of considerable strength.

This became evident from the nature of direct Soviet intervention in Egypt's Canal War with Israel in 1969. At the time, the Americans and Israelis assumed that the Soviet intervention was intended to help Egypt against Israel's deep-penetration raids. They failed to recognize that these Soviet moves were only the beginning of a far more ambitious plan designed to minimize Israel's position of power as an ally of the United States.

Our failure at the time to comprehend Brezhnev's purpose was understandable, for we were receiving disturbing evidence of the ongoing Soviet intervention and participation in rebuilding Egypt's military effectiveness and infrastructure. The immediate threat was considerable enough to warrant our undivided attention, as the so-called Canal War escalated into the War of Attrition. We now know that this was as a result of Soviet aid and advice, but we did not realize at the time, in 1970 – nor did Sadat or his military advisers after Nasser's death – that this was but a stage in Brezhnev's much more elaborate plan to diminish Israel and thus eliminate American influence in our region.

Thus, within two years of the end of the war on 12 June 1967 and in the wake of the arrival of the Shelepin mission in Cairo in February 1969, the

Soviet Union had carried out what Lawrence Whetten, a leading American authority on this period, has described as 'one of the most decisive great power acts since the Second World War'. Within two weeks of the end of the war, over 200 crated tactical aircraft were air-lifted to Egypt and Syria with a promptness and efficiency that belied later Egyptian complaints – not least by Sadat – about the inadequacy of Soviet aid. In his last May Day speech to the nation, Nasser paid colourful tribute to the contributions Brezhnev was making to Egypt's survival. 'Without the Soviet arms which we received after the June disaster,' he told Egypt's National Assembly, 'Moshe Dayan would now perhaps be living in Cairo.'

However, when we now assess the Canal War from June 1967 to August 1970, its most striking feature is that it does not make sense in any of the three phases into which it has been categorized by the Egyptians: the period of defence from June 1967 to August 1968; the period of active defence from September 1968 to February 1969; and the period of attrition from 8 March 1969 until the cease-fire of 8 August 1970. The massive cost in resources and men had no identifiable end result for either Egypt or Israel; what is more, it had no recognizable purpose except one, which was not particularly evident at the time and was only later explained by Brezhnev.

Both Egypt and Israel were suffering grievous losses without in any way changing the status quo. They were expending – or rather wasting – resources on a scale as if there were no tomorrow. At the height of the Canal War, Egyptian guns fired on average 1,000 high explosive shells in order to kill one Israeli and injure two. It was not unusual for an Egyptian barrage to fire more than 10,000 shells at an Israeli position over a period of two or three hours. The Egyptians did not have to worry about ammunition for these massive artillery barrages were supplied by the Soviet Union, who, according to Heikal, 'did not seriously try to restrict ammunition supplies at this time'. The military impact was minimal in terms of the balance of power.

Israel's counter-strikes were militarily far more devastating. When, in December 1969, the then Vice-President Sadat and War Minister General Fawzi were sent to Moscow with an urgent request for massive aid, they had to tell the Russians that Egypt's situation was desperate. The War of Attrition had backfired. Over a million civilians had had to be evacuated from the Canal zone, more refugees than all the displaced Palestinians. The morale of the armed forces had plummeted after Egypt had lost a third of her first-line aircraft only recently resupplied by the Soviet Union; and virtually all her SAM missile defences, installed by the Russians, had been destroyed at the cost of a single Israeli aircraft – a Piper Cub! But none of this was either militarily or politically decisive.

Therefore, this was a frustrating, exhausting and unrewarding interlude for Israel despite her unquestioned local military success. A contemporary analyst aptly assessed Israel's seemingly impregnable position – and its flaws. Israel had never been stronger or more dominant. She could not be forced to act against her own interests, not by the Americans, nor by the

Russians; not by the Egyptians, nor by the Palestinian Fatah. But for all that, Israel could not achieve a real peace so long as she had to deal with a weak Egypt on her borders incapable of independent action free from Soviet, Arab League or terrorist pressure.

This was an accurate snapshot, a static picture of the situation on the ground at the height of the Canal War in 1969 and 1970. But it missed the dynamic behind it; it could not discern the chess master behind the scenes, moving his pawns into calculated positions. Brezhnev was not going to be rushed or stampeded into the open by Egypt's premature action or by her cries for help. Even Nasser could not fully comprehend Brezhnev's interest in and concern for the War of Attrition. When at last Nasser queried the purpose of this strange war without objectives, Brezhnev told him that this War of Attrition 'was a military and political necessity'. What Brezhnev did not add was that it was so for Brezhnev's even more than for Egypt's benefit. Brezhnev, in fact, had achieved his primary objective in the War of Attrition. On 22 January 1970, some six months before the August cease-fire which marked the end of the War of Attrition, a desperate Nasser made a secret journey to Moscow to ask Brezhnev for help in manning the surface-to-air missiles and interceptor aircraft with which the Soviet Union was equipping Egypt's armed forces.

Before Nasser's talks had advanced very far, Brezhnev had manoeuvred the Egyptians into the position where he wanted them: Nasser presented the Soviet leader with a formal request for assistance to defend Egypt with Russian forces. Moscow's dividends from the War of Attrition were now coming in. As a result, according to Commander el-Hussini and General Farouk Abu el-Ezz, a complete Soviet air-defence system with missiles and fighter planes was installed in Egypt with over 20,000 Soviet troops to back it up, including a contingent of some 700 KGB and GRU intelligence specialists. (There was no make-believe any longer about 'technicians and advisers'.)

Airfields and missile sites came under virtual Soviet jurisdiction. In fact, most of the more advanced MIG 21–25 aircraft were placed in the airfield attached to the Soviet-controlled naval base near Alexandria. Brezhnev and the Politburo then played an elaborate charade of 'considering Egypt's request for Soviet troops' before giving Nasser an affirmative reply. But the Egyptians were not fooled. They understood that Brezhnev needed this Egyptian alibi so as to remove American and other suspicions about a Soviet predetermined decision. He had not been idle while waiting for Nasser to formalize Egypt's military relations with the Soviet Union. Some 1,500 tanks had already been delivered since the end of the war in June 1967. So had 350 combat aircraft and over 1,000 guns by the time the War of Attrition ended. Preparation could now begin for the more serious business of Brezhnev's War.

When the cease-fire came into force in August 1970, the Soviet Union was considered, by expert Egyptian observers, to have achieved 'a comfortable position in Egypt': storage and maintenance facilities for the Soviet navy;

the general use of air bases, even for operational missions in the Mediterranean; and Soviet personnel exercising a predominant influence in every section of Egyptian society, particularly in the administration of the armed forces. There was a commensurate Soviet naval presence in Alexandria, Port Said, Sallum and, later in 1970, Marsa Matruh; moreover, there was strong land-based air cover for the Soviet flotilla in the Mediterranean. Last, but by no means least, Egypt allowed the Soviet Union free and unhindered transit facilities for arms and military supplies to African countries, and the Alexandria shipyards were engaged in building ships on behalf of the Soviet navy. All in all, it added up to a formidable Egyptian contribution to the establishment of a Soviet presence at this nodal position in Eurasian strategy.

This was, by any standard, no mean achievement. The Soviet leaders had every reason to be content with their position of strength in the Middle East. There was, however, one significant loophole: Israel, whose military eminence had once more been so tellingly demonstrated. The need to 'eliminate the consequence of Israel's aggression' and to rebuild the strategic role of the allies of the Soviet Union, Egypt and Syria, increasingly occupied the attention of Brezhnev, Grechko and the all-powerful Communist Party apparatus in Moscow.

As a textbook, Brezhnev had before him a highly confidential study prepared 'for his eyes only' by D. Chuvakhin, a former colonel in the KGB who had been his special agent and Soviet Ambassador in Israel before the outbreak of war in June 1967. When Chuvakhin returned home after Brezhnev had broken off diplomatic relations with Israel in June 1967, he was withdrawn from active foreign service, given a salary increase that raised him to the status of a government minister and attached on special assignment to the 'International Studies Department' of the Institute of Oriental Studies in Moscow, an institution often used by Brezhnev as an unofficial part of his personal 'Think Tank'. Chuvakhin's brief from Brezhnev was to assemble all relevant information about the origin and course of the 1967 war, and about the role played, however indirectly, by the Soviet participants, especially those in intelligence and security; and to provide a comprehensive survey of Israel's politics, her economic condition and the state of her armed forces. It took Chuvakhin a considerable time to complete his task, despite the massive assistance provided, on Brezhnev's instruction, by the Institute of Oriental Studies and by a number of involved government agencies. In the end, Chuvakhin's report spanned over 1,000 manuscript pages and his colleagues were left wondering whether Brezhnev would ever really read it, or let anyone else read it.

Be that as it may, there was no doubt that Brezhnev had absorbed the succinct summary with which Chuvakhin had wisely prefaced his exhaustive and lengthy text. Chuvakhin concluded that Egypt would not be able to strike a decisive blow against Israel so long as Egypt was not in full possession of the Sinai Peninsula; Syria, on the other hand, could do so – under certain conditions. It was therefore the Soviet Union's role to provide Syria with these conditions. Brezhnev was said to have been impressed by Chuvakhin's arguments, which were backed by a wealth of documentary support.

However, Chuvakhin's thesis was challenged by the Soviet military establishment. It ran counter to all its thinking and actions based on the centrality of Egypt in the strategy of the Middle East. It had invested a great deal of military hardware and its reputation in the restructuring of Egypt as a military power on land, at sea and in the air. It took some time, therefore, and the War of Attrition on the Suez Canal, before the implications of the 1967 strategy, and with it the reversal of the respective strategic priorities of Egypt and Syria, were fully appreciated and accepted by the Soviet military establishment. Brezhnev and Grechko did not wait for that. They were more concerned to set their new policy in motion without delay, but without making it necessarily apparent at this stage. They could do that quite easily under cover of their all-embracing formula of 'eliminating the consequences of Israel's aggression' without having to show their hand to anyone except their innermost circle.

We can now trace the beginning of this seminal strategic switch on which the Soviet leaders were to embark. Syria's armed forces had been decimated by the 1967 war. When it was over, she had only twenty-five serviceable aircraft and less than 200 – mostly ageing – tanks; and she had lost most of her artillery. Barely a year later, the Syrians had an establishment of 150 combat aircraft, 800 tanks and 700 guns – with Brezhnev's compliments. Moreover, Soviet technicians, advisers and troops had gone to Syria even before they started moving into Egypt, and were already exercising both influence and authority before the then air-force commander, Hafez el-Assad, seized power in 1970.

In fact, the congruence of these factors were seen by many Syrian officers as not altogether unconnected. Assad seized power at the moment of the second great surge in Soviet military aid to Syria, when the armed forces were virtually doubled and the new President's air force increased almost tenfold over what it had been at the end of the 1967 war. Compared with the 200 indifferent tanks which were left over in 1967, Syria by the end of 1971 had some 1,200 of the Soviet Union's most recent tanks. Brezhnev was, in fact, implementing the new strategy on the ground. The theory would take care of itself in due course.

By the early 1970s both Egypt and Syria, bolstered by the massive military aid which Brezhnev had so generously bestowed upon them, were ready to start the countdown for their next war with Israel. This time, however, it was to be a very different affair from the previous débâcle in 1967, because the Soviet Union was to be involved in all planning and preparatory stages.

One of the major preoccupations of the Soviet Union, Egypt and Syria was to keep their plans well shrouded from the prying Americans and Israelis. A key element in what became an ingenious disinformation campaign mounted by Egypt was the secret 'back-channel' link which the

Egyptians established with Henry Kissinger, President Nixon's National Security Adviser in 1972 and 1973, with the State Department and with Nixon personally.

The Egyptian Chief of Staff, General Shazli, had noted in his diary in December 1971 that Sadat could not be believed when he reported on his conversations with Soviet leaders or even with the Soviet Ambassador. Yet it is largely on Sadat's evidence that most of the contemporary history concerning Egypt and the Soviet Union is based. Sadat's version was in some important instances reinforced by emissaries despatched by him to relay his flawed view of events – most confidentially, of course – to important foreign leaders and statesmen. Two examples in particular stand out: the secret 'back-channel' link with Kissinger and a similar channel to King Feisal of Saudi Arabia.

It may have been on the suggestion of his Soviet advisers that Sadat hinted to the American representative in Cairo, Don Bergus, that he would like to have a private channel of communication with Kissinger. Sadat nominated Kissinger's opposite number for this purpose, his National Security Adviser, General Hafez Ismail, an impressively presentable officer in his forties whom, according to his own account, Kissinger found almost as irresistible as Sadat himself.

Before going to Washington, he had been in Moscow and discussed his mission with Brezhnev, Grechko and Kosygin. He advised Brezhnev of the message Sadat wanted him to convey to reassure the Americans about Sadat's frustrations and unhappiness with the Soviet connection. This suited Brezhnev to the hilt, for the Soviet leader had recognized the possible danger in Kissinger's appointment and wanted it neutralized. It was not difficult for Ismail to establish a position of extraordinary influence in Washington, for when he confidentially advised Kissinger of his arrival, he at the same time informed the Secretary of State, William Rogers, and – equally confidentially – the CIA of his presence in Washington as Sadat's personal envoy. Everyone wanted to talk to him and they were all anxious to hear what he could tell them about Moscow's intentions and Sadat's policy.

There was yet one further bonus for Ismail. According to Kissinger's memoirs, it was then the prevailing practice of the Nixon administration that the State Department, the National Security Adviser and the CIA did not exchange information about consultations such as those with General Ismail. They did not even tell each other that they had met with him. Thus, it was only Ismail, and Sadat to whom he reported later, and Brezhnev and Grechko whom he went to see in Moscow on his return, who were fully informed of Egypt's new multi-channel secret connections with the men who counted in Washington. Judging by the subsequent reports and policy decisions by Secretary of State Rogers, and by the usually so sophisticated Kissinger, they had – unwittingly – swallowed Sadat's message as delivered by his envoy, hook, line and sinker.

In particular, they gave full credence to Sadat's version of his unhappy relations with the Russians: his vivid accounts of Soviet untrustworthiness, of their failure to meet supply dates for arms required by Egypt and of much else that was wrong, which gave the Americans the overall impression that Egypt's military apparatus was beset by seemingly insuperable difficulties, information which the Americans passed on to their Israeli counterparts. Judging by the assessment made by the Egyptian visitor, by the State Department and separately by Kissinger, it can be seen just how successful Ismail had been in directing American – and Israeli – attention away from the one topic which neither Egypt nor the Soviet Union wanted them to note: the actual preparations for war against Israel.

Ismail was particularly convincing because his stories of Egyptian dissatisfaction with the Soviet Union were to a large measure true. The Egyptians were miffed by the preference which the Soviet Government gave to Syria. They were annoyed by the condescending attitudes of Soviet experts and advisers. They felt affronted by the behaviour of the Soviet troops and advisers in Egypt, who kept to themselves and restricted social contact with their hosts to a minimum. Moreover, unlike Nasser, Sadat disliked socialism almost more than Zionism. One reason for Ismail's success was given by Kissinger, though in a different context. The rival pretensions and cross-currents of the different American authorities with which Ismail had to deal, Kissinger concluded, 'demonstrated to the Egyptians at least that we too could be Levantine without half trying'.

But however much Sadat was coming to dislike his Soviet allies, he needed them for his preparations for the coming war against Israel, because what had been happening during these preparations was a gradual awakening to reality by General Shazli and his senior colleagues and by Brezhnev and the Soviet commanders.

The reality was, as we shall see, that Egypt – even with all the Soviet assistance made available and despite her great numerical superiority in men and arms – would not be able to mount an attack which would 'liberate the Sinai Peninsula' from Israeli occupation and threaten the heartland of Israel. When Sadat was persuaded that there was no other way, he agreed to the concept of an Egyptian 'meat-grinder' that would destroy Israel's armed might on the banks of the Suez Canal. He also agreed reluctantly to the concept of according to Syria the prime role of the hammer while Egypt played the costly supportive part of the anvil – the Verdun on the Nile.

The first documented evidence of this process – and of the Levantine double-dealing between allies which accompanied it – is in the diary of the then Egyptian Chief of Staff, General Shazli. He describes the preparation for the mission of Egypt's Deputy Minister of War, General Abdel Kader Hassan, to Moscow on 21 September 1971. Hassan was given a formidable shopping list of arms required, which he was to present to Brezhnev and Grechko, together with Egypt's plans for 'Operation 41'. This was the ambitious outline plan for the crossing of the Suez Canal to be followed by the occupation of the key Sinai passes some forty-five kilometres from the Canal. The plan was also known as 'Granite One'.

However, Shazli, the Minister of War, the ailing General Ahmed Ismail, and his deputy, Hassan, did not really believe that 'Operation 41' could be executed by Egypt's armed forces. They knew that Egypt did not have the capacity, the arms or the trained personnel for such an operation. All the same, it was to be presented to the Soviet leaders in the belief or hope that so ambitious a plan would extract still more weapons and other assistance from the Soviet Union. Little did the Egyptians know their Soviet counterparts, but they were soon to learn.

Meanwhile, however, Shazli and his planning colleagues had taken a much more significant decision – without telling the Russians. In place of the plans for 'Granite One', which had been taken to Moscow, they set in train detailed planning for 'Granite Two', a much more modest operation which was targeted on crossing the Canal and occupying a shallow beachhead on the Israeli side of the canal. However, this was to be done in great force defensively equipped with Soviet arms and training so as to entice the Israeli land and air forces into its prepared killing fields within range of the air-defence screen set up by Soviet specialists. It would be a virtual ambush on a grand scale for the Israelis; in Shazli's colourful concept it would be the 'meat-grinder' that would mince the Israel Defence Forces. Shazli could not have known when he planted that seed as a way of misleading the Russian leaders over Egypt's real plans and capability that he was playing straight into Brezhnev's welcoming hands. For Brezhnev was at least as well informed about Egyptian intentions and capacities as Egypt's Chief of Staff.

The Soviet leaders took due note of Egypt's request for arms and equipment, but they paid even more attention to the dummy plans for 'Operation 41', which Hassan had brought with him. Brezhnev replied simply that time was required for the study of the Egyptian plans. However, it would be desirable for Sadat to come to Moscow soon so as to participate in these consultations. It took just three weeks for Sadat to arrive in Moscow on 11 October 1971, with a large team of senior military and political advisers. They met the Soviet leader the following day. It was a critical meeting for Sadat, though, curiously, there is no record of it or comment on it in all his writings, memoirs and speeches, or in his later meetings with Begin or Kissinger.

Whatever the uncertainties we had to contend with at the time, we now have the full authoritative account of the Moscow meeting with Brezhnev and Grechko on 12 October 1971 based on the record kept by the then Egyptian Foreign Minister, Mahmoud Riad. He was present at the Moscow meetings in the fortunate role of an objective observer. Unlike Sadat or the military, he had no axe to grind or to present. He could afford to sit back, listen and record the proceedings, which he did. It is particularly interesting to compare Riad's first-hand account of this meeting with the apocryphal version given by Hassanein Heikal in his *Road to Ramadan*, a much-quoted but often dubious source to the war of 1973.

Brezhnev opened the meeting with his customary probing questions.

This time he wanted to know what the Saudi position was with regard to launching a war against Israel; and what about the other Arab countries? But what evidently really interested the Soviet leader were the details of Egypt's contacts in Washington. Brezhnev suggested that it would be profitable to cultivate the American connection, particularly with Nixon, Kissinger and the CIA, so as to obtain relevant insights into American and Israeli thinking.

Then it was Sadat's turn. He told Brezhnev that he had come to Moscow because Egypt felt that the time had come to reopen the question of beginning with a limited military operation against Israel. To make this possible, Egypt requested the Soviet Union to assist her in establishing military parity with Israel as a necessary prerequisite. Brezhnev listened politely to the Egyptian presentation of the military situation, which had been tailored to back up Sadat's plea. When this was over, Brezhnev replied by asking Sadat a question and then, without waiting for the answer, he called on the Soviet Defence Minister, Marshal Grechko, to give him his considered assessment of the situation. Grechko was ready with a detailed analysis of the Egyptian military preparedness to go to war. He addressed himself particularly to Sadat's request for military assistance which would give Egypt parity with Israel. 'I would like to point out', Grechko said, turning to Sadat, 'that you already have actual superiority over Israel in the number of your soldiers and in the arms at your disposal.'

Then reading from a prepared document, Grechko compared the combined strength in men and arms of Egypt and Syria with that of Israel. Still addressing Sadat, he gave specifics showing that Egypt alone had a superiority of two to one in the number of men under arms and in the equipment and arms at the disposal of Egypt's armed forces, especially in the number of tanks, guns and air-defence missiles. In terms of aircraft, Egyptian superiority in numbers was not quite so decisive but it was still almost two to one. In naval terms, Egypt had overwhelming superiority. She had received engineering equipment adequate for nine bridges across the Suez Canal, as well as sophisticated electronic aids to detonate minefields and jam enemy radar.

After the then Egyptian Chief of Staff, General Mohammed Sadek, had confirmed the accuracy of the figures presented by Grechko, Brezhnev told Sadat that there clearly was no cause for Egyptian complaint as to equipment. However, Egypt would have to do a lot herself before her armed forces were capable of making effective use of the equipment supplied by the Soviet Union – and especially of the sophisticated new weapons that would be made available to her. In short, both Brezhnev and Grechko impressed on Sadat that it was Egypt's unreadiness to go to war that was the cause of the hold-up, not lack of equipment. The conclusion which Brezhnev had drawn from this encounter with Sadat and Egypt's military chiefs he later made clear to Egypt's War Minister and Chief of Staff: there could be no war before 1973 in view of the condition of Egypt's armed forces.

But that was only one half of Brezhnev's decision. All his doubts about Egypt's capacity to wage effective war were confirmed when, after further intensive consultations, the Soviet leader met again with Sadat in Moscow on 27 April 1972. Sadat was persuaded to stay longer than usual, during which time he was closely observed by Brezhnev and Grechko. They had been increasingly concerned by reports of Sadat's public and privately expressed opinions on the eve of his visit to Moscow. Brezhnev was particularly interested that nothing should interfere with the policy of détente which he intended to finalize at a summit meeting, barely a month away, in Moscow with President Nixon and Kissinger. To meet the new situation, Brezhnev and Grechko took two decisions concerning Egypt, but without telling Sadat at the time. The first concerned the scaling down of Egypt's strategic role in the planned war against Israel in relation to the new role allotted to the Syrians. The other was to complete arrangements with Sadat – as the record of these Moscow meetings shows – to 'expel' about half the Russian personnel in Egypt without revealing that it was done in collusion with the Soviet Union.

All this, it must be remembered, was taking place in October 1971, two years before the Yom Kippur War, and continued in April 1972 with Soviet participation at every stage. I find it, therefore, quite incomprehensible that many Kremlinologists and military specialists concerned with the Middle East can still argue that there was no Soviet involvement or direct participation in the preparation – not just in the planning – of the Yom Kippur War. Thus, while Sadat was in Moscow, the Soviet generals with their Egyptian counterparts were fashioning a major switch in the plans for the forthcoming war. Brezhnev was now exploiting the secret decision of Egypt's General Staff (about which he was supposed to be unaware) to opt for plan 'Granite Two'. It was just what Brezhnev wanted to fit in with his strategy based on the reversal of the battlefield role allocated to Egypt and Syria.

It was at this stage that the points of emphasis of Egypt, Syria and the Soviet Union began to diverge.

It was Sadat's objective, with his dramatic crossing of the Canal, to draw the Israeli forces into a carefully laid ambush – Shazli's 'meat-grinder'. Here on the Canal, the unsuspecting Israeli air force and armour would encounter this massive and overwhelming defence force, ready, waiting and equipped with the most sophisticated and unexpected Soviet weapons. The ensuing battle would be bloody and indecisive. But, according to Sadat's plan, the shock and surprise of this unanticipated blood-letting would shake Israel and stir the superpowers to intervene. They would have no choice but to settle that Arab conflict with Israel on terms relating to Egypt's successful crossing of the Canal and to Israel's anticipated heavy losses in aircraft, armour, men – and in her reputation for invincibility. Sadat then expected to gain his major war aim by political means with the help of the superpowers. Although the operation was to be tactically limited, the strategic ultimate objectives were wholly unlimited: the defeat of Israel's

22

defence forces and the 'liberation' of all territories occupied by Israel in June 1967 – Sinai, the West Bank, Gaza, the Golan Heights and Jerusalem.

For Brezhnev, this proposed Egyptian crossing had a different objective. He was no believer in Sadat's 'shock' theories. He knew enough of the effects of shock to be aware that it is not a permanent state and can wear off very quickly, especially when applied to superpowers or to a country and people such as Israel. Admittedly, the immediate tactical aim of both Assad and Brezhnev was the same as Sadat's: to draw the greater part of the Israel Defence Forces into the Canal trap, to hold them there and to weaken them as much as possible. But beyond that, their target was strategically different from Sadat's. For the Syrian and Soviet leaders, the designated holding action on the Canal had an altogether more fundamental purpose than Sadat's planned psychological 'shock' for the superpowers.

In their scheme of the war, the dramatic crossing of the Canal in great force was to tempt Israel to launch her main armoured and air forces against this attack and consequently to denude the northern front with Syria. This was the joker in the pack which Sadat reluctantly had to accept. Israel's military intelligence was focused on the Canal as the decisive war front. Brezhnev's was focused on the seemingly neglected north, on Syria and the Golan front. On the eve of the war, in October 1973, Israel had only 12,000 men and 170 tanks deployed along the entire northern front to face 60,000 Syrian troops with 1,300 tanks, 1,000 guns, 500 missile launchers and over 300 combat aircraft.

It was this Syrian strike force, with its overwhelming local superiority barely ten miles from the Jordan crossing into eastern Galilee, that was to be the pivot of the lunge at Israel's heartland. This was to take place while the Egyptians were creating what was really a diversion on the Canal and holding the greater part of the Israel Defence Forces – and the attention of the world – in its thrall. This was the essence of the strategic switch, the reversal of fronts and priorities in preparation for the decisive battle. This was to be the most crucial battle ever to be fought by Israel. It was to settle the Arab conflict with Israel – and Israel's future – on Brezhnev's and Sadat's terms, not Kissinger's. Sweet balm for the humiliation of 1967!

Brezhnev, however, was not a man who would place his trust in luck; nor would Assad, his principal associate in the execution of the strategic switch. Both men had planned this 'come-back' with great skill and stealth. According to Riad, Brezhnev had cautioned that they would have to be 'two hundred per cent certain of success' before the combined operation on the Canal and on the Golan Heights was authorized. By midsummer 1972, the signs were favourable and the countdown began in earnest for the opening of hostilities causing a series of false alarms in Israel. In Cairo, Sadat played his part by noisily proclaiming the expulsion of Soviet advisers and troops stationed in Egypt.

Both Egypt's Foreign Minister at the time, Mahmoud Riad, and the then Chief of Staff, General Shazli, have provided documentary evidence of repeated Soviet requests by Brezhnev himself, by senior Soviet military commanders and also by Prime Minister Kosygin for the repatriation of Soviet personnel before any fighting began.

In fact, the withdrawal of Soviet personnel from Egypt was fully discussed with Sadat, as was the manner and presentation of the departure of the Soviet troops and advisers. It can now be seen as a key to the sudden burst of Soviet diplomatic activity in preparation for the impending visit to Moscow of President Nixon, which was due towards the end of May 1972, almost immediately after Sadat's departure. The Middle East was to be an important topic and Brezhnev was concerned, as we now know from detailed accounts of his talks with the Egyptian leaders, to clarify his relations with Egypt before starting a serious affair with Syria's President Assad and meeting with Nixon.

The Soviet leaders had been particularly worried by Sadat's declared view – which had been faithfully reported to them by their own man in Cairo – that he would bring about a settlement of Egypt's dispute with Israel on his own terms by forcing a confrontation regarding Egypt between the United States and the Soviet Union. One of Brezhnev's principal objectives at the Moscow summit with Nixon and Kissinger was to forestall any such move on Sadat's part. He did. Sadat admitted later, on the day after he formally announced the expulsion of Soviet troops and advisers from Egypt, that following the Nixon–Brezhnev talks in Moscow in June, he found that he now had to deal with a new phase in his friendship with the Soviet Union and had to abandon his earlier concept of bringing about a superpower confrontation, which would compel them to intervene in the Middle East on lines acceptable to him.

Contrary to the official announcement and communiqué issued at the time by Moscow and Cairo, Sadat had stayed in the Soviet Union much longer than the two days claimed. He had arrived on 27 April and did not leave until 6 May – an unprecedented ten days shrouded in secrecy. The principal subject of his discussions with Brezhnev and Grechko was Brezhnev's Middle East programme, which Soviet Foreign Minister Andrei Gromyko planned to present to Kissinger as the basis for a superpower agreement on the Middle East. It was, in its way, a remarkable document, which must have shocked Sadat when he was shown the first draft, even before it had been amended by Kissinger.

In its final and very secret version, which was not made public at the time, the agreement proposed by Gromyko had nothing in it that a responsible Israeli Government could not have accepted. But the eight points of the Middle East section of the agreement were not meant for Israel; they were primarily designed for Sadat: they were meant to shock him into a state of greater realism concerning the superpowers. They reaffirmed their support for a peaceful settlement in the Middle East on the basis of UN Security Council Resolution 242. It was to be a comprehensive agreement, which was to be negotiated by the parties concerned on a voluntary basis. This could be done in stages and on a priority basis so as to end the state of belligerency and to establish peace.

It was enough to make Sadat realize that any hopes which he might have entertained of exploiting a superpower conflict for Egypt's ends were unrealistic and unwelcome in Moscow. He was also given to understand by Brezhnev, and even more so by Grechko, that Egypt was in no military position to launch any kind of major war against Israel, be it for limited or unlimited objectives. Sadat would have to wait until late in 1973 before the Egyptian armed forces would be able to embark on such an expedition; meanwhile, the Soviet Union would supply arms and training as required. However, judging by his own account, Kissinger was totally unaware of this Brezhnev–Sadat understanding to prepare for war.

Ironically, the superpower agreement in Moscow, for what it was worth, had been largely made possible by Sadat himself. He had scared the Russians and the Americans by his public pronouncements before coming to Moscow, and especially the speech he made on the day before his departure from Cairo. By this time next year, Sadat told a wildly cheering audience on 26 April 1972, he would have liberated all Arab territory including Jerusalem, which belonged to the Islamic nation. And the speech he made immediately after his return to Cairo from his talks in Moscow confirmed for both Brezhnev and Kissinger the importance of the agreement they had concluded on the Middle East. Sadat told the Arab Socialist Union Assembly in Cairo that henceforth his goal would be not merely the liberation of occupied Arab territory but also the destruction of the intolerable Israeli arrogance: 'I am prepared to sacrifice a million men in the next war; Israel should be prepared to do the same.'

As I have already mentioned, we now know from Egyptian and Soviet sources a good deal more about these extraordinary Brezhnev–Sadat talks in April 1972 and of Sadat's very outspoken conversation with the Marshal Grechko. Sadat was not in the least hostile or critical of the Soviet Union but, in the Soviet view, he was over-ambitious and quite unrealistic in the light of the confidential information about Egypt's armed forces with which the Soviet leaders were fully equipped. Both Brezhnev and Grechko were clearly determined that the Soviet Union should not come into conflict with the United States as a result of Sadat's headstrong and ambitious plans to involve the superpowers in Egypt's planned war against Israel. This possibility had been anticipated in Moscow for some time. Preliminary soundings had been made in Damascus behind a screen of great secrecy and dissimulation since February 1972. With Assad's enthusiastic approval, the entire concept of the war against Israel was revised and its strategic centre of gravity switched from Egypt to Syria.

The most telling argument for switching was that Egypt, for all her great manpower and massive Soviet help, was not strategically able to constitute a threat on land or in the air to the Israeli heartland; she could not even reconquer the lost Sinai province. Syria, on the other hand, given adequate military support and training, could launch a surprise attack which could carry her into eastern Galilee within forty-eight hours. The prospect and the temptation were irresistible.

25

The first necessary step was the ostensible Soviet disengagement from Egypt's war preparations. Most of the discussions during Sadat's stay in Moscow were devoted to finalizing the arrangements for the withdrawal of the majority of Soviet personnel from Egypt. Those who remained would no longer be autonomous and would come under Egyptian authority. What Brezhnev had not anticipated was that Sadat was going to make such an anti-Soviet meal out of the expulsion, which with Egyptian encouragement, was construed in the West as a sharp departure from the pro-Soviet policy that Egypt had followed during the previous thirty years.

The Egyptian army commanders were taken completely by surprise by Sadat's announcement that the Soviet military personnel had a week to pack their bags and leave. They noted that the Soviets made no objections. The commander of the armoured corps, General Kamal Hassan Ali, invited all the top Soviet advisers in his corps for a farewell tea party. 'You have lived with us over the years,' he told them, 'shared our hardships, helped us to prepare for the coming battle. We shall always be grateful to you. But we cannot ask you to remain here when we face the supreme test.'* General Ahmed Ismail heard of the farewell party and gave orders to all the corps commanders to follow suit.

The strategic switch was carried out with masterly timing and in total secrecy. All the complicated and sometimes Byzantine moves were co-ordinated like intricate clockwork during the summer and the latter half of 1972.† By the end of the year, virtually all the basic equipment required for the preparation and training for their respective roles had been delivered to Syria and Egypt. But special treatment was reserved for the Syrian President: he was given an apartment in the Kremlin with direct access to Brezhnev whenever he came to Moscow on his frequent brief visits during this preparatory period in which Syria was geared up to act as the cutting edge for the planned attack. All that remained was the training of the two Arab armies to use the sophisticated new arms and to deploy the Soviet equipment which had been delivered. We now know that Egyptian troops were trained in crossing the Suez Canal on a site on the distant Karakoum Canal to the south-east of Tashkent, which was prepared as a replica of its Egyptian counterpart.

Despite his constant public accusations of Soviet failure to deliver promised arms and equipment, Sadat was complaining to his Chief of Staff when the year ended and the countdown to war began in January 1973 that Brezhnev 'was drowning him' in Soviet military supplies. However, it would take another eight months, General Shazli explained, before Egypt's armed forces would be fully conversant with and able to deploy the new Soviet equipment. They would now have only a discreet rump of Soviet advisers, left behind for this purpose, to help assimilate the new equipment.

* Told to me by General Kamal Hassan Ali.
† The intermediary between Sadat and Assad was the Egyptian Military Attaché in Damascus, Mohamed Bassiouni, later to become Egyptian Ambassador in Tel Aviv.

Although they had been late starters compared to Egypt, the Syrians were in a far better position, for they were the beneficiaries of Sadat's expulsion. Many of the specialist Soviet experts and troops withdrawn from Egypt in the summer of 1972 were, in fact, transferred to Syria – in all almost 5,000 men. The Soviet infrastructure which had been so effective in Egypt was simply moved to Syria with all the advantages this entailed. Brezhnev had staked everything on the Syrian strike force equipped by the Soviet Union and trained by the Soviet expeditionary force largely brought in from Egypt. The planned Syrian attack was fully dovetailed to Sadat's planned crossing of the Canal. In this way it was proposed to engage the bulk of the IDF in a self-destructive and costly attempt to halt the Egyptian advance without the Israelis being aware of the Syrian intention until it was too late for them to regroup.

It was about this time – with preparations for war fully preoccupying Sadat, but not quite yet at their peak – that Israel's Prime Minister, Golda Meir, made one more attempt to induce Sadat to make peace. She decided that Israel should make a dramatic offer to him in order to reach Israel's goal of direct negotiations for peace in order to halt the drift into another war.

In the spring of 1973, Kissinger advised Mrs Meir that he had a back-channel to Sadat and that he was hopeful that a really substantive Israeli peace initiative would receive serious consideration by Sadat. Accordingly, Mrs Meir persuaded her Cabinet to go beyond the terms she had stipulated when she met with Kissinger and Nixon in Washington early in 1973. Soon afterwards, the Israeli Government addressed a formal offer to Sadat through his secret emissary in Washington, General Hafez Ismail. The message said that Sadat could have back the whole of the Sinai Peninsula without firing a shot and without the loss of a single Egyptian soldier in return for a peace settlement with Israel. But in 1973, on the verge of what he believed would be a victorious war, Sadat was not inclined to agree to terms which he was only too anxious to obtain four years later. Therefore, he would not entertain Israel's peace offer. The Sinai alone was not enough; Israel would have to withdraw from all occupied territories to the 1967 boundaries. In return, Egypt would abandon the state of war, but no more: there would be no recognition of Israel, and no diplomatic or normal relations. Kissinger commented at the time that, in fact, Sadat had handed the power of veto to the PLO and they did not want peace. The Israeli initiative had offered Sadat a chance to draw back, but by then his preparations for war were going ahead and his mind was set on war, not peace.

Brezhnev had calculated every detail of his equation. He had proposed to the Syrian President, but not to Sadat, that the Soviet Union would table a request for a cease-fire immediately after the initial Syrian breakthrough into Israel so as to forestall the anticipated Israeli counter-attack, especially by Israel's superior air force. By nightfall on that fateful Yom Kippur day, 6 October 1973, Soviet satellite and electronic intelligence reported that Israel's defences on the south-western Golan front were

27

THE LAST OPTION

crumbling; they did. The conclusion drawn by the Soviet liaison staff in Damascus was that by nightfall on the following day, Syrian armour would have crossed the River Jordan frontier into Israel's eastern Galilee heartland. That would be the time to call for a cease-fire in place and so pre-empt the anticipated Israeli counter-attack and leave Syrian troops in occupation of sensitive areas of the Golan Heights and of a limited zone of eastern Galilee – valuable bargaining counters in the making of an imposed peace.

This was to be the highlight of Brezhnev's War – the objective of the Six Year War fought by Egypt and Syria to undo the gains of Israel's Six Day War. It achieved nothing, despite the enormous effort made by Egypt, which had mobilized a million men for this war, and by Syria, chosen to spearhead the fatal thrust at Israel.

If the planned invasion of northern Galilee had not been halted and the Egyptians forced back across the Canal, who can tell where the war would have ended? It did not happen. But one may wonder what might have happened had we not turned the tide at the last critical moment before the Syrians reached the bridge over the Jordan.

The battle to prevent the Syrian breakthrough into eastern Galilee on which the Soviet–Arab plan was hinged turned into an epic struggle by the Israeli forces, greatly outnumbered and outgunned by the Syrians. For the Israelis, it was a battle of individuals; at the height of the crisis – between 7 and 9 October 1973 – every man was his own commander. Every officer, soldier and airman was aware that the fate of Israel was in his hands and by a superhuman effort they made certain it stayed there. The Israeli few had halted the Syrian onslaught. The second generation of Israelis, the sons and daughters of the Israeli class of 1948, had come of age. Like their fathers they paid a heavy price for Israel's independence.

It was touch and go for Israel in 1948 and it was no less so in 1973. Living thus always on the brink has conditioned us. However, before we turn to the transformation of Israel as a consequence of that fateful war, we need to consider the impact of a revolutionary new factor which took over when the Yom Kippur War had failed – Kissinger's diplomacy of compromise.

2
Kissinger's Compromise
1973–5

THE YOM KIPPUR WAR was a crisis waiting to happen in Israel at that moment. It shook our establishment and our over-confident and complacent society into recognition of the reality that was still with us and which had not gone away with the military success of the Six Day War. It made us reconsider military realities much as the *intifada* forced us fifteen years later to come to terms with political realities that would also not go away. But what we found most disconcerting in the months following the Yom Kippur War was a parallel situation in Egypt and in other Arab countries: an inability – or it may have been an unwillingness – on the part of the Egyptian leaders to see that what mattered most in October 1973 was the *end* of the war, *not the beginning*. So much attention has been concentrated by Egyptian and western publicists on Egypt's Soviet-assisted, meticulous preparation for the Canal crossing and on the shock element of the initial surprise thus created that the basic features and lessons of the war have come to be seen altogether out of focus, not least by the Israeli public.

In truth, Israel came of age as a nation during the Yom Kippur War; we matured and suffered grievous losses; we agonized over mistakes and might-have-beens; we mourned almost 3,000 dead and some leaders who were found to have feet of clay. But we withstood the greatest challenge any people could be called upon to face against impossible odds: surprised, hopelessly outnumbered and outgunned, we stood our ground and, in the end, compelled our most powerful adversary to make peace with us. It was no mean achievement. For this time – in October 1973 – there was no room for complacency or for over-confidence: we were really fighting for survival; and we survived. We had our friends, good friends that stood by us – and none more so than the American Secretary of State, Henry Kissinger, who played the lead in the complicated manoeuvre of simultaneously ending the war and laying the foundations for peace. He also taught us the meaning of realistic diplomacy – something quite foreign until then to Golda Meir's Government despite the valiant efforts of Minister of Defence Moshe Dayan. But he could not influence the Prime Minister or the ruling establishment.

In particular, Kissinger attempted to make the Israeli Government understand – not always successfully – that in war, as in chess, it is the endgame that matters. In our case, there were at that point four players who carried weight: Brezhnev and Kissinger, and the armed forces of Egypt and Israel. During this crucial end phase, neither President Sadat nor Prime Minister Meir played any significant role in the interplay between the four contestants. Kissinger's successful diplomacy was rooted in the movement of Israel's armed forces, which had crossed the Suez Canal and virtually immobilized Egypt's military power. Yet, for all the importance of these last moves of Israel's war with Egypt, we must not forget that they were actually of secondary significance, that they were merely playing out a scenario – the ending of which had already been decided: not on the Nile, nor in Jerusalem, but some two weeks earlier on 9 October on the Syrian bank of the River Jordan – and in Moscow at a historic meeting of the Soviet Politburo which continued for three days from 12 to 14 October. Forty-eight hours later, the Soviet Prime Minister, Alexei Kosygin, was in Cairo. It was at this meeting, as we were to learn some time later from a detailed transmission by Moscow Radio, that Brezhnev's full authority over Soviet policy was powerfully displayed.

Brezhnev had expected that the Yom Kippur War was to be the shortest major war on record. The timing of the initial operations had been finely tuned with the Syrian leaders, President Assad and his Defence Minister, General Tlas, and co-ordinated with Sadat's plans, as was subsequently demonstrated in the triangular public recrimination which erupted between Egypt, Syria and the Soviet Union. Within six hours of the initial Syrian breakthrough, the Soviet Union would request a meeting of the UN Security Council so that it could order an instant cease-fire. According to Soviet calculation and manipulation, this would take some forty-eight hours, which would allow time for the Syrian armoured thrust to reach and cross the River Jordan into Israel and establish itself in upper Galilee. The cease-fire would come into effect before Israel could mount a successful counter-attack since her armour and air force would be tied down in resisting the massive Egyptian crossing of the Canal and would be in the process of being decimated in General Shazli's 'meat-grinder'. Thus, Israel's northern front would be wide open with Syrian troops inside Israel and on the Golan Heights, and the Government in Jerusalem would have no option but to accept a cease-fire ordered by the Security Council and subsequently to pay the territorial price for a Syrian withdrawal.

In the event, it did not happen that way. The Syrian assault failed to break Israel's northern defences, because, contrary to Syrian anticipation, Defence Minister Dayan did not walk into their cleverly baited trap.

Inspired by his own belief in the old Arab proverb that in order to catch a fish you have to think like a fish – and reinforced in his conclusion by the alarming reports coming from his commander of the northern front, General Itzhak Hoffi – Dayan reasoned, after war had broken out, that the Egyptian armed forces, despite their great strength on the Canal, constituted no immediate threat to Israel. The main thrust of the attack and the principal danger to Israel would be in the north. He therefore ordered units of the air forces and of the armoured forces destined to move south for the Egyptian front to turn round and move north in great haste to reinforce the depleted northern front. Their arrival at the critical moment was decisive.

By 9 October, when Brezhnev had expected to have the planned cease-fire from the UN Security Council and to be in a position to dictate terms to Israel from a position of strength of the Syrian army, he had the perspicacity to recognize defeat before anyone else had done so and act accordingly. It was an unexpected and unusual situation, which was fully – though guardedly – reported on the Home Service of Moscow Radio. Brezhnev had come to far-reaching conclusions – quite revolutionary in Soviet terms – and it took three full days before the Politburo authorized him to go ahead and despatch Kosygin to Cairo on the difficult mission of implementing the new policy.

When the Politburo meeting ended on 14 October, Kosygin was instructed to insist that Sadat should agree to the standstill cease-fire which the Americans had tentatively proposed, but which Egypt and Israel still opposed. Brezhnev's policy was much more profound than outside observers were prepared to allow. He had seen enough of Egypt's and Syria's military prowess, beefed up as they were by Soviet arms and training and with Soviet advisers and troops to assist them, to be able to discount the propaganda. He concluded that there would have to be a radical change in Soviet thinking if the new policy, which had led to détente with the United States, was not to be jeopardized. It was a policy which Brezhnev considered absolutely vital for the Soviet Union for political and even more for economic reasons. If he had to choose between détente and Egypt, Soviet interest dictated that he must opt for détente. Sadat had been quite right in June 1972 when he sensed danger for Egypt in Brezhnev's decision to give détente the highest priority.

Accordingly, Kosygin's brief for his talks with Sadat in Cairo was based on the failure of Brezhnev's strategic switch, the collapse of the Syrian option and the urgent need to cut Soviet losses. All this happened *before* the Israeli crossing of the Canal, which played no part in Brezhnev's initial instructions to Kosygin and in his presentation to the Politburo on 12 October. It was the failure of the Syrians to overcome the Israeli defences in the north during the first forty-eight hours of the war, and the Soviet Union's inability as a result to actuate the cease-fire trigger and halt the fighting while the Israelis were at a serious disadvantage, that convinced Brezhnev of the need for a radical diplomatic U-turn.

In short, Kosygin's mission to Cairo was to lay the foundation for a speedy Soviet disengagement, not only from the war, but also from all further involvement in Egypt, and to arrange for the take-over of former Soviet responsibilities in Egypt (but not in Syria) by the United States. Brezhnev had concluded that Egypt had become a political, financial and military liability. She was no longer a Soviet asset; let the Americans have the responsibility and the burden of looking after her. But then the unexpected happened. Kosygin arrived in Cairo during the afternoon of 16

31

October, just as realization began to dawn among the Egyptian General Staff – but not yet with Sadat – that the Israeli crossing of the Canal was not a minor raid mounted for publicity purposes but an invasion which could transform the hitherto confident prospect of an Egyptian victory into certain disaster.

General Shazli's counter-offensive against General Ariel Sharon's troops, which had crossed the Canal into Egypt, was ineffective. His fellow officers later accused Shazli of having bungled it, while Sadat said that Shazli had had a nervous breakdown; in turn, Shazli accused Sadat of interfering in the conduct of the war. There was chaos and anger and a degree of panic when cool heads and unemotional reasoning were called for. Instead, Shazli urged Sadat to recall immediately all Egyptian troops that had crossed the Canal into Sinai. To this, Defence Minister Ismail replied that, if the army commanders dared do this, the people would have horses drag them through the streets of Cairo; it would be better if the generals died fighting at the front.

Sharon's crossing of the Suez Canal 'into Africa' had thrown Egypt's Supreme Armed Forces Command into total disarray. Before being dismissed by Sadat, Shazli issued an urgent general appeal to Egypt's Arab allies and to Marshal Tito of Yugoslavia for armour and aircraft, but none materialized before the end of the war.* It was into the midst of this military and political confusion that the Soviet Prime Minister arrived in Cairo.

As we have seen, Kosygin had been instructed, as a first step, to propose to Sadat that he accept the American plan for a cease-fire, which would have left Egypt in possession of both sides of the Canal and in a favourable bargaining position. But by the time Kosygin began his discussion with Sadat, Egypt's bargaining position was eroding by the hour. Kosygin had also been instructed to ensure instant Soviet disengagement from all further developments concerning the fighting; he was to leave the managing of the Egyptian end of the crisis to Kissinger. As the awful truth dawned on Sadat and his military advisers, they grasped at the American straw that Brezhnev had held out to them; Kissinger was now in business in Cairo by courtesy, to no mean extent, of Brezhnev. Kissinger would now have to learn the Brezhnev lesson the hard way: Egypt had become a liability – at least for the time being. We were to watch with fascination as Kissinger gave Brezhnev and the Israelis a demonstration of how to handle, with political finesse, a hot potato served the Russian way.

Brezhnev was too experienced in these matters to imagine that so drastic a revision of policy affecting the United States and Egypt, and two men of the calibre of Sadat and Kissinger, could be carried out without a good deal of stage-managing and real or imaginary outside pressure. But having decided on disengaging the Soviet Union from the war and from undue involvement in Egypt, Brezhnev went all the way. His arguments for doing

* According to General Kamal Hassan Ali, help did arrive, including 100 tanks from Yugoslavia. However, it was too late to change the course of the battle.

so had meanwhile been reinforced by the report brought back from Cairo by the Soviet Prime Minister. Kosygin had been witness to a display of all the principal weaknesses and faults of the Sadat regime. If the Egyptian President's worst enemy had stage-managed the events which occurred following Kosygin's arrival in Cairo on 16 October, he could not have bettered what actually did happen. Kosygin saw the Egyptian Third Army disintegrating; he saw the High Command in disarray and unable to control the battlefield; he saw Sadat in a state of ignorance of the growing Israeli threat developing in close proximity to Cairo. Kosygin could clearly see the disastrous end of the war becoming a reality any day now bringing with it further discredit for the Soviet Union.

If Brezhnev had still entertained doubts about his proposed Soviet disengagement from Egypt, these were put at rest by Kosygin's devastating report. At the same time, Brezhnev did not want to be the unwilling party to another extraordinary Israeli victory over Egypt and her Soviet sponsor. The only relief in sight for Brezhnev, his last hope so to speak, was the uncanny ability and the never failing vanity of Kissinger. Brezhnev, the master tactician, now turned to Kissinger and prepared him for the role of becoming Brezhnev's *deus ex machina*.

By the time Kosygin had returned from Cairo on 19 October, the Egyptian situation had become desperate. That same evening the Soviet Union, with Egypt's heartfelt support now, appealed to the Americans for an instant cease-fire that night. Without waiting, at 10 p.m. in Moscow, Brezhnev proposed direct talks with the United States. He invited Kissinger to come to Moscow at once and with full authority to act. At this point, it has become clear, the Americans misread Brezhnev's move. Kissinger and his experts were convinced that Brezhnev was trying to save the Egyptians from another Israeli defeat and wanted American support for the imposition of an instant cease-fire which Sadat had requested. In fact, we know now that Brezhnev had altogether more far-reaching intentions. However, at this point Brezhnev had to confront both an Egyptian short-term and a Soviet long-term crisis.

For the resolution of both crises, Brezhnev turned to Kissinger: he wanted to save Sadat and the Egyptian Third Army from disaster and to free the Soviet Union from the Egyptian entanglement. Only Kissinger could achieve both objectives without causing undue damage to Brezhnev's reputation and Soviet interests. Brezhnev was in a hurry. However, Kissinger wanted to play for time, to allow the Israeli forces playing havoc with the Egyptian defences on the Egyptian side of the Canal to create additional facts on the ground and so strengthen his negotiating posture. They did. Both Brezhnev and Sadat were now desperate for an instant cease-fire; Kissinger dawdled while the Israelis advanced and fuelled Egypt's desperation.

Though it was not evident at the time, in the midst of total confusion in Cairo and Damascus, and excitement in Jerusalem and Washington, Brezhnev kept his head and recognized his opportunity. In a skilful and subtly worded message transmitted to Kissinger in Washington, he conveyed the impression that the Soviet Union was about to intervene militarily unless the Israeli advance on the Egyptian side of the Canal was immediately halted. It was a model of a message that seemingly said everything but actually said nothing. Simultaneously, reports reached Kissinger from his own intelligence sources that the Soviet authorities had alerted some 50,000 airborne troops in southern Russia and in Hungary for immediate transport to Egypt. Kissinger was also informed that Sadat had requested troops from the Soviet Union and the United States to supervise the cease-fire. Brezhnev's message had said the same. Assad also requested Soviet troops to protect Damascus against the advancing Israelis. Both Sadat and Assad later denied, somewhat unconvincingly, that they had made such requests.

Be that as it may, what really mattered was that we were about to witness a unique superpower charade devised by Brezhnev and with Kissinger as impresario. Kissinger recognized Brezhnev's ominous message not merely as an empty threat but as an empty threat with a purpose. Whatever that was remained obscure in Washington that night of 24 October 1973. Characteristically, Kissinger decided to go along with Brezhnev, but at the same time to cover himself just in case he had misread Brezhnev's intention.

Accordingly, Kissinger played the trump card Brezhnev had wanted him to play: with the consent of President Nixon, he ordered a nuclear alert. Confronted thus by the prospect of nuclear war, Brezhnev had no option but to deny Sadat's plea for Soviet troops and gracefully withdraw from his involvement in Egypt. No one – not even Sadat – could blame him for stepping back from the nuclear brink. With Kissinger's help, the Soviet Union was able to disengage from her responsibilities in Egypt and, in effect, hand them over to the United States and to Kissinger. And with Brezhnev's help, Kissinger was able to convince Golda Meir and her colleagues to halt the Israeli advance and to accept the cease-fire. This was the whole point of the so-called nuclear alert. The question never put or answered was: 'Who had masterminded this nuclear emergency?' Was it Brezhnev or Kissinger? Or both?

In the event, it really did not matter. The result served both masters: the Russians wanted to get out of Egypt and the Americans wanted to get in. Both got what they wanted. It was the real turning-point of the Yom Kippur War. It set the stage for the years that were to follow, and it installed Kissinger as the unchallenged stage-manager. Even a moment's pause for rational reflection would have convinced Kissinger's worldwide critics – and especially his European NATO allies – that there had never been any real threat, nuclear or otherwise. At the point when the Egyptian and Syrian war effort against Israel was in a state of collapse, when the Politburo had decided even before the event to suspend further military aid to Egypt, a Soviet airborne intervention with 50,000 troops would have been absurd.

All it would have achieved would have been a confrontation with a far more lethal American mobilization – the one thing Brezhnev's policy was tailored to avoid. And for what would his precious policy of détente with the United States, and the Soviet Union's security and well-being, be placed at risk? Were the ambivalent friendship of President Sadat and the questionable benefits of the Soviet Union in the Arab world worth the price? One need only formulate the questions, as Kissinger did in the privacy of his office, to arrive at the self-evident answer. It made the agitated Europeans who sought to distance themselves from American policy look singularly ridiculous.

By comparison, we who had a ring-side seat could not fail but admire the deftness and professionalism with which Kissinger had conducted his diplomatic orchestra. He had taught us a lesson which we would not lightly forget: that to be effective even the most telling diplomatic moves had to be backed by commensurate power – real power; rhetoric was no substitute. Moreover, for the first time at the conclusion of the four wars we had fought, we were heading for a political settlement – a possible peace – instead of a kind of military no-man's-land where we were left with neither peace nor normal relations with our neighbours. It was an exciting realization that in the wake of Kissinger we were travelling along a new road, even though neither of us knew for sure our ultimate destination. The feeling we had then, and the confidence we had in Kissinger, created a mood in which everything was possible – despite the extraordinary display of self-flagellation in which Israelis were indulging back home.

However, we had an early warning – and so did the Americans – that it was not going to be an easy ride. The 'peace conference' agreed upon in the cease-fire agreements took place in Geneva at the end of December 1973. It was more of a parody than the real thing and was essentially an occasion for some self-serving speeches by those who attended and for denunciation by those who refused to attend, in particular Syria and the PLO. Having delivered the mutual denunciations and after a characteristic set-piece oration from Israel's Foreign Minister, Abba Eban, the chairman, Dr Kurt Waldheim, adjourned the conference never to meet again.

Meanwhile, the post-war climate in the Arab countries had assumed a familiar characteristic which we had first experienced after the Sinai War in 1956 (for us it was the Sinai; for the British and French it was Suez). It happened again after the Six Day War in 1967 and now once more following the Yom Kippur War. Only this time it was accentuated to the point of becoming ridiculous.

In short, as the weeks passed, the Egyptians, the Palestinians and the other Arab countries were beginning to behave as if they had won a famous victory over Israel in the October War. Reading Sadat's immediate post-war speeches in which he spelled out Egypt's terms for a 'just settlement', one had the impression that a conquering hero was dictating his terms; they were the same terms that had been demanded before the war with one important difference: Sadat and the Arab world in general this time really believed that they had won a historic victory; they were not play-acting.

They had restored the honour and power of Arab arms; they had wiped out the memories of the defeats in 1967 and, most important of all, they had exploded the myth of Israeli invincibility. The American-engineered cease-fire had saved Sharon's armour from being destroyed by a planned Egyptian counter-attack; and in the north, on the Syrian front, the tide had been about to be turned by the imminent arrival of Iraqi reinforcements. Sadat and Assad had been robbed of the glorious final victory by Kissinger's intervention. It was an alibi that won acceptance not only in the Arab world, but also by sophisticated publicists in London, Paris and Bonn. No one mentioned that the Syrian army had been pushed back to a point where Damascus came within range of Israel's guns or that the Israeli army was only seventy miles from Cairo.

It would be wrong though to ridicule Arab propagandists for again successfully turning a battlefield defeat into a political victory; it had happened in 1956 and 1967, and this time the transformation was even more effectively executed. In part, Kissinger was to blame; he did rather overdo his apotheothis of Sadat and his encomiums of Sadat's great states-manship and of the military expertise of the Egyptian armed forces. Admit-tedly, they had prepared well with Soviet help and under Soviet direction, and they had fought well, but they had still lost the fourth war against Israel, despite all the soothing syrup applied by Kissinger and the chorus of praise from western European and American publicists. These apologias did not help Sadat or Egypt. They merely left them suspended in an unreal dream world from which they had to be roused the hard way. They had to learn for themselves. But meanwhile wishful thinking continued to play havoc with the Arab cause. It delayed the time of reckoning and made it all the harder when it did come. It also jeopardized Kissinger's patient peace-making. After months of being all things to all men in order to get them to talk and act rationally, the whole peace-making process which he had so painstakingly initiated in the wake of the Yom Kippur War began to fall apart. It did so because no Arab leader, not even Sadat, was willing to contemplate peace with Israel on any terms even remotely acceptable to the United States, let alone Israel. Israel had, after all, according to Arab thinking, been cut down to size by the great Arab victory in the October War. There was no lack of prophets of doom forecasting Israel's decline and eventual downfall.

This mood was accurately reflected at the 12th Palestine National Council when it met in Cairo early in June 1974, seven months after the end of the October War. David Hirst was there for the then *Manchester Guardian*, one of the most experienced and perceptive sympathizers with the Arab cause. When the conference ended, he noted that there had been hardly a delegate there – a guerrilla leader, independent, notable, intellectual or West Bank deportee – who had not believed that Israel was now doomed and that the October War marked the beginning of the end of Zionism. Hirst then went on to explain that many Palestinians were really hoping that there would be no agreement with Israel and that the Arab states, having seen the futility of trying to achieve one, would return once more to the battlefield.

The decisions of the Palestine National Council, the highest decision-making body of the PLO, had been quite specific about PLO policy. It allowed for no fudging. It was such as to be wholly unacceptable to Israelis of whatever plumage – hawks or doves. It suggested, moreover, a policy of duplicity towards the United States, in order to win support for the PLO's undeclared and far more extreme demands. In effect, it restated PLO insistence on a solution that would embrace all of historical Palestine and which would involve the liquidation of the 'Zionist state'. It refused recognition of Israel. It rejected negotiation with Israel. It denied acceptance of any boundaries, secure or otherwise, of an Israeli state. Riding on the assumption of the great Arab victory in the Yom Kippur War, it 'went for broke', as the saying goes. There were to be no concessions, not even to reality.

The decisions of the National Council made us re-evaluate the Arab situation, for everything would depend on the manner in which the Arab summit, which was due to meet some three months later in Rabat, Morocco, confirmed or rejected the extremist demands of the Palestinian leadership. It was a test of strength and credibility for the Arab heads of state, for there was no evading the issue now that they had been openly challenged by the PLO. The Palestine National Council had declared at its Cairo meeting that Israel was the ultimate enemy to be overcome, but that the immediate target for the PLO was King Hussein of Jordan and his regime. Both would have to be replaced by a national-democratic regime dominated by Palestinian Arabs. Other unnamed Arab regimes – presumably Gulf rulers – were similarly threatened. The PLO was to be the sole legitimate spokesman of the Palestinian people in future wherever they may be. King Hussein was to be excluded from any say in Palestinian matters.

When the Arab heads of state met in Rabat in October 1974, they meekly fudged the issue and accepted the primacy of the PLO and its demands on the question of Palestine and, somewhat more ambiguously, on the question of Jordan. It was total surrender by the Arab Kings and Presidents – including King Hussein. Two weeks later, Yasser Arafat was given a hero's welcome by the UN General Assembly in New York. His PLO leadership had been moved centre-stage. With it came the Palestinian claim to independent representation, self-determination and an effective veto in Arab policy-making concerned in any way with Israel and with the Palestine question.

This new turn in Arafat politics, as reported by PLO lobbies in London, Paris and Washington, resulted in their claim of 'the tremendous new power wielded by the Palestinian Liberation Organization which was indicative of the almost universal belief in the Middle East that a fifth Arab–Israeli war was now inevitable'. This was undoubtedly the belief held by euphoric PLO leaders and Arab publicists; and it was fostered in the hope

of influencing the American administration. But there was no such assessment of the post-Rabat situation in Israel. Nor was it the view of Sadat or
Kissinger. However, it was no secret that some members of Sadat's entourage and some of Kissinger's officials at the State Department did privately
accept the PLO's alarmist forecast of coming events.

The Palestine Arabs, and some of the very intelligent young hardliners whom Sadat kept as intimate advisers and as foils to his own more
imaginative inclinations, were guilty of making the kind of mistake
against which Richard Crossman, then a British Member of Parliament,
had warned the Israelis in the 1950s: 'Never believe your own propaganda,'
he cautioned them, 'it could be fatal.' It was – for the Palestinians after
Rabat. Time and again, they fell victim to their own wishful imagination.

Ever since their rejection of the UN Resolution in 1947 which authorized
the establishment of a Palestinian Arab state in the partitioned Palestine at
the same time as a Jewish state, the Palestinian Arabs have consistently
refused to negotiate a political settlement with Israel, which would have
been far more favourable to them than anything achieved as a result of forty
years of war and terror against Israel. The real tragedy of the Arab summit
in Rabat in October 1974 was not so much the elevation of the PLO into a
role it could not fulfil, but that it institutionalized Arab attitudes and with
them the 'fatal' assumption that Israel was in decline and doomed, and that
Arab power henceforth resided in the PLO fuelled by 'oil dollars' and by
the worldwide deference accorded to it.

The rich and powerful Arab rulers settled for this at Rabat and agreed
to pay the financial and political tribute demanded from them as the price
for PLO preparedness to carry the brunt of the continuing war against
Israel. In this connection, the Palestinian rank-and-file, if not the leaders,
might have noted a shrewd comment by Sadat's long-time political adviser
and trouble-shooter, Tahseen Beshir. Speaking to Fuad Ajami, one of the
more perceptive of contemporary Arab writers, some time after the Rabat
summit, Beshir explained that for the rich, oil-producing Arab rulers, the
war against Israel was 'a spectator sport'. Having helped to subsidize
Egypt's war in 1973, they wanted the war to last longer; 1973 was to them
only one battle in an ongoing and sustained military encounter, which
presumably would henceforth be conducted by the PLO. As part of this
process, King Hussein was temporarily reprieved as the next target of the
PLO, but deprived at the same time of all effective power in shaping
Palestinian policy.

Sixteen years later, as we record these events of not so long ago, it is
difficult to believe that intelligent men and women in positions of authority
and influence should then have seriously propagated their conviction that
Israel's coming demise could be realistically anticipated. Yet when we now
look through our papers for that period, we can understand how logical and
convincing that prospect must have seemed to Arafat and to his Palestinian
colleagues. There were so many seemingly authoritative voices raised in

confirmation of the accuracy of the PLO's prognosis of Israel's inevitable decline.

Foremost among these was unquestionably the collective voice of the Arab world expressed with all the authority of the Arab heads of state assembled in Rabat in October 1974 – just one year after the Yom Kippur War. All the accumulated deviousness, cowardice and mutual disloyalty which have characterized relations between the Arab heads of state in so many previous crises found expression in the Rabat decisions, which confirmed and encouraged the extravagant claims to primacy by the PLO. Not one king or president attending the summit was prepared to denounce and oppose a policy which – if carried out – would have spelled political death for the Hashemite Kingdom of Jordan and King Hussein. None stood by him. On the contrary, they unanimously endorsed the PLO's policy calling, in effect, for the overthrow of regimes disliked by the PLO; but Jordan was the only one actually named and singled out for early action. The spinelessness of the Arab leaders in the face of this PLO threat, which in its way was addressed to all of them, is difficult to comprehend.

But it is undeniable that it gave the PLO a great boost, a feeling of invincibility and unchallenged authority. At every stage Kissinger was made aware of the new factor that had to be absorbed: the refusal of the new Palestinian leadership both to negotiate on any terms but full acceptance of its demands, or to deal directly with Israel on any terms. After Rabat, when all the Arab heads of state had underwritten this policy, there was nothing left to discuss or to negotiate for either Kissinger or Israel.

It is revealing, however, to recall just two very representative expressions of western opinion of that time to demonstrate how impossible the situation had become for Israel, despite the remarkable effort put in by Kissinger and his team in their endeavours to break the deadlock. They never had a chance after Rabat. Within weeks of the summit, one of the most respected of American academics, considered to be very much a spokesman of the alternative school of thought to that of Kissinger, the prestigious Director of Studies of the American Council of Foreign Relations, Richard H. Ullman, published a presentation of how the non-Kissinger establishment saw the Middle East situation after Rabat. It was vividly revealing in many ways. The position of Arafat and his colleagues at Rabat was described as that of genuine moderates in their willingness to abjure terrorism and even to recognize Israel's existence as a state. This was 1974 – not Geneva 1988. One outcome of the Rabat summit was, therefore, a possible harmonious relationship between Israel and the Palestinians. But Dr Ullman thought this was not likely. His reasons for not expecting peace to break out in the wake of the Rabat summit were interesting and instructive of a state of mind at one of the principal policy-making centres in the United States.

Ullman developed his policy perspective in this way: Rabat, in effect, symbolized the ascendance of the assumption that history belongs to the Arabs, not to their enemies. New and vastly greater oil revenues now made it possible to shorten the time-span of this 'history' from decades to years, and perhaps even to months. Moreover, as the flow of funds to Israel from Jews abroad had declined to a derisory trickle compared to the enormous stream of oil dollars, Arab resources were now many times those of the Israelis. Final Arab success on the battlefield was at last near at hand. These developments were seen to spell the failure of Kissinger's attempts thus far to bring about a Middle Eastern peace. It was not surprising that at Rabat the most uncompromising stand against Kissinger was that of the Saudis, whose colossal oil wealth provided them with enhanced standing among the Arab states. Riding high on their mammoth piles of oil dollars, the Saudis exuded self-confidence and determination to maintain the Arab consensus against any compromise with Israel. Thus, with the Palestinians playing a newly pivotal role in intra-Arab politics and with the Arab world as a whole convinced that oil would turn the tables on Israel, the Rabat summit and its aftermath seemed to have made a new war much more likely.

This scenario as seen by the Director of Studies at the American Council of Foreign Relations was not one that brought Israel much reassurance and made us wonder who spoke for the United States if it came to the crunch: Kissinger or the Council, whose views were so tellingly reflected by Ullman. He spelt out his scenario for the post-Rabat years without fudging it. What worried Israel's leaders about it was not so much what it might do to the Israelis, but what wrong signals it would send to the Palestinian Arab leaders.

Ullman's conclusion was that the vast transformation in the relative abilities of the two sides to command resources, together with the gradual but steady improvement in the fighting abilities of the Arab forces, had worked and would continue to work to undermine the credibility of the American commitment to Israeli independence. The global configuration of power had changed so much that, given their vast new wealth, the Arabs might never be induced to accept the existence of an Israeli state within their midst.

Ullman continued to explain that the post-Rabat Arab leadership, especially the Palestinians, would not insist upon the annihilation of the Israelis, in the sense that Hitler sought to exterminate the Jews; rather, they would seek the destruction of the Israeli state, with its inhabitants (but not necessarily all of them) 'departing', as Ullman delicately phrased it. Then, he went on to say, with all the authority of one of the State Department's most prestigious advisory bodies, that

rather than uphold the anomalous Israeli state, enlightened American statecraft should act to facilitate the inevitable transition in accord with the new realities of power, and should work to provide not only for the resettlement of the Palestinians but also [ironically] for the resettlement of the Israelis.

I must admit that we did not pay undue attention to these thoughts; they seemed to us to be so way out as to allow us to simply shrug them off. But what we did not know at the time was that Ullman was reflecting the mainstream of Arab thought more accurately than did Kissinger.

The publication in the United States of Ullman's views in *Foreign Affairs*, the most authoritative foreign policy publication of the US policy-making establishment, within weeks of the Rabat summit, confirmed the Palestinian leaders in their state of euphoria at the Rabat decisions and made Kissinger's attempts to move a few steps further ahead in his peace-making even more fruitless.

I make no apologies for dwelling on the Rabat summit and its aftermath, for it was one of the most significant turning-points of this period. As a corollary to Ullman's scenario, it is necessary to consider the thinking of the PLO leadership as expressed publicly and privately. I can think of no better way to do this than through the exposition penned at about the same time by one of the ablest presenters of PLO policy, a close confidant of Arafat's and most PLO leaders, the then Foreign Editor of Paris's *Le Monde* and later France's Ambassador in Algeria, Eric Rouleau.

Writing of the Palestinian question after Rabat, Rouleau first restated the conditions on which the PLO would participate at an international peace conference:

It would have to consider the implementation of all the UN resolutions, including those of 1947 relating to the division of Palestine, and 1948 concerning the refugees' right to choose either repatriation in Israel or fair compensation, as well as, of course, the resolutions passed on 22 November 1967. If these demands, which are considered minimal are not satisfied, the Palestinian representatives would refuse to make peace with the Jewish state. In that case, the PLO would not formally renounce its 'strategic goal', that is to say, the establishment of a Jewish–Arab Palestine.

Rouleau, like Ullman, was too sensitive to spell out that a Jewish–Arab Palestine presupposed the elimination or destruction of the State of Israel. Writing at the same time and in the same place as Ullman, Rouleau said bluntly that at this point, in mid-November 1974, Israel had no choice. She must negotiate with the PLO sooner or later on the terms set out by the PLO. Refusal to do so would leave no outlet other than a war, 'which might well end in a political catastrophe for Israel, considering the world-wide economic, financial and diplomatic power at the disposal of the Arabs'. By way of a footnote, Rouleau added that also on the PLO's menu was the taking over of Jordan by the Palestinians.

All these were strong signals beckoning the PLO and its backers to regain with diplomatic and political means what had not been achieved by war or terror. But another signal was yet to come, addressed not to the PLO but to Sadat and the Egyptians.

In the early autumn of 1974, while preparations for the Arab summit were under way, it became evident that Brezhnev had reactivated Soviet policy in Egypt. After a brief visit to Moscow in mid-October 1974 by Egypt's Foreign Minister, just before the Rabat summit at the end of the month, Brezhnev renewed his invitation to the Egyptian Foreign Minister, Ismail Fahmy, and to the new Defence Minister, General Mohammed Abdel Ghani el-Gamassi. The Egyptians were feted in Moscow while Brezhnev reaffirmed the 'unchanging Soviet policy of overall aid and support for the Arab peoples, including the Arab people of Palestine'. The Egyptian Ministers for their part expressed the gratitude of President Sadat and his Government to the Soviet Union for her principled and friendly stand in support of the just cause of the Arabs.

In order to underline his renewed support, Brezhnev despatched two shipments of tanks and missiles left over from a previous order, which had been halted at the end of the October War when Egypt was desperately seeking a cease-fire. It seemed that the Russians were probing to find out just how far the Kissinger initiative had run into trouble and whether there was any useful fishing in troubled waters to be done. However, when at the critical moment Kissinger again displayed his own particular brand of successful negotiation with the conclusion of the Second Disengagement Agreement between Egypt and Israel, he effectively closed the door to any possible Soviet re-entry on terms acceptable to Brezhnev. He had made it clear to the Egyptian Defence Minister in Moscow that the war option, which might embroil the Soviet Union with the United States, had to be excluded from future Soviet–Egyptian relations. There was thus not much leeway in Brezhnev's political alternative, which had been effectively blocked by the Americans and by extremist demands from the Palestinians.

We were about to enter a new phase without being very clear what it would involve. It would still take time before it would take shape, but Israel was now convinced that all the war talk at Rabat, and before that by the Palestine National Council in Cairo, was pure bluff. Neither the PLO nor any of the Arab states was prepared or able to go to war against Israel; the Russians would not buy another war in which they would have to rely on Arab proxies. The Americans – though sometimes critical – were solidly behind Israel. Kissinger had been a trustworthy and staunch ally and friend, although we knew of two attempts by President Nixon, when Kissinger was away from Washington just before the Watergate climax, to create a forum for bringing pressure on Israel. No one can say what would have happened if Nixon had remained in office, but he did not. However, those Israelis who were aware of the occurrence believed that Israel should not treat it lightly. It taught us at the time not to take anything – or anyone – for granted.

But all this was being overshadowed by a far more exciting development. We were getting reliable information from Cairo that Sadat had been greatly shocked and upset by the developments which had culminated in the Rabat summit decisions. The growing assertiveness of the PLO and its spoiling demands, which would make any form of negotiation impracticable, had begun to worry him. So did the opportunism of the Saudi leaders, who were exploiting Palestinian and other extremist opinion for their own purpose. Sadat read their intention correctly. It was designed to block every possible path to peace, and to obstruct every move that could lead to a settlement short of meeting all the demands of the Palestinians and the Saudis.

Sadat had learnt a lot from his association with Kissinger. He knew that the alternative he now faced was not a comprehensive peace or a partial peace; it was either a separate peace or no peace at all. This conclusion by Sadat was the most important consequence of the decisions taken first by the Palestine National Council and then by the summit of Arab heads of state at Rabat. By blocking Kissinger's chosen road to a settlement and peace, they made certain that Sadat would decide to take his own road, the road to Sadat's peace.

3

Sadat's Conversion

1975–6

PRESIDENT SADAT HAD BEGUN to think of a new peace strategy during the horse-trading sessions that preceded and followed the Rabat summit. Sadat and his fellow Arab rulers still believed – or at least pretended to do so – that the American intervention after the Yom Kippur War, and in the cease-fire which ended the fighting, was targeted on appeasing Arab demands so as to prevent the outbreak of another war. The idea of peace with Israel had not entered their minds: the most that Sadat was prepared to concede was acceptance of the new status quo once all Arab demands, including those of the Palestinians, had been met. There was to be no peace treaty, no normalization of relations, no fraternization and no direct negotiation with Israel. Nothing much seemed to have changed.

However, there was an important new element in Sadat's thinking after the Rabat denouement: he clearly felt himself freed from responsibility for both the PLO and the Syrians. They had charted their own course at Rabat – and it was not Egypt's course. They had decided on what they considered to be best for the Palestinians; it was now for him to decide what was best for Egypt. But even so, alone and seemingly prepared to negotiate with Kissinger for what was to all intents and purposes a separate deal, Sadat was no pushover. He was determined to exact a high price, for Egypt's sake, and to flaunt his successful independent and separate negotiations before the critical and unsuccessful Arab rulers – and, not least, before his own dissenting ministers and officials.

When Kissinger returned to Egypt and Israel in February 1975, he found Sadat in a confident and demanding mood. He wanted much and offered little. He knew Kissinger wanted to round off his series of Middle Eastern shuttles with a successful grand finale: an interim agreement between Egypt and Israel that would ultimately pave the way to a peace treaty. Sadat had shrewdly concluded that, as a result, Kissinger had become vulnerable; he wanted something which was in Sadat's gift and, therefore, had become dependent on Sadat if he wanted further success. This was particularly evident after the June 1974 decisions of the Palestine National Council, which were later endorsed by the Arab heads of state at their Rabat summit in October 1974.

Their call for the liquidation of the Jordanian monarchy had ruled out any advance of the Jordanian option with which Kissinger had concerned himself for some time, and which was aimed at reaching an understanding between Jordan and Israel which would embody within it a solution to the Palestinian problem acceptable both to Jordan and to Israel. Evidently for reasons of his own, when he must have known that it was a non-starter, he continued to urge it on the Israelis as a way to settle the Palestinian question. But Sadat understood that what the Palestinians and the Arab heads of state had done at the Rabat summit – apparently without realizing what they were doing – was to leave Kissinger with only Sadat's Egyptian option as the way forward; and Sadat, for his part, wanted concessions from the Israelis and financial assistance from the Americans – not an 'Israeli peace'.

Sadat had told Kissinger that he would not support the planned deal with King Hussein because he was not prepared to wait an extra year or more before settling Egypt's claim for the return of the whole of the Sinai. We were naturally concerned and interested in the response which our Arab neighbours would make to the militant call of the Rabat summit, but our principal interest was concentrated on Egypt; and it was from Egypt that most of the sound and fury emerged in the first instance. We noted, however, with particular interest that Egypt was hardly speaking with one voice: there were stark contradictions early in 1975 in the comments emanating from President Sadat and from his Foreign Minister, Ismail Fahmy. They contradicted each other on major issues of policy towards Israel and on relations with the Soviet Union.

This conflict inside the Egyptian Government was best illustrated by its public pronouncements. As so often, we learned much more from these published statements by Arab leaders than from confidential talks between Arab spokesmen and third parties such as Kissinger or the British, or even with our people. The Arab politicians and publicists appeared to have a hidden urge to express in public what they really thought and sought to speak with far more discretion in private. We therefore paid close attention to public pronouncements coming at this time from Cairo.

In an interview on British television by Ismail Fahmy, given shortly before his departure for Moscow in October 1974, the Egyptian Foreign Minister fully endorsed the PLO claims which Arafat had made at the United Nations – and went much further. He called on Israel to accept the boundaries which had been proposed in 1947 and to transform the State of Israel into a democratic Palestinian state of Muslims, Christians and Jews, with an Arab majority. But first Israel would have to make good the losses suffered by the Palestinians for the past twenty-six years and recompense Egypt for her losses of oil production and for other damage suffered as a result of the 1967 war. Finally, Israel would have to undertake to freeze her population at its 1974 level: there must be no more Jewish immigrants for fifty years.

Having made this extraordinary pronouncement of Egypt's position in all seriousness, Fahmy departed for Moscow for his meeting with Brezhnev, which was to finalize arrangements for Brezhnev's visit to Cairo in January 1975. In Moscow, Fahmy was feted and emerged on the last day of 1974 with a joint Soviet–Egyptian communiqué, which turned out to be most revealing. It spoke of cordial relations between Egypt and the Soviet Union, but Soviet involvement in Egypt was limited to support for the recalling of the Geneva conference.

Here we found one of those subtle distinctions in which Soviet policy specializes. The joint communiqué said that Egypt and the Soviet Union were firmly in favour of the Geneva conference (of which the Soviet Union was joint chairman with the United States) resuming its work. However, the conference was only to 'examine' all aspects of a Middle East settlement and then to take appropriate decisions leading to a lasting peace. There was nowhere any mention of negotiating with Israel. With the Soviet Union and Fahmy insisting that the PLO was to be part of the 'examination' and with the PLO's and Fahmy's stated terms for a settlement, the whole affair was little better than a charade. Neither the United States nor Israel would take a second look at these Egyptian–PLO terms.

Sadat's Foreign Minister, who was clearly so keen to upstage his President, was encouraged to pronounce on Moscow television and radio on the gratitude felt by President Sadat and the Government of Egypt for the principled and cordial support which the Soviet Union had given the Arab cause. Both Washington and Jerusalem were aware that this was largely make-believe and were curious to find out what would come next. They knew that the real reason for Fahmy's Moscow visit was for him to be told of Brezhnev's illness and the consequent cancellation of his proposed summit with Sadat in Cairo. They did not have to wait.

Within twenty-four hours of Fahmy's return to Cairo, Sadat addressed a conference in which he reviewed Egypt's prospects until the year 2000. He echoed his Foreign Minister's conclusion that Egypt and the Soviet Union had embarked on a new relationship based on an absence of confrontation. They shared the same views on what had to be done next. Sadat reminded his audience of something he did not want them to forget: that he had concluded no agreements with Israel. 'Neither the cease-fire nor the Disengagement Agreement was primarily with Israel; both were concluded between Egypt and the United States.' He then made a remarkable admission that brought the Egyptian reality home to members of this conference. In a passage that revealed the real state of Egypt in 1973, before the outbreak of the Yom Kippur War, Sadat confessed that Egypt's economy had touched bottom, so much so that on one occasion it was not possible to provide bread for 1974. And he went on to make his point: 'Really and truly, it was the $500 million we received immediately after the battle [from the United States] which propped us up and helped us through the painful tribulation. Our economy had been completely drained during the six years which preceded the battle.'

This was another way of saying that no matter what Fahmy and Brezhnev had concocted in Moscow, there was no way forward for Egypt other than with United States' assistance. He hinted at this in reply to a question from one of the delegates. The Arab Foreign Ministers would be meeting in three days' time to co-ordinate their policies with the Palestine Resistance for the proposed resumption of the Geneva conference and to apply the decisions of the Rabat summit. But that, he let it be clearly understood, would solve no Egyptian problems, feed no hungry Egyptian bellies nor restore the vitality of the Egyptian economy. Sadat was soon to find that no one was prepared to heed his warning that Moscow could not provide for Egypt's real needs. His Foreign Office and Foreign Minister, his newspaper editors and his senior officials seemed set in believing that they could again call on the Soviet Union as an ally and dictate the terms of a settlement without the need to negotiate with Israel. The idea of peace with Israel remained utterly remote.

Sadat waited a week and then he spoke again to correct the false optimism about renewing relations with the Soviet Union as an alternative to the new American connection. In an interview with a leading Beirut newspaper *An-Nahar*, which was fully reported on the following day, 10 January 1975, in every Egyptian newspaper and on every Egyptian radio station, Sadat attacked Brezhnev and the Soviet Union. They had deserted Egypt in her hour of greatest need and had not supplied any military equipment for a whole year, though they had made good all Syria's losses in the Yom Kippur War. And, most strikingly, the Soviet Union was demanding $500 million for arms and services, while the United States had made Egypt a grant of $500 million to meet urgent needs. As a result, he had frozen all issues outstanding between Egypt and the Soviet Union.

Sadat seemed to be particularly worried by the sheer size of the Soviet rearming of the Syrians. The Soviet leaders, he feared, were encouraging Syria to reopen the war with an attempted reconquest of the Golan Heights – a war for which Egypt was totally unprepared and into which she did not want to be dragged. This was a nightmare for the Egyptian military about which they made no secret. Sadat was also asked about Egypt's immediate objectives in any negotiations, be they at Geneva or elsewhere. Again, he did not fudge: 'I cannot accept less than my boundaries, or less than all my land, all of Sinai and the Golan in full and Jerusalem.' The Israeli withdrawal from these territories must come before anything else.

A week later, Sadat was speaking again to *An-Nahar* and again his words were fully reported in Egypt and worldwide: 'I will accept nothing less than an Israeli withdrawal on three fronts – and within three months. If nothing is accomplished very soon, we will go to Geneva, all of us, including the Palestinians, and explode everything there.'

About this time, Sadat's – and also Nasser's – former political adviser and editor of the prestigious *al-Ahram* newspaper, Hassanein Heikal, was himself interviewed by the ubiquitous Arnaud de Borchgrave, Foreign Editor of *Newsweek*. When de Borchgrave asked whether Heikal could see the Arab world living in peace with Israel, he replied, 'speaking frankly', that he did not think peace would come that easily. No one in Egypt would accept a peace with Israel so long as there was

a land barrier between Egypt and the rest of the Arab world in the east. Israel is a barrier that isolates Egypt. Even if a Palestinian state were created tomorrow and Israel were to return to its 1967 borders, we Arabs will still be physically separated and that is something we cannot accept.

So, de Borchgrave asked Heikal, what was the real solution? In Heikal's opinion the only peace possible was one based either on the 1947 partition plan or on a 'Greater Palestine' in which the Arabs would be the ruling majority. Israel within her 1967 boundaries was still unacceptable because she would remain a geographical wedge dividing Egypt from the eastern Arab world. Clearly, then, we faced a bleak prospect on the eve of Kissinger's new mediation. However, an assessment of Egypt's position at that point was not all that plain sailing. The cross-currents ran much stronger than Israelis had suspected.

This became evident when Egypt's Foreign Minister returned to the charge in a report to the Foreign and Arab Affairs Committee of Egypt's Peoples' Assembly on 18 February 1975, shortly before Kissinger's arrival in Cairo. Fahmy directly challenged Sadat's accusation that the Soviet leaders had distanced themselves from Egypt following the cease-fire on 22 October 1973. Fahmy boasted of the successes of Egypt's foreign policy in recent months in every field and nowhere more so than in relations with the Soviet Union. Twenty-four messages dealing with all areas of mutual interest had been exchanged between Sadat and Brezhnev in the course of developing bilateral relations. There was no disagreement between Egypt and the Soviet Union, he insisted.

The President and his Foreign Minister were obviously assessing the basic relations with the Soviet Union in contradictory ways. It was an impossible situation for Kissinger's new shuttle and it was clearly necessary for Israel to do something to clear the decks. When Kissinger came to talk with Prime Minister Yitzhak Rabin in March 1975, he was evidently aware of the same problem. The one thing that would not further negotiations for an interim agreement was to make more concessions to Egyptian demands, for these had become a bottomless barrel. Instead, Kissinger and Rabin embarked on a complicated and difficult diplomatic minuet to avoid the Egyptian trap and the unwelcome pressure on Kissinger from his new President, Gerald Ford, who had taken over after Nixon's resignation in August 1974.

All these moves coalesced into a weekend of crisis for Egypt and Israel, and for Kissinger – 22 and 23 March 1975 – when all attempts to reach agreement with Egypt seemed to collapse. Kissinger had spent Saturday 22 March with Sadat and Fahmy at Aswan in a last attempt to reach agreement. Fahmy had already told some of his friends (and ours!) among the international press corps, which had been summoned to Aswan, that there would be no agreement: Egypt had rejected all proposals that were put forward by the Israelis through Kissinger, 'because they were in conflict with Egypt's Arab obligations'. Fahmy also confided to his newspaper friends that Kissinger had wanted to conclude his mission with this visit to Sadat, who was staying at Aswan. However, Fahmy said that he had so arranged matters that Kissinger would come first to Aswan and then go to Jerusalem to announce there the failure of his mission. The world would then understand that the responsibility for this unhappy conclusion to Kissinger's peace-making lay with the Israelis.

But the ever-impetuous Fahmy could not wait. For one thing, most of the foreign press corps were leaving Aswan early with the Kissinger caravan 'to be in at the kill' in Jerusalem. As a result, Fahmy's carefully manipulated scenario simply collapsed. He had planned to call his press conference and make his public announcement immediately after Kissinger had departed for Jerusalem, in the early evening of Saturday 22 March. But Kissinger had to postpone his departure until nightfall and the end of the Sabbath, before starting his talks in Jerusalem, thus leaving Fahmy to reflect on the unanticipated pitfalls of timing in international diplomacy: contrary to his carefully laid plan, he was telling the foreign press corps that Kissinger had failed even before Kissinger had arrived in Jerusalem and talked to the Israelis. It did not help when Fahmy delayed publication in Egypt of details of his press conference until after midnight; the international news agencies had already reported what Fahmy had said in Aswan about Kissinger's failure. Thus Rabin was alerted to Egypt's negative position even before Kissinger arrived in Jerusalem. It greatly strengthened the negotiating posture of the Israelis, and of none more so than that of the Prime Minister.

Fahmy had given the game away even before the negotiations began. Fahmy had in his own inimitable way publicly revealed Egypt's negotiating position, which allowed for no way forward for either the Americans or the Israelis. What is more, it temporarily closed the door to Sadat's private hopes for his own independent initiative. But Sadat was a master at timing his moves and for the moment he left the stage to Fahmy. While Rabin and his ministerial colleagues were locked in tense negotiations with Kissinger in another room, they heard Fahmy announce that the United States' mediation had come to an end with the failure of Kissinger's mission.

Accordingly, Fahmy then announced that Egypt would request the immediate convening of the Geneva conference and would consult with her Arab sisters and the PLO. The state of war with Israel would not end until a final and comprehensive Arab settlement had been concluded, which would involve the withdrawal of all Israel forces from all the occupied Arab territories and the establishment of a Palestinian state. Only then could Israel ask to be accepted as part of this region. This Egyptian position, he said, had been, from the very first, based on and determined by the resolutions of the Rabat Arab summit conference. Fahmy added that these points had been put into a written submission by Egypt and handed to Kissinger: the Palestinians must be invited to Geneva, and Egypt would not agree to peace with Israel so long as the Palestinians had not obtained their national rights.

During these tense negotiations with Kissinger – especially on this critical Saturday night of 22 March – some Israelis were inclined to accept Kissinger's criticism of Israel's finicky, obstinate and unimaginative diplomacy. At the time, Kissinger made out an almost unanswerable charge-sheet against Prime Minister Rabin, Foreign Minister Yigal Allon and Defence Minister Shimon Peres. Probably the Israeli negotiators were often difficult and sometimes unforthcoming in negotiations, but I do not believe that Rabin and Allon – both highly imaginative and innovative soldiers in their time – obstructed American proposals because of small-minded and fearful considerations, as Kissinger has suggested in an often quoted passage in his memoirs. Both Allon and Rabin had displayed an unusually acute understanding of, and sympathy for, the Arab in war and peace, and as a result had greatly contributed to the foundations of Israel's military success story.

Their reasoning had been much more subtle and more fundamental than that of 'pure' politicians and diplomats. Golda Meir, who had handed over the premiership to Rabin when she resigned, would probably have gone along with Kissinger – as he reflected later with evident nostalgia. Rabin, Allon and Peres did not. Whether they refused the Kissinger–Sadat offer on that historic night of 22 March for the right or the wrong reasons is now immaterial. What did matter was that they refused Sadat's territorial demands in Sinai without Egyptian willingness to complete a formal peace treaty with Israel and they thus changed the course of Israel's and Egypt's history. For this refusal placed the onus of action on Sadat; he was handed Kissinger's baton. It was now the responsibility of Egypt's President to make the final run. Kissinger could no longer do it, but he had done the next best thing before bowing out: he had paved the way for Sadat that would lead him first to Jerusalem and then to Camp David. It was a contribution Kissinger made at this critical parting of the ways for which he has not yet received his due credit.

As for Israel's Prime Minister, he had in effect laid down something akin to the 'Rabin Doctrine', which neither Kissinger nor Sadat was willing to accept during March 1975, but which became in September 1975, only six months later, the cornerstone of the Interim Agreement which Egypt and Israel signed, as we shall see, on 1 September – the final step before the signing of a formal peace treaty. This was the essence of the Rabin Doctrine, namely that until peace was signed Israel would not make the territorial concessions Sadat demanded.

Meanwhile, with the customary ingratitude of politics, Kissinger had come that same weekend under great pressure from the new Ford administration. The Ford men had begun to assert themselves and to require Kissinger to produce meaningful concessions from the Israelis. In bald terms this meant insistence that Israel should accept Sadat's territorial conditions for a new interim agreement with Egypt, the so-called Second

Disengagement Agreement. This American demand climaxed after the night-long session with Kissinger in Jerusalem when, in the midst of the Cabinet meeting on Sunday morning, 23 March, the Ambassador called with a personal letter from President Ford to Prime Minister Rabin.

The letter, dated 21 March 1975, advised Rabin in unusually forthright language that Israel's failure to reach agreement with Kissinger and Sadat had caused Ford 'profound disappointment' and that the failure of the Kissinger mission, which expressed the 'vital United States' interests in the region', would have a far-reaching impact on Israel's relations with the United States.

The implied warning was fairly explicit. But just in case Rabin was inclined to minimize the Ford administration's determination to compel the Government of Israel to make concessions which the United States considered necessary, Ford told Rabin that he had 'given instructions for a reassessment of United States' policy in the region, including our relations with Israel, with the aim of ensuring that overall American interests ... are protected'. The Ford letter ended with a curt 'You will be notified of our decision.'

This was strong stuff. The stick had taken the place of the consultative carrot. The ultimatum long sought by Israel's American critics had at last been delivered. Clearly, we now had to make our own assessment of the policies with which we were confronted – Sadat's, Kissinger's, Ford's and the waffling, sitting-on-the-fence policy of King Hussein. We had to take another look at the Rabat summit and its consequences. This was no time for an Israeli mistake. But how had we reached this disconcerting position?

The real climax had come late on that Saturday night of 22 March, the night before Rabin received Ford's ultimatum. What happened that night transformed not only Israel's diplomacy but also Kissinger's; and the initiative for that had come from the Israelis, not from the Americans. Egyptian–Israeli relations were launched on a new course from which there was no turning back.

The key to understanding that change was the now famous last words by Kissinger which ended that meeting at midnight on 22/23 March; just one brief sentence, we were told, uttered by Kissinger as a kind of sad farewell when it became evident that Rabin was not prepared to accept the terms proposed by Sadat. 'Had Israel accepted the proposals backed by the United States,' said Kissinger, 'the consequential agreement would have enabled the United States to remain in control of the diplomatic process.' But what Kissinger had failed to understand that night – a rare occurrence for him – was that it was just this that had begun to worry the Israeli Government. Rabin had not yet received the Ford letter, but the Israelis had been getting the message for some time from Washington that the winds of change were stirring, if not actually blowing. In view of this, Israel did not want the Ford administration to control the diplomatic process. We were prepared to go along with Kissinger; we trusted him even if we did not always agree with him. But we no longer trusted United States' policy as expressed by the Ford administration; there were too many ambiguities and uncertainties. In future, we wanted Israel and not the United States to be in control of the diplomatic process. That was at the root of the difficulties which Kissinger had with the Rabin Government during the critical months of 1975.

During these months, when Washington was reassessing its policies towards Israel, a series of events outside the Middle East contributed to the hardening of Rabin's inclinations against reliance on American assurances and on Sadat's undertakings.

For overshadowing our local consideration and casting grave doubt on the validity of American assurances was the contemporaneous expulsion of the United States from Indo-China. Even if nothing was said in our negotiations with the Americans, Israel could not but draw disconcerting parallels. The United States appeared powerless – despite assurances given – to sustain her friends and allies in South-East Asia. The Cambodian capital fell to the Communists on 17 April 1975. Twelve days later, American forces and diplomats beat a hasty and inglorious retreat from Saigon and Indo-China. American promises and innumerable guarantees were of no avail to the hapless people who had placed their trust in the United States.

It may have been a fortuitous coincidence of unrelated events, but they made their mark on Rabin and fuelled his determination not to make Israel's security dependent on decisions taken in Washington without Israel's participation and assent. There were other occurrences in our region at this time which seemed marginal then but which would become significant. King Feisal of Saudi Arabia was assassinated on 25 March, only days after he had pledged his support for Kissinger's effort. In Lebanon, a civil war exploded on 13 April. Israel's Prime Minister felt strongly that this was a time when he had to keep his hand on the tiller – no matter what the reassessors were saying in Washington.

Rabin's firmness surprised and shocked Sadat and his advisers. It also surprised and annoyed Ford and his reassessment team, which was singularly lacking in friends of Israel or, for that matter, of Kissinger. Rabin had refused to take seriously Sadat's warnings that there would be an 'explosion', and had refused to be panicked by the Ford reassessment. This left both Sadat and Ford suspended uncertainly somewhere in a diplomatic limbo. Kissinger was more than usually reserved about these developments, but it is more than likely that he felt pleased that Israel had not fallen for Sadat's ploy.

Without saying anything that might suggest that he was doing this, Kissinger was in fact carrying out one of his most remarkable and – in my view – most self-effacing diplomatic manoeuvres of his career. It must have been the product of a classic inner struggle with himself, a question of priority rather than loyalty. Had he abided by the conventional rules of forcing Rabin to accept the American–Egyptian terms for a settlement, he might have brought the Israelis to agree. But in Kissinger's view, at that time, such an agreement would have ruled out Sadat's future willingness to consider a genuine peace settlement with Israel without other Arab participation or approval.

Somehow, therefore, Kissinger had to desist from encouraging the Israelis to agree to a settlement which, in the long run, would not have been in their interest, nor in that of the United States and Sadat – even if that entailed a temporary loss of American goodwill for Israel. It was a very emotional dilemma for Kissinger, but his innate intelligence and his perceptive understanding of the real prerequisites for peace at that time led him to accept Rabin's obstinacy while to all the world he appeared to condemn it. In a sense, by that action alone, Kissinger and Rabin were the real godfathers of the Camp David Accords. The revised Interim Agreement, which was signed on 1 September 1975, was consequently totally different in character from that on which Sadat and Ford had insisted in March. We did not realize it at the time, but Kissinger and Rabin had set up the signpost that would lead us to Camp David.

At that time, it must be said, the conventional view of the Interim Agreement was that it was little more than a stop-gap to paper over the inability of Kissinger to reach any worthwhile agreement between Egypt and Israel. On this occasion, however, the hard-line Arab states, Syria, Algeria and even Jordan, and the PLO, were nearer the truth than the sceptical experts who wrote off the Interim Agreement. For they saw correctly that it was, in effect, the first political bilateral agreement between Israel and an Arab state and they furiously denounced it. Looking at the contemporary records, I doubt whether Sadat and his colleagues saw it as such; certainly few, if any, Israelis did so. I am sure Kissinger knew what he was doing, but in the prevailing political conditions in Washington – bent on reassessing United States' relations with Israel – such thoughts voiced publicly would have been unwelcome. But Kissinger was then no longer worried; he could afford to let go and be content to hand over to his successor.

For with this final act of his Middle East career Kissinger had, in effect, corralled Sadat and the Israelis. It was a remarkable achievement and end to a unique diplomatic experience that had begun the day war broke out on 6 October 1973. It was only a matter of time now before Egypt and Israel would understand what had happened when Kissinger made them sign this much denigrated Sinai accord on 1 September 1975 – two years and two months to be precise before Sadat was addressing the Knesset in Jerusalem.

However, the Israelis were still preoccupied by two recurring problems. The first was the continuing reappearance of the ghost of the Rogers' Plan of 1971 in a new guise. We had heard, and had been told, that the consensus of opinion regarding the reassessment of American policy towards Israel was that Israel would have to accept the principal Arab demand, based on the Arab interpretation of the Security Council Resolution 242 passed after the Six Day War in November 1967, that Israel would have to withdraw from all Arab territories occupied by her in 1967, including 'Arab' Jerusalem. Our second problem was concerned with Sadat's motives and objectives, which preoccupied our leading politicians, soldiers and intelligence services. The answers which we would give to both questions would, as it were, condition Israel's future policy in relation to Egypt.

There was a great deal of misunderstanding in the United States and in Europe concerning Israel's supposed unwillingness to withdraw to the frontiers of 1967. It was widely assumed that this was Israel's single-minded response to any suggestion of a settlement linked to an Israeli withdrawal from the territories then occupied. This was to mistake our position. At that time, under Rabin's premiership, Israel was prepared to withdraw to secure frontiers once these had been properly negotiated; these would entail an Israeli withdrawal to 1967 boundaries, but not in all cases. However, withdrawal could take place only under conditions of total peace and normalization of relations with the Arab country concerned. In our view, the UN Security Council Resolution in 1967 had clearly indicated these priorities when it stipulated that 'the establishment of a just and lasting peace' has to come first before any withdrawals from the territories occupied in 1967. It was this conditional proviso that was always missing from peace proposals made by Arab negotiators or by third parties involved in such negotiations. It was Israel's price that Sadat was not prepared to pay until he came to Camp David.

Our second problem concerning Sadat's motives and intentions was central to the discussions in the Cabinet and in the General Staff. All were involved in our own policy reassessment, which focused on the concessions Israel could afford to make. This discussion climaxed in the summer of 1975, some three months before the signing of the Interim Agreement with Egypt, in open differences in the Government and among its advisers. Among those who opposed the Kissinger–Rabin approach to the new agreement was Yuval Ne'eman, the special adviser to the Minister of Defence, Shimon Peres. He resigned from his post. Another, as a matter of particular interest in view of his later role, was Moshe Dayan. It was an apt illustration of what Dayan had often said: there is no such thing as a final position or a last chance. Circumstances were always changing as he himself would illustrate in the case of Egypt.

There was a general consensus at the time that Sadat wanted an agreement as a means to an end. But to what end? On the face of it, he needed an agreement, not because he wanted to make peace, but because he desperately needed money. The Americans had undertaken to loan him another $500 million once there was an interim agreement. But Sadat needed the money so badly that the United States advanced him $250 million in March without first seeking congressional authorization. The balance was to be paid in August on the understanding that the agreement would be signed within weeks. It had become evident to Israel that Sadat still wanted to attain his traditional objectives: to compel Israel to withdraw from all of Sinai and from all other Arab territories occupied in 1967. But despite his routine warnings to foreign diplomats and journalists that the alternative to an early Israeli withdrawal was another 'explosion', another war, we sensed that there had been a change of emphasis in Cairo – primarily of necessity rather than of inclination.

There had been a subtle change of atmosphere and we had been alerted to it by Kissinger's handling of the affair. It was becoming evident to us that Sadat was no longer a believer in the alternative of a war option, but he was still planning to get what he wanted without war and with American help. He was greatly encouraged by the tone and contents of Ford's letter to Rabin warning him of the proposed reassessment of American policy. Thus, during the summer of 1975, while negotiations for the Interim Agreement were hanging fire, we were confronted with one of these peculiar diplomatic affairs that occurred periodically in our relations with the United States and taught us a great deal about the art of negotiation.

We were still focusing our attention on Sadat and his plans when it became evident to us that Sadat was losing interest in any further resumption of the Geneva peace conference and that he had discovered another love: none other than President Ford. In fact, he was placing great hopes on a scheduled meeting with the President which was to take place in June 1975. Sadat was carefully preparing himself for this encounter – something which was not a normal practice for him.

By the time the two Presidents met in Salzburg, Austria, on 2 June, there had been a great deal of preliminary collusion between them. The result was not exactly Mozart to Israeli ears. The form of words which Ford used for his announcement shocked the Israelis – and many others. But even more disconcerting to them was the harsh tone which Ford gave his undertaking to Sadat that the United States would ensure that the Sinai Interim Agreement, which Kissinger was then negotiating, would be only the first step towards a full settlement that would be acceptable to Sadat.

What was particularly shocking to the Israelis, and also to Kissinger, was that Ford had reawakened thoughts and hopes in Sadat which we had believed had been effectively laid to rest. It was inevitable that Sadat would respond to Ford in kind; it was inconceivable now that he would steer a more responsive course when the American President had gone overboard with so irresponsible an undertaking. Sadat was all in favour of making the most of it; why not? All the more so when Ford repeated his Salzburg promise publicly in a theatrically televised telephone conversation with Sadat, in which he congratulated Sadat on concluding the Interim Agreement on Sinai.

When Sadat made his public response before the Peoples' Assembly in Cairo on 4 September 1975, he did not thank his old and hitherto trusted friend 'Henry'. He had been displaced by the man on whom Sadat now rested his hopes: 'I should like to take this occasion', Sadat said, 'to thank President Ford.' He added pointedly, to the accompaniment of well-rehearsed stormy applause from the invited audience, that Ford had 'stood honourably by his words and undertakings. His personal intervention has had a great effect on the accomplishment of this great step.' He, Sadat, would not allow international agreements or the policy of détente to freeze the Middle East situation. There would be no peace until Israel had withdrawn 'from every Arab territory and until the Palestinian people have a state of their own in which to voice their will and their right to self-determination'.

On the face of it, many observers in Israel concluded that Sadat's uncompromising words justified the sceptics who questioned the value for Israel of the Interim Agreement – among them Dayan and Ne'eman. But Kissinger and Rabin were not over much impressed by Sadat's words because they were by now convinced that Sadat had really no choice but to go along with the Interim Agreement. Rabin had stood firm and had refused any further concessions. The result was a low-key agreement with Egypt which served Kissinger's and Rabin's purpose. This was to impress on Sadat that he was not getting anywhere with his insistence – with Ford's encouragement – that peace was to be found in the company of Syria, the PLO and Jordan. On the other hand, the Interim Agreement had set out the signposts along the road on which Egypt and Israel would have to travel. The Agreement had stipulated

1. that the conflict between Egypt and Israel 'should not be resolved by military force but by peaceful means';
2. that Egypt and Israel would not resort to the threat or the use of force, or military blockade against each other; and
3. that Egypt and Israel were determined to reach a just and final peace settlement by means of negotiations.

The Agreement then specified the territorial adjustments to be made by Israel. These left ninety per cent of the Sinai Peninsula – the ace of trumps – in Israeli hands.

There had been, in fact, two main agreements. The first, negotiated by Kissinger between Egypt and Israel, had emphasized the purpose of the two countries 'to reach a final and just peace settlement by negotiations' and to that end they agreed on a number of measures. Israel returned the Sinai oilfields to Egypt and made some minor adjustments in the deployment of her forces in the Sinai Peninsula on which Sadat had insisted. In particular, Israel withdrew her forces from the two principal passes in the Sinai Peninsula, but insisted that these should not be occupied by Egypt. A buffer zone was agreed, controlled by the United Nations, with an early-warning system which was entrusted to the United States.

Basically, we had made two major concessions: the return of the oilfields and the Israeli withdrawal from the passes. But the gains to Israel were immeasurable. For alongside this Interim Agreement, Rabin had been negotiating through our Ambassador in Washington, Simha Dinitz, what in effect was a parallel agreement between Israel and the United States. In many ways this 'Memorandum of Agreement', which was signed by Kissinger and Israel's Foreign Minister, Yigal Allon, on the same day as the Interim Agreement was initialled, on 1 September 1975, was a most remarkable agreement. Without this separate 'Memorandum of Agreement', there would probably have been no Camp David. It became an integral part of the peace-making process. It gave Israel the confidence and assurances which enabled her, just two years later, to take the initiative and grasp the Sadat nettle.

The then secret (but not for long) 'Memorandum of Agreement' began by acknowledging that the United States recognized that Israel's withdrawal from vital areas of Sinai constituted an act of great significance on Israel's part in the pursuit of a final peace. Accordingly, the United States undertook to ensure Israel's oil supplies. She would also make available sophisticated military equipment, which was detailed in the Agreement, and a sum of $2 billion in aid. There were also a number of political clauses, two of which were considered by us to be central to the Agreement.

Paragraph Five said that the United States Government would not expect Israel to begin to implement the Agreement before Egypt fulfilled her undertaking concerning free passage through the Suez Canal. Paragraph Six was the shortest and most important. 'The United States Government agrees with Israel that the next agreement with Egypt should be a final peace agreement.' In a separate section on reconvening the Geneva peace conference – if and when – the Agreement reaffirmed that the United States would maintain her policy 'whereby it will not recognize or negotiate with the PLO so long as the Palestine Liberation Organization does not recognize Israel's right to exist and does not accept Security Council Resolutions 242 and 338'.

In the light of these achievements by the Rabin Government and Kissinger, the shameful antics of the right wing and Gush Emunim demonstrators who excoriated Kissinger in Jerusalem must for ever remain a blot on those who were responsible for this painful display of anti-Semitism in Jerusalem. All the same, Kissinger and Rabin had now signposted the route.

How, then, could Sadat proceed towards his foremost objective – the 'liberation' of the whole of the Sinai Peninsula – within the parameters of the Interim Agreement? His options were shrinking. The Arab League or its separate member states had nothing to offer him that might have helped. The radical Arab and Third World extremism on display against Israel at the United Nations was unrealistically negative. It condemned Egypt, and the whole Arab world with its burgeoning oil revenues, to noisy inactivity on the question of a peace settlement with Israel. Understandably, Sadat was feeling trapped. A man of action who liked to shock the world, he seemed to have nowhere to go and nothing to do other than the way Kissinger had charted. On one of his journeys to Cairo, Kissinger had brought Sadat a personal letter from Rabin, which proposed that the two should meet privately and seek to break the diplomatic impasse. Sadat did not reply, but Rabin's message had sown a seed, which took some time to ripen.

Meanwhile, after all these diplomatic excitements, 1976 was to be an altogether different year. Israel and Egypt were preoccupied with domestic problems, with our morale-boosting Entebbe rescue of the hijacked plane passengers, and with the coming presidential election in the United States almost as much as were the Americans. New names and unfamiliar parties took the international stage, which was itself transformed by the change of guard in Washington. Jimmy Carter was an unknown quantity in the political record book.

We were now confronted by a reassessment with a vengeance; so were the Americans and Egyptians. The only constant factor in the Middle Eastern equation was Sadat – and that alone said much for the degree of certainty with which we were now faced. If ever there was a new ball game, the outlook for 1977 was certainly it. It was not so much a turning-point in the history of the Middle East as a somersault. And it was not over yet; another general election in Israel, with its accompanying political waves, was yet to come.

For us, among many other noteworthy developments, it marked the end of the Kissinger era, which had been so rich an experience and which had laid the foundation for benefits which we were yet to reap. Kissinger's diplomacy by compromise was, in its way, a continuation of the trial-and-error diplomacy of Israel's first President, Chaim Weizmann – but with a superpower additive. Kissinger called it 'step by step', but it was the same thing. He had to learn what was possible as he went along and – even more importantly – what was *not* possible. He had to make his own theories and conditions.

Sadat faced a different problem when the Kissinger phase ended – and his brief and hectic liaison with President Ford proved to be no substitute for his departed friend. For Sadat, there was one overriding lesson: whatever Kissinger could do for Sadat – and he did a great deal – it was not enough. Sadat had begun to understand that Egypt would never regain the Sinai Peninsula so long as he had Syria and the PLO in tow. And by the time he had concluded the Interim Sinai Agreement, he began to realize that the kind of initiative he required could not come from the United States, be it through Kissinger or Ford. Only Israel could provide the kind of initiative and conclusion that he wanted as a basis for a lasting peace between Egypt and Israel. If Israel did so, then the United States would follow.

Israel was under no illusions: Sadat's ultimate and primary aim was a de facto alliance with the United States. No one else could help Egypt overcome her desperate social and economic problems. But Sadat realized at last, at the end of the Kissinger odyssey, that his road to Washington must pass through Israel. Israel was his key to the United States, not the other way round. With Israel at his side, he would be sure of American support; and with American support, there would be certainty of peace with Israel. The dialectic of Sadat's reasoning would have delighted Lenin. But even without Lenin, it set the stage, with new actors and with new lines, for the historic and almost incredible developments of 1977. At last, we were on the road to Sadat's peace. The new American President and his men would have a lot to unlearn before we finally met at Camp David.

4
Peace: The Wrong Turning
1977

THERE WAS AN ELEMENT OF Greek tragedy in the transition to the new-look Democrats in the United States. The manner of Kissinger's departure was one more classic example of the ingratitude of politics and of the incomprehension of those who were his principal beneficiaries, not only in Israel but equally so in Egypt, and – not least – in the United States. In Israel also, Prime Minister Rabin fell victim to circumstance and had to hand over the premiership to Shimon Peres; before long Peres, too, was overtaken by the political tide which carried Menachem Begin to power on 17 May 1977 and set Israel on a new and uncharted course. But it was Sadat who faced the most difficult challenge: how to disengage Egypt from the dead hands of the Syrian ruler and from the self-destructive policies of the Palestinians.

It was evident by the time that Carter took office on 20 January 1977 that Sadat now knew what he wanted and what he could get, following the Interim Sinai Agreement which we signed on 1 September 1975. But he still did not know how to get it. The fifteen months' interregnum since then had been the occasion for marking time and taking positions – but the period was marred by the absence of perspective in Jerusalem and in Cairo, and even more so in Washington.

In Jerusalem, the Government was beset by domestic problems, political scandals and the ever-lengthening shadow cast by the pending general election in May 1977. The Labour Alignment Government realized that it had to contend with many, and some serious, local difficulties, but neither the Peres Government nor its supporters, nor – I suspect – Begin's right-wing Likud Party, at this time in early 1977 ever imagined that the Labour Alignment, entrenched in power for thirty years since the birth of the state, was about to experience total electoral defeat at the hands of the Likud Party. It was clearly a period when Government and opposition alike were preoccupied with their own problems and inward looking rather than focusing on the prospects of peace with Egypt.

In Cairo, Sadat was undergoing a period of considerable personal and political stress as he observed his Arab allies and his principal colleagues in government, while contending with popular riots in the streets of Cairo. This state of stress was further aggravated by the unabated social and economic malaise of the Egyptian people. The war of 1973 had not brought the dramatic change he had expected; Sadat, in fact, was prone to much exaggerated expectations, as we ourselves were to discover before long. Instead, he found himself burdened and restricted by the intervention of the Arab states – especially by the Palestinians – at the United Nations. These seemed to widen the gulf between the Arabs and the Israelis, and especially with the United States. It reinforced his conviction that there was no salvation for Egypt to be found along this line.

There was cold comfort for Sadat when he turned for counsel to his ever assertive Foreign Minister: Ismail Fahmy was opposed to any accommodation with Israel; he had not been happy with the Interim Agreement and he was most active behind the scenes in all kinds of schemes to shepherd Sadat away from the Americans and to steer him back into the welcoming embrace of the Soviet leaders. Fahmy did not seem aware that this was the last thing Brezhnev and his powerful advisers really wanted. The more they saw of the condition of Egypt, the fewer were their regrets that it was the Americans who were burdened with Egypt's insoluble problems. What the Russians had sought from the ever voluble and gullible Fahmy was something quite different: when Gromyko met Fahmy in Sofia in November 1976, the Russian was much more interested in the United States' intentions in the Middle East than in Sadat's. Fahmy was subsequently invited to Moscow and treated with obsequious – and rather suspicious – hospitality, first by Gromyko and then by Brezhnev himself. The talkative Egyptian Foreign Minister must have been an unwitting gold mine of information about Egypt and her relations with the United States for the Muscovites. In any case, the Soviet leaders must have learnt from him all that they had wanted. After Fahmy's departure, Gromyko cancelled his visit to Cairo, scheduled for August 1977; shortly afterwards, Brezhnev also cancelled his official visit, scheduled for September. For the Soviet Union, Sadat was now dispensable; and Fahmy was clearly a spent force.

However, all this had become almost irrelevant as the new Carter administration took over in Washington. It did not take us any time to discover that 'continuity' was not a buzz word in Carter's vocabulary; all the more so since 'Kissinger' had become a dirty word in the White House: his policies, his method and his practice would have to make way for Carter's New Deal for the Middle East. It was not so much that Carter proposed a clean sweep of the Kissinger method as a sweeping back into the diplomatic arena all the impediments to negotiations which Kissinger, Rabin and Sadat had so painstakingly removed in order to make possible the Interim Agreement of 1 September 1975. After that came the presidential election year in the United States, a period of uncertainty and indecision in Israel, while Arab aggression towards Israel found relatively harmless and ineffective expression in denunciation and condemnation of Israel in the UN General Assembly.

But there was one particularly unfortunate exception to this in which the European countries, especially Britain, France and Italy, shared with the

Arab countries and the PLO the responsibility for doing lasting damage to Israel. They did not seem to consider that by doing so they were also inflicting untold harm on the Palestinians in the refugee camps in the Gaza Strip and in the Israeli-administered West Bank territories. The Europeans supported an Arab-sponsored resolution in the UN General Assembly on 23 November 1976, some two months before Carter assumed the presidency, which ordered Israel to halt an ambitious and imaginative plan to rehouse many tens of thousand Palestinian Arabs residing in the UN refugee camps in the Gaza Strip. A hundred and eighteen member states voted against the Israeli proposal and condemned these Palestinian Arabs to continuing misery in the camps. Only the United States and Israel voted for the scheme.

The majority certainly did not do anything by this action to alleviate the abject conditions of the refugees, which Israel had sought to do on many occasions, but they had at least the consolation that, more than a decade later, the continuing misery of these refugees provided convenient propaganda fodder for politicians bent on condemning Israel, such as the then British Minister of State at the Foreign Office, David Mellor, or the British Labour Party's spokesman on foreign affairs, Gerald Kaufman. They had probably never heard of the blocking action of their Government at the United Nations in 1976 before they rushed in where angels normally fear to tread.

For Sadat, the arrival of Carter on the scene was critical to his plans. He knew that, with Kissinger's assistance, he had been boxed in by Rabin's firm stand during the negotiations for the Interim Agreement. Sadat understood that there was no way now in which he could regain Egyptian possession of the Sinai Peninsula without first concluding a peace agreement acceptable to Israel. He was not yet ready nor willing to make that psychological leap. Moreover, he was a rare species: a patient politician and a born optimist; something would turn up. And he had his eyes firmly fixed on that 'something'. When opinion polls were foretelling a radical turn-around in the coming American presidential election, Sadat 'went for broke' and placed his money on Carter. Friends in the United States, close associates of Carter, had brought him encouraging previews of the Carter administration's proposed New Deal for the Middle East. For Sadat, Carter's entry into the White House was like manna from Washington.

This was reflected in his maximalist public pronouncements and even more so in the private brief he proposed to take to Washington for the meeting with President Carter, scheduled for early April 1977. Sadat was preparing to submit 'a definite peace strategy' to the Americans. It was evident that these proposals marked a retreat from a peace settlement as understood in Israel when we concluded the Interim Agreement with Egypt. The plan Sadat proposed to take to Washington was something quite different – it was a reversion to the maximalist Syrian and PLO policies, which, without saying so, would rule out any peace agreement with Israel. The 'peace agreement', in Sadat's presentation for Carter, provided for a Palestinian state on the West Bank and in the Gaza Strip, while Israel would have to withdraw from all the territories occupied in 1967, 'so that a formal declaration is made when we meet in Geneva, ending the state of war with Israel'.

This was the familiar Arab demand when Kissinger first started, which he had proceeded to demolish step by step. Now, Sadat was putting it all together again with added spice. We heard of this new version of Sadat's peace only after he had elaborated on it in his talks in Washington with Carter and his new Secretary of State, Cyrus Vance.

Sadat did not mince his words. He evidently felt – rightly so – that he was talking to a sympathetic audience. He insisted that there had to be an end to the Kissingerian step-by-step solutions. He recalls in his memoirs that he wanted a comprehensive settlement, a final peace, now that he had proved that Egypt, 'after eighteen years of confrontation with the United States', had responded to the American peace initiatives, while Israel, 'who is really America's step-daughter', was willing to sacrifice American interests so as to achieve Israeli ambitions. Carter was totally overcome by Sadat's human warmth and powerful personality: 'It was as if a shining light had burst on the Middle East scene.' For Carter, Sadat was a man 'whom I was to admire more than any other leader'. But these were early days yet for Carter; he had been President for just six weeks. It was left to Secretary of State Vance to probe more thoroughly into the meaning of Sadat's peace.

The Carter–Sadat encounter had been noteworthy for the contrasting ambience from that with Prime Minister Rabin, whose meeting with Carter had preceded Sadat's by only three weeks. Everything about that meeting had been different. Carter's approach to Rabin had been adversarial even before he had arrived. Carter wanted to know whether Israel would be prepared to withdraw to the 1967 borders. He informed Vance that Rabin would be told that Israel could not have the peace she wanted without such a withdrawal. It was Rabin's bluntly expressed opinion that Israel would certainly not get the peace she desired if she agreed to such premature withdrawal as requested by Carter, Sadat and the PLO.

Carter was uncertain and confused about the precise Arab contribution which he would seek in return for the Israeli withdrawal he had requested from Rabin. Rabin was impatient with Carter's somewhat half-baked proposals and he made no great effort to hide his feelings. Vance was of the opinion that the President and the Prime Minister jarred on each other's nerves. When Rabin left, Carter was angry. He described Rabin as stubborn, unimaginative and unwilling to take positive steps – or risks – for the sake of peace with Egypt. Rabin was more measured and substantive in his reaction to the first meeting with the new American President; but what mattered at that time was not the impression made by a lame-duck Israeli Prime Minister who was about to leave office.

The impression that did matter was the instant aura created by the charismatic President Sadat when he greeted President Carter on the White

House lawn three weeks after Carter's unhappy encounter with Rabin. It was evident that, as far as Carter was concerned, it hardly mattered what Sadat said: he was captivated by the outgoing magnetism of the Egyptian leader. 'He was a consummate actor,' as one of Carter's principal and more cynical Middle East specialists, William P. Quandt, was to comment during a subsequent performance by Sadat. But it served its purpose. Sadat had arrived and conquered the White House and its occupant, something which Rabin had failed to do. It was no mean problem for the Israeli leaders as they sought to cope with this novel experience of being upstaged in Washington by an Egyptian leader. Fortunately for them the next Israeli Prime Minister was Menachem Begin, and even more fortunate that behind Begin stood the imposing influence of Moshe Dayan – a match for both Carter and his Secretary of State.

Meanwhile, Vance, with his sixth sense for the practical and the essential, dispersed some of the misty euphoria which had enveloped the presidential dialogue; neither Sadat nor Carter was prone to precision when it came to political formulations. It was Vance who brought them both back to earth to face the Israeli reality.

In Vance's opinion, Sadat had come to Washington with one overriding aim, which was rather different from the objectives which he had proclaimed before and after his visit to Washington: Sadat wanted to know authoritatively whether Carter was serious when he offered to provide American leadership in the search for a Middle East peace. Sadat wanted to be absolutely sure that Carter was committed to his promised even-handed policy despite the domestic political problems he would have to face as a result – a polite way of referring to the 'Jewish lobby'.

Sadat told Carter that he was against concluding a formal peace treaty with Israel. Instead, he preferred peace 'agreements' out of which normalized relations with Israel would develop after Israel had withdrawn from Arab lands. But this would take many years. For the foreseeable time, even after Israel had withdrawn from all the territories occupied in 1967, there would be no normalization, no open borders and no exchange of ambassadors. Sadat was still, psychologically, light-years away from his journey to Jerusalem, which, in fact, took place only six months later.

Sadat assured Carter that, within this bleak framework of Egyptian policy, he would be flexible if Carter could assure him that Israel would seriously negotiate 'a comprehensive settlement'. By this, Sadat meant Israeli agreement to withdraw from all the territories occupied in 1967, including East Jerusalem, and Israeli acceptance of an independent Palestine Arab state on the West Bank and in the Gaza Strip.

Sadat emphasized that Israeli acceptance of such a comprehensive settlement would be dependent on the degree of American involvement. The 'peace' should be negotiated under American auspices, not in direct negotiations between Egypt and Israel. The United States would make proposals and Egypt would accept them and then go to Geneva 'simply to sign the agreements'. It was Sadat's unspoken assumption that the United States would ensure that Israel would do likewise. He told Carter that there was no point in going to Geneva to negotiate with Israel at an international peace conference. 'That process would take ten years and Egypt would get nothing.'

Despite Sadat's really extreme demands, Carter's demeanour to him was warm and generous – in contrast, Quandt noted, to his frosty manner towards Rabin only three weeks previously. Quandt also noted that Carter never seemed to understand that Sadat – and other Arabs – wanted the Americans to impose their plan for peace (as approved by Egypt) on Israel. The international conference at Geneva should then be primarily a formal signing ceremony at which Israel would accept the American peace plan. As Israel's leaders received very full reports on the Sadat talks with Carter from our usually well-informed Embassy in Washington, it was evident to them that not only had Sadat still to learn a great deal about the facts of life concerning making peace with Israel, but so had Carter.

Carter had told our people how, prior to the Rabin and Sadat visits, he had sought to acquire the necessary background information by 'putting in an awful lot of time studying the Middle East situation'. Even before he became President, he had been particularly concerned with the centrality of the Palestinian situation and he had, on his own showing, a sound and sympathetic understanding of the origins of the Palestinian problem and of Israel's difficulties relating to it. What greatly upset Rabin was Carter's total failure to understand the changed nature of the PLO and the extent to which this affected Israeli attitudes. Carter was not alone in this curious lacuna in his approach to our conflict with the PLO. His principal advisers – one of whom had written a major study on the political and military dimension of contemporary Palestinian nationalism – were similarly at fault, and with much less excuse.

What was most disturbing was not only the position taken by Carter on the Palestinian question, but the certitude of their own rightness and self-righteousness with which the Americans lectured us. They made no allowance for the possibility that Carter, or his National Security Adviser, Zbigniew Brzezinski, or Quandt might be mistaken or might not be aware of relevant facts. They were so sure of themselves that they knew what Israel must do about the Palestinians. We know from the available records that before meeting Rabin on 7 March 1977, Carter had been urged by his security and Middle East advisers to 'lay it on the line' for Rabin.

Carter did so in no mean manner. Brzezinski was present at the meeting with Rabin and kept detailed notes of the conversation. Carter was direct and 'forthright'. The United States wanted rapid negotiations with the Arabs, including the PLO. Israel would have to withdraw to the 1967 boundaries with minimal border changes. Five days later, on 12 March, while Carter's almost rude presentation to Rabin of his New Deal for the Middle East was being assessed, Carter added one more morsel he had refrained from putting to Rabin. Without first informing his Middle East staff, he told a press conference at Clinton, Massachusetts, 'that there has to be a homeland provided for the Palestinian refugees'. Israelis were frankly shocked not only by the implication but also by the manner of the statement. If this meant a total reversal of American policy and United States' support for a Palestinian Arab state, why had Carter not mentioned it to our Prime Minister only a few days previously?

We made formal and informal enquiries; we sought some clarification. We were not the only ones. Vance and Brzezinski had been as surprised as the Israelis by Carter's declaration. They felt that an explanation to fudge the statement or a clarification of its meaning would be advisable. However, before they could do or say anything officially, they received strict instructions from Carter that no elaborations or clarifications were to be issued concerning the meaning of the 'Palestinian homeland'.

I have devoted considerable attention to these opening gambits which were unknowingly to launch Sadat on his journey to Jerusalem as the preferred terminal to Washington. For behind Sadat's posturing, which so impressed Carter, there was a profound understanding of the Arab – and especially the Palestinian – condition, an understanding which Sadat found totally absent in the Carter administration's conception of Egypt's problems. Despite all the outward bonhomie of the encounter with Carter, the two Presidents were not really on the same wave-length. In his diary, Brzezinski had been rather dismissive of Sadat – 'a man who could not distinguish fact from fiction'. Sadat, for his part, was much too polite (so long as he was not dealing with fellow Arab rulers) to make such judgements; but he must have wondered, as he listened to Carter's exposition, whether Carter and his assistants were even aware of the fundamentals of the Arab conflict with Israel, which, as it happened, had been on public display in Cairo only days before Sadat had left for Washington.

The occasion was the conference of the 13th Palestine National Council, which met in Cairo on the day Carter made his 'Palestinian homeland' pronouncement. Sadat welcomed the PLO delegates along familiar lines. Before doing so, he had met Syrian President Assad and Sudan's President Numeiry in Khartoum to declare their joint support for the PLO position which was to be pronounced with unaccustomed clarity by this 13th Palestine National Council convention, which was about to open its five-day session.

The star role at this convention was reserved for the head of the PLO's Political Department, Faruq Qaddumi, who presented the political report at the beginning and the 'Political Declaration' of the Palestine National Council at the end. Both were rooted, he emphasized, in the 'National Charter' of the PLO, which postulated the ultimate elimination of the Israeli state. This was the PLO's only authoritative policy statement. It was natural, therefore, that we should set it alongside the Carter, Rabin and Sadat discussions which had been going on at the same time. It served vividly to underline the total divorce from reality of the talks initiated by Carter. There was no way in which Carter or Sadat could advance towards a peace settlement with Israel as long as they continued to insist on a

comprehensive settlement which included the Palestinians. Sadat understood this and, therefore, played magisterial games with the Americans, the
Arab countries, the Palestinians and the United Nations. He was playing
for time while he searched for a viable way out of the impasse without the
albatross of his fellow Arab rulers and the Palestinians holding him back.

For whatever else the Palestine National Council in Cairo may or may not
have achieved, its fifteen-point 'Political Declaration' and 'Final Statement'
proclaimed on 20 March were, in effect, a 'No Through Road' sign for
Sadat just two weeks before he was due in Washington. They blocked every
possible avenue by which he might have reached agreement with the United
States, even on Carter's terms; and they ruled out accommodation with
Israel on any terms.

These, then, were the principal policy decisions agreed and confirmed
by the Palestine National Council exactly fourteen days before Sadat's
arrival in Washington:

1. The PNC rejects UN Resolutions 242 and 338 and it rejects all forms
    of negotiation at the Arab and international levels based on these
    resolutions.
2. The PLO will continue its armed struggle and its concomitant political
    forms to achieve its national aims.
3. The PLO will strive to escalate the armed struggle.
4. The PLO will abort any negotiated settlement with Israel by an Arab
    country which does not fulfil the demands set out by the National
    Council.
5. The Palestine Revolution is entitled to establish itself on the soil of
    fraternal Lebanon.
6. The PLO will endeavour to liberate all Palestinian occupied territory.
    It will not seek conciliation and it will not recognize Israel. '*It will
    abide by its Charter, its principles and decisions.*'
7. The PLO demands independent and equal representation at all inter-
    national conferences on the basis of the UN General Assembly Res-
    olution 3236 of 1974 which provides for an independent Palestinian
    state for the return of some 500,000 Palestinians to their former homes
    in Israel.
8. The National Council confirmed its adherence to the PLO's 'strategic
    objective', the liberation of all Palestine from 'the racist Zionist'
    occupation so that it will become a homeland for the Palestinian
    people.
9. The National Council undertakes that all Jews 'who set aside their
    racist Zionist affiliation' will be permitted to remain in the Arab
    homeland.
10. The PLO, in conjunction with the Arab countries, will determine the
    method by which Jews who do not qualify or do not wish to remain
    will be repatriated 'to their homes'.
11. The PNC confirmed 'the Arabism' of all Palestine and especially of
    the City of Jerusalem.

12. Accordingly, the PLO will not participate in any political efforts to solve the Middle East crisis unless its principal demands are first conceded.

13. The PLO will launch a new campaign 'to isolate Israel at the international level' and to 'thwart American plans for a settlement' by getting Arab states to support the PLO initiative to have Israel expelled from the United Nations.

14. The PLO will refuse to attend the proposed Geneva International Peace Conference if it is convened on the basis of UN Resolutions 242 and 338.

15. The PLO will strengthen and develop its bonds of friendship with the socialist countries and especially with the Soviet Union and the People's Republic of China.

This PLO policy was laid down by its supreme policy-making body, the Palestine National Council, in Sadat's presence and on the eve of his departure for the meeting with Carter. Sadat must have been very surprised and rather relieved to find that his American hosts – Carter and Vance – were completely oblivious of these decisions taken in his presence and with his apparent approval. Carter and Vance continued to move in a kind of Palestinian dream world, which bore no resemblance to the real world Sadat had just left in Cairo. Sadat must have wondered how the Americans could be so uninformed and gullible about the Palestinians. It must have come as a shock – and as a warning – to Sadat because Carter was unwittingly playing the Palestinian game with his insistence on an impossible 'comprehensive settlement' which would also embrace the Palestinians. During his talks with Sadat, Carter showed repeatedly that he had no clue what the PLO wanted and what they meant by a 'homeland'.

Yet it had all been expounded with commendable clarity by the Palestinian leadership and broadcast to the world – if it wanted to listen – from Cairo.

This was a comprehensive and frank exposition of PLO policy. It made clear where the Palestinian leadership stood. Sadat – judging by his later comments – understood what this meant for Egypt and he had expected that Carter would have been similarly briefed about its bearing on the possibility of a comprehensive settlement which included the Palestinians. The CIA must have known, so must the Middle Eastern specialists of the State Department; but evidently not the President.

Why had he not been told? At least, that is how it seemed. And if he had been told, how was it that Carter appeared so blissfully unconcerned by the destructive policies of the Palestinians? Sadat wondered, but he had no answers. He kept his own counsel and continued to play political charades with Carter. Time would tell; meanwhile, he too needed time to await the outcome of the Israeli election on 17 May. Sadat returned to Cairo unaware as yet of the political storm that would engulf Israel in a matter of weeks and give a surprising new twist to his negotiations with the Americans.

There was thus a natural and welcome hiatus in the proceedings, which was hardly broken by the appearance of Israel's new Prime Minister, Menachem Begin, on the scene. He was an unknown quantity in Washington and Cairo. He arrived in Washington with Moshe Dayan in mid-July 1977 and met Carter on the 19th. It was hardly a meeting of minds or hearts as it had been between Carter and Sadat. There were no 'shining lights' this time. Both men were subconsciously suspicious of each other, if only because they did not know each other. Secretary of State Vance, who was present, noted that the two men did not spark the same degree of mutual trust as Carter and Sadat had done.

However, it was – in Israel's view – a definite advance on the seemingly total deadlock that followed Rabin's last visit. At least the Americans were curious. They wanted to get to know this prickly new Israeli leader, who had about him an air of old-worldly charm and politeness, which, in its way, was strangely attractive and which even Carter found difficult to resist altogether. But there was a hard core beneath Begin's charm, which Carter was to discover before long, when he explained to Begin the American view of a comprehensive settlement.

Begin had been apprehensive and somewhat defensive. This was an altogether new situation for him. After thirty years in the political wilderness during Israel's most critical years, he was transposed in one fell swoop to this meeting on equal terms with the President of the United States. For a man so deeply imbued with the drama of Jewish history, this was no ordinary encounter. Both men had to feel their way to each other and this was reflected in Carter's presentation of American intentions. He was much softer and far more even-handed than he had been with Rabin. Carter was clearly aware that he would have to live with Begin for a long time to come.

It is interesting now – in the light of later events – to recall how Carter presented the American position to Begin on this, their first meeting. He began by reassuring Begin that the United States would be prepared to mediate, but would never agree to impose a settlement on Israel or let any other third party impose a settlement to which Israel had not agreed. But then came a performance of Carter's typical even-handedness, which, as we were to discover, he used not only in negotiations with Israel, but also in his discussions with the Egyptians and with other Arab leaders. Thus, having reassured Begin on this count, Carter then startled him by telling him as a matter of self-evident fact that the basis for a settlement would be the 'peace for withdrawal' equation based on the UN Security Council Resolutions 242 and 338, and on direct negotiations. Dayan, who was present and watchful, was particularly pleased with Carter's definition of peace. It was not very different from the Israeli concept. Peace, Carter said, must include open borders, diplomatic recognition and full normalization of relations, which Israel was demanding. Furthermore, the final territorial boundaries would have to be negotiated by the parties themselves and would have to be militarily defensible. Finally, Carter told Begin that he was convinced that the Palestinian question would have to be tackled, but he was against the establishment of an independent Palestinian Arab state: he preferred a Palestinian homeland linked to Jordan.

Dayan immediately saw the positive elements in Carter's presentation of American policy, whereas Begin focused on the negative aspects, which served, as it were, to halt the process while all kinds of side issues and hobby-horses were addressed. Dayan recognized that Carter had given Egypt and Israel 'the first nudge' that set Arab–Israeli peace negotiations going. He recognized those elements in American policy which would keep the process moving ahead and – this was the crux in Dayan's eyes – steer it away from the one issue which Israel could not concede before there was a full and viable peace in operation: the withdrawal from territories occupied in 1967, but not necessarily from all such territories and not from Jerusalem.

It was this issue that was to be at the heart of the negotiations with Sadat before it was resolved at Camp David in September 1978, just as it was at the heart of our conflict with the Palestinians ten years later: the conditions of Israel's withdrawal from territories in her possession since 1967. That whole period of negotiations, moving like a travelling circus, from Washington to Aswan, from Jerusalem to Leeds Castle in England, to Geneva, to New York, to Riyadh, to Marrakesh and to Camp David and Cairo, always reverted in the last analysis to this one question. Yet the real issue was never properly formulated and never clearly stated: it was Israel's refusal – then and now – to surrender territories occupied in 1967 except under the most rigorous conditions. It was an attitude based on Israel's experience.

During the sixteen years from 4 July 1947, when David Ben-Gurion addressed the United Nation's Partition Committee, UNSCOP, until 19 July 1963, when Israel's Prime Minister, Levi Eshkol, addressed a message to President Nasser: 'I want to talk peace,' Israel's representatives had made 122 recorded offers of peace to her Arab neighbours. The answer was always the same: the offers were not rejected; they were contemptuously ignored. When we questioned the Arab leaders informally or through friendly third parties, the answer was invariably the same: Egypt, Jordan and Syria – there was no Palestinian representation – were not interested in making peace, for Israel had nothing to offer in return. The Arab countries managed quite nicely without peace with Israel; this was Israel's problem, not theirs.

But all this changed dramatically after 1967 once the full impact of the consequence of Israel's territorial gains had been absorbed by the Arab world, and after Egypt's attempt to restore the pre-1967 boundaries by force of arms had failed in 1973. Egypt, Jordan, Syria and the Palestinians now favoured 'peace'; but in their new vocabulary, 'peace' meant Israeli withdrawal to the 1967 boundaries, which would then lead to an end to the state of war. That was 'peace'; nothing more. And once Israel had withdrawn, then – in Sadat's words – it would be a long time before there could be any move towards normal relations, diplomatic missions and open borders. Sadat told Carter during one of their private talks that it would probably take at least a generation after Israel had withdrawn from the occupied territories before there could be normal relations.

This was the problem and remained the problem of Israel's relations with her Arab neighbours. The Americans – Carter, Vance and their Middle East establishment – were seemingly unable to see that this was the crunch of all negotiation on a Middle East peace. The position taken by the Syrians and Palestinians automatically excluded them from negotiations since they posited an Israeli withdrawal first and peace and normalization a long time later, when Israel would no longer have any sanctions that would compel the conclusion of an acceptable peace. Egypt was the exception largely due to the foundation laid by Kissinger during his initial negotiations: they were conceived as stepping-stones to peace and did not require an Israeli withdrawal without a prior peace agreement.

When the Carter administration took over, the President and his advisers did not at first appreciate this fine but fundamental distinction. As a result, Carter and Vance not only frightened the Israelis, but also Sadat with their insistence on a comprehensive settlement. For Sadat had a better idea than most of the real intentions of the Syrians and the Palestinians; and in his book King Hussein of Jordan did not count. Sadat considered him totally ineffective and unreliable. Therefore, every time Carter and Vance reassured him that they were working for a comprehensive settlement, Sadat began to explore possible and really viable alternatives.

It was not easy for him. He had no one now with whom he could consult on this since Kissinger's departure. His own officials and foreign politicians used to make fun behind Sadat's back about his reliance on 'his friend Henry'. He knew all about that and did not mind because he valued Kissinger's advice and trusted him implicitly, because Kissinger could tell him unpleasant truths to his face even if he dressed them up in diplomatic mumbo-jumbo. But 'Henry' never misled or betrayed him. Sadat never felt the same about Carter. The great display of warmth in which Carter basked so ostentatiously was essentially, as Quandt recognized, a 'performance'. Sadat never lost his inner reserve towards Carter. It was not so much that he distrusted Carter, but that he distrusted Carter's ability to comprehend the essentials of the problem we had to overcome. Every time Carter elaborated on his belief in a comprehensive settlement and in a solution for the Palestinian problem, or in a 'homeland' for the Palestinians, Sadat drew further back.

The President suffered from a curious inability to understand Sadat – a man he appeared to admire more than any other politician or statesman. Carter never came to grips with the real Sadat – not before Sadat's journey to Jerusalem nor in the build-up to the Camp David agreement and its aftermath. For a brief period before coming to Washington in April 1977 to meet the new President, Sadat had harboured hopes that Carter would be able to deliver the Israelis and get them to withdraw to the boundaries of 1967 and to agree to an independent Palestinian state in return for minimal concessions by Egypt. It did not take Sadat long to discover, after meeting Carter, that this was another white hope that had to be written off.

The Carter–Sadat relationship was fraught, not for lack of goodwill on either side, but by total lack of mutual comprehension. It was quite different between Sadat and Begin. They had not yet met. They probably did not like what they knew of each other, but, unlike Carter, they understood each other. Both were cast in a similar mould.

Both were extreme fundamentalists, not moderate pragmatists. Both had begun their political careers opposing British imperial rule. Both had been in conflict with the authorities. Both had resorted to extra-parliamentary methods. Both were addicted to grand political gestures. They were almost made for each other; they even disliked each other.

Meanwhile, Begin's Foreign Minister, Moshe Dayan, had made his own mark in Washington. He had greatly impressed Secretary of State Vance with his ability as a diplomat, his forthright honesty and his passionate desire to bring about a peace with Egypt. But in this involved interplay that had taken the stage in Washington it was Dayan, among all the participants, who correctly assessed Sadat's great frustration at his inability to make progress. Sadat was blocked by Carter's constant harping on the need for a comprehensive agreement, without understanding the implications for Egypt; by Begin's pedantic and unimaginative formalism; and by the Egyptian Foreign Minister's inability to see Egypt's needs as Sadat did. Dayan decided on a drastic step to help Sadat overcome his frustration. He had his reasons.

5

Jerusalem:
The Education of Anwar Sadat

1977–8

IT DID NOT TAKE Foreign Minister Dayan long to understand that a fundamental change had taken place in the search for a peace settlement with Egypt. It was one of his unique qualities, which Israel's first Prime Minister, Ben-Gurion, had recognized in Dayan some twenty years earlier; he had a remarkable instant grasp of essentials. Even while Begin was continuing his discussions in Washington and New York, Dayan had drawn his own conclusions from the conversation they had had with President Carter on 17 July 1977. He had concluded that the biggest obstacle at this stage to an agreement with Sadat was not the Egyptian but the American position. The sublime indifference shown by Carter, Vance and their staffs to the realities on the ground in the Arab–Israeli conflict prevented any serious discussion between Egypt and Israel – and there was no Kissinger to bridge the gap. Almost before he had left the meeting with Carter, Dayan became convinced that the way forward to peace with Egypt was to exclude, for the time being, the participation of Carter and his men with their fixed ideas about a comprehensive settlement.

Unaware of Dayan's thinking, Sadat in his own way was reaching a similar conclusion. Both were looking, in their separate ways, for a possible alternative to the Washington middle-men, who were unwittingly creating conditions and making difficulties that could result only in deadlock. Both Dayan and Sadat had realized that there could be no effective alternative policy without first excluding the Americans from the next stage of negotiation, and that there would be no resumption of the international peace conference at Geneva on the American terms on which Carter had set his heart.

Begin and Dayan were having second thoughts after their favourable first impressions of their encounter with Carter. They had left the meeting with mixed emotions. They were impressed by the President's evident and sincere desire to bring about an agreed settlement of the conflict between Israel and her Arab neighbours, but they also sensed that Carter would exact a price for American support which Israel could not afford to pay. This was initially only an instinctive rather than a reasoned assumption, but formal confirmation of Carter's price-tag came within a matter of days. On the day Begin returned home, a week after Carter had outlined American policy to him in Washington, Carter's Ambassador in Tel Aviv, Samuel Lewis, handed Begin a five-point memorandum. It proposed once again, to Begin's dismay, the familiar theme that Israel should withdraw from all territories occupied in 1967, and that a 'Palestinian entity' on the West Bank and in Gaza be established as a precondition for a future peace. These concessions by Israel were to serve, together with other more acceptable suggestions, as a basis for reconvening the Geneva conference.

Begin was angry and upset by these demands, which the Americans had sprung on him and which were in striking contrast to what Carter had said to him only a week earlier. It shook his faith and trust in the President and in American assurances generally. He turned to his Foreign Minister for advice, not one of Begin's favourite occupations. It was the opening for which Dayan had been waiting – and he was ready for it. He suggested to Begin that this was the time and the opportunity for direct action to establish contacts with Sadat without American participation or knowledge. Begin hesitated before giving his approval, for he was a cautious man, all the more so now that he had achieved high office and the premier position of power. But Dayan convinced him, and so the chain reaction began which was to bring Sadat on his historic mission to Jerusalem.

Meanwhile, Secretary of State Vance had the thankless task of travelling to the Arab capitals and conducting esoteric discussions with King Fahd in Riyadh and with Sadat in Cairo on the kind of language that would make Carter's proposals and the PLO acceptable at the Geneva conference when it resumed. We heard from the travelling Secretary of State that the Americans had told the Saudi King that all that was required was for the PLO to accept 'the American language', and thus publicly accept Israel's right to exist. Then the Carter administration could fulfil its commitment under the Interim Sinai Agreement and accept the PLO into the international community. There still appeared to be no awareness in Washington of the decisions taken by the Palestine National Council in Cairo in Sadat's presence barely five months earlier, which had rejected all but maximalist demands. It was evident that, if there was to be any progress, it would have to be along the course on which Dayan had embarked.

On 5 September 1977, six weeks after the return from Washington and the receipt of the memorandum setting out Carter's unacceptable policy, Dayan was in Marrakesh, meeting King Hassan of Morocco. He asked the King to arrange a meeting between Dayan and a representative of Sadat, or, alternatively, a meeting between Begin and Sadat. The request was sent and the answer came back from Cairo with unaccustomed speed, within four days, on 9 September; and seven days later, on 16 September, Dayan met Sadat's representative, Hassan el-Tuhami, Egypt's Deputy Prime Minister, with King Hassan acting as host.

It was a meeting that deserves more attention than it has so far received. The subject of meeting with Arab leaders was a constant preoccupation among Israeli Prime Ministers, Foreign Ministers and our leading diplomats. It was, as a rule, little more than diplomatic icing on a non-existent cake. And so it seemed to be at first in our search for a meeting with Sadat. Begin mentioned it to Vance; Vance mentioned it to Sadat; Sadat said he would be quite interested and there the matter might have rested, as it usually did. Begin, however, was keen and talked about it to the Romanian President, Nicolae Ceauşescu, during a brief visit to Bucharest on 29 August 1977. Dayan, on the other hand, took a typically more direct approach. He arranged his meeting with King Hassan 'as a matter of urgency'. Hassan was intrigued and curious.

Dayan explained Israel's problem and impressed on the King that Sadat's difficulties were not dissimilar to Israel's. He told Hassan of the conversation which US Secretary of State Vance had had with Sadat in Cairo some two weeks previously. Sadat had told Vance 'in no uncertain terms' that he now shared the Israeli interpretation of Security Council Resolution 242 on the question of Israeli withdrawal from occupied territories and on the nature of a total peace between Egypt and Israel. On the strength of their nearly identical respective positions, Dayan asked for the King's good offices in arranging a meeting between Sadat and Begin or between Sadat's representative and Dayan. At this stage, Dayan considered a meeting of representatives might be more fruitful than a direct encounter between the two unpredictable leaders. Dayan knew what he was talking about. Hassan wanted to know why Israel could not arrange such a meeting through the Americans with whom both Israel and Egypt had been negotiating the resumption of the Geneva conference.

Dayan now explained to the King the reasons why Israel believed that a resumption of the international peace conference as visualized by the Americans, under the chairmanship of the two superpowers, would mean the end of the peace process. It would give Syria and the Palestinians a power of veto and a platform for their maximalist demands. The Moroccan King was much better informed about the status and policies of the PLO and other Palestinian groups than Carter, and shared Dayan's negative assessment of their value to the peace process. Hassan agreed to forward Dayan's suggestion for an official but secret meeting to Sadat. That was on 6 September.

About the time Dayan was arranging his meeting with Hassan, Carter had a meeting with his Middle East advisers in Washington. He was angry and impatient with Israel, a mood shared by his Middle East specialists and by his National Security Adviser. They urged Carter that the time had come for a frank showdown with Begin. Israel was no longer going the same way as the United States; nor was Sadat. Both had to be brought back on track. The Americans were still on the road to Geneva and seemingly unaware that Egypt and Israel were in the process of constructing their own bypass of the proposed international conference.

Dayan returned to Jerusalem to report to Begin on 6 September. Three days later, he was informed by Hassan that Sadat had agreed to the meeting and his representative would be in Morocco within a week, on the 16th. Sadat wisely felt that it was best to wait before holding a personal summit meeting with Begin. In his heart, Dayan felt the same about a Begin–Sadat encounter, but he was greatly encouraged by the unheard-of speed with which Hassan and Sadat had acted. He prepared with meticulous care for the secret meeting in Marrakesh with Hassan el-Tuhami, who arrived a little late; otherwise all went according to plan. Sadat's ministers, including Foreign Minister Fahmy, had no inkling of his independent diplomacy; nor did Dayan's colleagues in the Israeli Cabinet, except for the Prime Minister. Nothing reached the many ears of the administration in Washington either through overt or covert channels.

Long after the event, insiders in Cairo, Jerusalem and Washington were debating the reason for Sadat's curious choice of Tuhami as his representative. Tuhami was an old and eccentric friend dating back to Sadat's early days in the terrorist anti-British underground, who later became a central figure in the Islamic movement. He had a fine, bearded presence, piercing fanatical eyes, the great self-assurance which comes with single-minded political ignorance and little experience in diplomacy despite his tenure as Ambassador in Vienna. He knew nothing of Israel other than the preconceived prejudices of his kind. He had hated Nasser, whom he believed had sold Egypt to the Communists and had led her into Godless ways. All manner of reasons were later advanced for his choice by Sadat by interested parties in Egypt and Israel, and by the rather miffed Americans, who had not known about the meeting and felt upstaged by Sadat and Begin. But the reasons for Sadat's choice were quite simple and perfectly understandable.

Foremost was the need for someone whom he could trust absolutely, who would not question his decision to engage in secret talks with the Israelis and would never be accused of being anything but an Egyptian and an Islamic patriot. Sadat was not really interested in what his fundamentalist Islamic maximalist said to Dayan: all he wanted to know was what message Dayan had brought from Jerusalem that would enable Sadat to pre-empt American plans for the international peace conference at Geneva.

Tuhami, because of his peculiar qualities and his absolute loyalty to Sadat, fitted the bill to perfection. No one would ever accuse him of being a party to a sell-out; he could be relied upon to provide a perfect Arab alibi for Sadat so long as the Israelis kept quiet; and for once they did – mainly because, apart from Begin and Dayan's personal assistants, no one knew about the encounter in Marrakesh.

In the event, beyond all the hours spent on real and apocryphal discussion and on consuming endless courses of oriental delights, the essentials of the encounter in Marrakesh were reduced to a three-line, hand-written message, which Dayan gave Tuhami for Sadat's eyes only. It said simply that Israel was prepared to return the whole of the Sinai Peninsula to Egypt in exchange for a peace treaty, open boundaries and normal relations. Just that. It sounded simple enough to Dayan and to Begin at home. Dayan probably understood – especially after listening to Tuhami – that this was anything but simple for Sadat, but he had sown the seed; it was now up to Sadat and Tuhami to take it further in their own way.

Tuhami reported to Sadat and gave him Dayan's message. Dayan returned to Jerusalem to report to Begin and within forty-eight hours he was in Washington for yet another meeting with Carter, Vance and Vice-President Walter Mondale. It was a stormy encounter. The Americans were still unaware of the meeting with Tuhami in Marrakesh and were annoyed by Begin's actions with regard to settlements on the West Bank. Carter and Mondale were particularly unfriendly towards Dayan and were still focusing on an early meeting in Geneva, where Israel would be willing to make concessions on withdrawal from the occupied territories and to the Palestinians. Dayan offered them no joy. Instead, he told Vance privately of the meeting in Morocco and of the offer he had made to Sadat. It did nothing to assuage Carter's fury with Israel's independent excursion into diplomacy.

Meanwhile, Sadat had also informed Carter's Ambassador in Cairo, Hermann Eilts, of the report which Tuhami had brought him. Eilts's reported comment at the State Department was that, if Sadat had been serious, he would not have chosen a man such as Tuhami. Eilts was one of the ablest envoys the United States has had in Cairo since the Second World War, but even the best can make mistakes. Although he was very close to Sadat and enjoyed his confidence, Eilts could not see what Sadat saw clearly: that Carter's policy, despite its fine dressing with all the right phrases, was not a way to peace for Egypt.

Then, to Dayan's amazement, came the aftermath of the revelations about the Morocco meeting made to Vance and Eilts: nothing. There was no reaction from the Americans and no undue interest in the substance of Dayan's talks, only annoyance that we had gone behind their backs.

Meanwhile, Israel's leaders had to acclimatize themselves to Sadat's often inexplicable and erratic ways. Two days after the end of Tuhami's meetings with Dayan, on 21 September, Carter received a very tough letter from Sadat demanding urgent action to get the Geneva conference under way and to stop haggling about details. Yet, at the lengthy meeting Egypt's Foreign Minister Fahmy had with Carter on that same day, Fahmy told Carter that Egypt was in no hurry about Geneva. Egypt was concerned that Israel should withdraw soon and that a Palestinian state be established before there were any further negotiations with Israel.

As so often happens in such discussions, especially with a talkative minister like Fahmy, important new sidelights emerged. In this case, Fahmy had been urging Carter to ignore pressures from the Jewish lobby and to talk with Arafat. It was important, he told Carter. The PLO leader had recently told Fahmy that the reason why the PLO could not accept UN Resolution 242 was the clause referring to 'the right of every state to live in peace'. Fahmy's own comment was almost as significant as was Arafat's statement. For once, he was quite succinct: 'Arafat *rightly* feared that if the PLO accepted that clause, it would in practice recognize the State of Israel and its right to live in peace.' This told us as much about Fahmy as it did about Arafat, and it did much to explain the problem with which Sadat had to contend.

Meanwhile, reports reached Jerusalem of a proposed joint statement to be issued by the United States and the Soviet Union about policy in the Middle East. The central figure in these negotiations was the able Soviet Ambassador, Alexander Dobrynin, in Washington. Ostensibly this was to be a statement of the two co-chairmen of the forthcoming Geneva conference, Vance and Gromyko. In fact, it was intended to be a virtual policy statement for the Geneva conference. The text had been shown to and discussed with Egypt's Foreign Minister, with the PLO and with the Saudis. Fahmy reported to Vance that the Arab leaders approved of it, that the PLO was enthusiastic and that Sadat welcomed it. Once again, this was yet another example of the dichotomy in Egyptian policy-making.

Three days after the joint American–Soviet statement was made public on 1 October, Fahmy delivered a personal letter from Sadat to Carter. It was an urgent, important and significant message, which Carter recorded in his diary entry for 4 October. Sadat's letter urged Carter 'that nothing be done to prevent Egypt and Israel from negotiating directly ... either before or after the Geneva conference'. It was Sadat's first positive reaction to Dayan's meeting with Tuhami. Unsurprisingly, Fahmy makes no mention of it; Sadat's message to Carter had totally undercut Fahmy's diplomatic campaign against direct talks with Israel.

Sadat's letter to Carter could not have been better timed. It arrived almost simultaneously with the beginning of a seven-hour intense discussion between Carter, Vance and their advisers, and Dayan. The Americans had thought that they had neutralized Dayan's possible opposition to the American–Soviet statement when they had discussed some parts of it with him before publication. But the Americans had foolishly withheld the most relevant parts from Dayan before seeking his approval. This was a mistake. Dayan was particularly incensed by the fact that the document had nowhere referred to peace as an objective of the Geneva negotiations; only to a 'settlement'. It also allowed for PLO participation without clearly saying so, and set an agenda for Geneva which would allow the Palestinian and other maximalists to place their pet demands on it. It would have turned the conference into an anti-Israeli propaganda forum without any practical outcome other than poisoning the political atmosphere and jeopardizing the Dayan–Sadat initiative.

The angry Dayan descended on Carter and Vance on 4 October and did not let go for seven hours, until the Americans had, in effect, scrapped the joint statement with the Soviet Union and replaced it with a revised document: an American–Israeli 'Working Paper'.

It was brief and to the point. It set out the agreed agenda for a resumed Geneva conference on terms acceptable to Israel with military brevity and precision. Curiously, it is the most unquoted agreement in the histories and reference books of that period. Its text was supposed to be secret, but

Dayan knew what he was doing when he informed the Knesset of the text of the Working Paper which he, Carter and Vance had signed. It had six short and uncomplicated articles. These stated that there would be a unified Arab delegation, which would include Palestinian Arabs. Once the conference had assembled, it would divide into five working groups: Egypt–Israel, Jordan–Israel, Syria–Israel and, possibly, Lebanon–Israel; the West Bank and Gaza would be discussed in a working group comprising Israel, Jordan, Egypt and the Palestinian Arabs. The conference was to be based on Security Council Resolutions 242 and 338 and all previous agreements concerning the conference would remain in force.

The Working Paper was approved by the Cabinet in Jerusalem, but only after Begin had thrown his full weight behind Dayan's presentation. The hard-line Likud core of the Cabinet wanted to have it rejected; in the Knesset it was the other way round. Shimon Peres, on behalf of the Alignment, called the Working Paper 'the most pessimistic programme ever presented by any Israeli Government' and accused Dayan of agreeing to a separate Palestinian delegation. The Alignment censure was rejected by the Knesset by forty-one votes to twenty-nine. It had been an odd experience for Dayan to have his Working Paper attacked in the Cabinet by the Likud Right and in the Knesset by the Alignment Left; neither understood what was going on, for they did not know of the web that Dayan and Sadat had begun to weave.

The opposition to Dayan in the Cabinet and in the Knesset was in good company. In Washington, the whole panoply of the policy-making, policy-analysis and intelligence-gathering apparatus had swung into action and uniformly misread what was taking place in Cairo and Jerusalem. The meeting between Dayan and Tuhami was treated as an esoteric side-show not worth a second thought. The Working Paper, which Carter and Vance had produced after their marathon session with Dayan, was recognized as a 'brilliant diplomatic triumph for Dayan', as Quandt assessed it, primarily because it met the basic requirements of all parties. However, the Arab leaders were angry; Gromyko and Dobrynin were stunned into unbelieving silence that the Israelis should have been able to replace their painfully produced joint statement with the United States, the result of many weeks of consultations and agonizing, in a single night's session between Carter and Dayan; the PLO was furious.

What followed required an unusual degree of 'insight', in every sense of the word, on Israel's part. Everything depended on having accurate and comprehensive information about this phase of the euphemistically called peace process. We were in the picture at last about all the competing policy strands in Washington. We were adequately informed about the thinking of the principal Arab leaders. The one major difficulty was, strange as it may seem, Sadat himself. In retrospect, I would say that the problem arose from the fact that Sadat himself would not let his left hand know what his right hand was doing. Even at this stage we found ourselves asking what Sadat's game really was? No one was as yet prepared to give a definite answer. What was perhaps not fully realized at the time in Israel was that Sadat was also still agonizing how to get what he wanted. He was prepared to try every way open to him: with Israel or against Israel, with the Americans or – as his Foreign Minister argued – with the Russians and against the Americans. All options were open in Sadat's book. Ironically, it was Carter and his team of experts who made certain that Sadat would have to plump for Dayan's Israeli solution.

Before Sadat had seen the full text of the joint statement, he called Carter on 1 October to say that Fahmy had – rather belatedly – told him about it. The very idea of being associated with the Soviet leaders had upset Sadat, but Fahmy had reassured him about the contents of the statement and he was prepared to go along with it. Having thus given his evidently reluctant assent, Sadat then raised a much more serious objection.

He told Carter quite bluntly that he feared the Americans were changing their position with regard to the Geneva conference. Sadat reminded Carter that they had agreed that all basic issues would be resolved along lines agreed between Carter and the Egyptians, and that the Geneva meeting would be essentially ceremonial – the formal signing by the United States, the Soviet Union, Egypt, Israel and possibly Syria of the previously settled agreement. However, Sadat's impression from the latest reports he had from his Foreign Minister was that it was Carter's revised intention to preside over the direct Egyptian–Israeli negotiations without anything being settled in advance.

It was Sadat's firm opinion that this negotiating process at Geneva would not resolve either of the two principal problems they had to settle: Israel's withdrawal and the establishment of a Palestinian state. What Sadat would clearly have liked to have said to Carter was that his new-fangled formula would not lead even to the restoration of the Sinai territory to Egypt, but Sadat evidently kept his counsel.

However, Carter and his advisers concluded – in our view with surprising rashness – that all Sadat was showing was some tactical reluctance to go along with the American preparations for Geneva. Sadat at this time was coming under severe pressure from his Foreign Ministry establishment to support the position taken by Fahmy, who was still hankering after the original American–Soviet statement, which he sought to 'improve' still further. Sadat was persuaded to write a letter to Carter on 19 October expressing support for Fahmy's efforts to go back to the first American–Soviet policy statement and to abandon the Working Paper agreed with Dayan. By now the Americans had become totally confused by the manner in which Sadat had begun to juggle with his various irons in the diplomatic fire.

Two days later, Carter tried a new ploy to bring Sadat into line. He sent him a personal hand-written note, which was brought to Cairo by a senior officer of the Egyptian Embassy in Washington. It was a simple, almost pathetic appeal from the President of the United States to the President of Egypt to make a public declaration that he supported Carter's proposals for Geneva. As if to take the sting out of Carter's letter, if there had been one, the American Ambassador in Cairo, Hermann Eilts, called on Sadat on the day after he had been handed Carter's sealed personal letter and told him that it was no longer possible for the Americans to make any changes in the Working Paper they had agreed with Dayan. It was the final word before Geneva. Thereupon Sadat replied to Carter's letter with a meaningful silence, which not even the White House could misunderstand.

It took Carter a little time to ponder the implications of Sadat's Trappist response. A week after his previous letter, on 28 October, he wrote again to Sadat and had the letter delivered to him the same day at Cairo airport as Sadat was about to embark for Bucharest, Tehran and Riyadh. Sadat would therefore have time and opportunity during his flight to contemplate Carter's latest and most extraordinary move. He did. Carter's letter proposed that, in return for Sadat's support at Geneva, Carter was prepared to jettison the Working Paper agreed with Dayan. He told Sadat that he no longer saw any possibility of reaching agreement on a paper acceptable to all parties. Sadat understood what Carter meant: he wanted an agreement with Sadat even if the Israelis did not go along with it, and he was prepared to go ahead without Israeli approval.

Carter told Sadat in this letter that, in order to remove any doubts on this score, he was prepared, if the Arab side agreed to the course of action he proposed in this letter, to make an unequivocal public statement that the Palestinian question, as well as the question of withdrawal and borders of peace, must be dealt with seriously at the Geneva conference with the aim of finding a comprehensive solution to all aspects of the Arab–Israeli conflict. Carter concluded his letter with the assurance that the United States and the Soviet Union would now ask the UN Secretary-General to invite all parties to Geneva.

The degree of incomprehension in Washington over what was already under way in our region was clearly monumental. Otherwise Carter could not have written this letter and his advisers could not have either inspired or approved of it. A senior Israeli official rated this as the equivalent of the Nazi–Soviet Pact of 1939 as applied to Arab–Israeli relations. It was an offer to Sadat that Carter was prepared to ditch his Israeli ally all along the line in return for Sadat's support at Geneva. But Sadat was no Stalin. He understood Egypt's problem in relation to Israel. Carter did not. For when it came to the crunch – and he sensed from Carter's letter that they were getting near to this point – only one issue mattered to Sadat: it was Sinai and nothing else.

Over a year later, Sadat told Dayan, when they met in Ismailiya, how he had pondered over Carter's letter on the round flight to Tehran and Riyadh. Everything he had read in that extraordinary document had convinced him that Carter did not understand Egypt's requirement any more than he realized the inappropriateness of his approach to the Palestinian question. In Sadat's considered opinion, he now had to do everything possible to prevent Carter from being let loose at the peace conference in Geneva.

Any doubts Sadat had harboured, when he embarked on the flight to Bucharest with Carter's letter still in his hand, were resolved by the time he flew back to Cairo from Riyadh on 3 November. There was no way Egypt could regain Sinai by following Carter's course. The alternative route led to Jerusalem. The key to Sinai was after all in the hands of the Israelis, not the Americans. That had been the message Dayan had sent him with Tuhami from Marrakesh. The time had come for Sadat to respond to Dayan's message. Sadat did that when he addressed the Egyptian National Assembly a few days later on 9 November. He was prepared to go to Jerusalem and speak to the people of Israel. It was only quite some time later that it was fully understood in Jerusalem how and why Sadat had reached this conclusion. It looked simple and straightforward; it was anything but that.

Anyone who had followed Sadat's speech-making since he became President in October 1970 must have noticed the element of spontaneous improvisation in his otherwise carefully prepared pronouncements. It was as if at the moment of his greatest intensity his innermost thoughts asserted themselves over the blandness of his speechwriters. There have been other prominent politicians, usually outstanding orators, who underwent such metamorphoses in the midst of a set speech; but among many such practitioners in our time, Sadat was outstanding. It was possible, therefore, to learn a great deal about Sadat from a careful study of his speeches.

Sadat had another quality which had to be linked with his improvisations when speech-making. He was a consummate chameleon and dissimulator. Nasser had spotted this in the early days of Egypt's revolution when he was able to make great use of Sadat. These characteristics were never more evident than in Sadat's two historic speeches of 9 and 21 November 1977. The first was made in Cairo before Egypt's National Assembly with Arab ambassadors and Arafat in the audience. At the end of a long tirade against Israel, he said, almost in an aside, that he was ready to talk to Israel in 'their house, the Knesset'. It was a total non-sequitur to everything that he had said before, and there was no further elaboration. The second speech in Jerusalem, addressing the Knesset and a worldwide television audience of many hundred millions, was almost the precise reverse of the first speech but – and it was a most revealing 'but' – the conclusion was the same; only the wrapping had been changed.

The first speech made to the National Assembly has been remembered only because of Sadat's one-liner that he was ready to go to the ends of the earth, even to Jerusalem, in the pursuit of peace. But Sadat said much more in this speech which has been generally overlooked and which was most important – especially for Israel. Sadat was an angry man when he spoke on 9 November in Cairo. He was particularly angry with Carter over the letter he had received on 28 October. As he saw it, Carter had suggested that if Sadat gave his approval to the Working Paper which the Americans had agreed with Dayan, Carter would be prepared to double-cross the Israelis on the question of the Palestinians, on the issue of withdrawal to the 1967 borders and on the matter of the peace settlement.

Sadat was outraged at the short-sightedness and foolishness of the Americans. If they thus deceived the Israelis, Begin and Dayan would simply walk away from Geneva, and Egypt would be left with nothing. The Cairo speech, which was in effect his report to Egypt's National Assembly, was quite unbending in relation to Israel. It was harsh and uncompromising. Its themes were most revealing. These were his main points until he came to his finale, the non-sequitur about Jerusalem:

* Israel has obliterated and distorted the Palestine question for the last twenty-five years.
* President Carter has succeeded in tearing this Israeli veil from the eyes of the American people.
* The American–Israeli Working Paper of 5 October was forced on the United States as a result of a feverish campaign by Israel and by her shameless and disgraceful attacks on President Carter.
* We do not fear confrontation with Israel because we have cut her down to size. Israel no longer stands as a power; she has been shrunken, and we can deal with her.
* We can surpass anything Israel can mobilize beyond her borders or in any planned confrontation.
* We now have enough knowledge of our Israeli enemy and his methods to ensure our victory in every case.
* We have undertaken to foil Israeli objectives and we refuse to play her game. We will impose on her a comprehensive confrontation.
* When we eventually go to Geneva, Israel will not be able to prevent us from making our demand for the return of the Arab territories occupied in 1967, or for the granting of self-determination to the Palestinians and the right to their own state.
* Regardless of Israeli hysteria, I am going to Geneva. They cannot dissuade me from what I want – the Arab territories and Palestinian rights.
* Israel fears the Geneva conference. No Arab need have any fear of it. Why? Because we have exported to Israeli society the division, fear, defeatism, doubt and suspicion, everything, in fact, that we suffered from in the past.
* I am ready to go to Geneva: 'I am ready to go to the ends of the earth if this will prevent a soldier or an officer of my sons from being wounded – not being killed, but wounded.'
* Israel will be astonished when it hears me saying now before you that I am ready to go to their house, to their Knesset itself, and talk to them.

Those who had heard Sadat's speech broadcast live from Cairo were not just 'astounded' as Sadat had suggested. We were; but we were also very puzzled. This was best expressed by former Foreign Minister, Yigal Allon. Speaking before he was certain whether the Sadat journey would materialize, Allon asked what had happened to Sadat between May Day 1972 and November 1977. Just over five years earlier, Sadat had told his vast May

Day crowd in Alexandria that he would crush the intolerable arrogance of Israel. He was prepared to sacrifice a million Egyptian soldiers in the next war; Israel should be prepared to do the same. In 1972, he was willing to pay any price in Egyptian blood to destroy Israel; now, in 1977, he was ready to come to Jerusalem to prevent a single Egyptian soldier being wounded. What had brought about such a conversion? Israelis were all asking the same question. Their puzzlement was even greater after Sadat had delivered his Knesset speech on 21 November.

Sadat had come to the Knesset in a state of euphoria. He had defied everyone who had urged him not to undertake the foolhardy journey to Jerusalem: his family, his ministers, his friends, some Americans, the Syrian President, the Saudi King and the ever-concerned British Ambassador. Before going to the Knesset he had already spent eighteen hours in Israel and had prayed at the el-Aqsa Mosque in the Old City of Jerusalem. He had been overcome with surprise and pleasure by the tumultuous welcome he had received in Israel from Jews and Arabs alike. He had not expected it and his entourage could not really believe it. The informal friendliness and tremendous enthusiasm was something to which he was not accustomed. There were no cheer-leaders, no rent-a-crowd. It was genuine and it was heart-warming, but it was misunderstood by Sadat. It confirmed his mistaken assumption with which he had come to Jerusalem.

But before we come to consider that critical flaw in the journey to Jerusalem, we need to take a closer look at Sadat's speech to the Knesset, only twelve days after that to the National Assembly in Cairo.

Sadat began by reflecting on the great psychological gulf that divided Egypt and Israel and the incredulous disbelief that had greeted his decision to go to Jerusalem; he then proceeded to make his presentation. It was evident that he was aware that he was not so much addressing the Knesset or even the people of Israel but the great mass of people watching the proceedings on television in the United States and Europe, and in the Arab world where curiosity triumphed over censorship. Rarely has any politician had so large a captive audience. He said that:

* They had wasted long months in arguing about useless differences.
* It was his duty to save Egyptians and other Arabs from further wars and suffering.
* We must rise above all forms of fanaticism and self-deception and get rid of our obsolete theories of superiority.
* We must be frank with each other; how can we achieve a just and lasting peace?

Having asked the fundamental question, Sadat proceeded to dampen any premature hopes which the Israelis might have deduced from his decision to come to Jerusalem. The Arab nation was not proceeding from a position of weakness or instability; quite the contrary: its strength and stability was such that it could afford to make peace. But then he warned his worldwide audience: 'I did not come to conclude a separate agreement with

84

Israel.' Moreover, without a just solution of the Palestinian question, Israel would not be able to obtain the lasting peace she wanted. Sadat concluded this section on a somewhat patronizing note. But evidently this was how he read our situation and we had to take account of it even if, at times, it made us squirm. But Sadat was quite uninhibited:

* You want to live with us in this area of the world. We welcome you with all sincerity. We used to reject you and your kind. We had our reasons and grievances against your 'so-called Israel'.

Then, about half-way through his speech, he passed from the softening-up process to the hard reality. At this point we began to appreciate that he was not addressing the Knesset in Jerusalem but Congress in Washington, the White House and the great American public. This clearly was what mattered to him. The Knesset provided the stage and the 'extras'; the real converts had to come from the wider audience – the Americans and, not least, his fellow Arabs. The remainder of his speech was designed to that end. We began to understand: Sadat had come to Jerusalem not to embark on direct negotiations with Israel, but to elude them, to escape from the web that had been spun for him, first by Kissinger in the Interim Sinai Agreement, and lately by Foreign Minister Dayan in Marrakesh. Not only had we underestimated Sadat and misunderstood his reasons for 'confronting' Jerusalem, but so had his Arab critics and Carter. The rest of his speech showed very clearly Sadat's convoluted intention.

He began by asking us a simple basic question: 'What does peace mean for Israel?' And then proceeded to provide us with his own answer: 'To live securely within its borders together with its Arab neighbours.' This formula was to provide Sadat with the springboard he wanted for the elaboration of his concept of an Arab–Israeli peace.

* Israel would have to face these fundamental facts with courage and clarity. 'There is an Arab land which Israel has occupied by armed force. We insist on complete Israeli withdrawal from this land and from Arab Jerusalem. It must become a Free City.'
* 'I have not come to beg you to withdraw your armed forces from the occupied territory because this is a self-evident condition, a matter about which there can be no discussion. Peace will have no meaning if you occupy Arab lands by armed force, and there can be no peace without the Palestinians. It is essential that you face the Palestinian problem.'

Then as part of his dramatic finale, Sadat set out the priorities of what had to be done: 'Imagine the peace agreement which will be concluded in Geneva.' The order in which these settlements were to be concluded told us a great deal of Sadat's thinking on this all-important matter. First, there was to be a peace agreement based on Israel's withdrawal from the Arab territory occupied in 1967. Next would come the realization of the basic rights of the Palestinian people, including the setting up of their own state. After that would come the right of all countries in the region to live in peace, the non-use of force between states and, lastly, the ending of the state of war.

There was no mention of open borders, diplomatic relations and normalization. In Sadat's understanding – though he did not refer to this in his Knesset speech – this was music for the future, perhaps five or ten years later, possibly it could take a generation or more. It was, in fact, a revealing and daunting agenda for peace; the reality of Sadat's Jerusalem journey which we had been inclined to sweep under the welcoming red carpet. Our education in the art of peace-making had begun; Sadat's was still to come. We were left wondering whether Sadat realized this as we pondered over his closing words: 'I have come to deliver a message. Have I delivered the message?'

Some of the very knowledgeable Israelis were convinced at the end of Sadat's speech that he had cleverly manipulated Israel to provide him with a convincing stage-setting from which he could speak to the Americans – his main concern – and to the world at large, including his fellow-Arab rulers. In the light of the considerable knowledge about Sadat that we have since acquired, I do not believe that this was his only reason for coming to Jerusalem. The clue to Sadat's journey was altogether different.

Cyrus Vance, the shrewd Secretary of State and an outstanding judge of character, noted that some weeks after the Jerusalem odyssey Sadat was still convinced that he had given Israel 'her fundamental requirement' when he went to Jerusalem and addressed the Knesset. What he had said there was of secondary importance; what had mattered was the 'recognition of the legitimacy of Israel by its major Arab neighbour'. It was at the root of Sadat's concept of Israel, something which Begin never really understood. For Sadat – as for most Arab leaders and especially for the Saudi Kings – Israel had been an illegitimate intruder in the Middle East, who had to be expelled from the region.

Sadat's journey to Jerusalem marked the formal abandonment of this hitherto fundamentalist view of Israel. It was, in Sadat's eyes, the greatest possible gift he could bear to Jerusalem, something that Israel needed more than anything else. He was saddened and surprised that Begin and the Israelis could not recognize it in this way. The Israelis had been outcasts in Arab eyes and Sadat had brought them legitimacy and acceptance. What more could Begin want? Sadat brooded over such Israeli non-comprehension. It would take Sadat just about nine months to discover the answer which had eluded him in Jerusalem by having first to unlearn many deeply ingrained beliefs and prejudices. So, for that matter, had Begin.

It was clear to us from Vance's account of Sadat's conversion which led him to Jerusalem that it was based on a fundamental misreading by Sadat of the Israeli position and on his resulting assumption that all Israel wanted and needed from the Arabs, or at least from Egypt, was a form of recognition – not even acceptance. This flawed assessment by Sadat was rooted in an innate Egyptian self-assurance of national, if not racial, superiority over the Jews, Zionism and Israel, which had survived the defeat of 1967 (after it had been rationalized away) and the failure of the October War in 1973 (which had been transformed into triumph and success by a similar perversion of history). On the basis of this reading of recent history and a total incomprehension of the nature of modern Israel, Sadat expected that Begin and Israel would agree to all his demands with alacrity and gratitude in return for the honour bestowed upon Israel by the President of Egypt condescending to come to Jerusalem and bringing us this message in person.

It was not going to be like that. The road ahead to Camp David was harder and it would not provide Sadat with another experience such as his arrival in Israel. One such experience is enough for any man in his lifetime. However much it had been misread by Sadat – and by us – at the time, it was a glorious and unique moment in history and, undoubtedly, the cornerstone in the making of peace between Egypt and Israel soon to be consummated. At last we were on the way, because, as we shall see, Sadat had yet another very powerful reason for taking the road to Jerusalem.

6
Washington: The Education of Menachem Begin
1978

Sadat's visit to Jerusalem was unique: the people took over when he landed in Tel Aviv, when he moved through Jerusalem and when he returned to Cairo. For a brief spell – but what a spell it was – even the politicians were human, swept along by the tidal wave of common popular yearning for peace, real peace. It did not last, but it was genuine: a moment in history when the people had their say.

No one took all that much notice of what Sadat actually said in his speech to the Knesset; what mattered was that he was there addressing Israel's Parliament. No one really cared what Begin said in response, which perhaps was just as well; what mattered was that he was playing the engaging host to the President of Egypt. Had the Israelis really listened to Sadat's speech to the Knesset and had the Egyptians taken heed of Begin's unimaginative response, there would have been little joyous celebration either in Jerusalem or in Cairo. But during those unforgettable twenty-four hours, the act spoke louder than the words – and then the politicians took over once again.

Even so, in the immediate aftermath of Sadat's visit everyone in Israel was convinced that at last we were heading for peace, as indeed we were. But we had no inkling of the bizarre road that lay ahead of us. We were about to be taught the difficult art of negotiating a 'peace process' that meant something fundamentally different to each of the principals involved.

Sadat did not want peace as we understood it; he wanted the Sinai Peninsula returned to Egypt above all else; and – if he could get it – he also wanted the Israelis to withdraw from all Arab territories occupied in 1967, including East Jerusalem. But he knew that this was not on the cards. In return, the Egyptians were prepared to settle for a kind of peace that was, in effect, a state of no war, in which the State of Israel would be tolerated rather than accepted and formally recognized. The other Arab Governments – Syria, Jordan, Saudi Arabia, Lebanon and Iraq – and the PLO simply demanded an immediate Israeli withdrawal from all occupied territories, including Jerusalem. But they refused to negotiate or to recognize Israel, or to make any specific and direct commitment to a peace with Israel.

The Begin Government was also ambivalent in its search for peace. For Begin and his principal Likud colleagues in the Government, peace would be secured and assured by the preservation of the status quo in all the 'administered territories' – Judea, Samaria, the Gaza Strip and the Golan Heights. Any change would be bad. Accordingly, Begin was against any initiative which called for mutual Israel and Arab concessions. From the Israeli standpoint, this made Begin an ineffective or even counter-effective negotiator for a real peace, despite praise heaped on him as negotiator by William Quandt, Carter's house historian at Camp David, who was himself strongly opposed to Sadat's peace agreement with Israel.

Carter's State Department and National Security Council advisers were firmly against a separate Egyptian–Israeli peace agreement; Sadat's new Foreign Minister, Mohammed Ibrahim Kamel, and his senior Foreign Ministry staff were totally opposed to any formal peace with Israel. On the Israeli side, there were also conflicting opinions, but the alignment was different. It was the head of the Israeli delegation, Prime Minister Menachem Begin, who was willing to make concessions in Sinai, but he was not prepared to tamper with the status quo in Judea, Samaria and Gaza, nor to respond to any proposal initiated by President Carter that called for Israeli concessions in these territories, however minor. Fortunately for all concerned, Begin's Foreign Minister, Moshe Dayan, ably assisted by Attorney-General Aharon Barak and Defence Minister Ezer Weizman, repeatedly saved Begin from himself and thus also saved Israel's peace with Egypt. In many ways, the distinctive relationship between Begin and Dayan was the key to Israel's peace with Egypt and to Carter's role in bringing it about. Dayan, however, did not gain Sadat's trust; nor was he ever receptive to Sadat's charm. This role was reserved for Weizman, whose own brand of charm, candour and passionate search for a peace settlement won him a special place in Egyptian hearts and particularly in Sadat's.

Begin was in awe of Dayan, so were Carter and Sadat. They did not like or understand Dayan, but they respected and even feared him. Dayan knew this and it gave him the inner strength to play the part of a loyal Number Two to a Prime Minister whose politics and manner he disliked and distrusted, but whose strength as a national leader he admired and supported. It was a complex association in which Dayan sought, uncharacteristically, to lead, self-effacingly, from behind and, in this way, carry Begin along with him. Because Dayan never allowed himself to be used by Begin's adversaries – either by the Americans or by Sadat – as Weizman, Peres and some other Israeli politicians had done, Begin never doubted Dayan's loyalty or questioned his motives when he dissented or when he advocated policies which were contrary to the Prime Minister's chosen course; he always preferred Dayan's judgement to that of his Likud stalwarts, such as Shmuel Katz, who was vetoed by Dayan as Information Minister.

In the event, it was Dayan – not Begin – who played centre stage in fact, if not in name, in the making of the Camp David agreements. It was he and his brother-in-law, Ezer Weizman, who saved the negotiations when failure seemed inevitable. Carter's Secretary of State, Cyrus Vance, recognized the significance of the discreet role which Dayan had allocated to himself; at times of crisis in the negotiations he invariably turned to Dayan, who never failed him. Vance admired not only Dayan's diplomatic ability and suppleness, but even more his integrity and reliability.

The Begin–Dayan relationship encompassed the whole gamut of Israel's peace-making diplomacy following Sadat's departure from Jerusalem. Even before Begin had met there with Sadat, Dayan had his reservations about the advisability of the two men being allowed a head-to-head meeting. He had cautioned King Hassan of Morocco against it during his preliminary talks with Sadat's envoy, Tuhami, in Marrakesh in September 1977. It was then that Dayan realized that Israel's earlier belief that she would be more successful if she dealt directly with Sadat without American participation was no longer tenable. One reason for this was Begin's uncompromising opposition to the appeasement of some of Sadat's less extreme demands. Unfortunately, Begin would not admit Dayan's interpretation that the extreme demands which Sadat had made were actually in the nature of a smoke-screen for Sadat's real objective. This had become clear to Dayan during his talks with Tuhami in Morocco: Sadat wanted a pro-forma peace with Israel, a peace of sorts, but not as a desirable end in itself. In addition to Sinai, Sadat wanted peace with Israel as the entry ticket to the special relationship with the United States to which he aspired. And to this, Dayan had no objection.

It had taken the Israeli leaders some time before they understood that this had been one of the principal objectives of Sadat's coming to Jerusalem, and that what followed during the ten months which led to the Camp David agreement was part of the same bizarre scenario. But there was one big and all-important difference: after the Jerusalem drama, the lead role in the construction of the Sadat–Washington axis passed from Sadat to the Americans, to President Carter and his influential team of diplomatic activists. Henceforth, in preparation for Sadat's planned triumphal visit to Washington on 4 February 1978, it was they who wrote the script, allocated the parts and set the tone. Sadat's hard-line advisers, including his new Foreign Minister, Kamel, were content to let Carter and his men do the running – and it was some run, about which, at the time, we knew nothing. As for Sadat himself, he kept his own counsel for the time being. He was preparing yet another 'shock' – this time for his own Foreign Ministry inner circle and for their American opposite numbers.

Carter's Middle East advisers – Brzezinski, Harold Saunders, Ray Atherton and Quandt – had been sorely wrong-footed by Sadat's shock decision to go to Jerusalem and to end the charade maintained by Washington that peace in Israel's conflict with Egypt had to be sought at the moribund Geneva international peace conference. It had not met since its initial deadlocked meeting inappropriately held on Christmas Day 1973. With the disappearance of Kissinger, who had been the link between the President and the officials of the State Department who were the effective policy-makers, the still inexperienced Carter had no choice but to follow their counsel. They argued that it was in the United States' national interest to go all-out for a comprehensive peace settlement which would embrace not only Egypt but also the Palestinians. Only that would satisfy the Saudi rulers to whom the Americans were greatly indebted, politically and financially. The Saudis had impressed on Sadat that they preferred no peace agreement rather than a bilateral peace agreement between Egypt and Israel.

The reasons for this – like all explanations concerning the Saudi ruling families – were complex and mysterious. They had little to do with the nature of Egypt's peace settlement with Israel; but they had much to do with the besetting fear of the Saudis of the PLO's capacity for making trouble in Saudi Arabia, especially among the large number of Palestinians then working in the oilfields. In order to contain it, the Saudi rulers paid hundreds of millions of dollars in regular instalments to the PLO; we saw it as a form of protection money to ensure that the Palestinians caused no trouble to the nervous Saudi ruling families. What mattered was that Carter was being dragged into this same Palestinian syndrome: in order to keep the Saudis happy, which was a major American national interest, Carter's advisers were pressing him to give priority to the Palestinian factor in his talks with Sadat.

Carter was willing, but he had also to count the cost. The suspicion that the Carter administration was unfriendly to Israel was gaining ground and the message was not lost on the President himself when his most influential Democratic Party friends had to abandon two fund-raising banquets in New York and Los Angeles because of the large number of cancellations, which were presumed to come from supporters who were friends of Israel. If this was a warning signal, the reality was rather more serious. The Americans were clearly foxed and worried by Israel's refusal to budge on the two issues which were central to American and Saudi thinking: an Israeli withdrawal from all territories occupied in 1967 or at least a formal undertaking to do so, and Israeli agreement to the establishment of a Palestinian 'homeland'.

Carter's advisers had been thinking around this problem for some time, even before Sadat's Jerusalem 'shock'. Their great problem was that any overt move considered hostile to Israel would be counter-productive on Carter's home front and not least in Congress. Shrewdly assessing this dilemma, Carter's National Security Adviser, Zbigniew Brzezinski, decided to establish a new Israeli identity which he called 'Begin'. This was to be the unacceptable face of the new Israel, inflexible, assertive and unaccommodating, which had divided the Jewish community in the United States and the Israeli people at home. This new Israeli persona, 'Begin', had the further advantage of being a credible Aunt Sally; unyielding to the point of dogma when a more forthcoming negotiating stance would have been greatly to Israel's advantage. In short, the Americans believed that opposition to Begin would not be construed as being anti-Israel.

Far from preparing the administration for an attack on Begin, which might have been popular among some American Jews, the Carter administration had unwittingly drifted into deep water. Its spokesman explained to members of Congress and other curious enquirers from the media that the two basic demands for a major Israeli withdrawal from all occupied territories, including Jerusalem, were not Carter's idea. These were, the Carter people claimed, Sadat's absolutely minimal demands if there was to be a peace process in the wake of his Jerusalem trip. This was Carter's iron-clad alibi with which he confronted Begin.

In fact, as we knew from Dayan's talks with Tuhami in Morocco and from other well-placed Egyptian sources, Sadat was intent on a double-track diplomacy: when dealing with his own people in his Foreign Ministry and in the armed forces and – officially – with the Americans, he maintained the customary Arab demands, which the Americans had taken on board and which suited them and the Saudis. The Saudi factor, it must be remembered, was all important at this stage of the negotiations. It reinforced the Carter team's total opposition to a separate Egyptian–Israeli settlement. It was this American posture that was at the heart of our diplomacy at that time.

This was also Dayan's most worrying personal problem as Foreign Minister. He understood now, at the beginning of 1978, after his encounter with Sadat in Jerusalem, that there could be no agreement between Begin and Sadat without United States' mediation. The two men were, by nature and character, so alike that they were politically and psychologically mutually incompatible. But Dayan also realized that at that time the United States would not support a bilateral Egyptian–Israeli agreement based only on the return of the Sinai Peninsula to Egypt without reference to other Arab issues. It was this fundamental contradiction that had to be overcome, in Dayan's assessment, before there could be credible peace negotiations.

But unbeknown to Dayan – or to Begin – Begin was being set up for diplomatic slaughter by the master butchers in Washington, while Israel was being taken to the cleaners by the experts of the National Security Council and the Middle East specialists of the State Department with active participation by the Egyptian Foreign Minister and his principal senior officials. They had, moreover, the apparent blessing of the two Presidents, Carter and Sadat, for this bizarre and clumsy attempt at collusion designed to force Israel to abandon her refusal to withdraw from territories occupied in 1967, including Jerusalem, and to agree to the establishment of a Pale-stinian state. This plan – prepared behind Israel's back and without her knowledge – must rank as a unique attempt in United States' diplomatic history of short-changing a friend and ally by deceit and manipulation in order to assist her adversary, at that time Egypt.

This assessment of the American plan, which we shall describe in greater detail in due course, is not exaggerated. The Israeli Government has often been accused of being almost paranoic in its suspicion of our American friends, sometimes justifiably so. We do tend to be over-sensitive, but not always without reason.

In retrospect it is now evident that this carefully planned and structured collusion between Carter and Sadat to compel Israel to accept the proposed American–Egyptian terms for a comprehensive peace was an unusually naïve attempt at manipulated policy-making. It was to give expression to United States' interest in the Middle East by gaining the goodwill not only of Egypt but also of Saudi Arabia – America's most important financial ally in the world: the financial well-being of the United States was, in 1978, largely dependent on Saudi benevolence.

Already in early December 1977, only three weeks after Sadat's speech to the Knesset, the Saudi and Jordanian rulers – King Khaled and King Hussein – advised Secretary of State Vance of their private hopes for the success of Sadat's initiative and of their fears of what could happen should it fail. They asked the United States to help them to 'build on Sadat's initiative'. Khaled explained that if the United States failed to do so, Saudi Arabia and Jordan would be forced to break openly with Sadat. The administration took Khaled's appeal on board and the President's National Security Adviser and the State Department's Middle East advisers acted accordingly.

At this time Israel was not the prime concern in Washington. The Arab connection, especially the secure availability of Gulf oil and the goodwill of its Arab producer-governments, was of far greater immediate preoccupation, and this greatly influenced Washington thinking on the Arab–Israeli conflict. It reinforced the urge for an American initiative that would reassure the Gulf rulers and ensure a secure Arab flank for the United States and for the Shah's Iran – an effective Egypt–Saudi Arabia–Iran axis. The key to this was a satisfactory accommodation with Egypt. This need gave added impetus to use manipulative or coercive measures to bring a recalcitrant Israel to heel.

In the meantime, however, the peace process was taking on a momentum of its own. When Begin went to Washington on 16 December 1977, he dramatically transformed the discussion with Carter and gave it an altogether new direction, which was to have a profound effect on Carter and a lasting impact on the ultimate peace with Egypt. Vance has recalled that on that day Carter was still focusing on resuming the international peace conference in Geneva, 'when Begin showed his instinct for the essential. He offered an Israeli withdrawal from Sinai and Palestinian Home Rule for a start without going into details about boundaries or the Palestine question.'

American concern to keep the process on a path acceptable to Saudi Arabia and Egypt became all the greater a month later when a sudden and inexplicable crisis threatened the entire procedure: the Egyptian–Israeli Political Committee (which had been established as a follow-up to Sadat's Jerusalem visit) collapsed on 17 January 1978. Sadat had inexplicably recalled his Foreign Minister and withdrawn the Egyptian negotiators from Jerusalem. His real reasons for this arbitrary action became clear only very much later. He had realized that it would be disastrous to his future plans if he left negotiations with Israel in the hands of his Foreign Ministry

'Mafia'; he would have to handle these matters himself in due course, but the time was not yet ripe to reveal his negotiating cards – either to Israel or to his own Foreign Minister and his officials.

The abrupt ending of the Political Committee appeared to provide proof to the Americans that drastic steps were needed to get the peace process back on track. Carter demanded instant answers from his officials. The reply he received was what I would like to call 'Operation Begin'. I shall now describe and document it, for without the requisite official documentation of this chapter of American diplomacy, no one would believe that such things could happen in the Government of the United States of America.

7

Collusion: Carter as Balaam*

1978–9

ON 12 JANUARY 1978, three days before the Egyptian Foreign Ministry delegation arrived in Jerusalem for the first meeting of the Egyptian–Israel Political Committee, William Quandt had minuted his chief, Zbigniew Brzezinski, that at this time they should move towards closer co-operation with Sadat to help bring pressure to bear on Begin. In conjunction with Sadat and 'in total confidence, we should develop a strategy for developing a mini-crisis, which will be resolved by an American proposal which Sadat will accept'. It would be necessary to get Sadat's assurance in advance that he would agree to the American compromise proposals so that pressure could then be mobilized against Begin. Carter and Vance were wary at first and disinclined to use 'such manipulative techniques' of diplomacy, but they succumbed to the temptation of the rewards of such a diplomatic coup by means of collusion.

Just two days later, on 14 January, the President's National Security Adviser had a private talk with Carter in which he developed 'our new and highly secret strategy'. This is how Brzezinski explained it to the President: an invitation to Sadat to meet Carter at Camp David would be the occasion 'to precipitate' this new policy. 'We should urge Sadat to come forth publicly with a reasonable proposal.' But this Sadat offer to Israel 'should deliberately contain one or two maximalist demands'. These would then be declared unacceptable by the United States and would be followed by Carter insisting on Egyptian concessions. The stage would thus be set for public pressure on Israel to accept Carter's proposed reasonable compromise, which had been previously and secretly co-ordinated with the Egyptian Foreign Ministry and had received its approval and that of President Sadat. Brzezinski summarized these thoughts in a memorandum to Carter, who 'expressed approval' for the policy that 'would enable us to generate the greatest public pressure on Israel'.

---

* The attempt at 'strategic collusion' has been authoritatively documented: by Brzezinski, the father of the proposed collusion to trap Begin, in his *Power and Principle* (London, 1985), the first Carter official to refer openly to 'the secret strategy of collusion', on pp. 240–44; by William Quandt, in his *Camp David – Peace-making and Politics* (Washington, 1986) pp. 163 and footnotes 31, 34, 166, 168–74; by Egypt's Foreign Minister Kamel's account of *The Camp David Accords* (London, 1986) pp. 80–86, 273–9 of the English edition and pp. 134–40, 149–51 of the original Arabic version. President Carter himself in his autobiography *Keeping Faith* (New York, 1984) on pp. 306–8 is less precise than his aides.

Let us repeat here that Israel knew nothing of these backstairs plots in Washington and Cairo while she prepared for bona-fide negotiations with Egypt and the United States in the Political Committee which was to meet in Jerusalem, on 15 January, the day following Brzezinski's private talk with the President. In fact, the Israelis had enough to think about when the Egyptian Foreign Minister, Kamel, arrived in Jerusalem before dawn, clearly wishing to avoid too much friendly attention from Israelis, without worrying unduly about the esoteric scheming of the Americans. Kamel had hardly set foot on Israeli soil before he charged into the diplomatic fray like a young bull in a minefield – and with similar consequences, though he did not seem aware of what lay in store for him.

Later that evening, while Kamel and his staff were relishing the Israeli official discomfiture following his blistering criticism of Israeli policy in his formal arrival speech at Ben-Gurion airport, a coded message arrived for the Foreign Minister from Sadat. He had considered the Foreign Minister's airport speech and held it to have been violent and uncalled for. Sadat told Kamel 'to control himself and refrain from outbursts and to show patience in the negotiations'. These were tough warnings. Next morning came another, this time from the Vice-President, Hosni Mubarak. It warned the Foreign Minister that the President hoped that 'you will maintain your calm and that your speech be deliberate and controlled'. There can have been few foreign ministers who have received such a dressing down from their head of state and survived.

Neither the Egyptian delegation, nor the American Secretary of State, Cyrus Vance, had any clue what lay in store for them during these forty-eight hours, until the Egyptian Foreign Minister was rudely shaken out of his deep afternoon siesta on 17 January to be handed a telegram from his President. Without mincing words, it ordered Kamel and the entire Egyptian delegation to return to Cairo immediately. They were stunned, and so were the Israelis. Why had Sadat done this? It was only much later, as we have already explained, when we came to understand fully Sadat's extraordinary role in the making of the Camp David agreements, that we also understood his cavalier recall of the Egyptian delegation from Jerusalem. It was a necessary precaution in his eyes to save the deal which Dayan had offered him during the secret encounter with Tuhami in Marrakesh – the return of Sinai for an Egyptian–Israeli peace.

As Sadat read the speeches which his Foreign Minister was making in Israel, he understood that Kamel and his senior officials – Ahmed Maher, Nabil el-Araby and Osama el-Baz – were deliberately setting out to make impossible any peace settlement with Israel, thus frustrating Sadat's hope of regaining the Sinai Peninsula. They had probably been encouraged in this course by the American collusion proposals: the Egyptian Ambassador in Washington, Ashraf Ghorbal, had been reporting in great confidence to Maher at the Egyptian Foreign Ministry of the substantial progress these had made. In the opinion of the Egyptian Foreign Minister and his principal advisers, all that Egypt had to do to assist events was to play hard to get, talk tough, sit tight and let the Americans exert pressure on Israel to agree to a settlement on Egyptian–Palestinian terms. Sadat, however, realised that he had to act quickly, and alone, to halt the potentially destructive role of his Foreign Ministry officials on the Political Committee.

Sadat's swift and decisive action put an end to this distraction and compelled Carter's team to concentrate on Sadat's impending visit to Washington and on their planned collusion between the Presidents without the discordant noises from Sadat's men on the Political Committee, which would have caused Begin to end all further negotiations. However, in the light of our brief experience with Foreign Minister Kamel, Israel had some difficulty in understanding why Sadat still retained him. The machinations of the Egyptian political apparatus were becoming increasingly perplexing for us. We found it hard to read Sadat's game plan. However, we were in good company. Both Americans and Egyptians proceeded to draw all the wrong conclusions from Sadat's abrupt closing down of the planned political talks in Jerusalem.

Sadat let them; he made no attempt to enlighten them. Instead, he kept his own counsel, read the directives for his oncoming Washington visit with which his Foreign Ministry had equipped him, ignored them, looked misleadingly morose, and prepared to enjoy his Washington trip to the hilt. He knew what he wanted from Carter. He knew also that it was not what Carter and his officials wanted, but he knew that it was what Begin and the Israelis wanted: a bilateral peace agreement between Egypt and Israel. Once again, as before his decision to address the Knesset in Jerusalem, Sadat was playing solo, confiding in no one, dissimulating and preparing patiently for the right moment in Washington. This was his own intensely personal preparation for his meeting with Carter.

The Americans, meanwhile, were preparing with more enthusiasm than discrimination for collusion with Sadat's men rather than with Sadat. On 20 January 1978, Carter consulted Brzezinski about a possible summit at Camp David with Sadat and Begin. This was the last thing wanted by the advocates of a special strategy to isolate Begin. Two days later, on Sunday morning, Carter called his National Security Adviser and requested an early meeting of the Middle East group to consider further the proposed Camp David summit. As it happened, by one of those fortunate coincidences that are a frequent feature in manipulated diplomacy, Brzezinski noted that just at that time 'a message came in from Cairo from Ambassador Hermann Eilts pointing out that Sadat was becoming increasingly disillusioned with Carter's unwillingness to push the peace process forward'.

Brzezinski knew that Carter held his Ambassador in Cairo in high esteem; he also understood manipulative diplomacy better than most. He therefore sent Eilts's despatch to the President, together with his own assessment of the situation. 'We have reached a point', he wrote to Carter, 'where ... we can begin to lay the groundwork for a concerted strategy.' For this purpose, however, it was essential that they should meet with Sadat but without

Begin. Carter was impressed and called for a high-level meeting for that same evening, 22 January, to review 'the entire Middle East policy' of the United States.

The group agreed to invite Sadat, but not Begin, to a meeting with Carter at Camp David on 4 February 1978. In fact, the Carter State Department – National Security Council team – Brzezinski, Quandt, Saunders and Atherton – had already set in motion the 'special strategy' of consultation with Sadat's Foreign Ministry without waiting for Carter's approval and go-ahead. They had started to make plans on 14 January, ten days before Carter approved the invitation to Sadat.

These plans were discussed and co-ordinated with Ahmed Maher, the Egyptian Foreign Minister's *Directeur de Cabinet* and his staff. Carter's and Sadat's officials had already prepared (as far as we can tell, without either Carter's or Sadat's knowledge) 'an outline of what should be in such an Egyptian initiative'. This set out in great detail which elements in the Egyptian plan would be deliberately exaggerated so that 'the United States might then compel Egypt to compromise and apply maximum leverage on Israel' to agree to withdraw to the 1967 boundaries on all fronts and to accept a Palestinian settlement based on self-determination. The primary objective of the Camp David summit with Sadat was to provide a discreet opportunity for the two Presidents and their advisers 'to jointly shape the complementary US–Egyptian initiative'.

In all this complicated preparation to 'set up' Begin by means of a meticulously co-ordinated American–Egyptian planning, it became evident that this was very much a case of Hamlet without the Prince: Sadat was at no stage an active participant in the making of this joint American–Egyptian 'new strategy'. Carter was; so were Brzezinski, Quandt, Saunders and Atherton; Egypt's Foreign Minister Kamel was part of it; so were his principal officials, Maher, Baz and Araby. But not Sadat. He was the fly in the American ointment, as the protagonists of collusion were to discover to their distress. But meanwhile they prepared for the meeting with Sadat and for the consequential discomfiture of Menachem Begin and the Israelis.

On 30 January 1978, Brzezinski gave Carter a 'detailed scenario' for the meeting with Sadat now only a few days away. It set out the proposed co-ordinated steps by the United States and Egypt towards 'a just settlement', but which were in fact designed to increase pressure on Begin culminating in a showdown with him sometime in April or May. Carter was becoming impatient with the slow rate of progress. 'I don't want to play grab-ass with Sadat all weekend,' he told his assistant Hamilton Jordan in one of his lesser biblical glosses at the foreign affairs breakfast on Friday, 3 February, the day of Sadat's arrival. However, Carter would soon discover that there would be no need for so unbecoming an exercise.

It was Sadat who took charge of affairs at the initial private meeting at Camp David on 4 February before the American and Egyptian advisers and officials were invited to join the two Presidents. It was to be a momentous private meeting. No notes were taken or kept either by Carter or Sadat, but the political impact on Carter of Sadat's presentation, when it surfaced some weeks later, was to be fundamental for the peace process.

However, in the run-up to this Camp David summit scheduled for 4 February, the American officials and Sadat's Foreign Ministry and military advisers were too busy 'fleshing in' the details of their collusion to give a second thought to Sadat's uncharacteristic reticence. He puffed at his pipe and listened with seeming attentiveness to the last-minute directives from his Foreign Minister which were to guide him in his private meeting with Carter, but he said nothing. And so they met at Camp David on Saturday 4 February. In the morning Carter and Sadat were alone; later, the other members of the American and Egyptian teams joined them. Then came the first significant oddity.

When Carter formally opened the full session some time later, he began by reviewing his discussion with Sadat and, in the recorded words of the Egyptian Foreign Minister, 'to pass on his understanding of what President Sadat had been telling him, so that the matter should be clear to all'. For over half an hour, Carter dazzled his Egyptian and American audience with a clear presentation of their previous private discussion. He was particularly strong in his recounting of Sadat's contribution. He had assured Carter that the Arabs, including Saudi Arabia, the Egyptian people and the other friends of the United States, were indignant with the United States. They felt that Israel's intransigence would not have been possible without American military and political aid. But in his record of this briefing by Carter, Foreign Minister Kamel also expressed understandable surprise that Carter should reveal to the larger meeting details of his supposedly private talk with Sadat.

A closer look at Carter's briefing of the summit's participants, however, clearly revealed its intended purpose. Carter was concerned to justify Sadat's position while distracting his associates at Camp David from the real nub of their private talk. In fact, Carter had been badly shaken by Sadat's private presentation. It was altogether different from the expected participation in the planned collusion on which Carter's and Sadat's officials had been working in great secrecy. He pleaded for time to consider Sadat's proposal and urged him to maintain the utmost discretion concerning the purpose of their conversation. For briefly during this private meeting with Carter, Sadat had dropped his mask of dissimulation, which he had kept in place throughout the Jerusalem episode – and since.

For the first time, he revealed to Carter the reality of his intention. He wanted Sinai even if this meant a bilateral peace with Israel. This made nonsense of all the carefully laid plans by Brzezinski, which Carter had enthusiastically endorsed and embraced. Carter needed time to extricate himself from the diplomatic labyrinth in which his Middle East advisers had landed him. He had also learnt enough about Washington to know that there is no fury greater than that of a senior official whose advice has been scorned. He did not wish to risk that; nor did Sadat.

Thus, as the Camp David summit opened, there developed a second, surreptitious collusion between Carter and Sadat alongside the major structured collusion mapped out by Carter's and Sadat's officials. There was only one difference between them: the main collusion, which was the principal business of the summit, was aimed at Begin and Israel; the private Carter–Sadat collusion was aimed against their respective senior officials and advisers. It was an intriguing situation.

Both Carter and Sadat were politicians singularly versed in the importance of correct timing. Both Presidents agreed that, for the moment, it was best not to show their hand but to go along with the collusion plan against Begin and Israel, and wait for a suitable opportunity to ditch it in favour of Sadat's private plan for a Sinai settlement with Israel.

For the present, therefore, the summit proceeded as planned with the collusion charade as advocated by Brzezinski and approved by Sadat's Foreign Ministry officials, who were all blissfully unaware that, in this Washington spring, their masters' thoughts had turned to altogether different fancies. Sadat clearly knew what he wanted; Carter took some time to make up his mind and, for a while yet, it was to be Carter's ambivalence which troubled the peace process and the collusion aimed at Begin. It was to take Sadat another six months before he prevailed over Carter's hesitation – before Balaam Carter was at last prepared to bless rather than damn Sadat's faith that a separate bilateral peace with Israel was the only peace that was attainable.

Meanwhile, the formal meeting at Camp David proceeded according to plan. American and Egyptian officials agreed before the summit ended that they should now move on to Stage Two of their plan to bait the trap for Begin, our unsuspecting Prime Minister.

Brzezinski had succinctly, and without false niceties, outlined how they were to manipulate this next phase. We cannot improve on the language used by President Carter's National Security Adviser to explain how he proposed to place the noose round Begin's neck:

On Monday, Sadat would emerge as a moderate. On Wednesday, the US would back him publicly. Next, Carter would meet with Begin.

Sadat would then come out with his comprehensive peace plan including the Palestinians as previously co-ordinated with him and agreed by the United States.

Begin was certain to reject this.

Then the United States would go public with its compromise formula which had been previously co-ordinated with and agreed by Egypt.

Begin would be isolated as pressure was mounted in Congress, the media, the American Jewish community and in Israel to compel him to accept the American–Egyptian compromise.

But something went wrong from the start. It was all too well-arranged to be credible. Sadat was supposed to launch the combined American–Egyptian attack on Begin with a speech to the National Press Club on the day after the Camp David meeting had ended, on Monday 6 February. Sadat had told Carter at the outset of their formal session on Saturday that, on the advice of his officials, he would announce at this meeting with the American and international press that Egypt would no longer negotiate directly with Israel, only through the United States. Egypt no longer believed that Israel, and especially Begin, really wanted peace.

Carter, Vance and Mondale all argued passionately with Sadat not to do that; it would be very damaging to their collusion plans. Sadat, in fact, agreed with the American assessment, but his planned announcement had been in the directive which his Foreign Minister had given him before the meeting at Camp David. It was part of the tough brief which the Egyptian Foreign Minister's assertive *Directeur de Cabinet*, Ahmed Maher, had prepared for him and which he appeared to have loyally followed, much to the delight and satisfaction of the Egyptian officials who were evidently greatly relieved that the danger of peace breaking out had materially receded. And then something went horribly wrong.

They had carefully programmed Sadat for the public meetings on Monday, when he was to appear first before the press and then before the US senators as a moderate leader seeking peace in the face of the inflexible and expansionist Begin. In order to do this, Sadat was to abandon his customary Arab mannerisms when speaking in public and conform to the American public-relations stereotype. The Egyptians or their American hosts (we do not know who was responsible) employed two of former President Nixon's speech-writers to write Sadat's speeches. It was evident to most of his audience on Monday that when Sadat addressed the assembled domestic and international press he had probably not seen the speech he was about to give until it was handed to him.

When he did come to deliver it, this was not the Sadat we knew so well from his numerous long, rambling, endearing and most informative speeches, often extemporized or improvised in part. This Washington performance was not Sadat in style, content or presentation. It contained some important statements – grave errors in fact – which Sadat would never have made. The trouble was clearly that the American speech-writers did not really understand Sadat and his ability for fine-tuning when making speeches. As a result, he was made to call on the American media to understand that, as far as the peace process was concerned, Egypt 'has already fulfilled its share of the bargain'. If there was to be a compromise, then clearly it had to come from Israel. Egypt had conceded all that could be asked from her; there was nothing more on offer.

The Israeli negotiators were left wondering what exactly was going on in Washington? This was not the Sadat who had talked to Dayan and Weizman and with whom we had achieved considerable rapport. The Israelis decided that in this situation they had best hold their fire and see what would emerge; they were still totally in the dark concerning the covert collaboration between Egypt and the United States to isolate Begin and compel Israel to abandon her minimal position that there would be no Israeli withdrawal to the 1967 line on any front before there was a formal and total peace signed and seen to be working on the ground. This was not just Begin's position; it encompassed all of Israel. There was probably no other national issue on which there was a similar consensus. It was therefore a singular failure on the part of the Americans and the Egyptians that they could not come to grips with this essential element in Israel's negotiating position and assumed instead that this basic national interest could be erased by an artificial concoction of diplomatic 'dirty tricks'.

But, in retrospect, there could be an altogether different question that ought to be asked. Perhaps the real objective of this exercise in collusion was not the achievement of what every American and Egyptian diplomat involved must have known was an unattainable will-o'-the-wisp – a comprehensive peace including all Arab states and the Palestinians. The thought now occurs that the object of the exercise was quite different: to make sure *that there would be no separate peace* if a comprehensive peace on Arab terms could not be achieved.

As we shall see when we come to the denouement seven months later at Camp David, this was to be the last-minute thrust by Carter's and Sadat's advisers. It was a measure of the statesmanship of the two Presidents that they both recognized the inherent folly and danger of this course and also the risks they took in resisting this mainstream Arab policy.

Carter and Sadat understood this, though Sadat did so before his host became aware of it. Carter's re-education began at the private meeting with Sadat on the morning of 4 February at Camp David, when Sadat initiated Carter into the intricacies of Arab diplomacy and politics in relation to Israel. He found an appreciative but critical pupil in Carter, who wanted to consider every step carefully before it became irrevocable. Carter, moreover, had already begun to move away from his previous attitudes after his meeting with Begin on 16 December 1987, when Begin told him that he was prepared to withdraw from Sinai and agree to Palestinian Home Rule in exchange for a peace treaty with Egypt. While Sadat clearly knew what he wanted, he was anxious not to show his hand prematurely. He knew that most of the members of the delegation would go to great lengths to prevent him from concluding a peace – any peace – with Israel and there were some who might go to any lengths to do so. Sadat, therefore, continued puffing his pipe and without commitment went along with his Foreign Minister and his team bent on confounding the Israelis. He gave no inkling of the distaste he felt for the Foreign Ministry officials and for the negotiating directives which they inflicted on him as an essential element of the collusion discipline which they had worked out with the Americans.

Sadat found the first memorandum prepared by Maher particularly offensive in tone and inept in content. It was handed to Sadat on the flight to Washington on 3 February by his Foreign Minister. Sadat looked at it and even so thick-skinned a bureaucrat as Kamel should have recognized the disdain with which Sadat treated this document purporting to teach him how to suck eggs. The memorandum was ultimative in form and tone. Sadat was to warn Carter that unless the United States pledged to take positive action against Israel to compel the Israelis to accept the 'Egyptian peace terms', Sadat would cease all direct contact with the Israelis. Kamel was so filled with his own importance that he reported back to Maher that Sadat would be using the memorandum for the presentation to Carter at the plenary meeting at the summit next day. Sadat did. But his purpose, as we now know, was not to impress Carter (he had already told Carter in private what he really wanted at their meeting in the morning), but to pacify his own Foreign Minister and his team of advisers and to get them off his back – for the time being.

Sadat did not suffer fools lightly or for long. In this preliminary February canter, forty-eight hours was just about his limit. The talks at Camp David finished on Sunday with seeming total agreement on proceeding with the Brzezinski–Maher six-point collusion to snare the Israelis. Even before Sadat moved to Blair House in Washington next day, he summoned the President of the Egyptian National Assembly, Sayed Marei, his trusted friend and brother-in-law, together with Egypt's Ambassador in Washington, Ashraf Ghorbal, one of the few Egyptian diplomats who enjoyed Sadat's confidence.

He told them to get hold of Carter's National Security Adviser and to draft with him an outline strategy for the coming weeks. They were to have it ready for him the next day, 7 February. Sadat then proceeded to dictate the general 'strategy' which was to be the main thrust of the agreement. Sadat enjoined Marei and Ghorbal to total secrecy, not even Egypt's Foreign Minister was to be told or consulted until the document was complete and ready for presentation. This was typical of Sadat. His caution was hardly surprising for the strategy which he now proposed was totally at variance with the collusion scenario which the summit had only just approved at Camp David. It was also quite different to the official communiqué issued at the end of the summit, which was harmonized with the next phase of the planned collusion.

Brzezinski was understandably puzzled by Sadat's request and the tenor of the 'agreement' which he was asked to draft jointly with Marei. He cleared Sadat's request with Carter, who gave instant approval, much to Brzezinski's surprise and discomfiture. All Brzezinski could do was lamely note in his journal that he had an uneasy feeling that neither Carter nor Sadat 'fully understood' what their advisers were trying to do following the decisions taken at the Camp David summit. It was an understandable lament.

Sadat's outline for the Brzezinski–Marei 'Strategy for the Coming Weeks' first posed the need for a comprehensive declaration of principles, which was clearly unattainable because it presumed the inclusion of Jordan, Syria, the Lebanon and 'representatives of the Palestinian people' – not the PLO. This was Sadat's way of underlining the wishful thinking of his Foreign Ministry, and of current American thinking as expressed by Carter and his men at the summit. Having done that, he turned to the essentials: he set out the terms of a Sinai agreement with great precision and clarity, which would be negotiated directly between Egypt and Israel with American help and which had to be concluded 'as soon as possible'. The remainder of the

'Strategy' conformed to the wholly unrealistic requirements for processing the collusion theme.

Sadat was clearly aware of this and did not care. As far as he was concerned, all that mattered was to reopen the door to a separate Sinai agreement which his Foreign Ministry had sought to shut firmly in his face. This Sadat did with the new strategy memorandum agreed by Brzezinski on 8 February. When Kamel discovered that Sadat had authorized this post-summit policy paper without consulting him or his Foreign Ministry, he erupted and stormed into Sadat's private rooms, only to emerge soon after a chastened and wiser man and with Sadat's new strategy in place. Brzezinski, Quandt and, to a lesser extent, Carter himself tried to reconcile the irreconcilable – Sadat's Sinai policy with the American–Egyptian collusion – to achieve a comprehensive settlement which would satisfy at least the Palestinians.

Carter and Vance talked with Dayan later that February and, abrasively, with Begin on 21 and 22 March. Both Dayan and Begin were firm and clear: there would be no Israeli withdrawal anywhere before there was a negotiated formal peace in place and seen to be working for a considerable time; and there would be no Israeli acceptance of an independent Palestinian state, however described, based on the West Bank and including East Jerusalem as its capital.

It was at this point, soon after Begin's meeting with Carter in Washington, that Carter began to have serious doubts about the advisability of the collusion policy. He had gone all the way to intimidate Begin in direct confrontation and he had indicted Israel's policies before a full hearing of the US Senate. But it had been to no avail. The Israelis stood firm despite the rough and tough confrontation that had taken place between Carter and Begin. Carter had been advised by Brzezinski 'to make no effort to paper over the differences between the United States and Israel'. There would have to be a direct clash 'and we should choose the best ground for it'. This should not be too difficult, Brzezinski told Carter:

For the time being Begin was a real asset to us because his lost standing in American public opinion made it easier for us to move forward on the other key components of our Middle East policy – the development of a military relationship with both Egypt and Saudi Arabia.

Carter's meeting with Begin had been 'generally unpleasant'. Carter launched a strongly argued attack on Begin's negative attitude on every single issue. For the moment, he seemed to abandon Sadat's plea to keep the Sinai door open and not to be tempted to seek a Palestinian solution first. At that painful meeting for the Israelis, Carter appeared to have embraced the entire collusion scenario. He told Begin that he would denounce his policies as counter to American interest. Begin's policy, Carter informed them, had been a shock to him. It had undone 'everything we have been seeking'. Because of Begin's intransigence, Carter could 'see no prospect for negotiations'.

Brzezinski was delighted by Carter's performance. Collusion was again on course. Israel's friends in the Senate and in Congress were badly shaken. The Israelis accompanying Begin were in a state of shock, at least in Brzezinski's estimation; he noted with evident satisfaction that 'the stage was thus set for the execution of our plan'. The Israelis were now on the defensive, Congress was evidently moving to support Carter against Begin, and 'the moment of truth was nearing'.

Carter, Vance and their advisers met soon afterwards for their customary foreign affairs breakfast, and this time they made a meal of it. They agreed that all was set for the next stage. They would ask Sadat to make his public move towards the end of April as had been arranged at Camp David in February. Sadat would unfold his peace plan, which would include some maximalist demands. Again, according to plan, the American response would then follow, after it had been approved by Sadat, about the middle of May. 'This was to be done in conjunction with an address to the nation by the President.' This would emphasize that a peace settlement in the Middle East on the lines proposed by Sadat, and as modified by Carter, 'was in the American national interest'. The pressure on Begin and Israel to accept these terms would then be total and irresistible. The collusion would be in place.

The idea of a bilateral Egyptian–Israeli agreement, based on a Sinai deal with which Carter had flirted briefly after the Camp David meeting with Sadat in February, did not survive the contrary pressure from Carter's National Security Council and State Department advisers. All was thus set for the showdown with the Israelis, which the American and Egyptian presidential advisers had programmed.

It was not to be. The Americans became involved in other matters that preoccupied them, not least a major entanglement with the Israeli lobby over arms sales to Saudi Arabia. As a result, the collusion time-table was badly disorganized.

A more serious difficulty, however, was the draft of the Egyptian peace plan when it finally arrived some time in June, instead of in early April as the Americans had anticipated. The contents were even more disconcerting for the Americans than the delayed arrival. These fell far short of what had been agreed by the Americans in February. The Egyptian draft offered no possible basis for the proposed American compromise that was to trap Begin. As a result, Brzezinski drafted a hard-headed memorandum for the President on 18 July 1978, which summarized the new reality and the likely domestic and international consequences if they were to become involved in a diplomatic brawl with Israel.

He proposed that they should discuss these ideas at the foreign affairs breakfast two days later on 20 July. It was to mark a watershed in Carter's thinking. Having spent six months manipulating policy in order to corral Begin with the help of the Egyptians, Carter now argued that in view of all the facts and, not least because Sadat's Foreign Ministry had failed to meet the commitments which Kamel and Maher had made in February, it was necessary to reconsider their previous positions: 'Instead of working against Begin, we should try and work through him.' It was agreed that preparations should begin without delay for a summit at Camp David with Carter, Begin and Sadat.

There was another meeting ten days later on 30 July. This time it was attended by Vice-President Mondale, Secretary of State Vance, Defence Secretary Harold Brown, the President's special assistant, Hamilton Jordan, and their respective officials. Arrangements were formalized for the summit to be held at Camp David in early September. But there was still a strong undercurrent of confrontation with Israel. While the President had clearly abandoned all thought of further collusion with Sadat against Begin, Brzezinski was still bent on confrontation as offering the only prospect of a settlement which would be acceptable to the Egyptians – but which Egyptians?

This attitude was admirably reflected in the pre-conference memo which Brzezinski sent to Carter on 31 August, barely a week before the opening of the summit. He told Carter that the President would have to exercise strict control over every aspect of the proceedings at Camp David 'and thereafter pursue a deliberate political strategy designed to bring about significant changes in both Egypt's and Israel's substantive position'. Brzezinski warned Carter that 'Begin probably believes a failure at Camp David will hurt you and Sadat, but not him. He may even want to see Sadat discredited and you weakened, thus leaving him with a tolerable status quo.' At this stage, Brzezinski's policy advice to Carter was entirely related only to a Palestinian settlement.

Alongside the Americans, but without consulting them, the Egyptian Foreign Ministry officials – quite distinct from Sadat himself – were also laying their plans for the summit. Almost at the same time as Brzezinski had counselled Carter to beware of Begin, the Egyptian Foreign Minister addressed a 'highly confidential' memorandum to Sadat, in which he set out the strategy proposed for 'the Tripartite Camp David Meeting' by Sadat's Foreign Ministry advisers. It was dated 28 August 1978.

This was its argument. The conference, which was to take place at Camp David, had been brought about by Egypt's successful diplomacy. Its objectives were 'to expose Israeli intransigence before the United States and the world', and to force the United States to abandon her role as mediator and to act as a full partner with Egypt in seeking to bring about a settlement. The conference should also rally Saudi Arabia and Jordan in support of Egypt. The memorandum then described at length Israel's underhand designs to prevent such an alignment of Egypt and the United States, which was the principal purpose of the forthcoming conference. Egypt's political objectives at the conference were recalled in some detail. They did not vary from those of the PLO. In conclusion, it urged Sadat to take a hard stand at the outset and to be prepared to put all the blame for the failure of the conference on Israel. 'Peace' as the objective of the conference was not mentioned, nor considered.

It was an extraordinary document, which Israel did not see until long after the event. As a statement of Egypt's intended strategy, it provided us later with a remarkable insight into Sadat's Foreign Ministry. We knew a number of Sadat's principal advisers and we respected them for their ability and understanding. Among them were the Prime Minister, Mustapha Khalil; the Chief of Intelligence, Kamal Hassan Ali; the Minister of State at the Foreign Ministry, Butros Ghali; and the doyen of Egypt's Foreign Ministry officials, Osama el-Baz, a stern critic of Israel, but a man of great intelligence and integrity. How could these men have subscribed to a document so devoid of understanding of either the United States or Israel? Had they been consulted in its preparation as Foreign Minister Kamel – Mohammed Bey to his intimates – had claimed?

Had Sadat acted in accordance with this directive for the summit, the Camp David conference would have broken up within forty-eight hours; most likely it would never have started. There would have been no peace treaty with Israel for Egypt, no return of the Sinai Peninsula and no special relationship with the United States.

Sadat understood this. Two days after he had received his Foreign Minister's memorandum, on 30 August, he summoned its author and his principal advisers to meet his National Security Council at his rest-house at Ismailiya. Kamel arrived expecting a full discussion of his strategy paper for the summit. But Sadat was clearly furious with the tenor and substance of the Foreign Ministry memorandum and even more so with the assumption by the Foreign Minister that the President should or would take heed of his directive. Sadat responded in his own inimical and devastating manner reserved for those at the receiving end of his annoyance. Moreover, he had invited the leading television and press representatives to the meeting. For those who knew Sadat, this meant that he was about to put on a special show with a very real purpose; and this he did with his customary gusto.

In front of the assembled ministers, senior officials and press, he treated the Foreign Minister's strategy directive with demonstrative disdain. He did not even mention it; instead, he spoke of his own intentions at Camp David. This was vintage Sadat. At this important and normally top-secret meeting of the National Security Council, the President ostentatiously distanced himself from his former close friend, the Foreign Minister, and his team. He laughingly and cruelly mocked the Minister in front of everyone – television, press, subordinates and colleagues. 'Do you imagine yourself a diplomat, Mr Mohammed?' And, still laughing, Sadat responded to the patronizing advice the Foreign Minister had offered him at the outset of their meeting. Kamel had warned Sadat that as the Camp David talks might go on for a full week, it might be advisable for Sadat to take a much tougher line at the outset than had been provided in the Egyptian project.

Sadat had never taken kindly to juniors telling him how to conduct his negotiations. His biting response to Kamel was evident to all those present – but clearly not to Kamel, to whom it was addressed. Sadat just laughed very loud and said to his Foreign Minister: 'What week are you talking about? I intend to spring my project on them, wreck the conference and return to Egypt within forty-eight hours.' Solemnly, Kamel noted in his memoirs, apropos this encounter, that Sadat was 'a national disaster that had befallen Egypt'.

All this did not augur well for Egyptian diplomacy at the coming summit. Admittedly, Israel also had her problems, but they were manageable compared to Egypt's. However, there was considerable significance in this preliminary skirmishing in Washington and Cairo in preparation for the planned summit at Camp David, for something of decisive significance happened to both Presidents which was to make possible the agreement that was to come. This was the fact that by the end of August both Carter and Sadat had freed themselves from the programmatic straitjacket into which they had been forced by their advisers and officials. Carter and Sadat were thus free to negotiate without undue 'guidance' from their advisers. Begin, for his part, was also in a straitjacket, but it was of his own making; it was essentially ideological and theological – and virtually irremovable. He had to undergo traumatic difficulties before he managed to free himself from these self-imposed restraints.

Begin presented a bizarre problem. It was almost Sadat's position in reverse. Begin's advisers and officials were to a man determined to achieve a genuine peace with Egypt – and none more so than his Foreign Minister, Moshe Dayan, and the Defence Minister, Ezer Weizman. In Israel's case, the problem was not with the officials but with the Prime Minister. He wanted peace, but he wanted the status quo even more. He wanted to be a world statesman, but he was hidebound by the slogans and attitudes of a long political career mostly in irresponsible opposition. He was tied to his own propaganda image of himself and conditioned by his colleagues, his rivals, his friends and his followers. He was afraid to do anything which they might consider a betrayal of this ideal. He was aware at the same time that there were powerful critics in the wings waiting for him to slip.

Begin was not the firm, tough, inflexible negotiator depicted by some of the American participants. He was inhibited by and afraid of his own Likud constituency at home. This was a much more formidable force to overcome than Carter's Brzezinski, or Sadat's Kamel. But between them, all these constraints weighed like an albatross on the three principals and for long restricted the negotiating capabilities of Carter, Begin and Sadat.

Looking at the record now, after the event, it is not too much to say that, left alone, Carter, Begin and Sadat could have reached the same Camp David agreement in a matter of days instead of months without the hassle, the agony and the time-consuming manipulation. It was not possible, however, because the hard-to-get debates were necessary at Camp David so that Begin could have an alibi with which he could placate his noisy and critical Likud status quo constituency in Israel; so that Sadat could pacify the angry resistance to a peace with Israel from his increasingly hostile Foreign Minister and his team of officials; and so that Carter, at last, could square up to his principal advisers, whose hostility to Begin – and to Israel – was such that it exceeded the accepted norms of the American foreign service. When they discovered that the agreement was imminent and that Sadat's aides had failed to prevail on him not to sign, some of Carter's aides decided to take independent action.

According to Quandt, some of the Americans then quietly approached Sadat on their own initiative: 'They told Sadat he need not sign the agreements as they stood. He could say to the Arabs that he had refused to sign a deal that would have secured the return of Sinai because he had been unable to obtain a suitable deal on the Palestinian issue and that he would continue negotiating until he did.' At that point, Sadat lost his temper and shouted back at the Americans who were advising him not to sign the Carter peace: 'No, no, never! I cannot do that to my people.'

Sadat had made up his mind, and his decision to sign the agreement with Israel was to lead to a remarkable confrontation on the last day at Camp David. His Foreign Minister, Mohammed Kamel, resigned. His legal adviser, a man of keen mind and quick tongue, who several years later was to prove his mettle in his handling of the Taba arbitration, was encouraged rashly to attempt a last-minute conversion of Sadat to the views of his Foreign Ministry critics. Nabil el-Araby went to see Sadat, waited impatiently while he continued a lengthy conversation with Begin, and then bearded the President in his Camp David hut. Sadat, as always, was excessively polite and invited Araby to take a seat and to explain his problem. Araby, encouraged by Sadat's courtesy, spoke for a full forty-five minutes, stressing that in his legal opinion the letters which Carter had asked Sadat and Begin to sign were legally worthless. He therefore advised Sadat not to sign the Camp David Accords. When Araby had, at last, finished, Sadat asked him whether there was anything else he wanted to say? Araby said 'No.'

Sadat replied:

Then listen to what I have to say. I heard you out without interrupting you, so nobody can claim that I neither listen nor read! However, I would like you to know that what you have just been saying has gone in one ear and out of the other. You people in the Foreign Ministry are under the impression that you understand politics. In reality, you understand absolutely nothing. I do not propose, in future, to pay any attention to either your words or to your memoranda. My actions are governed by a higher strategy which you are incapable of either perceiving or understanding. I do not need your insignificant and misleading reports. And now your Minister Kamel insults President Carter in my presence; does he not realize that President Carter is my trump card?*

The last-ditch efforts to prevent agreement had failed, and the Camp David Accords, paving the way to peace between Egypt and Israel, were signed by Carter, Sadat and Begin in a grandiose ceremonial gathering at the White House on 17 September. As we look back on the Camp David talks

---

* Quoted in Mohammed Ibrahim Kamel, *The Camp David Accords* (London, 1986).

with all their agonies, and on their follow-up in Jerusalem in March 1979, which ended with the signing of the Peace Treaty in Washington on 26 March 1979, we must conclude that these were surely the strangest peace negotiations in modern times. The alignments and the loyalties were mixed and the ultimate purpose confused to the end. Peace emerged, as it were, virtually by accident. And if we have to give a name to that accident it has to be 'Moshe Dayan'. But all that mattered on that historic day was that now there would be peace between Egypt and Israel.

The game of collusion had come to an end – like Balaam's mission; the intended curse had become a blessing. In the event, the Americans had risen to the occasion. The tireless efforts of Carter, Vance and some of the other American officials present time and again prevented the talks from stalling. Throughout the protracted negotiations there had been crises: over Jerusalem, the question of settlements, and over the linkage between a separate peace between Egypt and Israel and moves to a comprehensive peace settlement involving the Palestinians. Both Begin and Sadat repeatedly threatened to pack their bags and return home over these issues. And each time Carter succeeded in finding a way round seemingly insurmountable difficulties. At Camp David Carter the statesman showed that his ultimate objective was a Middle East peace and not simply to side with the Arabs against Israel, as some observers had come to suspect. He had colluded against Begin because he believed Begin was an obstacle to peace as Carter then understood 'peace' – a comprehensive dream peace encompassing all the players. At Camp David he found the strength to forgo the unattainable and to bring Sadat and Begin to agree to a formula acceptable to both, and in doing this he completed the edifice whose foundations had been laid by a man he disliked and distrusted, Henry Kissinger.

Sadat had accepted Carter's version of peace so long as it served his Egyptian interests, which were that peace was an instrument to achieve Egypt's national objective – the return of the Sinai Peninsula to Egyptian sovereignty and, where possible, an Israeli withdrawal to the 1967 boundaries. For Sadat, it was the Sinai that mattered; all else was salad dressing. Carter's often repeated concept of a comprehensive peace was a meaningless abstraction for Sadat. The peace sought by his own Egyptian officials, and especially by his Foreign Ministry, was akin to the peace advocated by Brzezinski and, for a time, by Carter himself. This envisaged cutting Israel down to size for the benefit of the Palestinians. Such a peace, Sadat had argued strongly, was not only unrealistic but also unattainable.

We had often suspected that the opponents and critics of Sadat would go to any lengths to make certain that there was no peace with Israel, for without Sadat there would have been no peace. He was the real peacemaker and he was a great Egyptian. He also confirmed, by his action, the wise counsel of Ben-Gurion, who was convinced throughout his premiership that Egypt would make peace only when she had no other alternative. It was Sadat's greatness that he understood this – and acted accordingly.

8
Sadat's Peace
1979–81

THE PEACE TREATY was signed on 26 March 1979 in Washington. It heralded for most Israelis the beginning of a new era in our history, a period of brotherhood with Egypt and close co-operation in all fields. Expectations were high.

In Egypt, expectations were mixed. Many Egyptians believed that peace would put an end to Egypt's economic difficulties and lead to a period of prosperity. Egypt's leaders, in particular, were convinced that they had set in train a process that would result in a more comprehensive peace, and that the autonomy talks to be held in accordance with the Peace Treaty would ensure that the Palestinian problem would at last be settled.

However, these expectations were partnered by fears and suspicions on both sides. Thirty years of enmity and war leave their scars. The Peace Treaty had established that Israeli withdrawal from Sinai would be implemented in stages, the last phase of the withdrawal to be completed not later than three years from the date of exchange of instruments of ratification of the Treaty. The last zone to be given up by Israel was the most sensitive and controversial from the Israeli point of view – it included Sharm el-Sheikh, the strategic outpost on the Gulf of Suez; the picturesque new town of Yamit built by Israelis; the string of agricultural settlements that had been laboriously established along the coastline north of el-Arish; as well as two large sophisticated air bases in which a significant part of Israel's air force was stationed.

As the date of the final withdrawal drew near – 25 April 1982 – Egyptian apprehensions intensified. By the beginning of April, there was hardly an Egyptian who was not convinced that Israel would conjure up an excuse to delay the withdrawal. When, however, the fateful day arrived, and the blue-and-white flag was hauled down and Sharm el-Sheikh, the air bases and the villages were handed over to the bemused Egyptians, only then did many in Egypt grasp that peace between Egypt and Israel had come to stay.

Begin had declared that he would fulfil the terms of the Treaty and he kept his word. But the price was high. He was forced to send the army to do battle with the Jewish inhabitants of Yamit, who were reinforced by nationalist right-wing elements from all over the country who angrily opposed the withdrawal. Our army's clash with the settlers who refused to evacuate their homes in Yamit coincided with Memorial Day for the victims of the Holocaust. That evening a particularly harrowing film about the Holocaust was shown on Israeli television.

The following morning Philip Habib, President Reagan's envoy, met Begin to discuss the situation along the Lebanese frontier. Begin began by describing the film to Habib and to the American diplomats and Israeli officials assembled in his office. After a few minutes an aide came in with a despatch from Yamit, describing the fierce resistance of the inhabitants to being evicted by the soldiers. As Begin read out the note, tears welled into his eyes and he began to cry – for Yamit, for the Jews slaughtered in the Holocaust, and for the years of exile and persecution that the Jewish people had suffered. Begin carried that suffering on his shoulders through his own private interminable Via Dolorosa, and that morning he gave vent to his grief before the stunned American diplomats.

The fears and suspicions, however, were not only on the Egyptian side. Begin, too, was deeply suspicious of Egyptian intentions. He feared that Egypt would not abide by the articles in the Peace Treaty calling for the demilitarization of the Sinai. The article in question had provided for limited force zones in Egyptian and Israeli territory, and for the United Nations forces and observers to supervise the implementation of the security measures agreed upon by the two countries. Begin's suspicions deepened when it became apparent that the United Nations had no intention of forming such a supervisory force in the Sinai.

This was an essential element in the Peace Treaty and Begin was not prepared to relinquish it, as the Egyptians had requested. For them, an international force on Egyptian soil entailed a limitation on Egyptian sovereignty, something which Sadat said repeatedly that he would never tolerate. When Begin demanded that a multi-national force be established in place of the United Nations force as envisaged in the treaty, the Egyptians at first totally opposed the idea. Later, they reluctantly agreed to the principle, but with the clear intention of having a tiny force with minimal duties for a limited time, in direct contrast to Begin's concept.

Begin appointed me to lead the Israeli negotiating team, and for a year I grappled with this problem holding weekly meetings with a formidable team of lawyers and diplomats, headed through much of the period by Osama el-Baz, until finally the MFO – the multi-national force and observers – was put in place in a manner that was satisfactory to Begin – no easy matter, given his penchant for fine legal details. Once more, the suspicions proved to be unfounded. Very few complaints from either side marred the uneventful existence of the MFO in Sinai – the world's most peaceful and smoothly run international force.

At the same time, in those first years following the signing of the Peace Treaty, we were busy giving life to the Treaty, transforming the long, dark period of war into the brightness of peace. Egyptian and Israeli officials of every conceivable ministry and branch of government met in Cairo and Jerusalem in order to conclude agreements of co-operation. More than forty agreements were signed covering such diverse fields as a regular air link between Egyptian and Israeli airports, tourism, trade, tele-communications, scientific co-operation, land and sea traffic, police co-operation, exchange of youth groups and the like. All these manifold meetings were hosted and stage-managed by the two Foreign Ministries, which put a tremendous strain on our tiny but highly professional staff. The two Defence Ministers, Kamal Hassan Ali and Ezer Weizman, met frequently to oversee these activities and became close friends, as did their aides, Generals Taha el-Magdoub and Avraham Tamir. Weizman and Tamir succeeded in gaining the confidence of the Egyptians, and Tamir in particular made many trips to Cairo in order to iron out differences which arose throughout that intensive first phase. I myself made thirteen trips to Cairo in my first year as Director-General of the Foreign Ministry.

Yet even in those early days the seeds of the cold peace that was to follow were being sown. From the outset there existed an influential opposition in Egypt to Sadat's peace with Israel. We have already noted the antagonism displayed by two successive Foreign Ministers, Ismail Fahmy and Mohammed Kamel, which led to their resignations. Many senior Foreign Ministry officials were disciples of Fahmy and felt that it was their duty to obstruct any expression of practical co-operation with Israel.

They were backed by the majority of Egypt's intelligentsia – authors, journalists, lawyers, doctors, teachers and engineers. Very few of them were willing to have anything to do with Israel or Israelis – in public. The editor of one of the leading weeklies explained this hostile attitude to me:

When I write a column for al-Ahram, I get thirty or forty Egyptian pounds for it. But if the same column is printed in Kuwait, Abu Dhabi or elsewhere in the Gulf, I get two or three hundred pounds. A doctor or engineer will work eleven months in Egypt; the twelfth he will work in the Gulf and earn more than he did throughout the year in Egypt. If the doctor attends a medical conference in Israel, he will not be able to work any more in the Gulf. If I write something positive about Israel, my column will no longer be published in Kuwait and Abu Dhabi. We are all afraid of being blacklisted by the Arab world.

There were, of course, members of the free professions who refused to meet Israelis for nationalist, ideological and even for racist reasons, but economic factors as described above played the larger role. There were in the 1980s over three million Egyptians working in other Arab countries; each one of them, plus his six or seven close relatives in Egypt, would have hesitated before having any contact with Israel.

Sadat himself held the Arab countries in poor esteem and especially other Arab leaders. On one occasion, during his visit to Haifa, he declared that 'the Arab countries need Egypt much more than Egypt needs the Arab countries'. He firmly believed this and rode roughshod over Arab sensitivities. Yet Egypt was tied to the Arab world with an umbilical cord, and every escalation of tension between Israel and the Palestinians, or with any of the Arab countries, had an immediate effect on Egyptian–Israeli relations. Moreover, after having been expelled from the Arab League and after virtually all the Arab countries had broken off diplomatic relations with her, Egypt's desire to be received back into the Arab fold imposed a limit to intimacy with Israel. We rather felt that Egypt was paying for her return to the Arab world with 'Israeli currency'.

The notion that bilateral peace between Egypt and Israel was the first step towards a comprehensive peace in the Middle East, which had been pioneered by Egypt, was at the heart of Egyptian thinking in the days after the Treaty was signed. The key to opening the door to a comprehensive settlement was to be the autonomy talks, to which both Jordanian and Palestinian delegates had been invited, in accordance with the provisions of the Peace Treaty. But when the talks opened on 25 May 1979, in Beersheba, it soon became apparent that, if the two contenders would not move substantially from the hard-line position they took, the talks would be doomed to failure.

Kamal Hassan Ali, then Egypt's Foreign Minister, insisted in an opening statement that self-determination was the 'God-given right' of the Palestinians, that 'Arab Jerusalem' was an integral part of the territory under review, that Israeli measures to change her status quo were null and void, and that our settlements had no legal validity. The Israeli chairman, Interior Minister Yosef Burg, had been deliberately appointed by Begin in preference to Dayan, the natural choice. Burg's uncompromising answering statement made it clear that autonomy did not imply any future sovereignty.

Thus, from the outset, there was something unreal and artificial about these autonomy talks. The Palestinians and the Jordanians not only refused to take part in the talks, but rejected the entire autonomy process. The Egyptians, therefore, were representing clients who did not want to be represented. In order not to be accused of betraying the Palestinians, the Egyptians adopted a maximalist approach, demanding much more from the autonomy talks than had been agreed at Camp David. They interpreted the transitional period of five years to which they had agreed as no more than a corridor leading to self-determination and a Palestinian entity, independent or associated with Jordan.

There had thus been a considerable hardening in Egyptian policy since the day the Camp David agreements had been signed, caused primarily by the negative reaction in the Arab world. In Israel, a similar process had taken place. Begin had to contend with a growing revolt from the nationalist right-wing elements, who constituted the hard core of his support. The fact that stalwart supporters such as Yitzhak Shamir and Moshe Arens had refused to vote in favour of the Camp David Accords in the Knesset was bad enough, but among his grass-root backers there was increasing apprehension that the agreement on Palestinian autonomy, as set out at Camp David, was quite different from his original programme. They saw it as endangering Israel's continued presence in Judea, Samaria and Gaza.

Begin's original plan for self-rule was open-ended, with a proviso that its principles would be subject to review after a five-year period. The Camp David formula was fundamentally different in that it prescribed 'transitional arrangements for the West Bank and Gaza for a period not later than the third year of the transitional period to determine "the final status" of these territories'. There were many people in Israel who felt that Camp David was a formula for an eventual abdication of the Israeli presence on the West Bank and in Gaza, and that the Palestinians were missing a great opportunity by refusing to accept the Egyptian–Israeli invitation to join the autonomy talks.

The Israelis were influenced by these apprehensions as the talks opened and were determined not to provide any opportunities for the fulfilment of these fears. Begin's die-hard approach led to the resignation from the Government of Foreign Minister Dayan and then, later, of Defence Minister Weizman. Without the moderating influence of these two principal architects of the Camp David Accords, Begin, Sharon and the national-religious politicians in Israel moved without restraint to positions which were completely unacceptable to Egypt. Thus, both Egypt and Israel moved on diametrically opposing lines as the autonomy talks got under way.

However, unbeknown to the Israeli negotiators, the Egyptians held an ace up their sleeves, and they were waiting to play it. The card was President Carter's tacit agreement that after the American presidential elections in November 1980, when Carter expected to be re-elected for a second term, he would be free to compel Israel to accept a settlement of the Palestinian problem on his and Egyptian terms, without having to fear the backlash of the American Jewish lobby. The one condition for this American–Egyptian card to be played successfully was the anticipated Carter victory in the election against Reagan. In those early days – before the Iranians took sixty-six American hostages at the US Embassy in Tehran – Carter and Sadat were still supremely confident that victory would be theirs.

Even before the presidential election, when Carter was still careful not to antagonize the large Jewish constituency, the American team at the autonomy talks was clearly showing its preference. Secretary of State Vance, Saunders, Quandt, Atherton and the others in the American team sided as a rule on all key issues with the Egyptians against Israel. As Vance explained it, 'our intent was to create a procedure that could, if used seriously and conscientiously, lead to a Palestinian homeland while at the same time taking into account Israel's legitimate security concerns'.

Throughout 1979 and 1980, Sadat's policy towards Israel was clearly influenced by his conviction that Carter's second term as President would initiate a period of uninhibited American pressure on Israel to settle the Palestinian question on lines agreed between the United States and Egypt. Carter's débâcle in the presidential election of 1980 thus became also the ruin of Egypt's adversarial policy towards Israel. Sadat was bitter about Carter's defeat, blaming the American President for his indecision in dealing with the hostage question. 'What sort of superpower is it that allows itself to be humiliated in such a way without reacting with real force?'

Carter's defeat was a terrible blow for Sadat. It ended his hopes for a successful conclusion – from the Egyptian point of view – of the autonomy talks. By the time the new US Secretary of State, Alexander Haig, took over, they had become so bogged down that they were beyond rescue. In fact, the Americans had hardly been in a position to pursue the talks with much vigour even before the presidential election. The overthrow of the Shah, the invasion of Afghanistan by the Soviet Union, the taking of the American Embassy hostages in Tehran and, finally, soaring oil prices had turned 1980 into a black year for the attainment of American foreign policy objectives.

Carter's dislike of Begin and his sympathy for the Palestinians were reinforced by the fact that the Iranian débâcle increased the importance of Saudi Arabia and of Saudi oil in the American national interest; in Carter's eyes, this legitimized his unevenhandedness and the greater support he gave the Palestinians during the autonomy talks.

These were never formally abrogated, but the autonomy teams stopped convening after the Israeli side insisted that the next meeting be held in Jerusalem and the Egyptians refused to agree because of the sensitive nature of the city's status. In retrospect, as we reconsidered these discussions, it was evident that the failure of the autonomy talks was one of the greatest wasted opportunities on the road to peace in the Middle East. This was particularly true for the Palestinians themselves. They had failed to rise to the occasion. Petty considerations prevailed – especially the fear of the PLO that free elections would bring to the fore a new alternative leadership to the one that had dominated the organization since its foundation in 1965. The Palestinians failed to grasp the advantages inherent in the transitional nature of the autonomy arrangements and allowed their anger at the Egyptians to blind them to the opportunity provided to them by the autonomy plan.

However, we cannot escape the feeling that Israel also had displayed undue caution in order to contain the threat of self-determination and of a Palestinian state. The arguments over the size of the self-governing authority that was to be elected was a case in point: the Egyptians had demanded a legislative assembly of 80–100 members, who would elect a council of 10–15 executives. Begin, quite correctly, claimed that such an assembly would be tantamount to a parliament, for which the Camp David agreement had made no provision – it alluded only to an administrative council.

A parliament, in Begin's eyes, was a forerunner to a state. He, in his turn, proposed that the size of the administrative council should be in accordance with the number of functions the council would be responsible for. He suggested that it should have thirteen members, but was willing to agree to any number below twenty. When Haig sought to overcome this obstacle by proposing a number between thirty-two and forty-five, Begin refused adamantly, claiming that this would be construed as a parliament. Luxembourg, Sri Lanka and Iceland have small parliaments of the size Haig was proposing, he pointed out acidly to Haig, and there certainly were not enough functions to fit such a number. The distinction between sovereignty and autonomy was decisive, and therefore Begin was sticking by his criterion, which was one used in autonomies the world over.

Haig argued that all this was irrelevant, as Israel could easily prevent any move towards sovereignty with the aid of her forces, which would still be stationed in the territories. His appeal to break the deadlock was in vain. Begin was adamant. He would take no risks. The exaggerated demands by the Egyptians only stimulated Begin's caution. This Egyptian extremism served Egypt's purpose of demonstrating to the Arab world that she was protecting Palestinian interests, but, in doing so, Egypt made it practically impossible to reach an agreement that would have benefited the Palestinians – even if it did not meet all their excessive demands.

Thus, the road to a comprehensive peace was blocked by the lack of vision of each of the parties – the Palestinians, Israel, Egypt and the United States. Egypt and Israel settled down to an uneasy cold and unsatisfactory peace – a pale and distorted reflection of the peace imagined by Israelis and Egyptians in the high-noon of the signing of the peace agreement. The breakdown of the autonomy talks, coupled with the Lebanese War, provided the Egyptians with the welcome excuse for not fulfilling all the agreements they had signed for the full normalization of relations between our two countries.

Yet the Peace Treaty held fast. Sadat had been gunned down in October 1981 by Muslim fanatics who had called for his death in a *fatwa*, not – as widely believed – because he made peace with Israel, but because he refused to convert Egypt into an Islamic republic governed by the laws of the Muslim *Shariah*. In Israel, the ultra-nationalists who had opposed the withdrawal from Sinai had falsely prophesied that the Egyptians would tear up the Treaty after Sadat's death; they were also convinced that, if Israel ever found herself at war again with an Arab country, Egypt would scrap the Treaty. By June 1982, both these eventualities had occurred, but Hosni Mubarak, Egypt's new President, scrupulously maintained the main features of the Treaty, even as relations between the two countries rapidly took on all the trappings of a 'cold peace' as Butros Ghali, the Egyptian Minister of State, aptly called it.

The Egyptians were careful to uphold those agreements that were dependent on the Government without the active participation of the two populations: commercial flights between Cairo and Ben-Gurion airports; bus routes between the two countries; the embassies and consulates in Cairo, Tel Aviv, Alexandria and Eilat; the sale of oil; the telephone link and, particularly, the demilitarization of Sinai. But agreements depending on popular support – tourism to Israel, trade, cultural agreements and the like – were left in abeyance on the grounds that the Egyptian Government could not force its people to visit Israel, to trade with her and to like Israelis.

In actual fact, the Egyptian Government did everything possible to discourage such activities. Egyptians wanting to visit Israel were subjected to an interrogation by the security service; those wishing to trade had to receive special permission, which was often withheld. Particularly annoying was the hostile press, often bordering on open incitement against Israel and on rabid anti-Semitism. Our frequent protests were always parried with the same reply – that the Egyptian press was free and, therefore, journalists could write as they wished: they were merely giving vent to their feelings caused by the continued resistance of the Palestinians under occupation.

Hardly a positive word on Israel was allowed to appear on the state-run television or radio. Our repeated requests for balanced programmes on Israel to help eradicate the scars of the past were ignored. Yet these anti-Israeli tirades in the press made surprisingly little impact on the Egyptian public. In the first ten years of the Peace Treaty, some 300,000 Israelis visited Egypt and, except for one ugly incident, were received courteously and treated in a friendly manner by the Egyptians.

The peace with Egypt had a telling impact on Israel. The claustrophobic obsession caused by being hemmed in on all sides by hostile forces was at last broken. Israelis flocked to the land of the Nile. Even I, an experienced and blasé traveller of the world, felt the twinge of excitement and wonder when I landed at Cairo airport in an El Al Israel Airlines plane, or used to drive through the streets of Cairo in our Ambassador's car with the blue-and-white pennant of Israel proudly in place. After so many years of enmity, when a visit to Egypt was as likely as a visit to the moon, the change has been startlingly uplifting.

From our point of view, even a cold peace held many advantages. The fact that there was quiet on the southern Egyptian front afforded Israel much-needed respite and allowed us to make large cuts in our massive defence budget. This, in turn enabled the Government to overcome a 700 per cent inflation. More important, Israel's strategic situation was transformed by the Peace Treaty: the withdrawal of Egypt from the 'circle of hostility' which surrounded Israel in effect ended the threat of another war on two fronts. The Peace Treaty also brought about a psychological revolution which affected the entire region. The stationing of Egyptian diplomats in Israel and Israelis in Cairo, and the exchange between Egyptian and Israeli politicians and officials, created an aura of peace and normalcy which had a profound effect on the Arab world: for the first time since the State of Israel had been established in 1948, we were formally accepted as an existing reality.

Until Sadat's visit to Jerusalem in November 1977, the word 'Israel' was rarely used in the Arab media – such colourful phrases as 'the cancer in our midst' or 'the Zionist usurpation' were customary descriptions. By the early 1980s, however, the Arabs seemed to have come to terms with Israel's existence. 'Israel' was no longer a dirty word. A contributing factor to this was the ever-growing threat to the Arab world posed by the fear that Khomeini might export his Islamic Revolution. American diplomats touring the Arab countries soon after the overthrow of the Shah recalled that their Arab interlocuters hardly mentioned Israel – in marked contrast to previous visits. Arab attention was concentrated on the ominous events in Iran.

This Arab change of attitude towards Israel was seen by us as a welcome signal heralding, for the first time, possibilities of reconciliation. The focus was shifted from the old aim of annihilation to the possibility of coming to terms with Israel. The change was by no means uniform and there were, of course, painful exceptions: there was no softening of Syria's stance, nor of Muamar Qaddafi's, while the hard-line PLO continued to consider the destruction of Israel to be its great, albeit unavowed, aim. But by and large, as a result of the peace with Egypt, the relationship between Israel and the Arab world in the 1980s had changed to what could best be described as one of hostile co-existence. 'Peace' ceased to be an obscene word in the Middle East, even if it still had many faces.

Yet relations between states are usually made up of minor, mundane issues. None more so than the Taba affair, which cast its shadow over Egyptian–Israeli relations throughout most of the 1980s. The dispute over a small coastal stretch of rock and sand, less than one square mile in area, a virtual suburb only five miles from Eilat at the head of the Gulf of Akaba, took on surprisingly unexpected proportions – though there was more to it than met the eye.

The dispute began innocently enough. The border between Egypt and Ottoman Palestine had been demarcated by a joint Anglo–Turkish boundary commission in 1906; the British acted on behalf of Egypt, which was then British-occupied territory. The description given of that demarcation showed that the disputed land at Taba was to the east of the boundary of 1906, in Ottoman Palestine and not in British-occupied Egypt. When this fact was brought to the attention of Prime Minister Begin after he had signed the Peace Treaty with Egypt, he gave permission for a large hotel to be built in the Taba area, which was, according to the 1906 demarcation, within Israeli territory. Egypt, however, disputed the relevance of the 1906 agreement. The Egyptian Government claimed that facts on the ground – the actual frontier between Egypt and the British Mandate of Palestine, as well as maps drawn up during the Mandate and even by Israel after her establishment – showed Taba to be indisputably on the Egyptian side of the frontier.

Israel counter-claimed that the 1906 border was the only legitimate frontier; it had been clearly and precisely identified by the joint Anglo–Turkish boundary commission. This boundary had been arbitrarily and illegally adjusted on maps produced by the British during the First World War, when Turkish forces occupied the whole of the Sinai Peninsula including the disputed area of Taba, in order to improve future Anglo–Egyptian claims in relation to the Turks, who were at that time advancing on the Suez Canal. Egypt, however, relied on Article 1 of the Peace Treaty with Israel, which stated that 'the permanent boundary between Egypt and Israel is the recognized international boundary between Egypt and the former mandated territory of Palestine'. Both sides presented a wealth of evidence to support their claims before the International Arbitration Tribunal, to which the dispute was eventually brought. After lengthy hearings, the Tribunal decided in Egypt's favour, and Taba was duly handed over to Egypt in 1989.

The story, however, was not that simple. For Israel, with less than eight miles of coastline on the Red Sea, hemmed in between Jordan and Egypt, the extra mile of beach gave Eilat much-needed breathing-space. The Eilat inhabitants would point to the 100-mile virtually empty stretch along the eastern coast of the Sinai Peninsula and failed to comprehend why Egypt was making so much fuss about an additional mile at Taba to which Egypt's historical claim was, at best, doubtful.

For Egypt, Israel's refusal to hand back Taba aroused dark suspicions regarding Israel's acceptance of the legality of Egyptian sovereignty over other parts of the Sinai, about which many doubts had been voiced in past years, not least by the British Foreign Office. Nabil el-Araby, the dour but able head of the Egyptian negotiating team on Taba (who had resigned his office as legal adviser to Egypt's Foreign Ministry in protest of Sadat's signing of the Camp David agreement, but was later reappointed to this post), once illustrated these fears in a typically Middle Eastern manner, by telling me a story about Joha, who in Egyptian lore holds the place of part-clown part-folk hero:

Joha sold his house to a neighbour. After the deeds were signed Joha said to his neighbour: 'Please allow me to keep this nail on the wall. It holds sentimental value for me.' The neighbour, being a kind man, agreed. One day, Joha knocked on the door of his former house and told his neighbour: 'I want to hang my hat on my nail on your wall.' The neighbour could not object because it was, after all, Joha's nail. After that Joha's appearances became more frequent and his jacket and then his coat were hung on the nail. Finally Joha appeared leading two donkeys into his neighbour's house and tied them to his nail. You [Araby concluded] want to use Taba as Joha's nail.

The problem was compounded by the fact that very few Egyptians had any notion where and what Taba was. President Mubarak admitted to me that he had never heard of Taba before the dispute began. Most Egyptians, he told me, were sure that Taba comprised a large area; very few would believe that all the fuss was over one square mile.

'Abrasha' Tamir, the Director-General of the Prime Minister's Office, and I acted as co-chairmen of the Israeli team negotiating Taba and we spent many hours arguing with the Egyptians in Cairo and in Jerusalem before the issue was taken out of our hands and sent to the arbitration tribunal. Our effort to link our agreement to go to arbitration with Egyptian willingness to be more forthright on the normalization process was not particularly successful. We demanded that the Egyptians cease the hostile propaganda against us on the state-run media; that the Egyptian Ambassador who had been withdrawn from Israel after the Sabra–Shatilla massacre in Beirut be returned; that the Egyptians allow free movement of people and goods in both directions; and that the political dialogue at ministerial level, which had been decided upon in March 1982, be institutionalized. In the event, even after we agreed to arbitration, the only concrete conciliatory measures taken by the Egyptians were the return of their Ambassador,

Mohammed Bassiouni, to Tel Aviv, and the agreement to hold a per-
functory summit meeting between Mubarak and the new Premier, Shimon
Peres, which was singularly unproductive.

The Egyptians had promised to act otherwise. I recall a long meeting
with Mubarak in September 1985 in which he painted a rosy picture of the
relations we would have once the arbitration process got under way. At the
time we still had not come to an agreement with the Egyptians on the
compromis, or term of reference of the arbitration. As negotiators, our
difficulties lay not only with the Egyptians, but also with the conflicting
instructions we received from the two opposing wings of our so-called
National Unity Government. Nothing can illustrate more the agonies of a
civil servant endeavouring to serve his country faithfully under the exigencies of a two-headed government than the Via Dolorosa we went through
over Taba.

Peres, conscious of the damage being done to our relations with Egypt,
wanted to move to arbitration as speedily as possible. Foreign Minister
Yitzhak Shamir, relying on the Peace Treaty, insisted that we should agree
only to conciliation, which would give us a better chance of keeping Taba.
Shamir, moreover, was incensed that the Egyptians were not keeping all
the bilateral agreements they had signed, and demanded that our Taba
talks be linked to the 'other eggs in our basket', as we put it to the Egyptians.
He also had to contend with the demands of his own party colleagues –
Sharon, Arens and Yitzhak Modai – who opposed any concessions on Taba.

Thus, Tamir and I would go to Cairo with two different sets of instructions and our endeavours to maintain a united front were not always
successful. On one occasion the Prime Minister, while hosting a lunch for
Under-Secretary Richard Murphy at his residence in Jerusalem, addressed
me in English so that Murphy could understand and chided me for not
speeding up the negotiations. 'Why is it taking so long?' he asked testily.
Two days later, while discussing our next Cairo meeting with the Foreign
Minister, Shamir reproached me for moving too quickly on Taba. 'Why
are you running so fast?' he asked. This impasse was finally settled when
the Israeli Cabinet, in a marathon thirteen-hour session, accepted the
Premier's demand and agreed to accept arbitration.

But that was not the end. We also had to contend with the intervention
of the Americans. They were particularly insistent about the terms of the
compromis, on which issue they tilted heavily to the Egyptian side. Finally
the lawyers took over – Robbie Sabel, the legal adviser of the Israeli Foreign
Ministry, and Nabil el-Araby, who had ably led the Egyptian team from
the start, with a panel of five arbitrators; and Israel lost her case, which,
we were convinced, had been historically far stronger than Egypt's.

Taba was handed over to the Egyptians in 1989, but the cold peace
between our two countries did not become appreciably warmer. The Alexandria summit between Peres and Mubarak in September 1986 – Peres's
swan-song as Prime Minister – had been no more than an interlude, a
momentary ray of sunshine temporarily warming the chill. Temperatures

dropped after Shamir took over the premiership shortly after the Mubarak–Peres summit, and they failed to recover after the Egyptian flag had replaced the Star of David at Taba. Taba had been an important symbol for Egypt, for only in 1989 could she claim that she had restored all of Egyptian territory to Egyptian sovereignty. And whereas this was what really mattered to the vast majority of Egyptians, the issue at stake for the Government was a comprehensive settlement which would enable Egypt to remain harmoniously in step with the rest of the Arab world and would remove the stigma of the separate peace concluded by Sadat.

Thus Mubarak energetically pursued a policy of support for Arafat and the PLO – much to the chagrin of Shamir – and refused to meet the Israeli Prime Minister. Egypt became the driving force behind the Arab peace offensive of 1989, about which I shall have more to say. By maintaining Egypt's relations with Israel on as low level as possible without actually endangering the peace agreement, and by wooing the Arab countries in general and the PLO in particular, Mubarak sought to restore Egypt to her former position as leader of the Arab world without having to sacrifice her peace with Israel.

One Arab country after another reopened their embassies in Cairo – the Saudi Embassy incongruously next door to Israel's. The climax came in May 1989, when Egypt's President took his place side by side with the Arab Kings and Presidents who convened in Casablanca for a summit conference of Arab League members. Egypt had been ignominiously ousted from the Arab League after the Camp David Accords; now she was back, as the key player, urging the others to follow in her footsteps on the road to peace.

It had taken little more than ten years from the time Sadat had set foot in Jerusalem to the triumphal return of Egypt to the Arab fold. Israel naturally welcomed Egypt's success, for it revealed how deep a metamorphosis had occurred in Arab thinking as a result of the Peace Treaty. Egypt had been outlawed in the Arab world because she had dared to break the Arab consensus which forbade any contact with the Israeli enemy. Her renewed acceptance in the Arab world meant that the consensus against Israel no longer existed. Peace might still be a chimera, a distant goal on the horizon, but in May 1989 a formidable obstacle was moved aside, and peace moved perceptibly nearer. It could be said that at the Casablanca summit, the Arab heads of state, without being aware of it, had rehabilitated Anwar el-Sadat – however, without as yet committing themselves to a realistic peace with Israel.

PART 2
Israel and Lebanon

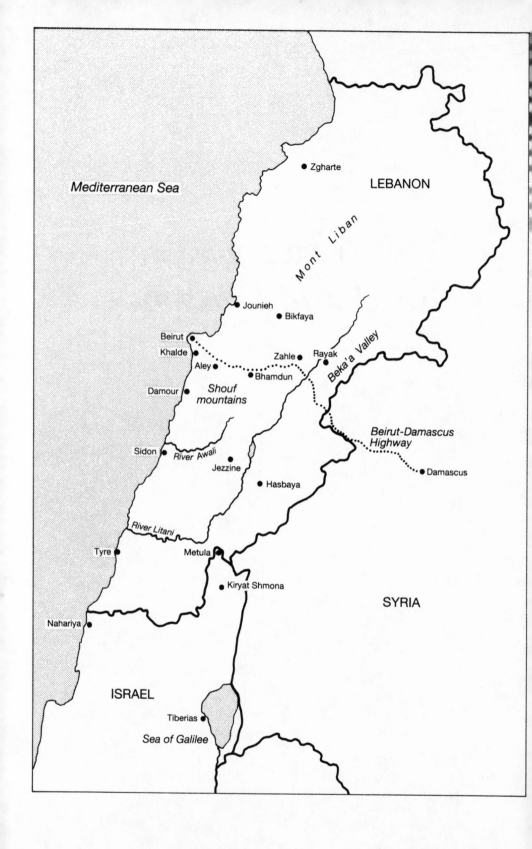

9
Beginning without End
1975–82

Two MEN, patriarchs in their respective countries – one, Menachem Begin, newly elected Prime Minister of Israel; the other, Camille Chamoun, had served two terms as President of Lebanon – met, in August 1978, for the first time, in Begin's modest Jerusalem home. There was an instant understanding between them as if each had recognized the charisma in the other. It was more than the customary encounter. Begin explained that, under his new administration, Israel would be prepared to expand her assistance to the Maronite Christian community in Lebanon beyond the limits set by his predecessor, the Labour Party's Prime Minister, Yitzhak Rabin.

Under the Rabin administration, Israel's position towards the Christian community in Lebanon had been clearly and restrictively defined. Israel would not intervene directly or actively in the conflict between the Christian and Muslim communities, but would help the Christians to help themselves by providing them with arms and training facilities. But now, in August 1978, Begin assured Chamoun that the Israeli air force would intervene if Christian positions were attacked by Syria from the air. Both these experienced politicians understood that such an undertaking could only mean that this was but the opening move in a new relationship between Israel and Lebanon.

Chamoun left for home hugely satisfied by this first encounter with Begin. But as Israel's Premier bade him farewell at the door, the ageing Chamoun paused for a moment as if he had forgotten something. He turned to Begin and in slow deliberate tones cautioned him not to make the mistakes 'we made in the Lebanon'. Chamoun recalled: 'The French imposed on us a Greater Lebanon. When we became an independent state, they compelled us to annex territories which were populated by Muslim communities. That was the source of our trouble. Do not add territories and Muslims to your land, or you will find yourself facing the same problems that we have.' Begin said nothing then or afterwards about this piece of telling and probably unwelcome advice. The Lebanese party, which included the young Christian militia commander, Bashir Gemayel, left for a quick tour of Jerusalem's Old City before returning to Beirut by helicopter.

Chamoun had good reason for counselling Israel to take care. In the course of his long life, he had seen the Christian majority – and the Christian domination of Lebanon – eroded, collapsing under the sheer weight of Muslim numbers. Unlike other countries with different religions and ethnic origins, such as Switzerland, the seventeen distinct religious communities in Lebanon have never achieved a sense of national identity, let alone a political consensus. They have never been able to overcome their sectarian allegiances; they have never really tried to do so. On the contrary, they are far more concerned to preserve them, no matter at what cost to the Lebanese state.

The ten years or so before the Begin–Chamoun meeting materialized in Jerusalem had been a traumatic experience for Lebanon, though neither leader realized just to what extent the worst was still to come. For during these years, Lebanon's sectarian divisions were markedly increased as each community looked outside for a reliable 'protector'. The most sought-after 'guardian' for the Muslim communities was, of course, Egypt's President Nasser, who played a key part in the preparation of Lebanon's recipe for disaster – even after Nasser and Egypt had suffered the catastrophic defeat in June 1967 at the hands of Israel. Syria, likewise, seeking new fields to plough, at first played second fiddle to Egypt. It was only later, in the mid-1970s, that she began to exploit the political and social turmoil in neighbouring Lebanon in her own interest and especially in that of her now emerging ruler, Hafez el-Assad.

However, neither of the old stabilizing 'protectors' had remained. The French, who had looked after Christian interests, and the British, who had safeguarded Muslim interests, had gone and left a power vacuum, which had been simmering as if awaiting the arrival of the Palestinian factor. In retrospect, the Palestinian arrival in Lebanon at this point was no accident in history, not just an unfortunate aftermath to the expulsion of the PLO from Jordan after it had attempted the overthrow of King Hussein's regime in 1970. It was, in fact, a ruthlessly calculated scheme to suit the governing circles in Cairo and Damascus, in Saudi Arabia and in Jordan. The failed PLO uprising in Jordan merely provided the pretext, much as the attack on the Israeli Ambassador in London on 2 June 1982 provided the occasion for the launch of the long-prepared 'Peace for Galilee' invasion of Lebanon.

Contrary to a widely held opinion, it was not the Palestinian flight from Jordan after the débâcle in September 1970 that led to the disastrous introduction of the Palestinian factor into domestic Lebanese affairs; it was the decision taken in Cairo in November 1969 by the principal Arab League countries to support the PLO's drive for control of Lebanon. All through 1969 clashes between Palestinian militia units and the Lebanese army had increased in number and intensity. The Lebanese Government had come under continuous pressure, accompanied by threats of economic sanctions from Syria, Egypt and Saudi Arabia, and by the Arab League states in general, radical and moderate. In the forefront of this campaign to undermine the independence of Lebanon and to provide the PLO with a base for operations against Israel was Egypt's President Nasser, still smarting from his own defeat. Another very active supporter of this policy was King Hussein. Documentary evidence is still understandably scant, but evidence from the Arab League secretariat shows clearly that Hussein was an enthusiastic backer of Nasser's planned summit for November 1969, which was to compel the Lebanese to accept an institutionalized Palestinian presence as an independent power factor in Lebanon. Hussein saw the Cairo formula as a safety valve that would relieve him of the PLO pressure in Jordan. He prepared himself accordingly for the confrontation between his army and the PLO, which had become possible in the wake of the secret Cairo Agreement concluded between the Lebanese and the PLO, under Arab League pressure and Nasser's supervision, on 3 November 1969.

There was now an escape route for the PLO in Jordan, which had not existed until the conclusion of the Cairo Agreement, for, as Hussein saw it, the PLO in Jordan could now be expelled as they would have somewhere else to go – to neighbouring Lebanon. Until the secret Cairo Agreement had compelled the Lebanese Government to provide free movement and all necessary facilities for the Palestinians, the PLO had nowhere to go; Egypt, Syria, Saudi Arabia, Libya and Iraq refused to provide shelter, let alone facilities, for operations against Israel. The Cairo Agreement, concluded on the initiative of Nasser and the Saudis, was thus, in effect, a declaration of war on the Lebanese state and on Israel – not by the Arab states who were most unwilling to take such risks so soon after the 1967 débâcle, but by the Arab leaders on behalf of the PLO. Not only the Lebanese, but also the PLO were the fall guys in this most secret Cairo Agreement. They were scheduled to take the brunt of the punishment which the Cairo Agreement had made inevitable. It is time we had a closer look at it.

The Agreement had nineteen articles in all. It was marked 'top secret' and its contents were – understandably – not to be published. It was signed by Arafat for the PLO and by General Emile Bustany, the Christian Commander-in-Chief of the Lebanese army, who was cast by his Government and country to play the role of Judas. At least the Lebanese leaders and the Arab sponsors of the Agreement had enough sense of shame or discretion to insist that the terms of the Agreement should be withheld from the Lebanese people. That, of course, was an idle hope, but it gives us a revealing insight into the intentions of those who engineered this evil arrangement.

However, not even they could have foreseen the horror and disaster which this Arab deal would eventually unleash on the Lebanese state and on the Palestinians in Jordan and Lebanon. It was the fate intended for Israel; the PLO based in Lebanon had been the designated spearhead of Nasser's revenge for 1967. It did not work out that way, though at first events seemed to move according to the secret plans of the sponsors of the Cairo Agreement. It provided the PLO with the legitimacy and the means to attack Israel from bases in Lebanon, and with free movement in and out of Lebanon. It also set out the terms for a virtual Palestinian state within the Lebanese state.

While the PLO received these substantive concessions, the Lebanese received only assurances that their integrity and sovereignty would not be jeopardized. The concessions were real, the safeguards were meaningless. The takeover of Lebanon by the PLO was effectively formalized in Cairo on 3 November 1969. It took Hussein less than a year to complete his plans for the expulsion of the PLO to Lebanon, because, in the wake of the Cairo Agreement, Lebanon had become the designated dumping ground for all Arab problems and especially for the Palestinians, whom no Arab country wanted. Reports on the bloody clashes that ensued between Jordan's Arab Legion and the PLO in September 1970 vary: some claim that 'only' 4,000 Palestinians were killed in the fierce fighting and shelling that engulfed the refugee camps; PLO sources put the number as high as 20,000. Those lucky enough to escape made their way to the new haven opened up by the Cairo Agreement – Lebanon.

The Palestinian newcomers found in Lebanon what they fondly believed was a perfect situation for their purpose; a weak Government (there had been no Cabinet in office from April to November 1969 while the Cairo Agreement was concocted), a fragmented army and a live-and-let-live atmosphere convinced them that here there would be no danger of repression as there had been in Jordan. Moreover, there was already a hard-core Palestinian presence in Lebanon, estimated to be between 250,000 and 800,000. No one could tell for certain – least of all the United Nations. The sprawling refugee camps and the Palestinian-dominated quarters in southern Beirut – el-Fakhehani, Sabra, Shatilla, Bourj el-Barajne – already had centres for recruitment and military training authorized by the Cairo Agreement. Members of the leading terrorist organizations in the world, from Germany's Baader-Meinhof to Japan's Red Army, attended courses in terrorism and added to the heady atmosphere of power and might that characterized the PLO leadership in Lebanon in those days.

The seasoned Palestinian fighters who had been expelled by Jordan exacerbated an already intolerable situation, especially so in the south of the country. This area, adjoining Israel, had never been regarded by the Beiruti politicians as a fully integral part of the country. Inhabited by the more backward Shia Metwalis, it had been one of the territories added on to Mont Liban by the French to which President Chamoun had alluded in his farewell advice to Begin. In fact, Chamoun was the only Lebanese President who had visited the south, and this despite the minute size of the country.

But in the late 1960s and during the 1970s, southern Lebanon had been transformed into a bastion of the PLO, with its own military and police forces, taxation and media. Lebanese law ceased to be applied and the Lebanese people watched helplessly as the PLO took over large parts of the southern country.

PLO cross-border attacks against Israeli targets invited instant response from the Israeli air force and, occasionally, by commando raids, which further destabilized daily life. Tens of thousands of Shia villagers fled from the anarchy and violence in the south and made their way northwards to Beirut, where they crowded into the slum areas of southern Beirut, destitute Shia living alongside the wealthy Muslim Sunni and Christian Maronite families of West and East Beirut. Many of the Shia were influenced by their radical Palestinian neighbours living in the camps of southern Beirut – in Bourj el-Barajne, Sabra and Shatilla.

It did not take long before the Palestinian presence was felt in every section of Lebanese society. The traditionalist fabric of Shia society was torn apart, releasing revolutionary forces which led to the formation of the radical Amal movement and, eventually, to the fundamentalist Khomeinist Hizbollah organization. The more radical Sunni elements also found a new strength and encouragement from the heavily armed Palestinian militia among them – and from the large amounts of money which the PLO spent in Lebanon. This new-found self-confidence expressed itself in ever-growing hostility against the Christians, who – alarmed by developments – hastily set about organizing their own armed militias. Violence became endemic.

But a new level of violence was ignited by the Palestinians, when, on 13 April 1975, they opened fire on the Christian Phalange leader, Pierre Gemayel, as he was about to inaugurate a newly built church in the Beirut suburb of Ein Rumaneh. Four of his entourage were killed. His enraged supporters instantly retaliated, killing twenty-two Palestinians in revenge. Fighting spread across the country with radical Muslim militias linking up with the PLO in the onslaught on the Christians.

The 'civil war' of 1975 had begun. But 'civil war' was a misnomer; in reality, it began with a foreign element – the PLO – launching a carefully prepared attack against its Christian enemies.

From the outset the Christians were outgunned and outmatched; they fought desperately to prevent their positions and their homes from being overrun. It was a war in which no quarter was given, no mercy shown; terrible excesses were committed and massacres were perpetrated by both sides. In Damour, a Christian seaside resort south of Beirut, which was overrun by the Palestinians, those who did not flee were killed, including women and children. There were few survivors. The Christians retaliated when, several months later, after a long siege, they captured the large Palestinian camp of Tel el-Zatar, strategically placed along the main highway linking the Christian quarters of Beirut with Mont Liban.

In the south of the country the Christian villages and towns were in ever greater danger because of the strong Palestinian build-up there. Villages near the Israeli border sent delegations across to Israel asking for help. As a result, two enclaves were formed of Christian villages depending on Israel for their safety and survival. Thus began a long chapter of co-operation between Israel and the local population of southern Lebanon; they were led by a Lebanese army major, Saad Haddad, who had been sent to the south by his commander to help the villagers organize resistance to the PLO attacks.

This alliance between Israel and the neighbouring Lebanese villages has since been depicted as planned and organized by Israel in order to create a security belt to the north of her border. In fact, during those first months the aid Israel was sending to the Christian villages was seen by many Israelis as a burden and a nuisance. In early 1976, the commander of the northern front, General Raphael Eitan, held a meeting of his senior officers at the northern front headquarters in order to decide whether to recommend to GHQ the termination of this aid. The majority present spoke of the difficulties caused by the Christian demands. After listening patiently to his officers, Eitan responded simply: 'You are forgetting what happened at Aishiya. We have a moral duty to continue our aid. We cannot turn our backs on people asking for our help.'

Aishiya is a Christian hamlet about ten miles north of the frontier. Shortly before that northern command meeting, it had been attacked by large forces of the PLO. The town leaders sent a delegation to Israel with a plea for help, but, by the time the Israelis got a relief unit under way, Aishiya had fallen. About eighty of the inhabitants who had sought shelter in the church in the town centre were butchered. Most of the others succeeded in getting away. Aishiya became a PLO stronghold until the town was restored to its inhabitants shortly after the IDF entered Lebanon in 1982.

Quite separately from these events in the south, the Christians of Beirut and Mont Liban were also looking for help from Israel. Israel had previously not had any visible contact with her neighbouring countries. No fraternizing with the 'Zionist enemy' was allowed by member-states of the Arab League, and contacts with Israel were of necessity strictly clandestine. Suddenly, bewildered officials in Israeli Embassies in Paris, Rome and other capitals found themselves in the unusual situation of being approached by citizens of an Arab League country asking for help – not for Lebanon as such, but for a political party or movement, for a religious order, for a village or town, or even for a large family. Armenians, Greek Catholics and Greek Orthodox, leading churchmen of the Maronite order, Jesuits, northerners from Zgharte paying allegiance to ex-President Franjiyeh, Beirut stalwarts of ex-President Chamoun's National Liberal Party, members of the elitist el-Tanzim and Guardians of the Cedars movements, and Kataeb-Phalange leaders – they all came asking for support and seeking urgent help.

Israel's leaders were taken by surprise by this sudden turn of events. It must be remembered that the Lebanese approach came four years before Sadat's visit to Jerusalem. In the atmosphere of near-hermetic isolation in which Israel had existed in the Middle East since her establishment as a state in 1948 such pleas for help from neighbours was little short of intoxicating, especially so as there had existed an influential school of thought in Israel which believed in the natural alliance between the Jews of Israel and the Maronites of Lebanon – two minorities in a sea of Islam –

each one struggling in its own hard way to live according to its heritage and tradition.

In a letter written on 27 February 1954 by Ben-Gurion to the then Prime Minister of Israel, Moshe Sharett, Ben-Gurion advised him to make the establishment of a Christian state within Lebanon's original borders 'one of the central tasks of our foreign policy'. Ben-Gurion wrote:

The establishment of a Christian state here is something natural, based on historical roots, which will be supported by powerful forces in the Christian world, Catholic and Protestant alike. In normal days such an action would be impossible ... but in an hour of confusion and revolution or civil war the situation changes and the weak will act as heroes.

Ben-Gurion had wanted to take advantage of the upheaval in Syria that had just occurred following the overthrow of Syria's President, Adib Shishakly.

A year later, in 1955, Israel's Chief of Staff, Moshe Dayan, again called for action on the part of Israel to help the Maronites create their own state. Dayan's pleas were not implemented at the time mainly because of determined opposition from Prime Minister Sharett. Now, almost twenty years later, there was once more confusion and civil war. This time the Christians were turning to Israel for help in their fight against Israel's enemy, the PLO. Understandably, Israel's first response was favourable, but cautious.

Conflicting attitudes emerged in the Government and in Israel's powerful defence establishment. There were those who said that the Christians were fighting Israel's enemies and should, therefore, be helped within the framework of that fight. Among those who held that attitude there was no particular sympathy for the Lebanese Christians as such; helping the Christians was another way of fighting the PLO – by remote control. However, there were Israelis who believed, as Ben-Gurion and Dayan had done, in the natural alliance between Israel and the Maronite Christians. For them, it was important that Israel should support any minority in the region. They preferred to see a heterogeneous Middle East made up of different peoples and religions rather than a Sunni Arab dominated region in which Israel herself would be an isolated minority.

Opposed to this position were those Israelis who argued that Israel would have to make her peace and learn to live with the Sunni Arabs and not with a mixed multitude of minorities. Therefore, Israel should fashion her foreign policy postulates accordingly. Common to all these schools of thought were strong moral considerations: how could Israel, with her own ravaged history of persecution, remain indifferent to and ignore the pleas of a neighbouring people, who – like the Jews over the ages – were being attacked because they were different from the majority around them?

In the event, the Lebanese in Paris, Rome and elsewhere were told that Israel wanted to meet the Lebanese leaders.

In particular, Israel wanted to meet Camille Chamoun and Pierre Gemayel, so as to make certain that the Lebanese approach had realistic and serious intentions. At the beginning of 1976, Prime Minister Rabin met former President Chamoun on board an Israeli missile boat off the Lebanese coast, and ground rules were set up for this new de facto alliance between Israel and the Lebanese Christians: Israel would supply the Christians with arms free of charge and would train their militias, but she would not intervene actively in the fighting. She would 'help' the Christians to help themselves. The liaison was entrusted to the two younger sons of the Chamoun and Gemayel families – Dany and Bashir.

Accordingly, close links were established with the other leading Christian groupings – with Tony Franjiyeh, son of the former President, with George Adwan, leader of the el-Tanzim, and with Etienne Sakr, known as Abu Arz, who commanded the shadowy nationalist Guardians of the Cedars movement. Groups of young Lebanese were sent for military training in Israel, while at night an Israeli patrol boat would sail northwards, hauling a barge laden with guns and equipment, which would be delivered to Dany Chamoun or Bashir Gemayel to be distributed among all the Christian factions.

The Israelis accompanying the arms would generally stay the night, for talks with the Christian leaders at Jounieh harbour, or in the home of the Gemayels at Bikfaya, or even in Beirut itself. These landings were frequently hazardous, especially after the Syrians occupied the area. On one such trip that I made to Beirut, our car was stopped by a Syrian patrol; the Syrian soldiers stared at me for a long minute before accepting the driver's explanation that his companion was a European journalist. When we reached a second Syrian post, the driver, Bashir Gemayel, crashed through the barrier. The Syrians were too surprised to shoot.

A special bond soon developed between the Israelis and the young Lebanese, with both sides feeling the common interest of our two nationalist entities, both of whom were fighting to maintain their own special identity in a region peopled by a Muslim majority.

Bashir, then a young man in his late twenties, was particularly articulate about this. 'I want to be free to live according to my own customs and traditions,' he would say. 'And if I want my children to learn physics in French and not Arabic ... that is my right.' Bashir was endowed with great charisma. He was enormously popular with his people and believed strongly that the time had come to create a different Lebanon, not dependent on the oligarchy of feudal patriarchs, who had dominated Lebanese life. He wanted a country in which all denominations would be able to live, true to their heritage; he wanted a cantonized federal country on the pattern of the Swiss confederation. He wished to see Lebanon neutral in the Arab–Israeli conflict and with regard to regional and global conflicts.

Lebanon could then become once more the playground of the Middle East, he would say. 'Our merchant and banking community will again thrive and we would stop fighting because there would be too much to lose for all of us.' The presence of the PLO spoilt this Lebanese pipe-dream. Bashir was convinced that unless he could get rid of the Palestinian hold on Lebanon, his vision would remain a vision – no more than that.

That is why Israel attracted him. Israel had the same aim: the presence of the PLO in Lebanon had become an unacceptable security problem for Israel; any group willing to fight the PLO was Israel's ally. For the same reason Israel also had made contact with the Shia communities in southern Lebanon, whose leaders watched with alarm as the PLO took over authority in their region. The Shia, however, were far more fragmented than the Christians. Israel failed to overcome the Shia divisions and consequently her attempt to forge a working connection with the Shia as a community did not materialize.

I had first met Bashir in his office at the Beirut headquarters of the Christian Kataeb Party in the summer of 1976. I had landed under cover of a dark night from a Lebanese fishing boat at Tabarja, north of Jounieh, and had been driven down to Beirut. The dark sky was lit by flashes of artillery fire; tracer bullets made weird patterns in the sky and the noise of exploding shells supplied an ominous and frightening backdrop to the meeting. Bashir was then twenty-nine, a young advocate dispensing free legal advice to members of his party in need.

Several months previously he had been appointed commander of the Kataeb military council and had devoted his time to the building up of the militia capability of the Kataeb, and then of all the Lebanese Christian forces. I met Bashir frequently, sometimes in the company of his father, and I was witness to his rapid rise to leadership. In a country where 'politician' was synonymous with venality, corruption and the upholding of an archaic feudal system, Bashir was refreshingly simple, direct and honest; he gave expression to the fears and hopes of his followers: to their fears of being overrun by the Muslims and to their hope for a new and different Lebanon in which the Christians would be responsible for their own security and destiny.

Bashir, however, was the product of the fierce, often brutal history of the Maronites and he ruthlessly suppressed opposition in order to weld together, by use of force, a united Christian militia under his command. Life was cheap in Lebanon; arguments and political dissensions were often settled by the gun. Having put his own house in order, Bashir felt more able to deal with his enemies, the Palestinians and the Syrians. He rejected the policy of appeasement practised by Lebanon's President towards the Syrians.

I used to visit Lebanon frequently at that time, coming in by sea north of Beirut and travelling up the hills or down to Beirut to meet the Christian leaders. I was impressed by their motivation and determination to live according to their customs and traditions despite the constant threat of being engulfed by Islam.

Their fear and hatred of the Muslims was vibrant, overpowering and steeped in the bloody history that characterized relations between the Christians and Muslims in Lebanon. During a visit to the Christian town of Deir el-Kamar in the Shouf mountains, I was given a blow-by-blow description, together with the minutest details, of a massacre of 2,000 Christians that had taken place in the centre of the town. The massacre had occurred in 1840, but the details of that terrible killing were related by the inhabitants with a vividness as if it had taken place only days before, and with a passion that was frightening.

As the war against the Christians intensified in 1975, it became evident that the PLO had the upper hand. They had unlimited supplies of arms from the Arab countries and the Soviet Union. The Christians had very few. Indeed, the Lebanese Christian community found that its traditional supporters and suppliers of arms – notably France, Italy and Spain – were standing aloof and withholding aid. However, the Christians managed to hold their own, ironically, largely as a result of the help provided by the Jewish state and of Muslim Syria's intervention against the PLO.

Syria, much more than Israel, was deeply involved in Lebanon. The Syrians have always considered themselves legally entitled to mix in Lebanese affairs since Lebanon had for centuries been part of the Syrian *Sanjak* – a province within the Ottoman Empire. Mont Liban, it is true, had been made a separate sub-province by the Ottomans under French pressure in 1860, but, when the French enlarged the country by annexing territories to the north, south and east in 1920, the Syrians objected. Syrian refusal to recognize the independence of Lebanon was expressed in her refusal to have diplomatic relations. This same concern with Lebanese affairs resulted in frequent Syrian intervention in Lebanon, yet throughout the 1950s and 1960s Lebanon prospered economically and consolidated her political standing, while Syria lurched from one coup to another, hardly in a position to dictate policy to her Lebanese neighbour.

This relationship changed radically with the destabilization of Lebanon caused by the influx of the PLO and with the seizure of power by Assad in Syria in 1970. Assad had two ambitions: to ensure the position of power in Syria of the esoteric Alawite sect, of which he was a faithful member, and to establish Syria as the leading Arab nation in the Fertile Crescent, on a par with, if not superior to, his chief rival, Egypt. He revived the concept of 'Greater Syria', along the lines of the old Ottoman *Sanjak*, which included Lebanon, Palestine and Jordan.

According to this concept, Syria would have to be, at the very least, the dominant factor in Lebanon; she would have to bring the PLO under her control; and she would have to bring King Hussein into the Syrian orbit. These, then, became Assad's foreign policy directives as he consolidated his power in Syria in 1971.

There was, however, more to it than that. He was an Alawite, a sect consisting of no more than twelve per cent of the Syrian population. The Alawites were considered by Sunni Muslims to be on the fringe of Islam, and many of the more orthodox Sunnis regarded them as heretical Muslims beyond the pale. Assad and his Alawite colleagues, who were placed in key government positions, in the defence establishment and in the security services, were suspect in the eyes of the Sunni majority within Syria and by his Sunni neighbours in the Arab world.

Therefore, he had to neutralize this in-built suspicion and opposition to him and his policies. To achieve this, he set out to outdo the Sunni Muslim leaders in Syria and, in particular, the other Arab leaders on the one topic which was sure to be effective – by being more anti-Israel than all the other Arab leaders. By heading the anti-Israel crusade, Assad kept his own Sunni Arab population in rein, for to oppose him would be construed as weakening the struggle against Israel, a treasonable offence; it also ensured Assad legitimacy in the Arab world. He wanted to eradicate his image as an Alawite sectarian and to be seen as a patriotic Arab leader cast in the mould of the great Saladin.

When tension increased between the Christians and the PLO in Lebanon, it was only natural that Assad, the super Arab nationalist, should support the PLO and its radical Muslim allies. When the Lebanese army tried to curb the Palestinians in the late 1960s, the Syrians immediately expressed their disapproval by closing the frontier with Lebanon, thus stopping the flow of goods from the Lebanese ports to the rest of the Arab world with resulting hardship for the Lebanese economy.

Initially, the Syrians were not displeased with the growing instability in Lebanon. It made it easier for them to intervene and support one Lebanese party against another. After holding protracted talks with President Franjiyeh and the leaders of the various warring factions, the Syrians declared a new political reform for Lebanon, which increased the Muslim share in the political power structure at the expense of the Christians.

It also attempted to regularize the relations of the PLO with the Lebanese state. The proposal was accepted by President Franjiyeh, but the Christian militias, alarmed by Syrian discrimination against them, stepped up their efforts to remove Palestinian strongholds from the Christian-controlled areas. In reply, the Syrians sent two battalions ostensibly to give support to the Muslim radicals and the PLO.

But the situation was soon to change. The Muslim Left and the PLO spurned the Syrian effort at compromise and refused to accept the Syrian Constitutional Document, as it was called. For them – and, in particular, for the leader of the 'Progressive Socialist Party', Druze Kamal Jumblatt – the Syrian compromise fell far short of their aims of completely scrapping the sectarian character of the Lebanese constitution and replacing it with a radical, Muslim-dominated regime.

They rejected the Syrian compromise and launched their own offensive, capturing Damour and a string of Christian villages to the south of Beirut, threatening Christian positions in the Beka'a and increasing their pressure along the 'Green Line' dividing Beirut. More significantly, the Palestinians with Druze backing moved into the heartland of Mont Liban, into the Metn mountains and into Kissrwan. The last thing the Syrians wanted was to see a PLO or a radical Muslim state set up in Lebanon in defiance of Syria; nor did they wish to have the balance of Muslim and Christian irrevocably upset. They were angered by Kamal Jumblatt's open defiance and mollified by overtures from the newly elected President, Elias Sarkis. Above all, however, they were exasperated by the Palestinians, who refused to listen.

On 1 June 1976, the Syrian Third Armoured Division, backed by elite commando units, moved into Lebanon. Its aim was to halt the Palestinian and Muslim advance, to bring the PLO leadership under Syrian control and to occupy most of Lebanon. But it was only four months later, on 18 September, that the Syrian forces attacked the Palestinian positions in Mont Liban. In typical fashion, the Syrians had waited patiently for a good excuse. It came when a PLO commando attacked the Hotel Semiramis in Damascus. Within twenty-four hours, the Syrians hanged the three PLO survivors in a public square in Damascus. Within forty-eight hours they launched their attack in the Metn, and the world witnessed the surprising spectacle of Syrian troops battling against PLO forces which had been receiving most of their weapons from the same Syrians.

Such are the twists and turns of events in the Middle East! The seemingly incredible Syrian attack on the PLO and on the Muslim Left was explained by President Assad in a remarkable speech to the Syrian Provincial Council on 20 July 1976. Speaking of the Constitutional Document, Assad accused the Palestinians and the Lebanese Nationalists of still not being satisfied after they had obtained all they had demanded. Instead they wanted the Lebanese President to resign and called for 'decisive military action', which, in the words of the Syrian President, would inevitably have led to Israeli intervention and to the partition of Lebanon. 'It would lead to the creation of a dangerous and oppressed Christian minority with a state of its own, more dangerous and hostile than Israel.' And, Assad continued,

I told Jumblatt and the Palestinian leaders that I could not see what interest they were serving by continuing to fight in Mont Liban. They are contributing nothing to the liberation of Palestine. Arafat agreed and undertook to halt the military operations. I must say that this promise was not implemented. *They did not understand that any talk about the liberation of Palestine without Syrian participation is either ignorance or a deliberate misleading of the Arab masses* [author's italics].*

Later, at a mini-summit conference held in Riyadh on 16 October 1976, Assad addressed Arafat in a remarkably direct and frank manner: 'Operation Semiramis cost you the "Mountain"; the attack on the Embassy in Rome cost you Bhamdoun. I shall continue to strike at you every time a Palestinian operation is directed against an Arab target, no matter which organization claims responsibility.' Such were the relations between the Syrian President and the PLO in 1976.

Syrian anger was directed against the PLO and also, increasingly, against the PLO's principal ally in Lebanon, Kamal Jumblatt, who, more than any other Lebanese leader, openly challenged the Syrian role in Lebanon. Syrian retribution was swift: on 16 March 1977, the Druze leader was

---

* Quoted in *Afro–Asian Affairs*, London, no. 35, 31 July 1976, p. 5.

assassinated, and there was no doubt in the minds of anyone in Lebanon that the killing had been ordered by Damascus. The disappearance of Kamal Jumblatt left a void which enabled the Syrians to strengthen their hold on the National Front, the alliance of PLO, the Druze and the left-wing Lebanese parties.

The entry of the Syrian army into Lebanon in June 1976 sparked the intervention of the Arab states. After much initial argument, the Riyadh mini-summit was convened in October to discuss the Lebanese situation. It was opened by the Lebanese President, Elias Sarkis, who, in his first international appearance as President, put the blame primarily on the shoulders of the Palestinians, but no less on the Arab states who had foisted the Palestinians on to Lebanon. He declared:

If the Palestinians had enjoyed better treatment in the Arab countries, Lebanon would not have been submitted to all these catastrophic happenings. Every time an Arab state restricted their liberty, they sought refuge in Lebanon. ... The Palestinians intervened in the internal affairs of the Lebanon, ignored the terms of the Cairo Agreement and incited one element of our population against the other.

Despite Arafat's opposition, the Arab leaders decided to create an Arab Deterrent Force (ADF) of 30,000 men and place it under the direct command of President Sarkis. For Assad, this meant the legitimization of the Syrian troops in Lebanon, for it was clear from the outset that this new Arab force would be overwhelmingly Syrian. With Sarkis openly following a pro-Syrian line, the Syrians could now act freely – and legally – in Lebanon. On 15 November 1976, Syrian troops in the guise of the ADF, and with the blessing of the Lebanese President, entered Beirut.

The Christians – in particular Camille Chamoun and Bashir Gemayel – welcomed them with mixed feelings. The veteran patrician and the young commander did not share the pro-Syrian, Arabist policy of their President. Their misgivings proved to be justified.

The uneasy truce of 1977 deteriorated in February 1978 into an open clash between units of the Lebanese and Syrian armies outside the Lebanese army barracks of Fayadieh, near the presidential palace in Beirut; more than twenty Syrian soldiers were killed. What became known as the 'Fayadieh incident' created an open clash of wills between the Syrians and the Christians. The Syrians demanded that the Christian officers of the Fayadieh unit be handed over for punishment; the Christians rejected the demand. Fighting between the Christians and the Syrians spread throughout Beirut. The feeble, timorous attempts of the Christian pro-Syrian President Sarkis to halt the fighting ended in failure.

The Syrians were determined. They insisted that the Christian officers involved in the clash be either handed over or executed. As the Christians had no intention of complying with this demand, the Syrians began to bombard the Christian quarters of Beirut with heavy artillery, killing many hundreds of civilians.

The Syrian attack reached its crescendo at the end of September, when

Ashrafiah and the other Christian quarters of Beirut, as well as the villages of the Metn and Kissrwan were subjected to an unprecedented deluge of shells. In Israel, the Cabinet became increasingly restless, while in the synagogues throughout the country the rabbis prayed for the well-being of the Lebanese Christians – a truly unique occasion! At the request of Begin, the Americans despatched a Note to the Syrians, warning them that Israel would intervene if the attacks continued. Finally, after more than three months of bombardment and fighting, on 6 October a truce was agreed between the Syrians and Christians. Thousands of Christians had been killed, tens of thousands had fled the country and widespread damage caused by the Syrian shells.

The shelling of the Christian quarters by the Syrians highlighted some of the weird contradictions which so characterized the Lebanese scene. The bombardment of civilian Beirut was carried out by the supposedly peace-keeping Syrian contingents of the ADF, whose commander, in theory at least, was the President of Lebanon. Sarkis had steadfastly followed a pro-Syrian policy, had refused to condemn publicly the Syrian onslaught on his people and had continued his visits to Damascus, much to the distress of his co-religionists in Beirut. Such were the peculiarities of Lebanon. Regional Arab rivalries were interwoven into the fabric of local sectarian politics: the fear that the PLO and the radical Muslim elements would ally themselves with Egypt or Iraq drove the Syrians into pre-empting such a move. At the periodic meetings of the supervisory Arab League Committee on Lebanon, the PLO became masters at exploiting the inter-Arab tensions and rivalries. These were exacerbated after the visit of Sadat to Jerusalem in September 1977 and even more so after the Camp David agreements a year later. There were no bells of joy ringing in Lebanon; on the contrary, the rival Arab factions turned her into their most convenient battle-ground.

The Syrians decided, at least for the time being, to end their confrontation with the PLO in order to join with the Palestinians in opposing the possibility of an Egyptian–Israeli alliance. This Syrian reversal of her attitude to the PLO had resulted in the worsening of her relations with the Christians. However, by October 1978, a month after the signing of the Camp David Accords, the Syrians were only too pleased to agree to a cease-fire with the Christians so as to be able to concentrate their efforts on frustrating of Egypt's unfolding peace with Israel.

The Christians, too, needed a respite. Battered and weakened by the Syrian onslaught, they had suffered heavily, but their spirit had not been broken. They made good use of the long lull that set in after October 1978, in order to rebuild, strengthen and consolidate their forces. In all this activity Bashir Gemayel came increasingly to stand out and to affect the rapidly unfolding events: he led the Christian opposition to the Syrians. He was determined to challenge their presence in Lebanon. The place he chose for his showdown with the Syrians was the city of Zahle: a town in the Beka'a Valley, populated by some 200,000 Christians, most of them Greek Catholics.

The Syrians were not prepared to tolerate Bashir's Lebanese forces occupying Zahle, so close to the Syrian frontier and in the heart of the valley, control of which they considered essential for their own security. Intermittent fighting erupted in the streets of Zahle on 1 December 1980. This escalated during April 1981 into a full-scale Syrian artillery bombardment of Zahle's ancient town-centre and – for good measure – also of the Christian quarters of East Beirut. Bashir rejected Syria's conditions for a cease-fire as the fighting grew in intensity, with the Syrians employing for the first time 'Gazelle' helicopter gunships against Bashir's positions on the mountain tops overlooking Zahle.

The messages which Israel and the rest of the world were receiving from the Christians were becoming increasingly alarming. 'The Syrians want to wipe the city of Zahle off the face of this earth,' Bashir declared. 'We shall not give in. We want to save all of Lebanon. We ask for outside help so that we can achieve our independence and our liberty.' 'Genocide' was mentioned. In Israel, Begin summoned the Cabinet. He recalled his promise to President Chamoun that he would intervene if the Syrians attacked the Christians from the air. He told his ministers that he would not idly watch while the Christians of Zahle were being butchered. For him, he declared, it was a moral challenge and not a question of politics. Begin gave the order and, within hours, Israel's air force shot down two Syrian helicopters transporting commandos to the strategic Sakhnin Heights above Zahle. What had been a local engagement had become an Israeli–Syrian confrontation.

The Syrians responded by installing ground-to-air missiles in Lebanon, thus threatening the freedom of the skies which the Israeli air force had enjoyed over the area. The Israelis considered this to be an essential factor in the defence of Israel, if only in order to have ongoing intelligence of possible hostile moves against her. Israel, for her part, warned that the deployment of missiles in Lebanon had changed the status quo; if the Syrians did not withdraw them, the Israelis would destroy them.

The fighting around Zahle thus made war between the two in Lebanon a real possibility. Had this been the intention of Bashir Gemayel? Had he deliberately exaggerated the danger of the Christians at Zahle? Had he provoked the Syrians in order to bring about an Israeli intervention? Bashir had, from the outset of the Syrian occupation of Lebanon, believed that only by direct intervention of Israel could the Lebanese free themselves from the Syrian presence. He was astute enough to realize that Begin would not remain passive in response to such a cry for help and the threat of a Christian massacre.

In retrospect, there were many in Israel who believed that Begin had, indeed, been tempted into the Zahle trap which had been baited by Bashir. The cries of genocide were undoubtedly exaggerated; but, for Bashir and for the Christians, Zahle had been much more than just a means to obtain Israeli intervention. The crisis had been a very real one and ended only because the Syrians did not want a confrontation with Israel. Neither

France, the traditional champion of the Lebanese Christians, nor the Vatican, nor even the Americans, and certainly not the UN Security Council or the Arab League, had reacted in any meaningful manner to the Syrian shells falling on Zahle, though the US Secretary of State, Alexander Haig, did go so far as to denounce 'the brutal action of the Syrians'.

Thus, in April 1981, the situation in Lebanon had once more been transformed. Syria and Israel were on the brink of armed conflict. On 30 April, the Israeli air force was given the order to attack the Syrian missile sites, and the army was put on combat alert in readiness for a possible Syrian counter-attack. But two hours before zero hour, low clouds still covered the target area and, with no likelihood of their dispersing, the Israeli attack was called off for that day. On the same evening the US Ambassador to Israel, Samuel Lewis, made an urgent call on the Prime Minister in Jerusalem. He told Begin that a special emissary of the President, Philip Habib, was on his way to the region, and that the US had every reason to believe that they would be able to convince the Syrians to withdraw the missiles from Lebanon. Reluctantly, Begin gave the order to the air force to postpone the attack. Low clouds and the last-minute intervention of the Americans had staved off hostilities. The spotlight now moved to the diplomatic scene as Habib arrived in Jerusalem.

Habib's first efforts were to play for time and prevent an Israeli attack on the missiles. The Americans feared that such an attack would have grave consequences for the entire region and could affect the recently concluded peace between Egypt and Israel. They were especially worried by a possible Soviet intervention. Only a few months previously, on 8 October 1980, President Assad had signed in Moscow a formal Treaty of Friendship and Co-operation, which called for regular consultations with the Soviet Union on bilateral and international issues of mutual interest, co-ordination of responses in the event of a crisis and military co-operation. If the Soviet-manufactured SAM missiles were destroyed by the Israelis, this might well test this Friendship Treaty at the very outset. The Syrian Government newspaper, *al-Baath*, warned that the Israelis would have to reckon with the Soviet-Syrian alliance if they dared attack Syrian positions in Lebanon.

The prospect of Soviet intervention was heightened when the Soviet helicopter-carrier, *Moskva*, sailed by close to the Lebanese coast; this was typical Soviet psychological warfare. It had its desired effect on Habib. He exercised all his undoubted skills to find an acceptable solution. The Israelis agreed to wait; the Syrians, however, refused to remove the missiles, possibly sensing their newly found advantage as a result of becoming the focus of international attention.

The Syrians had another objective in mind; for them the Egyptian–Israeli Peace Treaty was a mark of Cain that had to be excised from the Arab soul. The defection of Egypt from the ranks confronting Israel had left the Syrians dangerously exposed. With the Egyptians out of 'the circle of hostility', and the Iraqis increasingly occupied with their Iranian neighbour to the east, the Syrians were left to bear the brunt of any future Arab–

Israeli clash. The undoing of the Peace Treaty between Egypt and Israel, therefore, became a policy priority for Syria, and the Syrians were prepared to engage in risky brinkmanship in Lebanon to this end. At the same time, the Syrians were encouraging the PLO to be more aggressive against Israel in southern Lebanon, promising the Palestinians political and military benefits if they complied with Syrian wishes.

As the missile crisis was unfolding, the PLO's supreme policy authority, the Palestine National Council, met in Damascus on 14 April 1981. Emboldened by the backing he was again receiving from Assad, Arafat set the tone: 'We are the real strategic change in the Middle East. Let Reagan and all the people around him understand this,' he declared in his opening speech. 'We are the strategic change. We are a revolution in the most dangerous region in the world, in an area that has the biggest oil reserves in the world. We are a liberation movement that is not local.' And he continued: 'I have a friendly ally, the Soviet Union, by my side, and I hold the initiatives in the Middle East ... our rifles will create the new realities in the Middle East and we will deal with the whole world on this basis.' Arafat matched his words with deeds. Reinforcements swelled the ranks of the PLO in southern Lebanon; a steady flow of artillery, Soviet-made Katyushas and other weapons and equipment greatly reinforced the PLO positions facing northern Israel.

By July 1981, a situation of near-war existed along Israel's northern frontiers. On 10 July, the PLO launched a heavy artillery barrage against the towns and villages of northern Galilee, causing widespread damage. Israeli artillery had difficulty in silencing the hidden PLO guns and for two weeks the artillery duels continued intermittently, spreading havoc and terror on both sides of the frontier. In Kiryat Shmona and other towns and villages in the Galilee, hundreds of Israelis left for areas further south beyond the range of the PLO guns. Normal life came to an end as those who remained spent much of their time in bomb shelters. Once more, Habib was despatched to the region and, once more, he discovered that Begin was willing to be pliable and allow him the necessary time to patch together a workable cease-fire.

In those days the two men still worked well together: the jovial, somewhat theatrical Habib and the courtly, mannered, gracious Begin found a common language. But even as Begin agreed to Habib's cease-fire proposal on 24 July 1981, commanders of the Israeli army predicted that it contained the seeds of war. The cease-fire did not prevent the PLO from reinforcing the south, or from consolidating its fortified positions in this area; moreover, from the start there were differences over its interpretation. The Israelis claimed that the cease-fire called for a cessation of terror attacks against Israel or Jewish targets anywhere in the world; the PLO declared that it was bound only to desist from attacks on Israel from across the Lebanese frontier.

At a news conference given on the day after the cease-fire came into effect, Arafat declared that it would not entail any change of the PLO position. There would be 'no peace, solution or stability until all the PLO's demands were met'. With more guns going to the PLO in southern Lebanon, it became abundantly clear in Israel that, if the PLO resumed shelling the Galilee, Israel would have no choice but to ensure the removal of the PLO artillery. The only other alternative would be to allow the Galilee to be depopulated of most of its civilian inhabitants to become a sort of no-man's-land between Israel and the PLO gun emplacements; this was an alternative that no Israeli was willing to contemplate.

Thus, with the signing of the Habib cease-fire, the countdown for the Lebanese War began. It was now just a question of time when and under what circumstances the war machine would be put into motion. The alarm rang on 2 June 1982, when Palestinian terrorists ambushed Israel's Ambassador, Shlomo Argov, as he stepped out of London's Dorchester Hotel and shot him in the head.

10

The PLO Factor

1981–3

IT CAN BE ARGUED, with hindsight, that one of the factors which brought about the demise of the PLO in the Lebanese War was that it had tried to act like a regular army. Until the late 1970s, the PLO had been, for some, a liberation movement and, for others, a terrorist organization, but whether the one or the other it could not, by any account, be considered a regular conventional military force. Yet, by 1981, it had become just that in southern Lebanon. As a result, it had lost the suppleness and flexibility of an underground movement fighting unconventionally while gaining the advantages – and impediments – of a conventional war machine.

This change posed a threat to Israel which she could not ignore. Ongoing PLO terror attacks were something Israel could live with; but the PLO with batteries of guns trained on our towns and kibbutzim in upper Galilee was something entirely different. Unlike a sovereign state, a terror organization has no responsibility to anyone but itself. Its actions cannot be curbed by political means; neither the United Nations, the Great Powers, the Europeans, nor the Arab League had the power or influence to prevent the PLO from firing its guns at will at any Israeli civilian target.

As the military infrastructure of the PLO grew in strength, it became increasingly clear to Israel's political and defence establishment that her army would sooner or later have to destroy it. The Soviet-manufactured 130 mm guns, the Katyushas, the T-54 tanks, the underground bunkers and the fortified positions of the PLO in southern Lebanon all made 'Operation Peace for Galilee', the Israeli code-name for the Lebanon War, inevitable. The arguments of those who claim that all was relatively quiet in the cease-fire year which preceded the 'Peace for Galilee' action by the Israel Defence Forces completely miss the critical point at issue.

Throughout the latter half of 1981 and the first months of 1982, the PLO continued to strengthen its forces in southern Lebanon under the protective cover of Habib's cease-fire, which prevented Israel's air force and commandos from interfering as more guns, ammunition and equipment were deployed and more fortifications constructed. The PLO appeared to have an inexhaustible supply of weapons and of money, and it made good use of them while Israel's Chief of Staff, General Eitan, and his generals watched helplessly, their hands tied by the cease-fire. They were fully aware that this was not a question of military superiority; Israel had no worries about that. The problem was that the PLO guns poised across the frontier constituted an ever-increasing threat to the civilian population in upper Galilee, one of the most fertile and beautiful of Israel's provinces. In the wake of the PLO's bombardment of Kiryat Shmona, the largest town in upper Galilee, half the population had left the town in 1981; likewise, more than a third left Nahariya, Galilee's most popular coastal resort centre. Northern Israel was undergoing forced depopulation. No responsible government could tolerate sustained terror against its civilian population on this scale, least of all Israel.

Israel had a choice: either she could submit to the PLO terror or she would have to disarm the PLO threat in southern Lebanon. Thus, the PLO had made a military confrontation inevitable. Israel's leaders, and in particular Defence Minister Sharon and Chief of Staff Eitan, finalized plans and made little effort to disguise their intentions. Some months before the outbreak of the war Sharon had revealed his plans for dealing with the PLO in this impossible situation to a shocked Habib, when they met at the Israeli Foreign Ministry in Jerusalem to consider the situation in southern Lebanon. Habib and his deputy, Morris Draper, argued that they might succeed in obtaining a twenty-mile withdrawal of the PLO positions from the frontier, but they left the meeting with the impression that Sharon was not interested in more dubious palliatives. His mind was set on a more basic solution.

Sharon's plans were not confined to the conventional 'search-and-destroy' operations in southern Lebanon, similar to Israel's 'Litani' action in 1978 after PLO terrorists had landed on a beach in Israel and hijacked a busload of passengers, many of whom were killed in the subsequent shootout. 'Operation Litani' was mounted in order to remove the PLO from the territory bordering on Israel's northern frontier in an enclave stretching up to the River Litani. That operation had only been a limited success; as soon as the Israeli troops had withdrawn, the PLO returned. UN 'peacekeeping' units, UNIFIL, who had been moved into the area evacuated by the Israelis, were totally ineffective in ensuring 'peace' for Israel's northern territories.

For Sharon, the lesson of 'Operation Litani' was clear: Israel could not remove the threat to her northern settlements by limited local action in southern Lebanon; and the United Nations could not – or would not – do it. It would be achieved only by destroying the PLO headquarters in Beirut and eliminating the entire infrastructure of the PLO from Beirut to the south. These objectives became more feasible and attractive to Sharon as his conviction grew into certainty that he would be supported by his allies in the north – Bashir Gemayel's Lebanese Forces, the Israeli-trained and equipped Christian militia in East Beirut. In January 1982, Sharon had made a secret visit to Beirut, where he was given a royal welcome by Bashir. Together they went over the plans for the invasion. Sharon left in the belief that, with massive support from the Israel Defence Forces, Bashir's militia would take care of the capture and control of West Beirut, the heartland of the PLO.

Thus Israel was on course for war; it required only some inflammatory act by the PLO to light the fuse. However, not all Israel's Cabinet ministers and serving generals shared Sharon's conviction that there was no effective alternative to this war against the PLO. When Sharon presented his plans to the Government in January 1982, after a PLO attack on an Israeli settlement near the Jordanian frontier, a majority of ministers rejected them. When Sharon continued to pressure Begin, the Prime Minister did not accept his Defence Minister's arguments. Instead, he sent General Yehoshua Saguy, Chief of Military Intelligence, to consult with the Americans about the worsening situation. Begin did not want to upset the Americans more than he had already done.

Relations with Washington had become strained at the end of 1981 after Israel had, in effect, annexed the former Syrian Golan Heights. I was therefore sent on a special mission to meet the US Secretary of State, Alexander Haig, to evaluate Israel's position regarding the Golan and the Lebanon. Haig had already received Habib's and Draper's report of their meeting with Sharon at the Foreign Ministry in Jerusalem. Habib had warned Haig of the 'horrific' results on Israel and on US–Israeli relations which the implementation of Sharon's plans would have, but Haig had not been overly impressed by Habib's fears and he made no mention of them. In fact, Israel's political leaders, especially Prime Minister Begin and Defence Minister Sharon, had become convinced, during those spring months of 1982, that the Reagan administration was not averse to an operation in which the PLO, and perhaps even the Soviet-aligned Syrians, would be taught a lesson.

American officials have strongly denied the assertion made by Israeli journalist Shimon Shiffer that the United States had actively encouraged Israel to launch her attack against the PLO in Lebanon. Haig writes in his book *Caveat* that he warned Sharon of the 'devastating' effect on US–Israeli relations which an Israeli attack on the PLO in Lebanon would have 'unless there was an internationally recognized provocation'. There can be no doubt that a less ambivalent and more assertive stand on the part of Reagan, Haig and the CIA would have strengthened the hand of those Israeli ministers and military men who questioned Sharon's war option.

There was, in fact, no such resistance to Sharon's plans in Washington. This was due, at least in part, to a sympathetic American understanding of Israel's frustration and of her need to confront the PLO threat to her northern settlements. When Begin sent an oral message to Reagan in May 1982 warning that it might become 'imperative and inevitable' to remove this PLO threat, Haig's reaction was that the United States would probably not be able to stop Israel from attacking. And when Sharon met Haig in Washington later that month, Haig was reported to have told him: 'We understand your aims. We can't tell you not to defend your interests.'

The 'inflammatory act' materialized on 2 June 1982, when three Palestinian terrorists shot Ambassador Shlomo Argov in a London street. Israel retaliated against PLO ammunition dumps stored under the grandstand of a sports stadium in Beirut. Next day forty towns and villages in upper Galilee were bombarded by PLO guns in southern Lebanon. *It was this – not the attack on Shlomo Argov – that was the cue for Defence Minister Sharon.* On 6 June, Israeli troops and tanks crossed the frontier into southern Lebanon and engaged the PLO forces entrenched on Israel's northern frontier. 'Operation Peace for Galilee' had begun. But there was no agreement in Israel about its political aims or its precise military objectives.

From the outset there was no general agreement by the Government or the public with the position taken by Sharon and his principal military commanders. The Cabinet had approved an operation to drive the PLO from positions within artillery range of the Israeli northern frontier; it had expressly forbidden the Israel Defence Forces to engage the Syrian army in Lebanon unless provoked.

Begin had been explicit about this. In a note to Reagan and in his appearance before the Knesset, Begin had insisted that Israel would halt her advance within forty kilometres of the frontier. He told the Knesset that fighting would cease as soon as the IDF had secured a line which would place northern Israel beyond the effective range of PLO guns. The opposition parties and the general public supported the army action within this limited range; it was accepted as reasonable self-defence. Yet the Defence Minister and the IDF General Staff knew that the operation they had launched called for a link-up with the Lebanese Christian militia on the outskirts of Beirut, well beyond the agreed forty kilometre range. They knew also that the PLO positions in the eastern sector south of the forty-kilometre line were protected by the Syrian army deployment. Unless the Syrians persuaded the PLO to withdraw – which was unlikely – an Israeli clash with the Syrians would be unavoidable.

During the first forty-eight hours, Israel's armoured forces rapidly advanced according to plan along the coastal roads northwards, leaving the infantry to engage PLO positions left behind. By the evening of the second day, IDF forward units had advanced beyond the scheduled forty-kilometre line into the outskirts of the coastal town of Damour, a PLO stronghold. In the central sector, the Israelis were advancing on the strategically placed Christian town of Jezzine, which Lebanese Christian leaders had wanted to be linked to the south Lebanese villages of the Israeli-supported security zone, controlled by the 'South Lebanese Army' under Major Haddad.

In the eastern sector, facing the Syrians, the advancing IDF had cautiously moved forward only a few miles to take the Druze town of Hasbaya in order to avoid a frontal clash with the Syrian troops just to the north. Yet it was this Syrian force which prevented the IDF from removing the PLO gun positions threatening Kiryat Shmona and the settlements in upper Galilee. It would not make sense to destroy the PLO positions harassing Israel in the west, only to leave them untouched in the east.

Accordingly, Sharon sought to outflank these PLO–Syrian positions by advancing swiftly northwards in the central sector and then cutting the strategic Beirut–Damascus highway. This would threaten the Syrian positions in eastern Lebanon from three sides and make them militarily untenable.

When the Syrians saw our armour moving, they deployed an armoured battalion to Jezzine to forestall Israel's move. This Syrian column was photographed before it reached the battle zone by one of Israel's pilotless mini-planes. It was evident that, if the Syrians were to reach Jezzine, Israel would have to engage them. This was the kind of Syrian threat for which the Cabinet had made contingency plans: accordingly, Sharon ordered the air force to neutralize the Syrian tanks. The war in Lebanon assumed a new dimension.

The limited operation which the Begin Government had authorized had been overtaken by events – as should have been foreseen. Sharon explained to the Cabinet that battle conditions had compelled the IDF to advance and control a key sector of the Beirut–Damascus road; and the confused and uncomprehending Cabinet ministers reluctantly agreed. The Defence Minister was also authorized to destroy the Soviet ground-to-air missile sites which the Syrians had installed in Lebanon. Sharon and the air force were prepared for this. The following morning, special air-force units embarked on this unique, hazardous mission.

There were nineteen Soviet-installed Syrian missile bases in the Beka'a Valley. By the end of that day – 9 June – seventeen had been destroyed; the remaining two were demolished on the next day. The Israelis did not lose a single plane in this complex air attack against the missile batteries. In the air battles which followed, the Syrians lost eighty-six fighter planes; the Israeli air force lost none.

The lethal power of Israel's command of the air had once more been demonstrated. Syria's armoured forces were decimated. By the end of the week, Syria had lost 345 tanks – mainly the most sophisticated Soviet models. IDF units had come within striking distance of the highway linking the Lebanese and Syrian capitals and had joined up with Bashir Gemayel's Lebanese Christian militia on the outskirts of Beirut. It seemed at the time that the IDF had effectively destroyed the possibility of further PLO threats against the population of the Galilee.

American pressure now became intense. President Reagan telephoned Begin at 2 a.m.; Begin called a 4 a.m. Cabinet meeting at his home; and an ill-conceived, American-imposed cease-fire came into force at noon on 11 June. The Cabinet then issued an extraordinary statement, presumably to justify its inept decision. The Cabinet communiqué said: 'The IDF has achieved the mission assigned to it in full .... The stage is set for an end to the war.' There is no telling now whether Begin and members of the Cabinet really believed this to be true. Sharon did not; he knew better.

Intermittent skirmishes continued for another week, during which Israel's positions along the Beirut–Damascus highway were considerably improved. All the same, acceptance of this cease-fire had been a grave error on our part. It saved the Syrians from ignominious defeat. In Kissinger's opinion, this American insistence on a cease-fire was the great blunder which changed the course of the war.

One or two more days would have sufficed the Israelis to clear the Syrians from their position in eastern Lebanon, from Shtoura, Rayak and the Zahle region. This would have transformed the whole pattern of development in the Lebanon War. As it was, American diplomatic intervention and US demands for a cease-fire enabled the Syrians to maintain their positions, to reinforce them and to come back to confront the Israelis. The Syrians and their Soviet backers must have felt relieved and grateful to the Americans.

With the Syrians reeling, but by no means knocked out, the thrust of the war reverted to the PLO, now besieged in their strongholds in western Beirut. Together with General Tamir, I was given the task of opening negotiations with Habib on Israel's terms for the PLO's evacuation from the city. We would meet in the home of Colonel 'Johnny' Abdu, Chief of Lebanese Military Intelligence, in the Ba'abda suburb of Beirut, not far from the presidential palace. From the balcony of Colonel Abdu's house, we could see below us the panorama of southern and western Beirut, where Arafat and his PLO activists were concentrated.

Israel's terms were simple: all PLO fighters would have to evacuate Beirut and leave Lebanon either by road or sea. International or neutral supervision would guarantee their safety and they could take their personal weapons. We knew that these proposals had the backing of the Americans and especially of the Lebanese, who welcomed this opportunity to get rid of their uninvited guests. Indeed, a few days previously, actually when the Lebanese Ambassador called on the UN Security Council to order the immediate evacuation of Lebanon by Israel, a very senior Lebanese official came to see me in Beirut and appealed to Israel, in the name of his President, not to leave Lebanon before the PLO was forced out. Such were the vagaries of Lebanese diplomacy, which neither the Americans nor the Europeans seemed able to comprehend.

Our terms were handed to Habib, who passed them on to the Lebanese Prime Minister, who in turn sent them to the PLO leader. Habib was supremely optimistic. He assured us that the PLO evacuation would begin within ten days and his evaluation was passed on to Israel's Cabinet. However, as the days went by and nothing happened, it became evident to us that Arafat was playing games with Habib. One day the PLO leadership would agree in principle that the evacuation would be by sea and on the next day they would send a message cancelling their previous acceptance on the grounds that they could not risk their men becoming sea-sick; this went on for days and then for weeks.

We spent long hours on Colonel Abdu's spacious balcony discussing the ever-changing demands of the PLO: that they should be allowed to keep a Political Office in Beirut guarded by their own men; that they should be allowed to take their heavy weapons with them; that they should evacuate to Tripoli in northern Lebanon. and that their departure should be followed by the immediate recognition of the PLO by the United States. The list was endless and always, whenever it seemed that we had reached agreement, the PLO came up with new demands. Arafat was clearly playing for time, presumably to wear down the Americans – and they let him get away with it until Sharon called a halt.

Habib's undoubted negotiating skills did nothing to change this and his evident frustration with the PLO was matched only by his anger at Sharon, who came frequently to the Abdu residence to berate Habib for his failure to pin down the PLO to definite terms and a time-table for their evacuation from Beirut. By now, days had turned into weeks; it must have become evident to Habib – as it did to us – that the PLO had no intention of leaving Beirut. We heard of heated arguments among their leaders whether to withdraw or not. At first they believed that the United Nations would intervene and post observers in the city. But when the PLO realized that this was not to be, several among them wanted to negotiate in order to get the best possible terms before withdrawing.

There were others in the PLO leadership who had been misled by Israel's seeming reluctance to enter the city into believing that the PLO would be able to hold out indefinitely against the Israeli siege. These hardliners, who opposed evacuation, received unexpected support from the French Government. It had sent the Secretary-General of its Foreign Ministry, Francois Gutman, to Beirut ostensibly to act as a go-between, but – for reasons of their own – actually to encourage the PLO not to withdraw. We have the evidence of the Palestinian scholar and PLO supporter, Rashid Khalidi, who was in Beirut at the time and had access to the PLO archives. He quotes liberally from these in his study of the Beirut siege.* The French, he wrote, were encouraging the PLO throughout, using the PLO representative in Paris, Ibrahim Souss, as their channel. 'The American request for disarming the Palestinian forces has met with total French rejection,' Souss cabled Arafat on 26 June; a later Souss cable relates that the French told him that there was 'a lot of American double, triple and quadruple play' and that the PLO would not be defeated except by intense diplomatic pressure.

At the end of July, Gutman asked Souss to warn Arafat against the 'trap' of a US-sponsored evacuation agreement. Small wonder that Arafat sent a message expressing profound gratitude to the French. 'Our people will never forget it,' he wrote. As Khalidi points out, the French were much more pro-PLO than most Arab countries at the time. According to him, the Arab states, notably Syria and Saudi Arabia, 'had added their weight to that of Israel and the United States and their Lebanese clients in putting pressure on the PLO'. It was, in fact, one of Habib's most difficult tasks to persuade Arab states to give refuge to the PLO men about to be evacuated from Beirut. He told me, in typical Habib style, of talks he had had in

* Rashid Khalidi, *Under Siege: PLO Decision-making during the 1982 War* (New York, 1986).

Saudi Arabia regarding the PLO: 'When I suggested to them that they should take 2,000 PLO fighters, they looked at me as if they could hardly believe their ears, as if I had offered them a pork sandwich!'

In the end it was Sharon's tough tactic – the bombardment of Beirut – that convinced the PLO that it would have to leave. It had become evident to him that, unless he acted with determination, the PLO would stay on indefinitely in Beirut and make a mockery of the entire operation mounted by Israel; its salutary effects would be totally nullified. Khalidi's account of PLO decision-making in Beirut confirmed that Sharon's assessment of the situation in Beirut had been correct. Sharon was determined to bring the siege to an end and, if need be, make western Beirut untenable for the PLO. The inhabitants were deprived of food, electricity and water as a means of bringing pressure to bear on the PLO leaders. When Habib objected to Sharon at one of the meetings at the Abdu residence and demanded that he restore water and electricity, Sharon replied that it was 'better that they should be thirsty than dead'.

This was language which, in the end, Habib and Arafat could not fail to understand. The only way the suffering of the Beirutis could be ended was by fulfilling the conditions for the PLO's departure without further delay. On 5 July, Habib told us that the Lebanese Muslim leaders had met Arafat and demanded that he sign a document agreeing to the evacuation of all PLO personnel and to the transfer of all PLO positions to the Lebanese Armed Forces and to the multi-national force which was to supervise the departure. Arafat agreed in principle, but asked for guarantees to ensure the safety of Palestinian civilians not included in the evacuation. Habib immediately complied with this request. Sharon was happy; the curtain was about to come down on an unhappy phase of the war. He gave orders to cease all fire. We then waited for Habib to announce the arrival of the American and French contingents of 'observers' so that the evacuation could begin.

But this was not to be. The PLO again refused to abide by its undertaking and would not move. In retaliation, exasperated and frustrated and to demonstrate that Israel was not going to be fobbed off once more by PLO trickery, Sharon ordered a paralysing artillery and air bombardment on the Palestinian centres and on the hapless Lebanese in whose midst the PLO positions had been deliberately placed. Khalidi describes the results:

The intensive bombardment of Beirut from the air, land and sea and the attacks on the PLO headquarters and meeting places all over the city made it harder and harder for the Palestinian leadership to meet, while even consultation was often difficult because of communication difficulties.

Sharon's bombardment reached its crescendo on 12 August: the PLO leaders were convinced that they had no alternative left but evacuation. Seven long weeks after negotiating the agreement with Habib, the PLO decided to comply with its terms and leave Beirut. The cost of Arafat's imagining that he could play politics with Habib at Israel's expense was catastrophic for the Palestinians and for the Lebanese in Beirut. Arafat, and no one else, was responsible for the deaths and the destruction.

These seven summer weeks were the most difficult and ugliest of the Lebanese War. Sharon had been accused of heartlessly shelling the civilian population of western Beirut. As he saw it, he had no choice. His answer to his accusers was that the PLO had been offered an honourable and generous way out, even to the point of allowing PLO activists to leave with their personal arms. The Lebanese and Palestinian suffering would have been avoided had Arafat not reneged on every agreement he made with Habib, and if he had abided by the undertakings he had given the Americans. In the end, Habib found, as we did, that Arafat and the PLO could not be trusted.

However, Sharon found little understanding of his reasoning either at home in Israel or in the world at large. The nightly television pictures of the bombardment had a traumatic effect on both. The Israelis of all political shades had wholeheartedly supported the Government's decision, as it had been defined on 6 June 1982, to remove the PLO threat to the inhabitants of the Galilee. Accordingly, the PLO was to be cleared from a forty-kilometre swathe of territory along Israel's northern frontier. But when the battlefront moved further and further to the north, and when casualties began to mount in Kafr Sil, Aley, Bhamdun and other towns and villages well beyond the forty-kilometre range, many Israelis began to wonder what was going on.

Officially the objectives of the war remained unchanged, but the reality on the ground was very different as the fighting became prolonged and costly by Israeli standards. Doubts and dissent became increasingly vocal. On 4 July 1982, the 'Peace Now' movement, which spearheaded the active opposition to the war, organized a giant protest demonstration in Tel Aviv; more than 100,000 Israelis called for an immediate cease-fire in Lebanon and for the dismissal of Sharon as Minister of Defence. Throughout July and August there were protest marches and demonstrations in Tel Aviv and Jerusalem. Opposition to the conduct of the war also became evident among members of the Cabinet, many of whom objected to being told of events after they had happened without Cabinet consultation. Even Prime Minister Begin himself was not always fully informed by the Defence Minister and the IDF Command. When, on one occasion, he was asked about this by Deputy Premier David Levy, he reportedly replied that he was always kept informed 'either before or after the event'.

Sharon was in a difficult position in the Cabinet. Because of the outspoken opposition among some ministers to his policy in Lebanon, he could not always confide his plans to the Cabinet without the risk of 'leaks' to the media. He was forced, therefore, to give confidential information to the Cabinet in a roundabout way so as to avoid censure or risk breaches of confidence by his colleagues. However, worse was to come. The story that Sharon was keeping his Cabinet colleagues in the dark or that he was deliberately misleading them soon made the rounds, suitably spread and embroidered by dissident Cabinet Ministers looking for reinsurance. This fuelled the confusion and polarization of opinion among Israel's worried public.

At the same time, Israel took a worldwide public relations bashing the like of which it had never suffered previously. The Lebanon War was without doubt the most widely televised war in history – even allowing for Vietnam; the fighting was brought daily into the living-rooms of millions of people the world over. Whereas the British had succeeded in keeping the press at arms' length from the Falklands War, in Lebanon reporters and television crews were free to roam at will. Television, no matter how honest reporters and crew are, or claim to be, is a prism which can at times deflect and distort the truth. If one house in a row of a hundred is damaged, the cameras will zoom on to it and the viewer will have no idea that there are ninety-nine intact houses on either side; he will see only the damage done to the one house.

A colleague at the Foreign Ministry witnessed a spectacle in the main square of Sidon, which highlighted for me the meaning of 'impartial' television reporting. An enterprising reporter went up to a woman who was standing in the square holding a sleeping baby to her shoulder; after a short conversation between them, the woman took the baby from her shoulder and, holding her in outstretched arms, started walking across the square, followed by a camera crew. After about twenty paces, she was told she could put the baby back again, to its former sleeping posture. That evening the world witnessed the heart-rending sight of a woman carrying her 'dead' baby across Sidon square. The use of television as a means of propaganda and partisan reporting distorts the truth since it usually totally isolates effect from cause, with the result that it becomes little better than emotive incitement.

War at the wrong end of a gun or at the receiving end of a bomb is a terrible thing – be your cause just or evil. Thus the horror of war, as depicted on television, equated Israel as 'the invader and the oppressor'. Israel was placed in the dock of world opinion. It mattered little that, in fact, relatively few civilians were killed, that advancing troops had strict orders to do their utmost to prevent Lebanese casualties, that planes dropped leaflets calling on civilians to evacuate areas close to PLO positions before those positions were bombed, and that pilots and artillery gunners were pin-pointing PLO targets at great personal risk to themselves.

Typical of what was later to be called 'the media miscoverage' of the war were the reports of casualties put out after the first few days. The Palestine Red Crescent Society, which was headed by Arafat's brother, Dr Fathi Arafat, announced that 10,000 civilians had been killed in the first four days of the war; this figure was matched by the Lebanese Red Cross representatives in Beirut, who declared that an estimated 600,000 refugees were homeless or had fled the fighting in southern Lebanon. These figures were picked up and reported by every major American television network, by the BBC and ITV in Britain and by leading newspapers the world over.

No one bothered to check the accuracy or even the plausibility of these figures, or to consider the fact that the entire population of southern Lebanon was less than 600,000. David Shipler of the *New York Times*, who travelled extensively in Lebanon during the war, noted the 'extreme exaggerations' in the reporting of casualty figures, but he was the exception. For much of the world these were the figures to be remembered* and endlessly quoted until they assumed the mantle of truth by repetition.

Israel's internal dissensions and defamatory image in the international media fed on each other, each relying on the other to justify hostile denunciation of the actions of the Israeli Government in Lebanon. An added dimension to this was the disenchantment, especially in Israel, with Israel's Lebanese ally, Bashir Gemayel's Lebanese Christians. Throughout the seven years' civil war from 1975 to 1982, Bashir's forces had failed to gain the sympathy of their western co-religionists, even when the Christian population of East Beirut and the Metn were exposed to ruthless bombardment from Syrian guns, far worse than anything that western Beirut was ever to suffer from the Israelis. But there was no outcry from the media, from the politicians or from the Church. At that time, there was hardly a television camera or a reporter's notebook in sight.

Meanwhile, as the world media were becoming ever more hostile to 'Israel's war', many Israelis began to blame the Lebanese Christians for these negative repercussions. At a meeting between Sharon and Bashir Gemayel at Johnny Abdu's house in Beirut on 5 July 1982 (at which I was present), an acrimonious argument broke out in which Bashir charged that the Israel Broadcasting Services, *Kol Yisrael*, was as negative about the Lebanese Christians as was the PLO's *Voice of Palestine*. Sharon, for his part, accused the Lebanese Forces under Bashir of committing excesses against the Druze inhabitants in their Shouf mountain villages. Bashir was markedly impatient at Sharon's reluctance to move into Muslim western Beirut and forcibly expel the PLO from its stronghold there. Sharon pointedly reminded Bashir that he was still waiting for the promised help from Bashir's Christian militia in doing just that. Both men were noticeably frustrated by the stalemate.

At the time of this Bashir–Sharon confrontation, Habib's negotiations for the withdrawal of the PLO were still undecided. Sharon's earlier hopeful belief that he could leave the problem of Beirut to be settled by the Lebanese had been dispelled during Bashir's visit to Jerusalem at the beginning of the war, in June 1982. In many respects it was this visit that signalled the turning-point in relations between Israel and the Lebanese Christians. I recall a particularly poignant moment during the visit when Bashir and I were standing on the balcony of one of the top floors of Jerusalem's Hilton Hotel. Before us lay the Holy City in all its pristine

---

* Israel later published official casualty figures of Lebanese civilians. The slipshod and biased reporting of the Lebanese War is ably described by Ze'ev Chafets in *Double Vision: How the Press Distorts America's View of the Middle East*.

splendour. With a wave of his hand at the historic setting that lay before him, Bashir said to me very quietly: 'I want to come to Jerusalem as President of Lebanon and sign a peace treaty with you. I want to come as President and not as the head of a Christian gang.'

If ever there was a cry from the heart, this was it. Bashir had made up his mind to be the next President and he did not want to jeopardize his chances by openly joining with Israel in the fighting for Beirut. He had, however, in previous meetings with Sharon, promised to do just that and he was therefore in a quandary. He confessed to me his dilemma as we waited in the Hilton for his meeting with Prime Minister Begin. He reassured me that he had the necessary support to be elected Lebanon's President on 23 July 1982. 'After the elections I will come to Jerusalem as a second Sadat, to discuss a peace treaty,' he promised. Surely, he asked, Begin would understand the importance of him becoming President and release him from his promise to deploy his forces in south-west Beirut in order to drive out the PLO. 'If Begin does not see it my way,' he added, 'I will fight even if it means giving up the presidency. But then we shall have no choice but to carve a Christian state out of Lebanon and ask for a formal defence alliance with Israel in order to protect ourselves.' This was the voice of the new young Lebanon extending its hand in friendship and commonality to Israel – so different from the old leaders, Pierre Gemayel and Camille Chamoun, who had told Sharon in the previous January that 'no Lebanese Government could make peace with Israel'.

Later, Bashir was visibly nervous when he came to the Prime Minister's residence, where Begin was flanked by Defence Minister Sharon and Chief of Staff Eitan. (I also attended this meeting.) 'Today, I as Bashir cannot bring you the political victory you want, a full peace treaty,' he told Begin. 'I do not represent the Muslims, I cannot speak in the name of a government. But when I come as President, all will change.' Bashir reiterated his willingness to take part in 'Operation Spark', as the Lebanese participation in military operations in West Beirut was code-named. However, he cautioned us that should he join us in the attack on West Beirut, he would not be elected President. 'I am a Christian, and I will never be forgiven by the Muslim world,' he impressed on Begin.

Bashir's explanation of his difficulties was not well received. 'We all have to be ready to take risks. We certainly did,' Begin responded; 'in my opinion you, and not those who co-operated with the PLO, are the true representatives of Lebanon. Now is the time for brave decisions. It is important for Lebanon that the Lebanese Forces should be in the forefront in the liberation of the capital.'

However, it was Sharon, not Begin, who gave Bashir Israel's reply. Sharon and Bashir had met many times and a close relationship based on mutual respect had developed between them. Bashir had been certain that Sharon, much more than Begin, would understand his predicament. But Sharon had his own problems: he was frustrated with the situation in Beirut, in which the PLO seemed to be collectively thumbing their noses at him, daring him to move in and get them. He knew – and the PLO knew – that the Israeli Government baulked at the idea of the Israeli army fighting its way into an Arab capital city.

It was not a military problem, but a political one. The ideal way out of the Beirut impasse, for Sharon, was for the Lebanese Forces to launch an attack, which could then be massively supported by the Israeli army. That had been the idea behind 'Operation Spark' and Sharon was bitterly disappointed to hear that Bashir was trying to back out of his part in the operation. Turning to Bashir he gave voice to his own predicament:

We are under increasing public pressure ... we have mobilized some 200,000 men, and there is a growing chorus of voices here saying 'Where are the Christians?' ... The Prime Minister has said that we both have a common objective; you want to liberate your capital from the PLO fighters and we want to defeat our enemy. This operation can only take place if we both participate in it .... The Prime Minister does not see any possibility of our doing it on our own, but he believes it must be done, and as soon as possible.

Begin and Sharon promised Bashir that he would have Israel's support, but both insisted that the time had come for the Christians to do something for themselves in order to liberate their country. A cowed Bashir remarked bitterly: 'You are asking me to burn the entire investment that we have made over the past seven years. We will not be able to be effective any longer.'

By the time Bashir left Begin's home, the former idyllic relationship was no more. There had been a parting of minds, a gap never again bridged. Begin and Sharon could not understand how Bashir could go back on his promises after all that the Israelis had done for the Lebanese Christians from the very first consignment of arms and military training to the war itself. They considered Bashir's reluctance to commit his forces as an act of gross ingratitude, especially as it was an essential part of their joint plan. Bashir, on the other hand, was bitterly disappointed that the Israeli leaders had not understood that it would be folly on his part to jeopardize his chances of winning the presidency – as much in Israel's interest as in Lebanon's. Bashir returned to Beirut and, except for a small local fire-fight between his men and the PLO, he withdrew the Christian militia from this critical phase of the war, much to Israel's chagrin.

Would he really have jeopardized his chances by joining with Israel in the battle? Five years after the event I questioned some of the most prominent members of the Lebanese Christian community about this. In a way, the question was not fair to Bashir, for now they were only too conscious of the searing criticism of the Christian inaction which had engulfed Israeli public opinion after the war. The all-pervading feeling was that the Christians had been content to let the Israelis fight their war for them, but were not willing to lift a finger to help either themselves or the Israelis. The answers I received were clearly tinged by feelings of guilt. Bashir, I was told, had made a grave mistake by antagonizing the Israeli Government and public opinion from the Lebanese Christian cause. At that time of great Israeli need for assistance from the Christian militia, it was said, he should have come forward and he could still have been elected President.

This was the fairly general reaction to my question. The PLO was so unpopular at the time, even among Lebanese Muslims, that a Christian alliance with Israel would not have affected the elections. There can be little doubt now that it was Bashir's failure to act in that critical phase of the Lebanese War which brought about the disillusionment with the Lebanese Christians in Israel and the souring of relations that had once been so warm and understanding.

I am convinced, however, that Bashir genuinely believed that by joining the fight he would be jeopardizing something that would be of inestimable value to him and his people, and also to his future relations with Israel.

Little did we know that his days were numbered. They were to end in high climacteric – wild and heady days and nights of celebration. He was elected President by a majority of the members of Parliament on 23 July 1982. Hectic preparations followed to celebrate the day in September when his position would be consummated and he would become the seventh President of Lebanon.

Bashir, now President-elect, and I met for lunch in a Beirut restaurant in what was to be my last meeting with him in which we were alone. He was hugely satisfied with his success and very much cognizant of the fact that he would never have reached this pinnacle of his achievement without Israel's help. He was also worried about future relations with Israel, remembering perhaps the unfortunate meeting in Jerusalem. He pleaded with me, 'Please tell your people to have patience. I am committed to making peace with Israel and I promise you I shall do it. But I first need nine months, maximum one year, to consolidate my position as President of all Lebanon and not only of the Christians. I need to mend my fences with the Arab countries, in particular with Saudi Arabia, so that Lebanon can once more play its central role in the economy of the Middle East. I can do it in not more than one year.' In the meantime, he said, he would maintain close relations with Israel and we would be welcome to continue to operate our Foreign Ministry's Mission that had been established in the fashionable quarter of Dbaye to the north of Beirut.

But yet once more his hopes for an understanding with Israel's leaders were to be frustrated, this time by Begin himself. A meeting had been arranged between Bashir and Begin at the beginning of September 1982 at a security establishment near Nahariya in northern Israel. Begin was enjoying a few days of rest at a modest hotel in Nahariya and he had wanted to congratulate Bashir personally on his election and to discuss future relations. It was to have been a festive occasion and the leading figures of Israel's Prime Minister's Office, Defence and Foreign Ministries and Army who had relations with Bashir were all there. Bashir, in jovial mood, arrived with his closest associates, who, over the years, had remained by his side as the long struggle in Lebanon dragged on from those first days of fighting in 1975.

The only person missing was Begin himself. As the minutes ticked by, it became clear to those who knew of his penchant for punctuality that there must be a good reason for his being late. We were not wrong. By unhappy coincidence, the US Ambassador to Israel, Samuel Lewis, had asked for an urgent meeting with the Prime Minister in Nahariya on that same day. On arrival, Lewis handed Begin a message from President Reagan. It was, in fact, a finalized set of proposals for a Middle East settlement, which became known as the Reagan Plan.

'It was as if he had been hit in the solar plexus with a sledge-hammer,' a close aide later described Begin's reaction to Lewis's visit. It was not only the substance of the Reagan Plan that so shocked Israel's Prime Minister; hardly less offensive to him was the fact that a plan affecting Israel's future could have been finalized in Washington without consulting Israel.*

Begin talked of the stealthy, underhand manner in which the plan was conceived. No hint had come from Washington during the weeks when the planners at the State Department and the National Security Council were piecing it together. Begin saw it as a calculated act of deception designed to confront him with a fait accompli. This Reagan Plan destroyed the centre-piece of the Camp David Accords, and Begin rejected it outright. This centre-piece, it may be noted, in order to appreciate fully the shattering impact of the Reagan message on Begin, had found expression in a compromise formula which stipulated that the future of Judea, Samaria and Gaza would be freely negotiated by the parties concerned after a five-year period of autonomy in those regions. The new unilateral Reagan Plan now suddenly presented Begin with proposals which pre-empted the outcome of these negotiations: the West Bank – Judea and Samaria – would be federated with Jordan after the transitional five-year period. No one had asked Begin, no one had told him. It was a cruel bolt from the blue.

When Begin finally arrived at the meeting place near Nahariya, the waiting Israelis noted his black mood. Never before had I seen him so disturbed. Briefly, he spoked to us: 'We have been betrayed by the Americans, the biggest betrayal since the state was established. They have stabbed us in the back. We now have a completely different fight on our hands.' As we entered the room where the Lebanese were sitting, he was still in another world, preoccupied with the public response he planned to make to the American proposal.

Bashir, who had been anticipating a joyous occasion, immediately sensed the change of atmosphere. He saw Begin's grim face and could feel the tension in the room. Not knowing the cause of this unexpected change, he assumed the worst. What should have been a celebration, a toast to victory, turned into a catastrophe. Begin demanded an immediate peace treaty with

---

* Ambassador Lewis subsequently publicly criticized this aspect of the Reagan Plan, for which he was reprimanded by Secretary of State George Shultz.

Lebanon after Bashir's investiture; Bashir told him that his demand was unrealistic. After that recriminations began to fly in both directions; the meeting ended in dismal failure.

The damage done at Nahariya was, however, swiftly repaired by Sharon. Realizing that the meeting had got out of hand, he flew to Beirut for an all-night session with Lebanon's President-elect. Sharon spoke of the hopes and expectations in Israel which Bashir's election had inspired; Bashir explained the problems which he faced as newly elected President, the task of unifying the country, of gaining the support of the Muslim community and of consolidating the economy with the help of the Saudis. Both discussed the more immediate problem of deploying the Israelis in Beirut, especially at the airport. They agreed on the urgent need to reach an agreement which would bring about the evacuation of all foreign forces from Lebanon, including the Syrians. They also considered the challenge posed by the remaining PLO forces in the country.

This last Bashir–Sharon meeting restored the old intimacy between the young Lebanese leader and his Israeli friends. But neither Bashir nor the Israelis were to reap the fruits of the new understanding. A few days later, on 15 September 1982, a bomb shattered the building of the Ashrafiah Kataeb Party headquarters. Bashir had arrived several minutes earlier for a victory celebration with old friends, led by the Ashrafiah party boss, Jean Nader. Both Bashir and Nader were among the dead, buried beneath the debris. Buried too were the hopes of the young Lebanese Christians – and also of many young Muslims – for a different and better Lebanon under the dynamic and charismatic leadership of Bashir Gemayel. He had planned to put an end to the self-destructive politics of the old oligarchies. He was prepared to fight and stamp out corruption, so deeply rooted in Lebanese society, especially among the feudal barons who still maintained absolute rule over much of Lebanon's countryside and its deprived population.

It was not to be. The powerful, remote-controlled bomb, planted by a member of the Syrian-controlled Partie Populaire Syrien, destroyed Bashir's life and, with it, hope of a new and better Lebanon.* It also destroyed Israel's one hope of Lebanon becoming the second neighbouring state to sign a peace treaty. It was a devastating blow for us and – as events would show – also for the Lebanese, far more so than we realized at the time.

Bashir's popularity among the Christians can be measured by the grief that overwhelmed the Christian population. But expressions of bereavement and of loss quickly gave way to demands for revenge. An eye for an eye, blood for blood have been the governing imperatives of all Middle Eastern people since the days of the Old Testament, nowhere more so than in Lebanon, and no less so among Christians than Muslims. The enormity of the loss following so rapidly on the wild elation of the election victory

---

* One of the first acts of the Syrians when they entered the Christian quarters of Beirut in November 1990 was to release the man convicted of the bombing from prison.

created an atmosphere more ugly than any Beirut had witnessed in our time.

Revenge was in the air and, with Bashir gone, there was no one who could or would cool the sense of outrage and attempt to control a situation which was fast becoming uncontrollable. With a bloody reprisal appearing imminent, Sharon, always accustomed to decisive action, especially in times of adversity, ordered his troops to occupy the line dividing Christian and Muslim Beirut and to seize the main roads through the western half of the city. Only after having given the order did he inform Prime Minister Begin and the Cabinet, an 'oversight' for which he was strongly criticized, particularly by fellow ministers.

Sharon has defended himself against the accusation of irresponsible action by pointing to the tension which had gripped the city after Bashir's death and the necessity for immediate action, which would not have been possible if he had waited for the Cabinet to make up its unpredictable collective mind. However, his move would have been more acceptable had he taken effective measures to prevent any confrontation between inflamed Christians and the Muslim population following Bashir's death. Instead, he did just the opposite. Once he was in control of all Beirut, he immediately set his mind to the problem of driving out the 2,000 PLO fighters who, he was convinced, had evaded the evacuation and had 'gone civilian' in the large sprawling Palestinian enclaves in southern Beirut. This appeared to him to be the overriding need of the moment. Typically, again, he transplanted his concern into action. The Israeli army had been given strict orders not to enter the so-called Palestinian camps and search for the PLO remnants; instead, the Israeli command sought to persuade the Lebanese regular army to do so. When the Lebanese 'regulars' showed that they had no intention of engaging the PLO, Sharon, headstrong as ever and without consultation, submitted to pressure from the angry Christian militia leaders in Beirut.

He authorized the Christian Phalange, known as the Lebanese Forces, to enter the Palestinian districts of Sabra and Shatilla in order to flush out the remaining PLO fighters and thus complete the expulsion of the PLO from the Lebanese capital. On the evening of 16 September, special units of the Lebanese Forces, under the command of Eli Hobeika, moved into the camps. Early the following morning, reports reached the Foreign Ministry in Jerusalem that civilians were being killed. However, it was only twenty-four hours later that the last Phalangists left the Palestinian camps after the local Israeli commander had ordered them to do so. By that time some 600 men, women and children had been butchered by the Phalange. A wave of anger and revulsion swept the world. No less so in Israel, where Sharon's move into western Beirut had already set off a chain of demonstrations against the war in general and against the occupation of western Beirut in particular.

As news of the massacre spread, the groups opposed to the war, led by the 'Peace Now' movement, called for a mass rally in Tel Aviv's Municipal

Square to demand Sharon's resignation and the formation of a commission of enquiry to investigate the circumstances of the Sabra and Shatilla massacre. The anger which had been generated in Israel, primarily against Sharon, can be measured by the fact that some 400,000 people – more than ten per cent of the entire population of Israel – turned up for the rally on 25 September, the largest demonstration ever seen in the history of the country. With such public pressure against it, the Government submitted to the demand for a public enquiry into the responsibility of Defence Minister Sharon and Israel's armed forces, although it was accepted that no Israeli troops had been directly involved in the massacre of the Palestinians in Sabra and Shatilla.

The September killings of Bashir and his friends in Ashrafiah, and of the Palestinians in Sabra and Shatilla, displayed the degree of cruelty which was typical of the sectarian strife which had dominated life in Lebanon – especially since the outbreak in 1975 of the largely religious-orientated civil war. It had produced a sense of hopelessness and a frightening disregard for the sanctity of human life. I have witnessed pleasant, cultured and seemingly civilized Lebanese speak with incredible savagery and lust for the blood of their fellow countrymen of a different religion, sect or faction. I have seen cafés overflowing with people and with bonhomie, while only a short distance away their fellow countrymen were engaged in killing each other. Hatred within Lebanon has no limit. As Tom Friedman of the *New York Times* had put it, 'they hated each other more than they loved their country'.

The events of September dragged the country down to its lowest depths and extinguished any spark of hope. Bashir's elder brother, Amin, was sworn in as President; his was a thankless task. As the son of a domineering father, who was still ruling with an iron grip the Christian Phalange Party he had founded, and as brother of the martyred hero whose place he was asked to fill, Amin Gemayel faced insuperable handicaps. It was hardly surprising that he failed to overcome the religious hatreds and ethnic suspicions which divided the country.

Meanwhile, public opinion, as it is called with sublime disregard for reality, had all the answers worldwide. Israel stood accused. She had facilitated and condoned even if she had not directly ordered or participated in the massacre in Sabra and Shatilla. Every accusing finger pointed at Israel as the killer of innocent Palestinians. During the first decisive twenty-four hours when the world heard of the massacre and witnessed the first gruesome pictures, Israel was blamed as the perpetrator by proxy. The world had judged. The outcry against Israel was total and universal.

No matter that worse massacres had been perpetrated during the war in Lebanon by Christians, Druze and Palestinians. They passed with barely a mention or a notice. A different set of standards was applied to Israel. The reporting by the media was emotive and frequently inaccurate; the comments by foreign statesmen and politicians were both injudicial and harsh. In the face of such an onslaught Begin, who had been slow to recognize the extent of the worldwide condemnation, was forced to act and confront the world – and a greatly concerned Israeli public – with the facts of the Sabra and Shatilla massacre. On 28 September 1982, an independent judicial Commission of Enquiry was appointed under Supreme Court Justice Itzhak Kahan to establish responsibility.

The Kahan Commission presented its final report on 8 February 1983. It criticized Prime Minister Begin for failure to act when he should have done. It also criticized Defence Minister Sharon and Chief of Staff Eitan in much stronger terms, whereupon the Cabinet requested their resignation from office.

11
Sharon's Diplomacy
1982

AFTER THE DEATH OF Lebanon's President-elect and after the Sabra and Shatilla massacre, we realized that the Lebanese situation had changed dramatically and that we faced an entirely new state of affairs. Less than a week after the massacre, Philip Habib had lengthy discussions with the newly elected President, Amin Gemayel, in Beirut and with Begin, Shamir and Sharon in Jerusalem. The Israelis saw Amin as the obvious choice to fill his brother's place at the presidency. Habib exuded confidence and optimism. He came to see Sharon directly after his meeting with Amin. (I was also present.) 'I am a chronic optimist. There is no problem without a solution,' he began in his typical breezy manner. 'The important thing now is to strengthen the central authority in Lebanon. The next phase is to strengthen the Government and to make Lebanon fully sovereign.'

Later he assured Begin that 'Amin will surprise us all. He is no weak sister of the Syrians. He is on the right side of the political fence with the United States, Europe and Israel and he will also be on good terms with the Arab world.' Habib and the Israeli leaders were agreed that Amin should be helped to consolidate his position and Lebanon's sovereignty. The Israelis agreed to evacuate Beirut and to have their troops replaced by a multi-national force made up of contingents of Americans, French, Italian and British soldiers. Begin and Sharon agreed to discuss the withdrawal of all foreign troops from Lebanon, with the PLO leaving first and the Syrians and the Israelis withdrawing 'simultaneously'.

Begin expressed the hope at the conclusion of his meeting with Habib that all those 'foreign' to Lebanon should leave as quickly as possible. Israel, by now, was ready to close her Lebanese chapter. The PLO in Lebanon had been disarmed and expelled. The threat to the citizens of Galilee had been removed. The new President installed in Beirut was presumed to be friendly. Israel could now contemplate withdrawing from Lebanon, but only with two provisos: that all other foreign forces would also leave and that Lebanon and Israel conclude a formal peace treaty or, at the very least, an accord providing for secure and normal relations.

After meeting Begin on 24 September 1982, Habib and his deputy,

Morris Draper, were invited to Sharon's farm in the Negev. Following the sumptuous Shabbat meal, host and guests informally explored the new twists in the Lebanese enigma. Draper had met Amin the night before. Lebanon's newly installed President had explained to him, as Draper put it, that there would have to be changes in his relations with Israel. As President he could not continue to act as he and his brother Bashir had done. He was not a private citizen any more. He wanted good relations with Israel, but he would no longer be able to meet informally with the Israelis as he and his brother had done. Sharon understood: the jovial Shabbat meal was the occasion for Amin and the Americans to serve notice that the rules of the game in Lebanon were about to be changed.

Sharon also had a message for the Americans and the Lebanese. He told Habib, Draper and US Ambassador Lewis that Israel must begin negotiations for the necessary security and normalization arrangements. Moreover, these must include arrangements for the free movement of people and goods (customs, even veterinary services) and, of course, security. The sooner we reached agreement, he declared, the quicker Israel would be able to withdraw from Lebanon.

Sharon's proposals were formally embodied in a Cabinet statement on 11 October 1982, which called for direct negotiations with the Lebanese Government, with American participation if the United States so desired, to conclude the necessary security and normalization arrangements. The Cabinet also decided on the priorities of withdrawal from Lebanon: first, the PLO would have to leave; following that, Israel would withdraw to a line forty-five–fifty kilometres north of Metula, the northernmost town on Israel's frontier with Lebanon, provided the Syrians had withdrawn from their positions on Mont Liban. Israel would finally withdraw from southern Lebanon when two further agreements had been signed: one, between Israel and Lebanon; the other, between Lebanon and Syria, which would ensure the simultaneous withdrawal of Syrian troops from Lebanon.

Sharon insisted, however, on attaching a rider to this statement. This stipulated that the negotiating teams should be led by ministers and that the venue should be the two capitals, Beirut and Jerusalem: open negotiations between two sovereign states, precisely what Lebanon's new President was not prepared to contemplate.

Habib pleaded, rightly but in vain, that by adding these two conditions Israel was making sure that there would be no negotiations. It was a form of diplomatic hara-kiri. But Sharon was adamant and Begin went along with him. It was as if they did not want an agreement. Habib kept telling Begin and Sharon that he could, quietly and quickly, 'shuttle' between Beirut and Jerusalem; that the Lebanese were willing to make security arrangements with Israel which would provide for a de facto peace in the south if they could tell their people that this was the only way to obtain the withdrawal of all foreign forces in the country. Normalization could come at a later stage, once the PLO, Syrians and Israelis had left, Habib argued.

The Syrians, he told the Israelis again and again, would agree to withdraw their troops from Lebanon under these conditions.

Habib's proposal to postpone talks on normalization had particularly angered the Israeli ministers. They felt that once Israel had withdrawn her physical presence from Lebanon, there would be little chance of negotiating an agreement on 'normalization'. They did not seem to realize that there would be even less chance of concluding any agreement on the basis of Israel's amended Cabinet decision of 11 October. Anger has never been an effective basis for diplomacy.

Valuable weeks passed; the diplomatic impasse continued while Lebanese politics were not standing still. The forces opposed to peace with Israel were consolidating and growing in strength. The Muslim militias were mounting attacks on the multi-national forces stationed in West Beirut; the Druze under Walid Jumblatt increased their forays against the Christians in the Shouf and the Syrians were able to restore their lost strength and confidence with the aid of a massive resupply of arms from the Soviet Union. Three vital months, which could have provided the groundwork for an agreement with the Lebanese, were mindlessly frittered away.

During this time, the Lebanese Government, at first, wanted talks to be held by two delegations led by Israeli and Lebanese military personnel, a sort of upgraded version of the discredited and ineffective Israeli–Lebanese Military Armistice Committee, a body established by the United Nations in 1949 to report on frontier 'incidents'. This was completely unacceptable to Israel. The Lebanese then proposed that there should be military and civilian co-chairmen, but the Israeli Government was adamant. Members of the Government would have to head the negotiating team or there would be no negotiations. The delay this imposed on the peace-making process for the sake of ministerial *amour propre* was to prove terminal.

The deadlock was eventually broken in characteristic Lebanese fashion. Alarmed by the deterioration of relations with Israel and under strong pressure from the Lebanese Forces to do something about it, Amin sent one of his closest friends to Israel on a secret mission: to negotiate the framework for an agreement between the two countries. Immediately code-named by the Israelis as 'The Emissary', Amin's friend was a handsome, intelligent Maronite patriot, whose polite and winning manner charmed the Israelis with whom he was dealing.

I had known him since the mid-1970s. We had spent hours discussing the situation in Lebanon, searching for solutions to seemingly insoluble problems; his creative mind never tired, examining one plan after another, trying them on for size before discarding them and picking another. 'The Emissary' was the ideal negotiator. The Israeli negotiating team, comprising General Tamir, myself, a Mossad operative and later, also, Sharon, prepared together with 'The Emissary' an impressive list of issues on which both sides had agreed.

After a great deal of commuting by the Lebanese negotiator between Beirut and Israel, a final draft was settled after an all-night session on

13 December 1982, forty-eight hours before Habib was due back from Washington. The timing was important for Sharon. His relations with the United States were perceptibly worsening. By the end of 1982, there existed a state of emotion-laden mutual aversion between him and Habib, Draper and Ambassador Lewis. I witnessed shouting matches between them and heard Lewis express himself about Sharon in a most unambassadorial manner. Sharon had got under their skins, while they, in Sharon's eyes, pursued a policy designed to deprive Israel of her rightfully achieved gains from the war in Lebanon.

This was the reason for Sharon's insistence on direct negotiations with the Lebanese. He distrusted Habib and his shuttle diplomacy. Thus, when we succeeded in concluding an agreement with the Lebanese 'Emissary' before Habib's return from Washington, Sharon was jubilant. It was in this mood that he confronted Habib and Draper in Begin's office in Jerusalem on 15 December. He visibly savoured the moment when the Prime Minister told Habib that Sharon had something important to say to him.

Sharon then read to them the text of a document, entitled 'Basic Elements and Guidelines'. It began with the forthright statement that 'both sides are in agreement that efforts should be made to achieve results at the earliest possible date regarding the following topics which should be considered as a package deal: normalization of relations, security arrangements for the south, withdrawal of Israel's forces'. Sharon's victory appeared to be absolute. He had, so it seemed, achieved something that Habib had said could not be done. Sharon felt that he had convincingly shown that the Americans had been obstructing direct negotiations for an agreement that would embrace normalization of relations and arrangement for the security of Israel's northern border.

But for victories to be complete they must be publicly seen and heard. It was therefore hardly surprising that the secret document and the fact that secret negotiations had taken place found their way into the Israeli media, to be followed by a blaze of publicity for Sharon, the star performer. Sharon was vindicating himself and his deeds in Lebanon, attacking his detractors and upholding his policies. After having been hounded by the press, especially since the Sabra and Shatilla massacre, his triumph must have been sweet indeed, but, alas, only ephemeral. The adverse consequences of this indiscreet publicity had more substance and were to be longer lasting – much longer than the short-lived public-relations 'triumph'.

The Lebanese were furious that their request for secrecy, to which Sharon had agreed, had been treated with so little respect. They refused to sign the agreement. Lebanon's new President told a close friend of his sense of shock. He felt that he had been betrayed by Israel's publication of the secret agreement. 'How can I trust the Israelis when they do something like that to me?' he asked. Amin, who was prone to dark suspicions, believed that the Israelis had published the document deliberately so as to embarrass him and drive a wedge between him and Lebanon's Muslims. He had always been aware that the Israelis had preferred his brother Bashir to him.

The openly displayed jealousy between the two brothers lived on long after Bashir's assassination.

The anger generated over the Israeli publication of the agreement was the beginning of the slide that was to lead to almost total estrangement between Amin and the Israelis. More personal misunderstandings on both sides widened the gulf, all the more so when Amin refused to meet Sharon and then his successor as Defence Minister, Moshe Arens. Yet it had been Amin who had sent 'The Emissary' to seek a secret agreement with Israel. Amin also appointed a close friend of his family, former Foreign Ministry Director-General Antoine Fattal, to lead a Lebanese delegation in official tripartite talks with Israel and the United States.

Begin had appointed me to head the Israeli delegation despite the strenuous objections of Sharon, who feared that I was too independent and had not always followed his directives. We had differed following a preliminary meeting between Fattal and myself, which we held, incongruously, in Muslim West Beirut. We agreed on the technicalities for getting the talks started, but Sharon felt, rightly from his point of view, that I had not insisted strongly enough that the talks be led by Israeli and Lebanese ministers and that we should meet alternately in Jerusalem and Beirut. I knew that Fattal would not be able to accede were I to make such demands, and I felt strongly that it was more important that the talks should start without further delay. The town of Khalde on the outskirts of Beirut was the Lebanese choice of venue. Begin, as always with an eye for the symbolic, chose Kiryat Shmona, the northern Galilean town which had suffered most from the PLO bombardment before the Lebanese War.

On 27 December 1982, the official talks at long last opened at the Beach Hotel in Khalde. The hotel was ringed with Lebanese and Israeli security forces because intelligence sources had reported that the PLO and its allies were planning to attack the Khalde negotiators. Ambassador Morris Draper headed the American delegation; the lugubrious Fattal had charge of the Lebanese; and I presided over the Israeli team, with General Tamir leading the military personnel in our delegation. Israeli ministers and officials, who had assumed the talks would now proceed speedily according to the guidelines laid down in the agreement with the Lebanese 'Emissary', were to be quickly disillusioned. It took the negotiators three full weeks merely to agree on the agenda. For five more months the delegations shuttled between Khalde, Kiryat Shmona and Nathaniya, when, later, a third weekly meeting was added.

Every word was hotly contested, every idea was challenged by someone. Moreover, the composition of the Lebanese delegation destroyed any thought of rapid progress; its chairman, Fattal, was a Chaldean by religion, his deputy and head of the military committee was a Shi'i; one of the other civilians was a Sunni Muslim and the other a Maronite Christian (another Shi'i was later added for good measure); the other members of the Lebanese delegation were a Sunni Muslim, a Maronite Christian and a Greek Orthodox Catholic. It was inconceivable for such a team to agree on any major issue. The problem was made worse by the fact that each member had to report to his respective community leaders and to ask for their approval before he could agree to anything. For example, the Sunni civilian delegate, Ibrahim Kharma, was a wealthy merchant – an ambassador who also happened to be a relative of Saeb Salaam, the veteran Sunni Muslim leader; he refused to accept any conference decision until he had ascertained Saeb Salaam's opinion. Fattal wrily pointed out to us that his delegation was more like a convoy which had to adjust its speed to that of the slowest ship.

Lebanon's President made even more difficulties for us. In view of the delicacy of his situation, he refused to approve of any agreement reached without the prior consent of his Sunni Prime Minister, Shafiq el-Wazzan. Amin confided to a friend that he did not intend to enable Muslims to disown any agreement with Israel by charging that it was an agreement with the Lebanese Christians and that the Muslims had nothing to do with it. Amin insisted that the Muslim leaders would have to share full responsibility with the Christians in the conclusion of a settlement. Thus, after hours of negotiating, Fattal would give his consent to an idea or the wording of a sentence. He would then report back to Amin, who would concur with what Fattal had already accepted. Amin would then place the proposed formulation before Wazzan, who would, in turn, confer with Saeb Salaam, the Muslim *éminence grise*, who had already received his own private report of the proceedings from Ambassador Kharma. I would on occasion send messages direct to Saeb Salaam through Kharma, in the hope of shortening this circuitous procedure, and I had the satisfaction of knowing that the Muslims – Sunni and Shi'i – were fully involved in the negotiations through Saeb Salaam and General Hamdan, the Shi'i head of the military committee, respectively.

The negotiations hinged primarily on the question of the normalization of relations between our two countries, and on security arrangements which would prevent southern Lebanon being used again as a base for attacks on Israel. The future of Major Saad Haddad and his South Lebanon Army was a particularly sensitive problem in this context. However, while our talks were making their painfully slow progress, normal relations were being restored. Thousands of Lebanese came to Israel on holiday. It was a novel sight on Israeli roads to see cars with Lebanese licence plates. Lebanese tourists crowding into Israeli hotels became common-place. Lebanese merchants found Israeli goods attractive, not only for the Lebanese market, but also to re-export to Arab countries after suitable repacking and relabelling. Trade between the two countries soared. It exceeded trade between Israel and many of her traditional European trading partners.

Israeli Foreign Ministry personnel stationed at the de facto Israeli Mission in Beirut, headed by Yitzhak Lior and Bruce Kashdan, were treated by the Lebanese much like normal diplomats accredited by a foreign country; political and economic questions were discussed; there were interviews on local and international radio; and the customary cultural activities and a great deal of socializing took place. Considering that we were technically still at war with each other, these functions of the Israeli Mission in Beirut were somewhat unique. At first we were housed in a mansion belonging to a Saudi princess; later we moved to a large house in Dbaye, north of Beirut. In a city prone to terrorism and violence, Israeli diplomats were a prime target of the PLO, the Islamic fundamentalists and other terrorist organizations and militia activists, yet Israeli security was such that there was not a single attack on our Mission. In fact, the prevailing anarchy in Beirut was actually helpful to the Israeli diplomats. Lior, for example, bought a large stock of Lebanese licence plates, which he could change every few days on the hired cars we used to confound potential terrorist attackers.

I used to visit Beirut every week, usually for talks with Lebanese personalities, to meet the American officials, or just to give encouragement to our Israeli diplomats. It became increasingly 'normal' to talk not only with Christian Lebanese – our traditional friends – but also with Muslims, many of whom had suffered greatly from the PLO presence and were grateful that the Palestinian militants had been evicted. There were many Lebanese who followed our negotiations with hope for a successful outcome, which would lead to peace and normal relations between Lebanon and Israel.

12
The Israeli–Lebanese Agreement
1983–4

GIVEN THE INCREDIBLE, mostly man-made difficulties which we had to overcome, the agreement we signed on 17 May 1983 was an impressive document. Our difficulties did not stem only from the Lebanese. A committee of ministers, presided over by Begin, with Shamir, Sharon and Burg, would meet after every session at Khalde or Kiryat Shmona. Any undue flexibility shown by the Israeli negotiators was immediately picked up and excised. When these tougher demands were then put to the Lebanese, they, in turn, would not agree, further slowing the progress; we therefore gained nothing. We had to understand that the Lebanese could not afford to be seen as too forthcoming. As Fattal put it: 'For us the wrapping is more important than the contents of the parcel.' It was difficult to convince our ministerial censors sitting in Jerusalem of this Lebanese fact of life.

Agreement was eventually reached with help from the US Secretary of State, George Shultz. He had come to participate in the last lap of the negotiations – 'to put the icing on the cake' – as he phrased it. On 17 May 1983, the three parties met in festive mood at Khalde and then at Kiryat Shmona to sign the document that should have brought security and a semblance of normalcy to relations between Lebanon and Israel, and which would have led to the withdrawal, within three months, of all foreign forces from Lebanon.

Ambassador Fattal's speech for the signing ceremony had been vetted by his President and it gave expression not only to the thoughts of Fattal, but also to those of Amin Gemayel. Thus Fattal reminded us that 'Lebanon intends to remain faithful to its Arab vocation, while ending its state of war with Israel'. This was no contradiction. With his President's blessing, he told us, 'Inter-Arab solidarity in no way impels Lebanon to copy its neighbours' behaviour,' and, quoting Paul Claudel, he concluded, yearningly for a Lebanese diplomat, 'I thought that there was something more immense than war, it is peace.'

In my answering speech, I spelt out our objectives of the negotiations – no less yearningly, I suspect: 'We wanted peace in place of war, friendship, not hostility, security in place of instability and violence.' Israel's wish was for a Lebanon with her sovereignty and independence fully restored and with a strong central government under President Gemayel exercising its authority over the whole of Lebanese territory. But this could be achieved only if the terms of the agreement which we were about to sign were scrupulously upheld. 'The alternative', I added, 'would truly be tragic.'

In the event, despite the fact that the Agreement was overwhelmingly approved by the Lebanese Parliament, by Christians, Muslims, Druze and all – with only three abstentions – it was eventually abrogated by the President under strong pressure from the Syrians. The chaos, anarchy and bloodshed that have characterized Lebanon's history since the abrogation of the 17 May Agreement were the predictable outcome of this Syrian veto. Probably, the Syrians wanted it thus.

This period between the ratification of the Agreement by the Lebanese Parliament in the summer of 1983 and its abrogation by President Gemayel in the spring of 1984 was one of lost opportunities, when everything appeared to go wrong in Lebanon for the Lebanese, the Americans and the Israelis. According to the terms of the Agreement, instruments of ratification were to be exchanged between the two countries after its ratification by the two Parliaments. The Agreement would then come into effect. Amin, however, refused to sign the instruments of ratification.

In conversation with a close friend during this period, Amin repeated his determination to see the Agreement ratified. It was, in his eyes, a historic landmark for Lebanon; he would allow no one to sabotage it or alter one word of it. But since its acceptance as a legal document depended on him, and on him alone, he saw no reason for haste. He wanted first to conclude his talks with the Syrians, which were to bring about Syrian agreement to withdraw from Lebanon just as the Israelis had done. Signing the instruments of ratification with the Israelis now would make it more difficult to persuade the Syrians to leave and would gain him nothing, as the Israelis were not prepared to withdraw until the Syrians did likewise. Without a Syrian withdrawal, the Agreement with Israel could not become effective.

Amin rejected Israeli arguments that, if he signed, he would demonstrate to the Syrians that the Agreement was an irrevocable fact and that further pressure on him would have no effect. It must be remembered, however, that Amin in those days had infinite faith in the Americans. When asked by a friend if he really believed that the Syrians would quit Lebanon, he replied immediately in the affirmative; the Americans, he insisted, were working hard at it and he had no doubt that they would succeed.

Amin's objective in that first year of his presidency was to achieve the withdrawal of all foreign forces from Lebanon. In effect, this now meant the PLO and the Syrians since Israel had already signed the 17 May Agreement. Amin was confident that this would unite all of Lebanon behind him. He was, I am convinced, sincere in his intention eventually to put the 17 May Agreement into effect, believing that, under the umbrella of an American presence, he would be able to achieve both his goals and, at the same time, have the 17 May Agreement validated. It is easy after the event to ridicule these naïve beliefs; we must remember, however, that in those days Israel still controlled the vital Beirut–Damascus highway, Lebanon's life-line. The Americans, for their part, policed Beirut with a contingent of marines as part of the multi-national force. Moreover, the Americans were represented in Lebanon by President Reagan's special emissary, who believed in the judicial use of force when needed.

Robert C. ('Bud') McFarlane's aims were the same as Amin's: the removal of all foreign forces and the re-establishment of a united and stable Lebanon under the authority of the President. Amin could not have guessed in those confident summer days of 1983 that within less than a year both the United States and Israel would abdicate their responsibilities and positions of influence in Lebanon and leave him to face the Syrians alone, with no cards to play with the exception of the abrogation of the 17 May Agreement, a move he had sworn he would never make. He was given no choice by his American and Israeli allies.

In order to understand this extraordinary *volte face*, it is necessary to take a closer look at the way the Americans conducted their Lebanese policy. From the outset the American administration behaved in Lebanon like an orchestra whose members were playing different symphonies and with a conductor who had no idea what was happening. The Department of Defense was at odds with the President's National Security Council and with the State Department to such an extent that senior American officials at the White House complained that Defense Secretary Caspar Weinberger was undermining American policy in Lebanon.

Weinberger wanted minimal American involvement. He feared a situation in which American policy and eventually troops would be drawn into a Vietnam-like situation, which would become uncontrollable. He liked to remind his colleagues that during his tenure at the Pentagon he did not want to see any American casualties. He was against using the marines as part of the multi-national force and even more reluctant to allow the use of force, if necessary. White House officials noted bitterly that under 'Cap' Weinberger, the motto of the marines had been changed to 'last in and first out'.

As against the Defense Department's negative inaction, National Security Council and State Department officials endeavoured to bring about the rapid withdrawal from Lebanon of the PLO and also of the Syrian and Israeli forces. This would strengthen Lebanon's central government and army. They were prepared to use pressure and a certain amount of force to achieve the objectives of this policy in total contradiction to the Defense Secretary's policy.

American policy-making had been further destabilized by the President's decision to send Philip Habib to the region as his personal emissary. Despite his Lebanese ancestry, Habib was not considered a Middle East expert by either the State Department or White House officials who looked askance at his appointment. The National Security Council, the State Department, the Pentagon and Habib were thus frequently, and without consultation, pulling in different directions.

The result was a policy that was often incoherent and contradictory. This was particularly true for the period before Alexander Haig resigned as Secretary of State. Defence Minister Sharon, at that time, felt he had the understanding, if not encouragement, of Haig and the President. He believed the Americans were content that the allies of the Soviet Union – the Syrians and the PLO – had suffered a serious setback in Lebanon. Yet we have seen how the Americans came to the rescue of the Syrians deployed in Lebanon when they saved them, through their insistence on an untimely cease-fire, from an Israeli *coup de grâce* during the opening phase of the war. In Sharon's perception, the policies advocated by Habib were far from friendly to Israel.

Habib urged Amin – rather like the British had done with King Abdullah in Jordan forty years earlier – that Lebanon should not endanger her position in the Arab world by formal good-neighbourly co-existence with Israel. However, Israel's mounting annoyance with Habib's interventions only erupted fully when it became evident that there was no substance to his oft-repeated promise to the Israelis that the United States would arrange, in due course, the evacuation of Syrian troops from Lebanon through a formal agreement between Syria and Lebanon similar to the 17 May accord with Israel.

The American's persuasive powers had stilled Israel's initial doubts. But now, when the Israelis realized that their reservations about Habib's assurances were justified, and that his promises to Israel and to Reagan were without substance and would not be fulfilled, Habib lost all credibility with Israel – as he did, curiously, also with the Syrians, who believed erroneously that he had double-crossed them when Israel attacked the missile sites at a time when Habib was in Damascus waiting for a meeting with Assad. He had thus exhausted his usefulness to President Reagan.

It did not surprise us, therefore, when Habib was replaced soon afterwards by the Deputy Head of the National Security Council, a former marines officer, 'Bud' McFarlane, especially after President Assad had refused to meet Habib again. One of McFarlane's first assignments was to go to Damascus and resume the dialogue between America and Syria. For reasons which we could not fathom at the time, McFarlane's trip was made under condition of total secrecy. Neither Secretary of State Shultz nor the US Ambassador in Damascus was advised of McFarlane's journey. It was not an easy position for McFarlane. His authority over the Pentagon, the State Department and other US agencies, overt and covert, was never defined. The absence of a perceived central authority and visible lack of co-ordination between the many US agencies operating in Lebanon was felt by us on many levels. It led to indecisive and often contradictory American action.

McFarlane was an activist. He believed that the United States could and should use its power to influence events in Lebanon; otherwise there was no point in the US presence. Yet when McFarlane wanted to deploy US naval guns against the Syrian-backed Druze militia in the Shouf mountains to halt the massacre of local Christian communities, he was told by marine commander Garrit that the marines did not take orders from him and that he was not in the recognized chain of command. Other attempted interventions by McFarlane were similarly frustrated, until he returned to Washington in 1983 to take charge of the National Security Council and to become Reagan's adviser on National Security Affairs.

McFarlane had been a compromise choice to either Jean Kirkpatrick or Howard Baker, both senior and influential politicians, while Don Rumsfeld, a former Secretary of Defense (under President Ford), took McFarlane's place as the President's personal representative in the Middle East. It was only after these changes had been made that the battleship *New Jersey* was authorized to fire its giant sixteen-inch guns at Syrian and Druze targets in the mountains, in circumstances neither desired nor chosen by either McFarlane or Rumsfeld.

Rumsfeld was flying to Damascus when he was told that the *New Jersey* was firing salvoes on Syrian targets. Astounded, he asked his companions whether they thought the Syrians would now shoot him out of the sky by way of retaliation? When he landed in Damascus, the Syrians were convinced that the naval bombardment had been co-ordinated with his arrival to add muscle to his visit. He remarked later that the Syrians would never believe that he had not been informed of the decision to open fire. It turned out, however, that the *New Jersey*'s guns had been fired in retaliation for Syrian guns firing at US F-14 reconnaissance flights over Lebanon and not as part of the strategic use of fire-power that Rumsfeld and McFarlane had been advocating in order to deter attacks by the Syrians and their allies on the multi-national forces and on government troops. The huge shells from the sixteen-inch guns missed their targets, for the US commanders had refused to supply spotter-planes to control the naval gunnery. The incident caused more damage to American standing with the Lebanese and further eroded American resolve to achieve the strategic objectives in Lebanon.

Defense Secretary Weinberger's orders to the US marines not to intervene in any way in the war in Lebanon had already caused much confusion; they were, in the event, to become the contributing cause for one of Lebanon's worst massacres, however unintended this may have been. The tragedy of the Shouf could have been prevented had Weinberger been more flexible, or if he had accepted recommendations of Americans on the spot in Beirut as proposed by McFarlane. The ultimate blame for the Shouf calamity, in which tens of thousands of Christians lost their homes and hundreds, possibly thousands, were butchered, rests, however, with the Lebanese themselves.

The tragedy began, unwittingly, with a decision by Israel in the summer of 1983 to withdraw her troops from Lebanon in stages, without waiting any further for a concurrent withdrawal by Syria, or for the implementation of the 17 May Agreement by the Lebanese. This was a consequence of the replacement of the Israeli hardliners – Sharon and Eitan – who had dictated policy at the Ministry of Defence and in the army. Their successors, Moshe Arens and Lieutenant-General Moshe Levy, were made of different fibre.

The new Chief of Staff, understandably, was not interested in the political in-fighting which had, unfortunately, been so much a part of the war in Lebanon. He wanted his troops redeployed so as to reduce casualties, and to cut the size of the army committed to the Lebanese front so that training programmes could be resumed. Neither calculated the cost of their action for the Christian population of the Shouf and for Israel's reputation, as we shall see, among these mountain people, who had put their trust in Israel's continuing presence.

In the summer of 1983, the new Chief of Staff and the new Defence Minister began to argue forcefully for a pull-back of Israeli troops to the more easily defendable line along the Awali River. Begin and the Cabinet agreed, and the Americans and Lebanese were notified of Israel's planned withdrawal. At first both welcomed the proposed Israeli move, but then they were made aware that there was a serious problem regarding our evacuation of the Shouf mountains.

These picturesque but inhospitable hills were the home of Druze and Maronite Christians, who had been warring against each other since contingents of the Christian militia, the Lebanese Forces, had been allowed by Sharon to set up operational bases in the Shouf during the opening phase of the war. The Shouf had been home for Druze and Christians and both now claimed it as rightfully theirs.

The Israeli army found itself in the unenviable position of trying to keep the peace between them and, as was to be expected, found itself caught up in the cross-fire. Understandably, our army wanted to get out and to do so as quickly as possible. But what would happen then? Who would fill the power vacuum: Druze or Christians? The Israelis tried to bring about an understanding between Druze and Christian representatives, which would ensure a peaceful evacuation of the Shouf – and a peaceful aftermath.

The Druze looked upon the Shouf mountains as their heartland, the nucleus of a Druze canton which one day would have autonomous status within a decentralized Lebanon, in much the same way as most Christians considered Mount Liban to the north of Beirut to be their canton. But the Druze claim was complicated by the presence in the Shouf of a sizeable Christian Maronite minority and by the deep antagonism between the Druze leader, Walid Jumblatt, and the Maronite President, Amin Gemayel, on personal and political grounds. It was not easy.

Israel's co-ordinator of Lebanese affairs, Uri Lubrani, spent many hours with the Druze putting together a political formula that would be acceptable to them; other Israelis, myself among them, endeavoured to persuade Amin's entourage to accept the formula. But Amin refused to make any deal with the Druze; he demanded their unconditional allegiance, which would be followed by the entry of the Lebanese army into the Shouf. The Druze refused to accept these conditions. They vowed to oppose the Lebanese army if it attempted to enter the Shouf on these terms.

Undeterred, Lubrani, in co-operation with McFarlane's American team in Lebanon, obtained Druze agreement to allow units of the Lebanese army

THE ISRAELI-LEBANESE AGREEMENT

in the Shouf provided that these were preceded by contingents of the US/French/Italian multi-national force. We felt that a solution had been found which would enable our peaceful evacuation of the Shouf. The departure of Israeli troops had already been twice postponed following American requests. In the late evening before the withdrawal was due to begin, Lubrani brought a Druze emissary to the Israeli Mission in Beirut to finalize arrangements.

While the Druze envoy waited, I met McFarlane, who was to have arranged for the participation of the multi-national force to enter the Shouf with the Lebanese army on the following day, 1 September. We met in the presence of a senior officer of the Lebanese army in the sumptuous Beirut apartment of a wealthy Lebanese politician. McFarlane was tense and downcast. In dry, almost pedantic tones he said that he did not have the authority to allow units of the multi-national force into the Shouf. He understood that we were trying to avert terrible and unnecessary bloodshed, and was impressed that we had a Druze emissary not a mile away awaiting his answer. But the purpose and tasks of the multi-national force had been strictly defined and these did not include chaperoning the Lebanese army into the Shouf. The answer was 'No.' We learnt later that McFarlane's positive recommendation supporting our proposals had been vetoed by Defense Secretary Weinberger. He would not listen to the arguments and pleas by McFarlane and his staff, Commander Durr and Howard Teicher of the National Security Council.

The withdrawal of the Israeli army could no longer be reversed and it evacuated the Shouf according to plan; no one took its place. The Lebanese army made no move to protect the Christian villages of the Shouf. As a result, armed Druze villagers easily overpowered the local Christian militia; entire Christian villages were sacked and destroyed, and their desperate inhabitants forced to flee, looking in vain for a safe haven. The churches in the south and in Beirut were crowded to overflowing with thousands of fearful refugees. The less fortunate were massacred. A nod from Weinberger to McFarlane would have saved them.

The tragedy of the Shouf was caused by a combination of circumstances: undue haste by Israel's High Command, who wanted to get out of Lebanon in a hurry; lack of sensitivity and responsibility of Lebanon's President and Government, who could have come to terms with the Druze, but refused to do so; the refusal of the American Secretary of Defense, Caspar Weinberger, to permit the use of the multi-national force for a humanitarian purpose; and, principally of course, the Druze themselves, who, in their frenzy to rid themselves of the Christian minority in the Shouf, perpetrated terrible acts of cruelty and brutality. No one was prepared to stop them.

It is a sad reflection on our world of double standards, but the fact remains that very little notice was taken of this massacre of Christians by the Druze. Many more Christians were slaughtered here than Palestinians in the notorious Sabra and Shatilla massacre, yet there was hardly a Christian voice of protest raised anywhere. Could the reason be that different standards were applied in this case and that the Lebanese Christians had, after all, long been singled out as the villains by the western media and politicians: this time they had no Palestinian stick to hand with which to beat the Israelis?

There was, however, another major aspect of the Shouf débâcle. The northern fringe of the Shouf is bounded by the Beirut–Damascus highway, its western hills overlook the outskirts of Beirut and the coastal road that connects the capital with the south. The Shouf is, to a large extent, the key to the strategic mastery of Lebanon. By surrendering the Shouf in this precipitate way without getting anything in return, Israel lost her position of power to influence the political outcome of the war; and the Syrians, despite their previous failures, won by default.

Not long before, Begin had insisted on a simultaneous withdrawal of Syrian and Israeli forces to be preceded by the departure of the PLO from all of Lebanon. His only point of pressure on the Syrians was his hold on the vital highway linking Beirut with Syria. By releasing the Israeli army's grip on it, and on the hills surrounding Beirut, Begin sacrificed all hope of influencing the outcome of the Lebanese War, on which so much effort had been expended and so much blood spilt. Fatigue, internal dissensions and leadership crisis had all taken their toll in transforming an Israeli victory into apparent defeat.

The Israeli departure from the Shouf in September 1983 helped the Syrians to achieve their one overriding aim, the abrogation of the 17 May Israeli–Lebanese Agreement. However, they still had to overcome the presence of the US marines in Beirut and also Amin's obstinate refusal to repudiate the Agreement, as the Syrians had demanded, instead of only refusing to sign the instruments of ratification. The Syrians addressed both problems in characteristically typical manner. With the heights of the Shouf on the outskirts of Beirut in Druze hands came the inevitable clash between the Muslim militias, supported by Syrian and Palestinian units, and the Lebanese army. At the same time, the Shia Amal militia defeated the Lebanese Army's 6th Brigade and took command of large parts of western and southern Beirut. The Druze, in turn, overcame the Lebanese 4th Brigade on the coastal road. Most of the Lebanese troops fled south towards Sidon, leaving behind their weapons and heavy equipment.

Thus, in one swift offensive the Syrian-backed Druze and Syrian Shia 'proxies' made a mockery of the Lebanese army, which American military personnel had been so painstakingly training and equipping. Indeed, one of the major differences between Israel and the United States had centred on their assessment of the ability of the Lebanese army to protect a strong central government. This was the basis of an argument in the conference chamber of the State Department in Washington during a visit there by our then Foreign Minister Shamir. The American officer charged with training the Lebanese army, supported by the CIA's Middle East expert Bob Ames, argued forcefully that the solution to the Lebanese imbroglio lay in strengthening the Lebanese army. The army would then restore order and take over the areas to be evacuated by Israel and Syria. The Israelis responded no less strongly that the Americans were living in a dream-world; the Lebanese army would split apart along communal seams at the first sign of crisis – which it did when Shi'i soldiers and officers of the Lebanese army's 6th Brigade refused to fight the Shi'i Amal militia; some deserted to Amal with their arms.

President Gemayel therefore had to rely on the Christian 7th Brigade to stem the critical Druze onslaught at Souk el-Gharb, the gateway to Beirut; and in the decisive test in 1984, the Lebanese army was no match against the Syrian-backed militias. The whole Lebanese governmental regime was in danger of total collapse. However, the Syrians, now conscious of their regained position of strength, agreed to a cease-fire engineered, with strong American support, by their pay-masters, the Saudis. The Syrians could now dictate terms after the victory of their proxies, the Shi'i and the Druze militias. They were fully aware, however, that it would not be in the Syrian interest to let all semblance of Lebanese central authority disintegrate. Accordingly, one of the conditions of the cease-fire called for a national dialogue between the leaders of all principal Lebanese factions, who were summoned to attend a conference at which representatives from Syria and Saudi Arabia would, in effect, determine future Lebanese policies.

Amin was to invite the National Salvation Front – Walid Jumblatt, Rashid Karame and Suleiman Franjiyeh; the Christian Lebanese Front – Camille Chamoun and Pierre Gemayel; the Amal Movement – Nabih Berri; and also, *ex officio*, three veteran leaders – Saeb Salaam, Adel Usayran and Raymond Edde (who declined the invitation). Some of these men – Karame, Franjiyeh, Chamoun, Salaam, Gemayel and Usayran – had played leading roles as Presidents, Prime Ministers and heads of political movements. They were the pillars on which the Republic of Lebanon had been built. Yet it took them a whole month of squabbling just to decide on where to meet. The opposition refused to come to the presidential palace, the obvious venue; the Syrians objected to having the dialogue in Saudi Arabia and, in the end, there being no place in Lebanon or in the entire Middle East acceptable to all, the conference met in far-away, neutral Geneva.

I was in Geneva when the group convened on 23 September 1983 and met some of the participants and Richard Fairbanks, the US envoy who had worked with McFarlane and with Rumsfeld in monitoring the events in Lebanon. From the outset the conference was dominated by the Syrian 'observers', especially her Foreign Minister, Abdel Halim Khaddam. He insisted that the principal item on the agenda should be the abrogation of the Lebanese 17 May Agreement with Israel.

The pressure was concentrated on Amin. Its focal point was a long way from Geneva, at Souk el-Gharb, where the Syrians, Palestinians and Druze were poised, waiting for the signal from Geneva to resume their onslaught on Beirut. The Christian leaders, President Gemayel, former President Chamoun and Pierre Gemayel, the President's father and mentor, were hard-pressed to submit there and then to the Syrians' demands. With difficulty they gained some time so that Amin could consult with President Reagan before taking a final decision. The conference adjourned with a request to Amin to 'carry out the necessary international measures and contacts to end the Israeli occupation and to ensure Lebanon's full and absolute sovereignty over all its territory'.

Syria's next move, therefore, had to be against the Americans – and against the French, who were also providing support for Amin: it was devastating in its savagery. On 23 October 1983, a week before the Geneva conference reconvened, a truck laden with explosives smashed into the US marines barracks in Beirut killing 241 marines. A second truck filled with explosives crashed into the building housing the French contingent of the multi-national force, killing fifty-nine French soldiers. The American presence in Lebanon had been challenged. Either the Americans now took up this challenge – and seek out the perpetrators of the attack on the marines and circumscribe the activities of opposition militia hostile to the Amin Government – or get out. Given the outlook of Secretary of Defense Weinberger, it was a foregone conclusion what the choice would be; the Americans departed – ingloriously.

In order to help the Americans make a decision, a second attack was mounted in similar fashion as the first: this time the target was the US Embassy in Beirut, where sixty-three people, including seventeen Americans, lost their lives. At the time, the Israeli–Lebanese negotiating teams were closeted in the conference room of the Four Seasons Hotel in Nathaniya, immersed in the intricacies of finding acceptable security arrangements for southern Lebanon. Morris Draper, the head of the US delegation at these talks, passed me a note while we were negotiating, which I still have. It said: 'Bob Ames is among the dead.' Ames, the CIA Station Chief in Beirut, was one of the most knowledgeable Americans on the Middle East and particularly on Lebanese affairs. He had been one of the central personalities in the making of Washington's Middle East policies over the years. We had spent many hours discussing and arguing with him. Now, he was one more victim of the Lebanese carnage at a time when America could ill-afford to lose him.

Four months after the terror attack on the US marines headquarters in Beirut, on 26 February 1984, the marines withdrew from Lebanon. Their departure meant that Amin had come to the end of the road. He was on his own, left by the Americans at the mercy of the Syrians and the terrorists. Within a matter of days Amin was in Damascus; and on 5 March, he announced the formal abrogation of the 17 May Agreement with Israel. By September 1984, the entire American military and naval presence in Lebanon had been liquidated by Defense Secretary Weinberger against the advice of the National Security Council. A frustrated Don Rumsfeld, the President's personal representative, who had won the respect of Israelis and Arabs against overwhelming odds, returned to Washington and was not replaced. With his departure, the United States ceased to have any part in the shaping of Lebanese affairs.

The American departure at this critical time was difficult to justify and even more difficult to understand. The Syrians, their principal antagonist, were experiencing great problems. President Assad was recovering from a heart attack; an internal power struggle was in progress in Damascus between Assad's brother Rifaat and the Alawi generals, Assad's principal supporters in the Syrian army; and the French were bombing Syrian positions in the Beka'a Valley in retaliation for the loss of French lives in Beirut. The Syrians were in total disarray. A more determined American stand, of the sort that Rumsfeld and McFarlane had proposed, could have transformed the political balance of power in Lebanon. Instead, the Syrians found that they were confronted by American forces imbued with acute withdrawal symptoms. Despite their initial disbelief and evident weakness, the Syrians were encouraged by this collapse of the American 'front' to show their then largely hypothetical muscle. It sufficed. In that deadly game of poker, the Americans had blinked first.

By the end of 1984, the situation in Lebanon had been radically transformed – one is inclined to say catastrophically. The Americans, with their ships and marines, had slipped ignominiously away, leaving behind the memory of political and military ineffectiveness and of almost 300 dead Americans, while the perpetrators of the terror attacks against them remained unpunished and triumphant. The Israelis, also, had gone from the Beirut scene. Their Mission in Dbaye had closed down, their patrols had disappeared from the streets of Beirut and from the nearby heights, and the IDF – so feared and dominant – was conducting rearguard operations far away to the south, on the banks of the Awali River.

Amin was left alone, isolated in his dismal palace in Ba'abda, President in name only of a country tearing itself apart; a country in shambles etched in beautiful surroundings. Yet large parts of the country were still occupied by Syrian forces. Damascus was calling the tune. And one big political 'achievement' which the Israelis could show for their costly war effort – the 17 May Agreement – had been nullified by a Lebanese President demoralized, as it were, primarily by the American and Israeli policies of retreat.

As head of the Israeli delegation negotiating with the Lebanese I had made a great effort to produce a viable agreement, freely accepted by Israel and by Lebanon. Had it all been wasted?

What we had concluded at Khalde was no mean achievement. We had signed a virtual peace agreement between Israel and Lebanon, and had signalled to each other our terms for peaceful co-existence. How else could one interpret the first two paragraphs of Article 1 of the Agreement?

1. The Parties agree and undertake to respect the sovereignty, political independence and territorial integrity of each other. They consider the existing international boundary between Lebanon and Israel inviolable.

2. The Parties confirm that the state of war between Lebanon and Israel has been terminated and no longer exists.

In return for the Agreement, Lebanon had obtained Israel's promise to withdraw to the international frontier, which they could justly claim to be a 'troop withdrawal agreement'. All the same, the other articles of the Agreement changed the previous state of hostility into good neighbourly relations.

The Parties ... undertake to settle their disputes by peaceful means ... [Article 2]

The territory of each Party will not be used as a base for hostile or terrorist activity against the other Party [Article 4]

The Parties will abstain from any form of hostile propaganda against each other [Article 5]

Upon entry into force of the present Agreement a Joint Liaison Committee will be established by the Parties ... [it] will address itself on a continuing basis to the development of mutual relations between Lebanon and Israel, *inter alia the regulation of the movement of goods, products and persons, communications etc.* [Article 8 – author's italics]

Each of the two Parties will take ... all measures necessary for the abrogation of treaties, laws and regulations deemed to be in conflict with the present Agreement [Article 9]

But more important than any single paragraph in the Agreement was its implicit overall message to the Lebanese: it provided Lebanon with an Israeli guarantee; in effect, it underwrote the independence of Lebanon. The Lebanese negotiators understood this when they signed the Agreement; the great majority of the Lebanese Parliament understood it when they approved the Agreement; the Syrian President Assad understood it when he showed his determination to do everything possible to prevent the ratification of the Agreement, which would thus ensure Lebanon's independence.

Without the Agreement and with 50,000 Syrian troops occupying more than half of Lebanon after the Israeli withdrawal, the hapless Lebanese had really no option but to submit to Syrian demands. The lukewarm and negative attitude towards the Agreement taken by the western powers, despite the energetic personal support from Secretary of State Shultz, and for which his departmental officials and ministerial colleagues showed no enthusiasm, was another disturbing element in the situation which merits further consideration.

The abrogation of the Agreement by Amin did not achieve any of the results or consequences which had been promised to the Lebanese. The Syrians did not go away, and communal and sectarian strife in Lebanon did not lessen; but both the United States and Israel began to distance themselves from the conflict in Beirut. Lebanon was left to her own devices and the Syrians were given free reign to do as they pleased in a country that was no longer able even to elect a new president when Amin's term of office expired. Lebanon's independence became a mockery. For long without a president, but with two opposing Prime Ministers – one Christian and one Muslim – and with virtually no army, Lebanon had ceased to be an effective sovereign state. When, finally, a new President, railroaded by the Syrians, was sworn in in 1990, the loss of effectual sovereignty was underlined.

President Elias Hrawi had been virtually unknown in Lebanon. He was chosen by the Syrians as a person who would follow unswervingly the dictates of his Syrian masters. Under his rule – and in particular after the independent-minded commander of the Lebanese army, General Michel Aoun, was ousted in a bloody battle between Lebanese loyalists and Syrian troops – Lebanon lost all semblance of independence. She had to all intents and purposes been transformed into a Syrian colony.

As I have shown in this account of the rise and fall of hope, it could have been otherwise, had Lebanon's President Gemayel acted with greater political foresight and had his western allies supported him. The 17 May Agreement with Israel was no dream, but it had come too late. Its backers – the United States and Israel – had lost their sense of purpose to help the Lebanese to peaceful co-existence. The Lebanese leaders had shown that they had no desire for a real settlement since Bashir Gemayel's tragic assassination by the Syrians in September 1982. His successor, his brother Amin, was no match for Syrian President Assad, who was prepared to destroy Beirut and its Maronite Christian population rather than allow the Lebanese to go their own independent way.

13

The Reckoning

As a civil servant, not as a politician, I had been at the nerve-centre of Israel's relations with Lebanon during its critical decade from 1976 onwards. It gave me an insight into the formal and informal development of our relations with the Lebanese and with the attendant American, Palestinian, Egyptian and Jordanian overtones. When I look back now on this decade, I am astonished at the manner in which, at the end of it, all the principals felt compelled to abandon our Lebanese enterprise. We simply cut our losses without attempting to salvage any political gains. The Lebanese morass, as it has so often been called, proved to be too strong for us. Yet a different ending would have ushered in a more promising prospect for Lebanon and Israel, which would have compelled the Syrian and Palestinian leaders to reconsider their position in relation to Israel with a much greater degree of realism.

I had few, if any, illusions left when we finally began to negotiate the agreement that was to be the formal end of Israel's war in Lebanon. Many weeks had already been wasted in pointless haggling about unattainable demands and by constant petty objections from the Lebanese and by more subtle obstructions from the American officials. Thus, when we did finally settle down to serious negotiations, alternately at Khalde and Kiryat Shmona, I found myself presiding over a bubbling witches' cauldron of conflicting interests and endless objections.

It was disconcerting to find that these objections were not concerned with the kind of peace agreement that was realistically possible, but rather the opposite. It was no less distressing to find that the Americans were advising the Lebanese President to make haste slowly, to think twice before concluding an agreement with Israel, and to consider the importance of Lebanon's relations with the Arab world before embarking on a rash embrace of the Israelis.

We know from the Lebanese that American and French officials pressurized Lebanese leaders not to commit themselves to any kind of exclusive agreement with Israel. This was not a new policy: we now have the authoritative evidence that some of the leading American officials taking part in the Camp David negotiations for a peace agreement with Egypt approached President Sadat privately and advised him that in the opinion of the United States there was no need to sign the proposed agreement with Begin; he could back off and say he was not prepared to sign until there was also a satisfactory agreement with the Palestinians.* Sadat shouted at the Americans that he did not need such advice. He could not do to the Egyptian people what the Americans wanted and abandon Sinai for the will-o'-the-wisp of a Palestinian settlement.

Unfortunately, President Gemayel did not enjoy the same position of strength as did Sadat. Sadat won peace and Sinai for Egypt – and respect. Amin lost the peace and Lebanon, and won only pity from his American, French and Arab 'allies'. Sadat may have paid with his life for what he did for Egypt; Amin was forced to pay with the lives of thousands of innocent Lebanese for what he failed to do for Lebanon, because he was forsaken by his allies.

The fact remains that our 17 May Agreement with Lebanon was an important achievement and not some inconsiderate irrelevance, as so many Israeli and western 'historians' and politicians have downgraded it. Whenever Lebanon – Christian, Sunni, Shi'i and Druze – regains her allotted role in the Levant, it will have to be on the basis of terms akin to those we agreed on 17 May at Khalde. For these terms alone can guarantee the people of Lebanon their separate and national existence alongside a strong and friendly Israel. It is tragic both for Lebanon and for Israel that, but for the many mistakes described in these chapters, this could have been one of the positive results of the war on which Israel embarked in June 1982.

The war in Lebanon was in many respects Israel's most controversial war. Israel had no choice in 1948 or in 1973; she had to fight or die. However, 1982 was in a class by itself; the alternative here was not as self-evident as in 1948 or 1973. Nor was it like 1956 or 1967 – justifiable pre-emptive war – about which it is possible to argue the pros and cons. The 1982 war against the PLO was entirely different; it was a war with political objectives without precedent in the conventional history of Israel. The alternative to war was not death, but a slow strangulation. Lebanon was, in fact, as much a victim of the PLO in 1982 as was Israel. It was no idle claim by Israel that the IDF, when it moved into Lebanon in June 1982, was in fact liberating the Lebanese villagers from their PLO overlords. Israel was then on the same side as the Lebanese. Unfortunately, there was no way of expelling the PLO from Lebanese territory without inflicting hurt on the Lebanese; the PLO had seen to that and the Lebanese in those first months understood it and were prepared to accept it.

The welcome given to Israeli troops in Shi'i and Christian villages in southern Lebanon was a measure of the hope the Israeli move had inspired among the local Arab population, which had been mercilessly harassed and exploited by the Palestinians. None of this was shown on television and yet it was one of the most significant elements of Israel's entry into Lebanon.

* See interview with William Quandt by Zahid Mahmoud in 'Sadat and Camp David Reappraised', *Journal of Palestine Studies*, no. 57, Autumn 1985, p. 77; see also p. 109 above.

Many thousands of Christian and Shi'i villagers, who had fled or had been driven north because of the PLO take-over of their homes, now returned from Beirut and other places of refuge to their ancestral homes where the Israelis had replaced the PLO.

It was one of the pitfalls of the war in Lebanon – especially for the Israelis – that the prolonged stay of the IDF and the very real concerns for tactical security considerations turned this very valuable goodwill into active hostility. The enormous political implications of Muslim goodwill were sacrificed on the altar of security. This sad fact was compounded by lack of imagination and understanding on the part of Israel's defence and security establishment, which had been prone to ride roughshod over political needs which did not conform to immediate security imperatives.

But if Israel's leaders had to submit themselves to some serious soul-searching into their lapses in the Lebanon operation, this was even more true of the PLO and its leaders, especially Arafat, the 'chairman'. He and his PLO colleagues exploited their Lebanese diaspora to the full. They enjoyed the fleshpots of Beirut, the high living of the huge bureaucracy they put together and the power they wielded over the weak Lebanese. Hugely satisfied with their new home in the Levant, they were not prepared to live modestly as guests, but insisted on flaunting in many ways that they and not the Lebanese were the real masters of the house.

The PLO was riding high in Lebanon, dictating policy – so it seemed – to the Lebanese, the Syrians, the Jordanians and even to Begin's Israel. There appeared to be no limit to PLO power; even President Reagan sent a special envoy, Philip Habib, to treat – albeit indirectly – with Arafat and seek his terms for agreeing to a cease-fire on Israel's Galilean northern frontier. The Soviet leadership under Leonid Brezhnev was supplying sophisticated weapons and rather less sophisticated encouragement to the PLO. When, in July 1981, Arafat concluded a cease-fire agreement with Habib, for which the Americans obtained Israel's acceptance, Arafat had reached the peak of his power. That was how it looked to him, to his PLO fighters, to the Americans and to Israel – and perhaps also to the Soviet leaders. The PLO was rich in financial resources and had massive reserves secured in Europe and America. Brimming over with self-confidence and self-satisfaction, Arafat and his colleagues felt that there was no limit to what they could do in Lebanon. But there was a limit, and in the end the Lebanese bubble burst with tragic consequences for the Palestinians.

The Lebanese War was the PLO's moment of truth. Arafat's bombast about his political victories and the longest war against Israel impressed no one at the end, least of all the Palestinians. The war had demonstrated the PLO's isolation in the Arab world. Having manoeuvred the Palestinians into Lebanon, they were gladly abandoned there by their Arab brethren, left to the mercy of the Israelis. Had they been left to the Syrians or Jordanians, they would have fared far, far worse. As the very perceptive PLO historian at Columbia University, Rashid Khalidi, wrote after the war in the PLO *Journal of Palestine Studies*, very few Palestinians had any residual illusion regarding the Arab regimes such as they harboured in the mid-1970s. These had been dispelled by the Lebanese War. There was now a much more sober assessment of what could be achieved. In Khalidi's view: 'If the Arab regimes are our enemies at times nearly as deadly as Israel, then certain things follow which were not obvious when it was believed that the Arab situation could perhaps be changed in favour of support for Palestinian nationalism.'

Khalidi adds a further cautionary warning which deserves attention not only by Palestinians; it applies to all concerned with the future of the Middle East, be it in peace or in war. It must be remembered, he says, 'the current configurations of the Arab world are not set in stone. The Arab regimes (with the exception of that in the Sudan) have been in existence for at least fifteen years. Many are unlikely to survive in their present form for very much longer.' It is against this background in the Arab world that future policy has to be attuned. That was written in 1985; time may be running out rather than marching on.

The Palestinians in Judea, Samaria and Gaza were not slow to learn the lesson of the abandonment of the PLO in Lebanon by the Arab states. Their subsequent uprising in December 1987 saved the PLO from the consequences it suffered in Beirut.

As for us, the Israelis, we need only ask ourselves what would have happened after 1981 if there had been no war in Lebanon; and no halting of the PLO's domination and control of Lebanon. Even so, Arafat continued to ride high, to intimidate powerless Arab regimes and to persuade the Americans that they could get results only by treating with him, in the hope of yet bludgeoning the Lebanese into submission and the Israelis into American-sponsored inaction. The cost of the war to Israel was considerable, but the cost of inaction would have been enormous.

We made many mistakes on every level during the war in Lebanon and during the negotiations for the 17 May Agreement. Yet, it was, in the final analysis, this unconsummated agreement that set the seal on the campaign. It demonstrated Israel's real intentions, it signalled Israel's close link with the United States and it set out the terms addressed to any Arab country on which it could achieve a settlement with Israel. In the event, Israel disengaged from the Lebanese swamp because the cost of staying was too high and pressure from our friends in the United States was too great. But, in truth, there was no longer any need for a rationale for Israel's departure. The people of Israel felt that they had had enough. The pendulum of friendly intervention had swung to the opposite extreme and 'Lebanon' had become a dirty word in Israel. Yet, when all is said, Israel held a unique opportunity for peace in the Levant in the palm of her hand – and she let it slip.

PART 3
Iran and Iraq

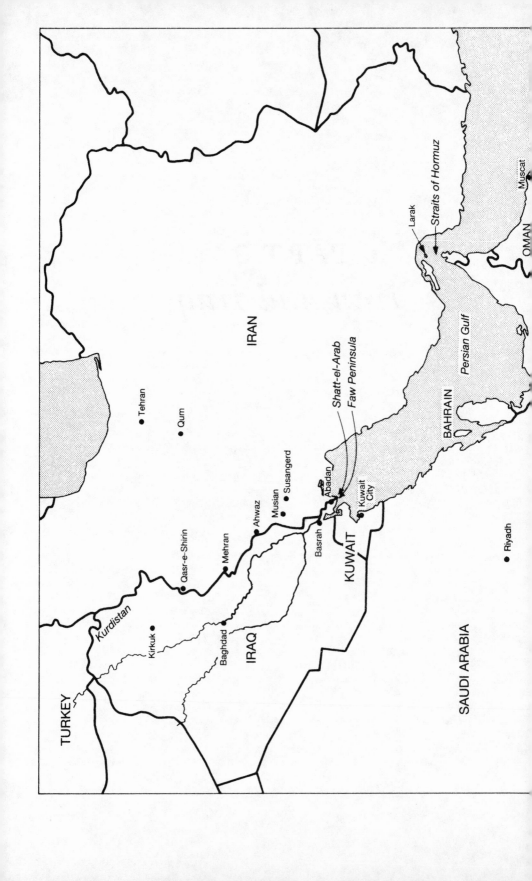

14
The Kurdish Option
1965–79

THE KURDISH PROVINCES of Iraq are renowned for their majestic beauty. Imposing mountains, barely accessible, look down on the lush green valleys below; villages nestle into the hillsides, half hidden in the contours of the mountains. In spring, the air is heavy with fragrant scents, as myriads of wild flowers carpet the fields and almond trees burst into blossom. The mountain streams rush down the hillsides, swollen with the waters of melting snow.

It was in springtime that we first met the fabled leader of the Kurds, Mullah Mustafa Barzani. The meeting took place in a small hut, which was bare except for heavy carpets, on which the Mullah sat, cross-legged, facing the Israelis. They had been sitting in that position for several hours – no mean feat in itself – discussing regional affairs and possible Israeli–Kurdish co-operation. They sipped endless glasses of tea, sucking the hot liquid through lumps of sugar clamped between their teeth in the old Russian custom. Outside, in the pale moonlight, the snow lay piled high.

This was in May 1965. The Israelis had been sent into Iraq to make contact with the Mullah. It had not been an easy assignment, because the Iraqis would not have taken kindly to an Israeli caught wandering around inside their country.

Iraq was the most aggressive Arab state in her verbal attacks against Israel. She was the only Arab state that had fought against the establishment of Israel in 1948 and had refused to sign an armistice agreement to end the war against Israel. Thus, Israel had a considerable affinity with the Kurds, who, under the leadership of the Mullah, had taken up arms against Baghdad after their demands for autonomy had been rejected. By 1965, the Kurdish insurrection had grown into a full-scale war, with a large part of the Iraqi army engaged in a determined effort to dislodge the Kurdish forces – the Pesh Merga – from the mountains. For Israel, there were obvious advantages in having an ally inside Iraq and with the Iraqi army committed far from Israel's eastern front, where its presence might have presented a threat to our security.

Any doubts that Israel had about the way the Kurdish leader would react to our proposal for a regular contact were soon dispelled. The Mullah understood Israel's position, and Israel understood his difficulties. The Kurds are Sunni Muslim, but apart from that they have nothing else in common with the Arabs among whom they live. They are of Aryan, and not Semitic, origin; their language is akin to Farsi, not Arabic. They consider the Arabs as enemies who have prevented them by force from living according to Kurdish custom and tradition. The Mullah, therefore, had no hesitation in dealing with Israel. In fact, it was evident that he knew a great deal about Israeli affairs and he admired our achievements. But above all else, his men were short of arms, food and money. He desperately needed outside help. An alliance between Israel and the Kurds was thus speedily consummated.

Very little of what was happening in northern Iraq was known in the outside world. The Kurds had no broadcasting facilities to publicize their battles and their victories, while the Iraqis were understandably reserved about their defeats; and very few journalists ventured into this inhospitable region without any of the customary conveniences to report an out-of-the-way war of little concern to readers back at home. The Iraqis had deployed over two divisions – some 25,000 men – against the Kurds. However, despite their overwhelming superiority in numbers and fire power, they made little headway against the Mullah's partisan army of 12,000 tribesmen; these had kept the Iraqi army at bay and caused it heavy losses.

Thus, in Jerusalem, the decision was taken to give the Kurds the help they needed. There was, however, another reason for Israel's willingness to help the Kurds, for there existed at that time a close relationship between Israel and the Shah of Iran. In the early days of her existence, Israel had sought to befriend the non-Arab periphery of the Middle East – Turkey, Iran and Ethiopia, as well as non-Arab Sunni and Shi'i minorities in the region. It was an understandable policy considering the uninhibited hostility of the Arab countries.

This de facto alliance with Iran was very much reciprocal. Iran was the largest non-Arab country in the Middle East and she had a century's old tradition of hostility with the Arabs. It was thus only natural that the leaders of Iran should look upon Israel as a potential ally with similar strategic aims. Both feared a too powerful and homogeneous Sunni Arab Middle East. Israel did not want an Iraqi army reinforcing Syria and Jordan in a future war; Iran did not want an Iraqi army massed along her southern frontier, where the Shatt-el-Arab waterway and the oil-rich, largely Arabic-speaking province of Khuzistan have been two very real points of friction between Iran and Iraq.

Iran was therefore interested in keeping the flame of rebellion burning in Iraqi Kurdistan and thus weakening her unfriendly neighbour in the west. This self-evident identity of interests was the strategic basis for the increasingly intimate ties between Iran and Israel.

So began a close co-operation between Israel and Iran, which enabled us to send aid to the Iraqi Kurds via Iran. Weapons, medical supplies, doctors and instructors made their way from Israel to Iran and from there to the Kurdish front.* Kurds came to Israel for training, also by way of

* Israel's Prime Minister, Menachem Begin, disclosed officially on 29 September 1980 that Israel had

Iran. Iran and Israel made common cause in this activity on behalf of the Kurds and, as relations between Iran and Iraq became more strained because of tension along the border-country in the south, the Iranians progressively increased their involvement with the Kurds in the north.

By the early 1970s, the south had become one of the focal points of tension as Iraq was conducting a massive campaign to subvert the population of Khuzistan bordering the vital Shatt-el-Arab waterway. The terrain and the circumstances were ideal for such propaganda and covert operations. There was no love lost between large segments of this population and the authorities in Tehran. There was also much cross-frontier movement in this region, with tens of thousands of citizens of one country living and working in the other. The Marsh Arabs living and working in the Iranian marshes to the east of Basrah used to cross daily into Iraq to sell their delicious flat cakes of water buffalo milk curd, a highly sought-after delicacy on the Iraqi side. Iraqi and Iranian agents mingled with this cross-border traffic as a result, and the intelligence war waged by both sides reached an intensity rarely seen elsewhere.

Khuzistan, or – as Iraq renamed it – Arabistan, was a prize of exceptional value, the heartland of Iran's oilfields, with Abadan, then the world's largest oil refinery, as the Jewel in the Crown. Iraq's Baathist regime of army officers, headed by President Hassan el-Bakr and his ambitious and ruthless nephew, General Saddam Hussein, developed a grand design in which Iraq would become master of the immensely rich oil region comprising Khuzistan and Kuwait together with the Basrah fields of southern Iraq.

Mastery over Khuzistan and Kuwait would transform Iraq into the leading oil power in the Middle East, with the resources enabling her to dominate the entire Persian Gulf area and the OPEC oil market. This grand design was translated into a forceful anti-western foreign policy. The Iraqis befriended the military Marxist regime of South Yemen and sent aid in money and weapons to the Dhofar rebels waging war against the Sultan of Oman and his pro-British regime in Muscat. They threatened and bullied the Kuwaitis and championed every movement directed against the conservative, pro-western Governments in the region.

Unsurprisingly, this policy attracted immediate support from the Soviet Union. In 1972, Bakr's deputy, Saddam Hussein, visited Moscow; two months later, a treaty of friendship and co-operation was signed between the Soviet Union and Iraq. Baghdad was casting an ever-lengthening shadow over the Gulf states as their rulers identified Baghdad, reinforced by its treaty with the Soviet Union, as the principal threat to their regimes.

At the same time, the Iranians were not idle. The Shah had his own ambitions. While Iraq had adopted Soviet military doctrine and went shopping for her military hardware in Moscow, the Shah turned to Wash-

provided the Kurds with money, arms and instructors and had assigned military advisers to help the Kurds. Israeli newspapers reported on 30 September 1980 that Mullah Mustafa Barzani had paid several secret visits to Israel. For a good collation of press reports on Israel's relations with the Kurds, see Jasim M. Abdulghani, *Iraq and Iran: The Years of Crisis* (New York, 1984), pp. 145–7.

ington. Buoyed by the windfall of soaring oil prices, which transformed Iran's economy after the Yom Kippur War, the Shah embarked on a buying spree for sophisticated military equipment. In 1973, Iran's income from oil exports had been worth $5 billion; two years later, by 1975, the annual oil income had increased fourfold to $20 billion; and in 1977, on the eve of the Shah's fall, it peaked at $24 billion.

The Shah's voracious appetite for high-technology weapons knew no bounds; it was matched only by the clearly unlimited flow of arms that Washington was happy and more than willing to sell to Iran on very favourable terms, including advance payments.

After meeting the Shah in Tehran in 1972, President Nixon gave orders to the US Defense Department to make available whatever arms and equipment the Shah desired to purchase – with the exception of nuclear weapons. In the five years that followed Nixon's visit, the Shah placed orders for an estimated $12 billion worth of the most advanced weapons in the United States' inventory, and he was still hungry for more.* The Americans were now content to let the Shah take responsibility for the security of the Persian Gulf area, all the more so as the British were preparing to withdraw their military forces from 'East of Suez' at the end of 1971. This planned British departure threatened to leave a power vacuum in one of the most volatile regions of the world.

The Americans welcomed the Shah's intervention and were happy to help Iran rearm with such profitable consequences for American defence industries. It was an ideal situation for the Americans. They were deeply disturbed by what they considered to be Soviet and radical encroachments into the region, but they were reluctant to commit American forces to take over when the British withdrew. The Shah's eagerness to expend billions of dollars and mobilize hundreds of thousands of Iranians, in order to safeguard the Gulf region, was to them the perfect answer.

The Shah was pleased by the far-reaching understanding he had concluded. American advisers, experts, instructors and technicians went to Iran by the thousand – by 1976, there were a reputed 24,000 Americans working in Iran.

Iran, in fact, had become one of the most valued and trusted allies of the United States with one of the largest armies outside NATO. By 1975, Iran had 250,000 men on active service and another 500,000 in the reserves. She was spending a greater proportion of her Gross National Product on defence than any other country except Israel – three times greater than that of the United States and four times more than the British.

The Shah took his new responsibility with great seriousness. He became a kind of patron and protector of the traditional regimes in the Gulf, who saw him as a form of insurance against radical and Iraqi attempts at

* See, for example, the testimony of Gary Sick, an Iranian expert who had served on the Staff of the White House Security Council: *All Fall Down – America's Fateful Encounter with Iran* (London, 1985), p. 15.

subversion, especially in Kuwait and in the Dhofar region of Oman. There was, however, a difference of perspective between Tehran and Washington. The Americans saw the Shah's role essentially in global and Cold War terms, while the Shah became increasingly preoccupied by what Iran considered to be the aggressive expansionism and subversion of the Baathist regime in Iraq. In particular, this found expression in the long-standing conflict with Iraq over freedom of shipping through the Shatt-el-Arab waterway, a vital link with the Gulf for both countries.

Persian and Arab hostility has a long history. Its origins are shrouded in the mists of the distant past, but the battle of Qadisiya, at which the Arab forces roundly defeated their Persian enemy in AD 638, is taught in all its real and apocryphal details to every Iraqi child and turned into a contemporary reality. Similarly, Iranian children learn that the Iranian national poet, Ferdowsi, who lived in the tenth century, had claimed that he had written all his works without resorting to a single word of Arabic origin.

This antipathy between Semitic Arabs and Aryan Persians received new impetus in the sixteenth century, when Shah Ismail founded the Safavid dynasty and declared Shi'ism to be its official religion. The Shia Persian and Sunni Ottoman Empires were soon in conflict over rival claims to religious truth and valuable territory. For a brief period, in the early seventeenth century, much of the land now known as Iraq – including Baghdad – fell under Persian occupation.

Throughout this period of tension between the Persian and Ottoman Empires, the question of sovereignty over the Shatt-el-Arab did not pose a problem; the waterway was accepted as the southern boundary between the two Empires and both used it freely. It was only with the arrival of the European powers on the scene – Great Britain and Russia – that the boundary on the Shatt-el-Arab became a subject of dispute. As a result of this outside pressure, a series of treaties regulating boundaries were concluded in the nineteenth and early twentieth centuries. These favoured the Ottoman Empire at the expense of the Persian.

It could be argued that most modern boundary disputes in the Middle East, Africa and Asia arose when clashing colonial power interests were injected into hitherto harmless local quarrels. This was the case in the Shatt-el-Arab. After the First World War, the British annexed large parts of the Ottoman Empire, including the territory which later became known as Iraq. The Iraqi port of Basrah, linked to the Persian Gulf by the Shatt-el-Arab, became an important link in British imperial communications with the Indian Empire. The number of British ships using the waterway far outnumbered those of all other nations combined. When, in the 1930s, the Iranians demanded that the international boundary be moved to the middle of the navigable channel of the Shatt-el-Arab – to the so-called Thalweg – it was the British more than the Iraqis who opposed this. They feared that, if Persia remained neutral in any future war, they might refuse passage of British warships to Basrah. It was an eventuality the British were not willing to risk.

It was, however, not until the late 1960s that these differences between Iran and Iraq assumed crisis proportions. In Iraq, the new Baathi regime was emphasizing the pan-Arab nature of the Baathi doctrine, while in Iran the massive build-up of the army and navy produced a new self-confidence and a much greater assertiveness. Inevitably these clashed. Moreover, by now the Shatt-el-Arab dispute had assumed symbolic importance, and neither side was any longer willing to compromise. In February 1969, the Iranians declared that the circumstances under which the 1937 Treaty was signed were no longer relevant, as they had not been implemented by Iraq. The Iraqis, for their part, decreed that Iranian ships using the waterway would have to lower the Iranian flag and that Iranian warships would no longer be allowed to pass through the Shatt-el-Arab. The two countries were on the brink of war. Thousands of Iranians living in Iraq were, in the words of *The Times* of 19 May 1969, 'taken away from work or dragged out of bed at midnight, taken to some military interrogation centre for interrogation and beating, then put into lorries to be carried like cattle to Iranian frontier posts'.

War was averted, if only because neither side was ready for it, but the tension continued. For the Iranians, the answer to this stand-off on the Shatt-el-Arab lay once again in the north, with the Kurds. Their military operations were now expanded, and the Iranians sent in regular forces across the frontier to support the Kurdish insurgents against Iraq. Iraqi army units were ambushed in the mountains and the Kurdish Pesh Merga, backed by Iranian troops, caused them heavy casualties.

Moreover, the Kurds were by now receiving additional help from the United States. Henry Kissinger had been kept informed of the Iranian–Israeli effort to encourage and strengthen the Kurdish insurgents. He was persuaded to join with us and support the Kurds against the advice of the State Department professionals, led by Morris Draper, who argued that America had nothing to gain from such a venture. Kissinger decided otherwise. He believed that the United States had a commitment to the Shah and should demonstrate her support for Iran. As a result, American aid made its way to the Kurds via Tehran, though not in the substantial manner which we had expected.

In Tehran, in those years, the depth of feeling against Arabs in general and Iraqis in particular was astonishing. As Israelis, we felt no particular animosity against Arabs, but we were constrained to fight against their ongoing threats to extinguish our national existence. All the same, it was difficult to stomach the expressions of hatred and sheer racial aversion that the Iranians voiced against the Iraqis. This enmity was focused at this time on the situation in the Shatt-el-Arab: the immediate aim of the Shah was to undo the wrong which he believed had been done to Iran when the Great Powers had granted sovereignty over the entire riverway to Iraq. The Shah sought to restore the old balance on the Shatt-el-Arab in the south by applying pressure on the Kurdish front in the north. His ploy proved to be successful beyond all expectation.

The Iraqis had no military answer for the situation in the north. Kurdish attacks became increasingly audacious; they had harassed Iraqi troops in the mountains for a considerable time, but now the Pesh Merga penetrated even to the oil centres of Kirkuk and Sulaymaniya. In the south, there was also growing unrest among the Shia tribes, who were incited by Shi'i agents of Iran's military intelligence. Violent discontent was turning to open insurgency at both ends of the country; Iraq was in danger of disintegrating. Iraq's rulers concluded that, under such conditions, they had no option but to come to terms with their Iranian enemy in the east.

It was this development which led to the shameful agreement concluded by the Shah in March 1975 at an OPEC summit meeting in Algiers. Iran abandoned the Kurds to their bitter fate at the hands of the Iraqis in exchange for the acceptance by Iraq of the Iranian proposals for a revision of the Shatt-el-Arab boundary.

Israel, Iran's ally in the Kurdish operations against Iraq, was not given any forewarning of Iran's intention to betray the Kurds. The deal had been worked out between the Shah and Saddam Hussein, the Iraqi leader, with the help of Algeria's dynamic Foreign Minister, Abd el-Aziz Bouteflika. Even senior army officers in Tehran and Savak, Iran's intelligence service, were surprised by the Shah's move. Iranian units serving in Kurdish territory in northern Iraq – two-and-a-half battalions of artillery and anti-aircraft guns – were summarily ordered back to the Iranian frontier with all their equipment. The commander of the Pesh Merga and the Israelis on the spot watched incredulously as their Iranian associates in the field packed up and walked away.

Iranian commanders informed our liaison officers that there was to be a routine replacement of troops; they were too embarrassed to tell them the truth. It was only a day later that the Israeli representative in Tehran was called to a senior Iranian official and was told of the details of the agreement. When the Israeli objected strongly to such a betrayal of their Kurdish friends, the Iranian gave him an object lesson in Middle Eastern politics: Israel's weakness, he told the surprised Israeli, was that she allowed sentiment to interfere with politics. Helping minorities should not be considered as an end in itself but as a means to obtain useful concessions from the majority, in this case the Iraqis. Good politics was to know when to terminate one's aid to the minority in order to obtain maximum concessions from the majority. We could not subscribe to such cynical *realpolitik*.

Thus, the Kurds were left overnight to face the Iraqi army on their own. Israel attempted to continue providing help, but this came to nought because, with the Iranian frontier closed, we no longer had access to the Kurds.

The Iraqis took full advantage of the sudden switch of circumstances in the north. They transferred virtually their entire army to the Kurdish areas in the north and launched a murderous offensive, which the Kurds were unable to contain. The victorious Iraqi soldiers wreaked terrible vengeance on the abandoned Kurds. Hundreds were massacred; many thousands more were forcibly displaced from their homes and transported to camps in the arid south of the country, while their own homes and villages were taken over by Iraqi Arabs.

The Mullah, his two sons and the hard core of the Pesh Merga command fled across the frontier into Iran. The Mullah was given an apartment in the north of Tehran, where Savak kept careful watch over his movements. He died several years later, in the United States, a broken and betrayed leader, forced to live out his last years in Iran among the very people who had betrayed him and his struggle for freedom for his people.

His death, however, was not the end of the Kurdish saga. Cruelly and arbitrarily divided by national frontiers, the twenty million Kurds of Iraq, Iran, Syria, Turkey and the Soviet Union have nevertheless sought – and fought – to preserve their identity and to live according to their own heritage. Israelis who came into contact with them soon felt a great affinity and respect for this proud, persecuted people.

When the Iraqis launched their attack against Iran in September 1980, the Iranian authorities once more prepared to seek the help of the same Kurds, who had been so shamefully betrayed by the Shah in 1975. The Kurds responded with a magnanimity not shown to them. The Mullah's younger son, Masoud Barzani, led the rebellion against the Iraqis now engaged in the war against Iran. He was joined by Jalal Talabani, the leader of a rival faction of Kurds. The old story was to repeat itself. The ink had hardly dried on the armistice between Iran and Iraq in August 1988, when the Iraqi army, once again freed from the southern front, launched yet another all-out offensive against the Kurds.

This time, however, the Iraqis chose not to fight their way into the mountains. Instead, they launched their air force armed with lethal poison gas. The Kurds had no defence and no answer as their homes and villages and what was left of the Pesh Merga choked to death. The rest of the story is yesterday's news: thousands of refugees succeeded in escaping the gas and the Iraqi soldiers by crossing into Turkey; many thousands of the less fortunate succumbed. They had responded to the Iranian appeal and again they were abandoned. Once more the Kurdish dream of an autonomous state in Iraq vanished in a welter of innocent blood and betrayal.

It is a sad story, but it was not the end of the line for the Kurds: demography, geopolitical realities and the character of the Kurdish people will enable them to survive despite the grievous losses inflicted by Iranian treachery and Iraqi brutality. For the Iranians, however, the Kurds had outlived their usefulness in 1975 and once more in 1988. Thanks to them, Iran had obtained the revision of the Shatt-el-Arab boundary. When they did so in 1975, the Iranian leaders felt that they had achieved their ambition. They failed to notice the gathering storm clouds.

Looking back on those twilight years of the Shah's rule, I find it hard to believe that we were all so blind. It was not as if we did not see the danger, nor that we did not feel the rot setting in. As far back as the late 1960s, the religious leaders of Iran presented a potent threat to the rule of the Shah.

They were as determined as the Communists and the feudal landowners to get rid of him, and were a great deal more powerful. They were willing to join forces with either conservatives or radicals in order to achieve their goal.

We could see the danger and smell the corruption and decay, but we could not believe that the Shah's powerful military machine would disintegrate so completely or so quickly, or that the United States would stand by idly and allow its Iranian ally – and its own reputation – to be so ruthlessly destroyed. The Iranian ruling elite and the Carter administration in Washington appeared to be oblivious to all signs and warnings of the danger ahead.

At the time when the streets of Tehran were filled with demonstrators shaking fists and shouting support for Khomeini, it was reported that the head of Savak, General Nematollah Nassiri, said that in his opinion the days of the Saudi regime were numbered. He was unworried by the prospect in Iran. However, he was quite sure that within three years – certainly not more than five – the Saudi monarchy would have disappeared. Within a year, Nassiri was dead, after having been horribly tortured by Ayatollah Khalkhali.* Nassiri, the powerful head of the Shah's all-powerful security and intelligence apparatus, had been as blind as all of them. Neither he, nor anyone else in the Iranian hierarchy, was willing to admit or even to consider that the Shah-in-Shah could be fallible. The leaders and senior officials of the country displayed total unquestioning subservience to every whim of the Shah. When it became evident that he was no longer in control when confronted by the tidal wave of popular opposition, neither the masterful Nassiri nor the hitherto powerful generals had the will or the self-confidence to act independently of the Shah. As the Shah went down, so did they: they sank together. They seemed to make no attempt to save what they could of their regime, or even their lives. They were military lemmings.

Did they know what had been hidden from the Americans, that the Shah had cancer and that, at about the same time as the revolutionary troubles became serious in the spring of 1978, he had been told by his French doctors that he was terminally ill? A former minister and close confidant of the Shah told me some time later that the Shah's illness was one of the most closely guarded secrets in Iran during those fateful days. Certainly none of the senior officials and influential sycophants, who were, in effect, the rulers of the country, had any inkling of it. Neither did Savak.

Israeli officials, however, had become aware that the much-advertised competence of Iran's intelligence service, and of its greatly feared head, General Nassiri, was strictly limited. It was amazing that such a seemingly all-powerful organization had such poor intelligence on matters vital to Iran; Nassiri himself, despite his elevated position, had mediocrity stamped

---

* Several months before the return of Ayatollah Khomeini, Nassiri was replaced as head of Savak by General Nasir Moghadam, who suffered the same fate as Nassiri.

all over him. Experience has shown that military generals often make poor intelligence chiefs, and Nassiri was a classic example.

Many of the army's senior officers and staff stationed in Tehran were inadequately educated in second-rate military colleges. Corruption was the norm. General Moghadam, the last serving head of Savak before the Shah's departure, was asked: 'What were you doing all these years?' He answered without hesitation: 'Buying and selling land' – a cryptic reference to corrupt practices that were the norm for getting rich quickly by the use of influence while holding a military or official position. It was an easy life and officials – military and civilian – were content to follow the Shah without asking questions. The Shah himself had by now deteriorated into an inept mega-lomaniac. Ministers, officials and generals dared not take decisions, and no one was allowed to express an independent opinion or take independent action – not even his wife. Nor could the Shah control the bureaucratic machine, with the result that chaotic disorganization had taken over.

The Shah's megalomania was encouraged by his Prime Minister, Amir Abbas Hoveyda, who dealt ruthlessly with anyone daring to disagree. The one man in his entourage who had stood up to the Shah and who could have helped him through the difficult days was his former Prime Minister, Asadullah Alam, who had served him loyally but not uncritically. However, Alam had died in 1977 before the great test of 1978.

The Shah, moreover, was inclined to panic under stress. He did so as a young monarch in 1953 during the Mossadeq period and again in 1963 during the Khomeini-instigated mass demonstrations. It was the firm hand of Alam who had saved the Shah then from his own follies and from those of his favourite advisers – foreign and home-bred. An irreverent story circulating in Tehran at the time reflected popular and insider opinion. The Shah, it was said, had asked Alam what he should do about these hostile demonstrations? Alam reportedly replied: 'I will weigh your Majesty's testicles. If they are heavy, I will smash the demonstrators. If they do not weigh much, then I will take the next plane out of Tehran.' Be that as it may, it was an accepted fact that the Shah was prone to panic and it did not surprise anyone when it happened.

Inexplicably, the Americans ignored these danger signs during the critical years of 1977 and 1978. Earlier in the 1960s, the CIA had made a strenuous effort to 'cover' Iran's internal affairs, but as Washington's confidence in the Shah increased beyond all reason, orders were given to cease this intelligence activity. The CIA began to rely on reports from Savak for its assessment of the situation inside Iran.

At the end of 1977, Hanan Bar-on, Israel's Minister in Washington and deputy to the Ambassador, presented the State Department, on behalf of the Israeli Government, with a detailed assessment of the situation in Iran, accompanied with a sombre warning. This was so startling that it was 'red-flagged' by the State Department and given wide priority dissemination, including President Carter. The report was read, filed and forgotten. Soon afterwards, King Hassan of Morocco, on a visit to Washington, expressed similar concern about the situation in Iran. He told American officials that the Shah had ceased to act in a strictly sane manner and overall conditions in Tehran were rapidly deteriorating. One point mentioned by Hassan, which the Americans remembered with considerable bemusement at the time, was that the Shah had not knelt in a mosque for the past thirteen years. Hassan told his American hosts angrily that the last time the Shah had visited a mosque he had sat in an armchair and had thus played straight into the hands of his religious detractors.

Hassan proposed to go to Tehran and talk to the Shah if the Americans backed his mission, but the offer was not taken up. Instead, the CIA together with the State Department decided to send Farsi-speaking operatives to Iran to find out what was happening. One of them spent a month in Iran in the spring of 1978 and came back with an unmistakeable message: everything was falling apart; within weeks the Shah's regime would be swept away. But, once again, the report was filed and no action was taken. Soon afterwards, the Ambassador in Tehran received authorization from Washington to leave Iran for his summer vacation.

Everything appeared to be coming apart in Tehran at that critical time in 1978 and Washington did not seem to take any notice. How could the CIA and the State Department ignore the bloody demonstrations, first in the holy city of Qum in January, and then spreading from city to city? Every death of a demonstrator ignited more trouble elsewhere. By mid-summer 1978, the Iranian authorities had lost control and the military proclaimed repressive martial law. When that failed to stem the tide, the Shah embarked on a policy of demonstrative concessions, which – far from appeasing the angry crowds – served only to encourage them to greater effort to bring about the overthrow of the tottering monarchy and its military props.

It was not until November 1978 that Washington began to realize the immense gravity of the situation. For the first time the leading players – President Carter, his National Security Adviser Brzezinski, Secretary of State Vance and CIA Director Stansfield Turner – began to have doubts whether the Shah could survive the crisis in Tehran and remain in power. But once more Washington was divided and uncertain on the course of action the United States should take. Brzezinski, Energy Secretary James Schlesinger and the White House officials urged total support for the Shah; Vance and the State Department were in favour of bringing moderate opposition elements into the Iranian Government as a prelude to trans-forming the Shah's autocratic rule into a constitutional monarchy. But it was too late now to halt the revolution that was engulfing Iran. Not even the belated agreement between the Shah and one of the National Front leaders, Shahpour Bakhtiar, could do that. As 1978 drew to an end, Bakhtiar was installed as Prime Minister after the Shah had agreed to quit the Peacock Throne – and the country.

This solution would have been received with popular joy only a few months earlier; but now it was unacceptable. Khomeini had proclaimed his fundamentalist Islamic policy and declared his opposition to any gradualist solutions. Neither Bakhtiar nor the United States could do anything to stop the Islamic storm that the Ayatollah and his mullahs had unleashed.

On 16 January 1979, the Shah left Tehran to go into exile in Egypt, while Bakhtiar, belatedly backed to the hilt by the United States, began his rearguard action to save Iran from the ayatollahs. He, like Carter and Brzezinski, were convinced that the Shah's army could still prevent the overthrow of the Iranian Government even if they had been unable to save the Shah. In order to strengthen the resolve of the new Government, Carter sent US General, Robert E. Huyser, to Tehran to advise the military commander. Brzezinski, in particular, placed his trust in the army. He believed that by backing Bakhtiar, it would prevent a take-over by Khomeini or, by staging a coup, it would pre-empt Khomeini from seizing power.

It was not to be. The generals lacked the will, the nerve or the competence to embark on independent action; they might by now even have had an inkling of doubt about the loyalty of their troops – a thought they would, until now, never have entertained. Whatever the reason, when Khomeini announced that he was about to return to Iran, they were paralysed. However, the decisive factor in the inaction of the generals and the army was unquestionably their conviction that they had been abandoned by Carter's America. Alone, by themselves, they felt, they would not stand a chance. They were right. When the crunch came, they dithered and, instead of agreeing a plan of action, quarrelled among themselves.

On 1 February 1979, Khomeini made his triumphant entry into Tehran, greeted by a tumultuous, hysterical and enraptured crowd. Eleven days later, the legal Government of Shahpour Bakhtiar was swept aside when the army withdrew its support. The *ancien régime* had come to an end. Iran's 'New Order' had arrived.

15

The Gulf War

1980–86

As THE ISLAMIC REVOLUTION began its grotesque course in Tehran, across Iran's western frontier one of the most autocratic and tyrannical regimes the Middle East has known in the twentieth century consolidated its grip on the Government of Iraq. There was an arbitrariness about Saddam Hussein's rule that had few parallels. Power was concentrated in his hands and in those members of his extended family or clan, the Takritis. Opponents of the regime were liquidated, as were many who were considered to be no more than a potential threat: members of his family, old friends, fellow soldiers or party comrades; no one was safe. Ruthless violence was the hallmark of Saddam Hussein.

Saddam's one outstanding failure had been the 1975 pact signed at Algiers, when a triumphant Shah of Iran had forced him – then Vice-President – to surrender ignominiously what he considered was Iraq's rightful claim to the Shatt-el-Arab boundary. The Shah's superior force, wealth and political strategy had brought about Saddam's humiliation, which rankled deeply. Not even the Shah's 'free gift' – the betrayed Kurds – compensated for the loss of Iraqi domination of the Shatt-el-Arab.

Relations between the two countries deteriorated rapidly after Khomeini assumed power. Two opposing ideologies clashed: secular, Arab nationalism against militant pan-Islamic fundamentalism. Khomeini, who had been expelled from Iraq by Saddam, had lost no time in broadcasting his views on the 'evil, reactionary, anti-Islamic' Iraqi regime from his safe haven in France, and had urged the Iraqi people to overthrow it. Insults and threats flew in both directions. For the Iranians, the Iraqis were atheists, racists, exploiters of the downtrodden and – the ultimate expletive of them all – Zionists. The Iraqis responded in kind. The verbal assault of Iran threatened to destabilize the fragile balance between the different ethnic and sectarian groupings that made up Iraqi society. The rapid escalation of the war of words soon led to renewed efforts of subversion; the Iranians supported the outlawed Shi'i el-Da'wa Party of southern Iraq, while in Khuzistan an Arabistan Liberation Front was created with active help from the Iraqi intelligence service. By 1980, these activities had led to border clashes, which grew in intensity and frequency.

In the end, it was an almost foregone conclusion that Saddam would resort to war, in revenge for the humiliation of 1975 and as retribution for the 'evil' done to him by the Shah, coupled with the fear that the Shi'i frenzy across the Iranian frontier could infect the large Shi'i population of Iraq. Even so, Saddam would not have plunged his country into a full-scale war had it not been for a report which Barzan el-Takriti, his half-brother and the head of Mukhabarat el-Am, Iraq's secret intelligence service, had put before him. In his report he painted a picture of chaos and anarchy within the Iranian army: hundreds of officers had been executed and hundreds more were in exile after fleeing for their lives; there were widespread desertions of officers and troops; and a breakdown of order and organization. Iraqi intelligence estimated that Iran would be incapable of waging war and that an Iraqi offensive aimed at taking Arabistan (the Iraqi name for Khuzistan) would reach its objectives within three weeks.

Armed with his brother's report, Saddam's desire for revenge assumed new significance. The dream could now be translated into reality, at no great effort – or loss – for Iraq. At the very least, Iraqi rights over Shatt-el-Arab would be restored and Iraq's superiority in arms over Iran would be effectively demonstrated. If Iran chose to fight, instead of capitulating immediately, then she would lose the province of Khuzistan and Iraq would become the major oil power in the region.

This was the essential Iraqi thinking which led to the launch of the surprise attack on Iran on 22 September 1980, when Iraqi forces crossed into Iran at four points along the southern border. All the evidence shows that the Iraqis expected a virtually uncontested walk-over, a lightning offensive and a speedy victory, with the Iranians coming cap in hand to the negotiating table, just as the Shah had forced the Iraqis to do in 1975.

Iraq's Foreign Minister, Tariq Aziz, wrote of his country's 'two aims'. The first 'concerns the sovereignty of Iraq over the Shatt-el-Arab waterway, which has been under Iraqi sovereignty until the 1975 agreement. The second aim is a nationalist Arab one and concerns the area of Ahwaz or Arabistan, that Iran calls Khuzistan.'*

Iraq's aims and motivations were clear, but they were based on an intelligence miscalculation which was to provoke the most bloody conflict since the Second World War. The two combatants suffered nearly a million and a half dead and wounded as their giant armies fought each other for eight long years, instead of the three weeks that Iraqi intelligence had estimated.

There have, over the years, been other instances of leaders failing to heed their intelligence services. 'Operation Barbarossa' – the surprise offensive mounted by the Germans after Stalin refused to believe the warnings that the Nazis would attack Russia in 1941 – is such an example. There have been fewer cases of leaders acting – or failing to act – because of faulty intelligence. Israeli military intelligence refusing to believe that Egypt was

---

*Tariq Aziz, *Iraq–Iran Conflict: Questions and Discussions* (Third World Centre for Research and Publishing, London, 1981), p. 8.

preparing to attack Israel in 1973 is a case in point. But the colossal misreading of the Iranians by Iraqi intelligence – and the tremendous damage and loss of life that this mistake caused – must surely rank as one of the outstanding examples of the fatal consequences of bad intelligence.

The Iraqis did, in fact, reach most of their objectives in less than the prescribed time. Two weeks after launching their attack, they were holding a line running from Khorramshar to the outskirts of Ahwaz and northwards through Susangerd to Musian. Further to the north, other Iraqi forces had invested the Mehran and Qasr-e-Shirin areas. The Iranians, however, far from implementing the 'cap-in-hand' scenario envisaged by Saddam and Iraqi intelligence, seemed unperturbed by their losses, reorganized and regrouped their forces. Ignoring Iraq's call to negotiate a settlement, the Iranians fought on.

By the time the Iraqis renewed their offensive, the Iranians were ready for them. They fought with a combination of patriotic and revolutionary Islamic fervour against their hated enemy. By November 1980, only some six weeks later, the eight-year stalemate had begun, brought about by a balance of weakness in which neither side was able to defeat the other. But it was by no means a static war. By May 1981, the Iranians were ready to attack the Iraqi invaders with very large, if not always adequately trained and equipped, land forces. In a series of massive attacks, the Iranians succeeded in driving the Iraqis from most of the Iranian territory they had occupied, taking many thousands of prisoners and inflicting heavy losses on the retreating Iraqi forces.

It was an increasingly bleak situation for the Iraqi leader, Saddam Hussein. His surprise attack had succeeded and had caused great damage and heavy losses to Iran; it all but destroyed the centre of Iran's oil industry, including its valuable refinery at Abadan. But his victim had refused to lie down and die. The Iraqi invasion had had the opposite effect to that intended. Far from weakening the Khomeini regime, the war turned out to be an Iraqi-sent boon for the ayatollahs. It provided effective and patriotic means to rally support for the Revolution; it kept the army, with its still uncertain loyalty to the ayatollahs, occupied far from the capital; and it provided convenient justification for economic shortages, which characterized Khomeini's post-revolutionary Iran. It also harnessed the strong nationalist and patriotic tendencies – which often had heavy anti-Arab overtones – which were a characteristic of most Iranians.

The irony of all this was that it really ran counter to the ideology of Khomeini and the mullahs, which was basically anti-nationalist and pan-Islamic. And far from demonstrating Iraq's military superiority to his Persian neighbours and to the world at large, Saddam was forced on to the defensive. He made repeated and barely disguised pleas for an end to the war, and offered to withdraw his troops from Iranian territory still held by Iraq in exchange for a UN-sponsored cease-fire.

For the Iranian ayatollahs, however, there were advantages to be had from the continuing war. Their success in containing the Iraqi assault had given them renewed confidence. They also believed that the war could become an effective vehicle for 'exporting the Revolution' to the Shi'i majority of the Iraqi Arab population* and to the large Shi'i minorities in the Gulf states, particularly in Saudi Arabia. By July 1982, the Iranians were set to expand the war into Iraqi national territory. Their July offensive code-named 'Ramadan', had as its objective the port of Basrah, the second largest city in Iraq, which had a Shi'i majority. For days, the fate of Iraq hung in the balance as the Iranians inched their way towards Basrah. However, the strong defensive positions which the Iraqis had built to protect their national territory stood the test and could not be breached by the Iranian army. In particular, Iran's Revolutionary Guards – the Pasdaran – whose revolutionary and religious zeal was equalled only by their dismal lack of military training, were no match for the sophisticated Iraqi defence. Their untrained enthusiasm led them to launch repeated, suicidal frontal assaults with the consequential terrible loss of Iranian lives.

It was the Iraqis who were now fighting with their backs to the wall. Basrah had come within artillery range of the Iranian guns and Baghdad itself was only sixty miles from the front. But the Iraqi soldiers proved themselves to be better in defence of their own territory than in offensive action on Iranian soil. Moreover, the Shi'i population demonstrated that its loyalty was primarily to the Iraqi state to which it belonged. The Shi'i uprising, which the Ayatollah had anticipated, did not materialize.

The failure of 'Operation Ramadan' against Basrah, in July 1982, on which Khomeini had staked everything, proved to be a critical turning-point in the war. It not only restored Iraqi confidence and halted the run of Iranian victories, but it also lifted the threat of the march of the Iranian Revolution across the Gulf into Bahrein, Kuwait and the eastern Shi'i provinces of Saudi Arabia. It heralded the long, static war in which repeated Iranian assaults were repulsed with heavy casualties on both sides. The Arabian Gulf states recovered their composure and recognized Iraq as their protector worthy of massive aid. Henceforth, these Gulf states would be financing Saddam's war.

The battle of Basrah proved to be the watershed for the ayatollahs, who never recovered from this setback. It marked the opening of a new and terrible phase in the war, in which hundreds of thousands of Iranian and Iraqi lives were sacrificed to no end. I find it difficult to dismiss these years of attrition in a few short lines, even though, from the purely military point of view, nothing much was gained or lost on either side from the launching of 'Ramadan' in July 1982 until the capture of the Faw Peninsula by the Iranians in February 1986. They were years of terrible carnage, in which up to half a million men were locked in battle as the Iranians used ever larger forces in their assaults while the Iraqis strained to contain them. But Khomeini remained the final arbiter. Nothing less than the downfall of Saddam Hussein, and the end of the Baathi regime, would satisfy him; he

---

* The non-Arab Kurds together with the Arab Sunnis give the Sunnis the majority.

was determined to defeat and overthrow Saddam whatever the cost in Iranian 'martyrs'.

In a desperate bid to loosen the Iranian grip, the Iraqis launched bombing and missile attacks against Iran's civilian centres, including Tehran. Iran countered with reprisal missile attacks on Baghdad. When these assaults on civilian targets in Iran had no effect, the Iraqis sought to undermine Iran's capacity to continue the war by attacking her supply routes, especially her oil exports. This 'tanker war' raged throughout 1984. In that year alone there were more than fifty Iraqi air attacks on tankers passing through the Gulf, truly a remarkable figure in view of the fact that nearly all these tankers belonged to neither Iraq nor Iran, but most of them were carrying oil from Iran or goods to Iran.

Yet these attempts at indirect warfare brought the Iraqis no respite from Iranian attacks on land; but despite the large numbers deployed by the Iranians, the Iraqi defences remained intact. There is no way of knowing the precise extent of Iraq's use of chemical weapons and their role in staunching the Iranian offensives. However, it has been established that Iraq made extensive use of poison gas against the Iranian attack in March 1985 and against subsequent Iranian assaults as well as against the northern Kurds.

Then suddenly, in February 1986, the situation changed dramatically. While Iraqi troops were defending the Basrah lines against yet another Iranian attack, an Iranian force succeeded in crossing the Shatt-el-Arab under cover of darkness, surprising the Iraqi defenders of the Faw Peninsula, to the south of Basrah. Within twenty-four hours, the port of Faw had fallen and the Iraqi soldiers were retreating, leaving large quantities of arms and equipment. A counter-attack by elite Iraqi Revolutionary Guards fared no better. The Faw Peninsula remained firmly in Iranian hands and Basrah was threatened as never before. In neighbouring Kuwait, there were signs of near panic as the Iranian revolutionary threat appeared to materialize.

The fall of the Faw – Iraq's window on the Gulf – was a terrible blow for Saddam. The fall of Basrah appeared imminent, with Iranian troops only a few miles from the outer suburbs. But, once more, Iraqi defences held firm. On the battlefront there was continuing deadlock. All the same, in 1986, the Iranian star was in the ascendant; for the first time, an Iranian victory had become a possibility. The outlook for the Iraqis was grim as one international effort after another to end the war was repudiated by Khomeini in Tehran.

Iran's success at Faw set alarm bells ringing in the capitals of the world, not least in the Arab world, and more so in the neighbouring Arabian Gulf states. Most Gulf regimes had not been displeased by the setback suffered by Saddam; but the prospect of an Iranian victory, which had become a real possibility, was another matter altogether.

Kuwait, in particular, felt threatened. With Iranian troops across the frontier at Faw, the city of Kuwait and all its oil installations had come within range of the long-feared Iranian take-over. Moreover, with her troops performing so badly, the Iraqi regime had sought to offset the danger that the new Iranian successes posed by redoubling Iraqi attacks against the Iranian oil terminals and against tankers of all nationalities carrying Iranian oil. The 'tanker war' reached a new intensity after the fall of Faw, and the Kuwaitis, with their oil ports so close to the battle lines, considered themselves to be particularly vulnerable to Iranian reprisals. The Iranians, for their part, would have preferred peace and quiet in the Gulf. With Basrah and her oil port under siege, the Iraqis had long ceased to make use of the Gulf sea-lanes. The Iranians, however, were shipping the bulk of their oil exports by tanker through the Gulf Straits of Hormuz. By disrupting Iran's oil exports, the Iraqis hoped not only to cripple Iran's fighting ability, but also to provoke retaliatory Iranian attacks against Arab shipping in the Gulf, which would, they hoped, internationalize the Gulf War and thus hasten its end.

In the event, this Iraqi calculation was justified. The Kuwaitis, alarmed at the rapidly deteriorating situation, appealed to the British for protection; when Britain refused, they turned to the United States and the Soviet Union. For the Soviet Union, this was an unusual and welcome request. For years she had been regarded with suspicion and hostility by the Gulf rulers; only Kuwait had diplomatic relations with her. It was, therefore, hardly surprising that Moscow reacted positively to the Kuwaiti appeal. Soviet interest, in turn, triggered an immediate American response, for it had long been axiomatic in Washington that the Soviet Union must be kept out of the Gulf. The Americans announced that they would agree to register twelve Kuwaiti tankers under the American flag and to give these tankers naval protection. With this declaration, the Americans ceased to be neutral in the Gulf War and sided with Iraq.

Once before during the Gulf War the Americans had saved the Iraqis from certain defeat, but they had managed to preserve the mantle of secrecy over that episode. On that occasion, the Iranians had secretly massed their troops for a major offensive. American satellite intelligence showed clearly that the Iranian attack was to be directed against the 'seam', the most vulnerable point between two Iraqi army corps. An attack along the 'seam' would, in American intelligence estimation, have enabled the Iranians to break through the Iraqi defence, with catastrophic consequences for Iraq's ability to continue the war. Faced thus with the prospect of an Iranian victory, the United States decided to forewarn the Iraqis. They redeployed and avoided disaster, thanks to the CIA's discreet intervention.

This action, which was by no means unique, underlined the inclination of the Pentagon, strongly backed by the State Department, to support Iraq throughout the war. This partiality was plain to us from the beginning of the war. Iraq's invasion, though an obvious violation of the sovereignty of another country, was not denounced by the United States or by the UN Security Council, which had always been so quick to condemn quite minor border forays by Israel. The Security Council was convened in 1980 by

Secretary-General Kurt Waldheim, but, as the former Under Secretary-General, Sir Brian Urqhart, describes in his memoirs, *A Life in Peace and War*, the meetings dragged on 'in a depressing and undignified way' with 'spineless pettifogging', so that nothing should be done by the United Nations to interfere with the success of Iraq's aggressive invasion of Iran. And the fifteen members of the Security Council – including Great Britain, France and the United States – did not even have the decency to be ashamed.

16
Iran without Contra
1985–6

SHORTLY AFTER THE MEETING of the UN Security Council, the nine – as they were then – Foreign Ministers of the European Community met at Luxembourg and decided, on the initiative of Lord Carrington, that there was no need for any European intervention to bring an end to the war. Iraq still appeared to be winning handsomely. Ironically, though, the Iraqis themselves were already at that time beginning to realize that their objective for a short war was not attainable and would have welcomed a European initiative. Pressure to end the war was to come later when it became obvious that the Iraqis were in an increasingly difficult situation. The American decision to send her navy into the gulf to protect Kuwaiti and other ships against Iranian attacks was a direct result of the unneutral desire of the Pentagon to favour the Arab side in the war.

This preference for Iraq became much more pronounced once Iran appeared to be winning the war. It stood, however, in direct contradiction to the American position in what became known as the Iran–Contra Affair. It is time, therefore, for us to examine this controversial affair more closely. I was directly involved in the Iranian half of this *cause célèbre* and have, therefore, first-hand knowledge of the origins and of the reasons that brought about Israel's connection with Iran in the summer of 1985.

A number of different factors and events came together that year which created the climate for our approach to Iran. Each of these separate components by itself would not have forged the chain of events that was to lead to the controversial climax of the Iran initiative, but together they composed the scenario which shaped the Iranian part of the Affair. American fear of Soviet encroachment into Iran; President Reagan's emotional involvement in the fate of the hostages; political in-fighting in the Reagan administration; Washington's alarming lack of intelligence about Iran; and, on the other side, the opportune arrival on the scene of Adnan Khashoggi with a man providing direct access to the Prime Minister's Office in Tehran, with all that this implied – these were the basic elements that made the Iran initiative practically inevitable. On the American side, William Casey, then Director of the CIA, and 'Bud' McFarlane, then National Security Adviser to the President, were increasingly concerned about the situation in Iran and in the Gulf region. They believed that Iran would become one of the most vulnerable and dangerous points on the globe for western interests if the Soviet Union were to extend her influence in the country and its new order.

Iran, with some 1,200 miles of frontier with the Soviet Union and another 530 miles of frontier with the then Soviet-dominated Afghanistan, was in a most exposed position. The Middle East experts of the National Security Council and, to a lesser extent, of the CIA felt that the United States was painting herself into a corner, and that by her policy of refusing to have anything to do with the regime of the Ayatollah, she had, in effect, cleared the ground of western players and allowed the Soviet Union free rein to play the field.

I had first encountered McFarlane's deep concern over Iran shortly after I became Director-General of the Foreign Ministry in Jerusalem in 1980. McFarlane was then serving as Counsellor at the State Department under Secretary of State Haig. We met regularly to discuss the political situation in various parts of the world. Iran figured very high on his list of potential danger zones for western interests. Daily anti-western tirades in Tehran, plus thirty divisions of Soviet troops poised on Iran's northern frontiers, gave him ample cause for concern. His dilemma was only too clear: the regime of this fanatic, die-hard Ayatollah was repugnant to the United States; it was thus unthinkable that America should be seen competing for the grace of the new rulers in Tehran. On the other hand, if Iran were to 'fall under Soviet influence', the Americans would be faced with their biggest challenge since Pearl Harbor.

In McFarlane's considered opinion, a Soviet-dominated Iran could become the catalyst for the Third World War. In fact, early in July 1981, an inter-departmental committee examining US policy towards Iran concluded that American efforts to discourage third parties to sell arms to Iran 'could increase opportunities for the Soviets to take advantage of Iran's security concerns and to persuade Iran to accept Soviet military assistance'.

Meanwhile, the war between Iran and Iraq was nearing its first anniversary and the dichotomy of interests between Reagan's National Security Adviser and the CIA on the one side, and the Pentagon and State Department on the other, was becoming evident. The Pentagon strongly opposed the committee's findings. In a strongly worded rebuttal, the US Joint Chiefs of Staff warned that any change of policy regarding arms sales to Iran 'would be perceived by the moderate Arab states as an action directly counter to their interests and could intensify the war with Iraq'. The policy of preventing the sale of arms to Iran by third parties was to continue unabated.

This remarkable statement by the Joint Chiefs of Staff introduced an altogether new factor. Was this Pentagon policy of continued unneutral support for Iraq based only on the designation of Iran as a sponsor of international terrorism? Or had the Joint Chiefs of Staff inadvertently let the 'cat out of the bag' and revealed the real reason for this policy?

Four years later the same situation recurred. Defense Secretary Weinberger's irritable rejection of a memorandum, written by Howard Teicher in May 1985, in which he recommended that the United States should encourage her western allies to provide 'selected military equipment' to Iran in order to 'blunt Soviet influence' provided a significant clue to understanding the statement by the Joint Chiefs of Staff, in which they opposed McFarlane's considered advice on the question of contact with Iran. Teicher had prepared his memorandum at the behest of McFarlane, who was becoming increasingly frustrated by what he considered to be American impotence in view of the growing danger of Soviet encroachment into Iran.

Teicher was the senior staff member on the National Security Council dealing with Middle Eastern affairs. Though only in his thirties, he had already attained wide experience in this field, having served under McFarlane and Rumsfeld in Lebanon and participated in virtually all American initiatives in the region during the previous five years. Like the National Security Adviser himself, he was convinced that the lack of any American leverage over events in Iran was highly dangerous; and that the virtual abandonment of Iran by the West had provided the Soviet Union with an opportunity she was bound to exploit. This view was reinforced by the fear that the death of Khomeini would touch off a succession struggle which would enable the Russians to support pro-Soviet elements in Iran, while the United States, because of her lack of influential contacts, would be helpless to intervene.

Teicher's views, together with those of the late Donald Fortier, then Senior Director for Political Military Affairs at the National Security Council, were dismissed by Weinberger out of hand. We know now a great deal more about this as we have had access to a mass of documentation released by official bodies who have examined evidence concerning the Iran–Contra Affair.

The documents make fascinating reading. They show how the concern caused by the strategic importance of Iran on the one hand, and a feeling of helplessness in the face of unknown factors on the other, brought such experienced and brilliant officials as Fortier and Teicher to encourage American involvement in the supply of arms to Iran. In those first months of 1985, there was no thought of an arms-for-hostages deal; National Security Council activity revolved exclusively round the strategic implications of the Iran situation as seen from the American national interest.

This was particularly true of McFarlane, the National Security Adviser himself. I consider him to be an honest, dedicated American patriot, who, in the affair of Iran, anguished over what he considered to be a dangerous weakness in the global strategic situation of the West. When Fortier continued to warn his superiors of the dangers inherent in uncharted waters of succession struggle, McFarlane wrote to him: 'I do consider planning for the succession to be one of our greatest failures and vulnerabilities so I am very glad you are turning to it.'

On 3 July 1985, I discussed these matters at length with McFarlane in his office in the west wing of the White House. There was no one else present and no notes were taken. We sat for a long time, two good friends, representing friendly countries, analysing, dissecting and evaluating the situation in Iran and in the Gulf region, and giving voice to our respective fears and objectives. As an Israeli, I did not always make the same judgements as McFarlane. A possible Iraqi victory in the Gulf War had very different implications for me; a possible change of regime in Iran had certain advantages for Israel over and above those to be gained by the United States or by the West in general. But overall we were in agreement that the international situation in Iran was fraught with danger.

When I told McFarlane that Israel had contacts with Iranians who had direct access to leading figures in Iran's political establishment and who had expressed a desire eventually to meet official American representatives on an unofficial basis, he enthusiastically encouraged us to continue these contacts. I warned him that, in all probability, we would be faced with a request for some American arms.

I have no intention of describing in detail all the facets of the Iran–Contra Affair. There has been a plethora of books giving blow-by-blow descriptions, many of them highly inaccurate and imaginative. My own role in this drama has been greatly distorted in most of these published accounts. I feel neither the need to justify my actions nor to apologize for them. But by describing my own involvement, I feel I can clarify how and why Israel and the United States embarked on the strictly limited Iranian undertaking which was later to cause such commotion in Washington.

I had gone to the White House to see McFarlane on that July morning at the request of our Prime Minister, Shimon Peres. He knew that I was going to Washington on Foreign Ministry business and, remembering my friendship with the National Security adviser, he called me to the Prime Minister's Office. There he told me briefly, in general terms, about the contacts that Israel had succeeded in making with certain Iranians, and about the request that had been made to him by a National Security consultant, Michael Ledeen, three months previously, to assist the United States in re-establishing contact with Iran. He advised me to talk to his friend, Al Schwimmer, who was his special adviser and who would put me in the picture. Peres then explained his own position in this matter: 'Dave, we owe the Americans so much that we have to do our utmost to help them; especially as they have come to us to seek our help.'

This was Peres's overriding justification for his involvement in this Iranian venture; he returned to this theme repeatedly in subsequent talks we had on the Iranian operation. 'Look what the Americans did to help us to bring the Falashas from Ethiopia,'* he once said to me; 'and look what efforts they have made for Soviet Jewry. The least we can do is to help them on Iran.'

Our then Foreign Minister, Yitzhak Shamir, to whom I reported our

* Black Jews living in Ethiopia, who were brought to Israel clandestinely in what was known as 'Operation Moses'.

conversations, fully concurred. There was nothing Machiavellian or under-hand, as some people have claimed, about Israel's role in the Iran Affair; on the contrary, from the very first conversations I had at the White House on 3 July 1985, we made it plain that we would continue our Iranian contact only if the United States wished us to do so; and then only if we could act jointly and in concert with the United States.

I have been asked on many occasions why we allowed ourselves to be drawn into an adventure which was to have such unsavoury overtones. For us Israelis, however, the situation was clear-cut: we were co-operating with the National Security Adviser, one of the most senior officials on the President's Staff, who had to report daily and in person to the President, and who assured us that he was talking with us about Iran with the full authority of the President. We had neither reason nor occasion to doubt the legality of the American request, nor to question the internal procedures of the United States Government. We felt no need to enquire whether Congress, the Pentagon, the State Department or the CIA were informed and supportive of the Iran operation; it was not our business to question the working of the US Government agencies. Nor did we know that money from the Iran connection would be siphoned off to the Nicaraguan Contras.

During my second meeting with McFarlane concerning our Iran oper-ation, in August 1985, I did overstep the boundaries of diplomatic etiquette by requesting that Secretary of State Shultz be informed of our joint American–Israeli–Iranian operation. We did not want Shultz, who had been a good friend to Israel, to be under the mistaken impression that Israel was conniving with Iran without the knowledge of the United States.

The intelligence we obtained from the Iranians was most welcome in Washington. McFarlane told me that it was of great value and much better quality than anything the CIA was getting on Iran. I had no reason to doubt his judgement. This American stamp of approval was convincing evidence that our Iranian connections did have access to valuable sources of information; they really knew what was going on in Iran.

Manucher Ghorbanifar may not have been a model of Evangelical righteousness, but then men playing his role seldom are. Ghorbanifar was a controversial figure. He was close to the top officials of the Iranian Prime Minister's Office and proved it by phoning them in our presence. Yet he neither accepted their political creed nor did he profess any religious affinity with the zealots who were his employers. Intelligent, fast-thinking and eloquent, Ghorbanifar was always ready with an answer, but we quickly realized that the accuracy of those answers was often open to question. Had the Americans said, once they had sampled Ghorbanifar's information, that they considered it to be fabrication, or worthless, we would have halted our joint operation there and then. But they did no such thing. On the contrary, their evaluation of the intelligence Ghorbanifar brought us was couched in superlative terms of approval.

In the event, it was Ghorbanifar who informed us of the imminent release of the Reverend Benjamin Weir after we had delivered 500 TOW anti-tank shells. By letting us know beforehand of the imminent release of a hostage, Ghorbanifar gave us convincing evidence that he had access to the decision-makers in Tehran.

The release of hostages held in Lebanon by groups with shadowy links to Iran had meanwhile become indirectly but inextricably enmeshed in Iranian requests for American-made arms as part of the Iran operation. When the Iranians told us that they wanted to improve relations with the United States, we replied: 'How can you talk of improving relations when you hold American citizens hostage?' The Iranians replied: 'How can we know that you are capable of bringing us together with the Americans? Prove your ability and your close connections with the United States by supplying us with some American arms.' Thus, the hostages and the arms became our respective 'visiting cards' – to prove our seriousness and ability to deliver; they were, at least in the opening months of the operation, a means to an end, not an end in themselves. That, however, was to change.

From the outset the operation moved along two separate tracks, with only Ghorbanifar linking the two. Hardly any of the Congressional investigators, committee members, journalists and authors who have dealt so extensively with the Iran Affair have grasped this fundamental feature, and this has been one of the principal reasons for the incredible inaccuracies and distortions which have characterized so much of Irangate literature and also the official reports.

One track brought us in contact with the Iranian Government. Ghorbanifar appeared as the Prime Minister's representative in Europe, reporting directly by telephone to Mir Hussein Mussavi, the Prime Minister, and to his special assistant, Muhssen Kangarlou. (Yaacov Nimrodi, one of Israel's former diplomatic representatives in Tehran, who speaks fluent Farsi and who played a leading role in the Affair, would monitor these telephone conversations for us.) It was the Iranians contacted through this channel who asked for arms, and they increased their demands after every token delivery we made. In this way, they transformed the secondary role of the arms-for-hostages arrangement into a central feature of this operation.

Ghorbanifar was also the means of access to the second channel, in which groups in opposition to the Prime Minister played a leading role. They had no interest in the supply of arms, which, they claimed, only strengthened the Government they sought to overthrow. Ghorbanifar, however, argued that in order to be able to retain the contact with us and to connect us with the second track – the opposition – he must satisfy his employers, Mussavi and Kangarlou, by providing them with some American arms. During the six months of my involvement in the operation, we kept the amount of arms exchanged to an absolute minimum – 500 TOW anti-tank rockets and seventeen Hawk anti-aircraft missiles.

Our major interest was in the second track, the group of pro-western mullahs, soldiers and politicians who planned to seize power once the struggle for the Khomeini succession began in earnest. According to our information, there were three groups jockeying for power. The first was a hard-line, radical, fanatical group which favoured a policy of 'exporting' Iran's Islamic Revolution to neighbouring Arab countries, together with a wide-ranging policy of nationalization in Iran. Leading members of this group were Prime Minister Mussavi; Ayatollah Ali Akbar Meshkini, one of the most influential men in the country; the then minister in charge of intelligence, Mohammed Rayshari; the Minister of the Interior; and the head of the High Council of Revolutionary Guards, Ayatollah Fazollah Mahalati. It was backed also by about fifty members of Parliament.

The second was a middle-of-the-road, or centrist, group. It was radical in foreign policy, but more conservative in domestic affairs. Its recognized leader was the then already powerful Speaker of the Majlis (Parliament), Hashemi Rafsanjani. He was supported by Ayatollah Mussavi Ardabili, head of the Supreme Court, and by Ayatollah Mahdi Karrubi, chairman of the Shahid, the Martyrs' Foundation. This group had strong support in the High Council of Justice and in the Supreme Court, and was reputed to be backed by the two favourite claimants for the Khomeini succession, Ayatollah Montazeri and Ahmed Khomeini, the Imam's son.

The third – and most pro-western group – was represented by the ayatollah with whom we were in contact through Ghorbanifar, who assessed it in the following manner: its adherents believed in free trade, the guarantee of personal wealth and the protection of private investment. They were totally against Communism. They wanted better relations with the West and with Islamic governments throughout the world. They did not support the export of Iran's Islamic Revolution either by force or through political influence. They asserted the principle of personal freedom within Islam and non-interference in the personal lives of the people in Iran or in neighbouring countries. Among the more prominent backers of this group were a number of influential ayatollahs and, according to Ghorbanifar, some sixty members of Parliament, senior officers of the armed forces, members of the police and civil service officials.

It would be wrong to describe this third group as moderates or as liberals. On the basic question of Islamic hegemony in Iran with the Islamic clergy as the final authority on all issues of church and state, they were indistinguishable from the two other groups. Yet, for all that, this group was politically much more palatable to Israel and to the West than the other two radical groups, if only because it renounced state-backed terrorism, opposed the policy of exporting the Islamic Revolution to its Arab neighbours and favoured closer ties with the West.

Ghorbanifar claimed to be a strong supporter of this third group, although his employer was Prime Minister Mussavi and his direct superior was the Prime Minister's assistant and head of foreign operations, Kangarlou, both of whom were leaders of the radical group.

I had an opportunity to assess this third group at first hand when, in the summer of 1985, we met in Hamburg with one of their leading ayatollahs. The meeting had been arranged by Adnan Khashoggi, the Saudi intermediary, and by Ghorbanifar; both actively participated in our discussion.

The Israeli side was represented by Prime Minister Peres's adviser, Al Schwimmer, Yaakov Nimrodi and myself as Director-General of the Foreign Ministry. Khashoggi's son and son-in-law, a member of a prominent Lebanese family, also took part in the midnight session.

I had been on my way home after meetings in Washington and had stopped over in Paris on 3 July. There I received a message from Peres, who told me to meet Schwimmer and Nimrodi in Geneva and to participate in a meeting of importance that had been arranged. When I arrived in Geneva, the two Israelis were in conference with Khashoggi and his entourage. We all left soon afterwards for Hamburg, where Ghorbanifar was waiting for us.

This was my first encounter with Ghorbanifar. I had not, until then, been involved in the discussions which had been taking place with the Iranians. I was naturally curious to meet this man of whom both Schwimmer and Nimrodi spoke so highly. I was impressed by this first encounter. Well-groomed and elegantly dressed, Ghorbanifar exuded self-confidence as he described Iran's political scene in colourfully impressionist terms. When he came to telling us of the ayatollah we were about to meet, he produced a photocopy of his passport to prove his identity, for he realized that we would wish to be quite sure of his bona-fide position and identity. Khashoggi, who was present, tried to persuade us not to reveal our identities; he feared the ayatollah's reaction when he found out that the 'westerners' that he was supposed to meet here were, in fact, from Israel. We refused. When we were later introduced to the bearded, turbaned man dressed in traditional black, he was clearly startled. I must admit it was indeed an unusual gathering in the plush surroundings of the Hamburg hotel suite – an Iranian ayatollah, a Saudi billionaire (as he was then) and a Lebanese Shia aristocrat in intimate consultation with three Israelis.

At the end of several hours of discussion a clear picture emerged: if the man we were facing was all he claimed to be, then we had before us a fervent patriot, who, for the sake of his beloved Iran, was willing to take immense risks, including the danger of being in contact with Israelis. He painted the future of his country in dark, bleak colours: if his group failed to grasp the reins of government and the 'other side' won the power struggle, then Iran would go in one of two possible directions: she would either disintegrate into a Lebanon-type anarchy, but with violence on a much greater scale than that witnessed in Beirut; or she would be transformed into a de facto satellite of the Soviet Union, with the extreme radicals, the rabble-rousers and the haters of the West in positions of authority.

In order to save Iran – and the world – from this, he and his friends needed our help. When the time was ripe, they would have to take over the Government. They also wanted help to renew ties with the United States. They wanted the West to become once more a factor and a moderating influence on the men who ruled in Tehran.

This was, on all counts, a heady message. If what the Muslim cleric was saying was true, then we were faced with a group of people – not fringe elements, but men close to the centre of power – who wished to lead Iran back into the family of nations, away from state-supported terrorism and subversion which was so much an integral element of exporting the Islamic Revolution. This was, after all, what we had been working for, a way to halt the runaway Iranian fanaticism, terrorism and radicalism.

In my report to Prime Minister Peres after the meeting, I warned that we had no way of establishing in an authoritative manner whether the man was all he claimed to be and if he was speaking the truth. But I recommended that we should maintain contact with the Iranian, in view of the great importance of this matter. My recommendation was accepted and henceforth this relationship with the spokesman of the pro-western group in Tehran became the central feature of our Iranian operation.

Through Ghorbanifar we maintained continuing contact with the ayatollah. A second meeting was arranged, in Geneva, and this time the Americans participated, with Michael Ledeen representing McFarlane. Meanwhile, however, the second and more official channel in the operation, the contact with Prime Minister Mussavi and his deputy, Kangarlou, which had been conducted by Ghorbanifar, was turning sour, for these radical leaders had discovered that the United States could be a soft touch for the extraction of more arms in exchange for their promises to release American hostages. The eager expectations of the President's men to see the hostages safely brought home as a result of their Iranian operation made their disappointment all the greater when Iranian promise after promise was broken, with the wily Ghorbanifar coming to each meeting with new excuses and new demands for arms.

In November 1985, McFarlane and I met again at the White House. Only four months had elapsed since the meeting when he had given the go-ahead signal for the Iranian operation. In that short time something had happened to the National Security Adviser. It became an open secret in Washington that he was considering tendering his resignation. I found him morose, irritable and depressed; his spirit broken. The problem was not Iran, although his anger and disillusionment smouldered brightly throughout our long talk. His main preoccupation was his relationship with President Reagan and with other members of the White House staff. It was another form of disillusionment, the feeling that he was not succeeding in convincing the President of the importance of foreign policy issues; in his eyes, Reagan was a great and wonderful president, who had an almost uncanny understanding for everything American but very little patience for anything outside the United States.

Deep down McFarlane felt that he was not getting through to the President, which in those weeks before the Geneva summit with Gorbachev had become critical. (The December 1985 summit was to bring about the first real breakthrough in Great Power relations, which heralded several years later the dawn of what we then believed was a new era.) It was this bigger

bigger issue and not Iran that led him to resign in December, and he would not be deflected from his decision.

McFarlane had been occupied almost exclusively by the preparations for this Geneva summit and had consequently delegated the overseeing of the Iranian operation to a member of his staff, Lieutenant-Colonel Oliver North. I had met North for the first time on that November day in 1985 when I went to the White House to see McFarlane. North was much more interested in obtaining the release of the hostages – which he knew to be of cardinal importance for the President – than in continuing the contacts with the Muslim cleric who represented the pro-western opposition to the rulers of Tehran, but who did not have in his power to free the hostages.

Shortly after McFarlane's resignation, I ceased to be involved in the Iranian operation; so did Schwimmer and Nimrodi. The new team – Admiral Poindexter, North and the Israeli adviser to the Prime Minister on terrorism, Amiram Nir – concentrated only on the contact with Mussavi and Kangarlou, while the all-important second channel was completely ignored; no more meetings were held with the Muslim cleric or with other members of his group.

I consider this to have been the greatest mistake in the Iranian operation. Until the change-over in 1986, McFarlane, Ledeen and the Israeli team maintained the strategic context of the operation as its primary objective, but once the new men had taken over, the Iranian operation was transformed into an arms-for-hostages deal. This conformed with the wishes of the Iranian radicals, who, however, played the game according to their own rules, which were quite different from those of the Americans. The new American–Israeli team accepted this revision of our earlier concept. They dispensed with Ledeen because he continued to stress the strategic aim of our initial operation and had opposed the arms-for-hostages format.

The efforts of Nir and North did lead to what might have become a singular success – a meeting between American and Iranian officials in Tehran in May 1986. McFarlane was called back from retirement to head the American delegation, but what could have become a fitting climax to the Iranian operation ended in dismal failure. The Americans had been told by Ghorbanifar that they would meet the Iranian Prime Minister and Rafsanjani; that the American hostages would be taken from Lebanon and assembled in Tehran in readiness for the arrival of the American delegation; and that the hostages would then be released in exchange for Hawk missile spare parts, which the Americans had agreed to bring with them.

Reality, however, was to be cruelly different. When the Boeing bringing the American delegation landed at the military section of Tehran's Mahrabad airport on 26 May 1986, there were no senior Iranian officials to meet them, not Rafsanjani – as McFarlane had been led to expect – nor, indeed, anyone else. Ghorbanifar, together with Kangarlou, arrived at the airport over an hour late to escort the Americans to their hotel. They fared no better during the rest of their stay. Neither Mussavi nor Rafsanjani met them.

217

The most senior official who eventually was allowed to meet the former National Security Adviser and his team during their four-day stay in Tehran was the chairman of the Iranian Foreign Affairs Committee of the Iranian Parliament, Mohammed Ali Hadi Najafabadi. There was no meeting of minds, no acceptance of one set of rules to guide the talks. McFarlane, perhaps more than anyone that I know, was eminently unsuited for the bazaar bargaining which so characterized Iranian negotiating postures. He was not one to suffer lightly the long rigmarole of walking away only to come back at the last minute to strike a compromise bargain, which is what the Iranians expected. 'Take two of the hostages,' they almost pleaded with him when they saw he was serious about leaving; 'the others will come later.' But McFarlane would have none of it; he demanded the immediate release of all the hostages and would accept nothing less. After four days of fruitless discussions, he left Tehran an angry and frustrated man without any hostages.

Could it have ended differently? The Iranians insist that they would have given up the two hostages and arranged a continuation of the dialogue if McFarlane had not left so abruptly. Be that as it may, the meeting was a fiasco mainly because it had not been prepared properly. The Americans relied blindly on the arrangements being organized by Ghorbanifar and made no effort to find out beforehand what would be the framework, the agenda and the likely outcome of the meeting. Henry Kissinger told me later that he would never have gone to such a meeting with Iranians without first having worked out with them the minutest details – including the results.

In the ensuing months, two hostages were released – the Reverend Lawrence Jenco on 26 July and David Jacobsen on 2 November 1986 – after more arms had been sent to Iran in direct contrast to the policy that McFarlane had followed in Tehran. The arms shipments and hostage releases came about after a series of meetings had been held through two separate channels – the old one with Ghorbanifar, in which North and Nir played a major role, and a new one with a relative of Rafsanjani, which had been initiated with the help of Albert Hakim without the knowledge of the Israelis.

The new 'Hakim channel', in particular, raised the hopes of the Americans. The Iranians had, in the summer of 1986, let it be known through two separate foreign governments that they were interested in better relations with the United States. Rafsanjani's relative proved to be forthcoming; at one of the meetings he discussed at length Iran's concerns about Afghanistan, the Soviet Union and the Persian Gulf. He proposed that a joint American–Iranian commission be set up to discuss, in secret, ways of improving US–Iranian relations.

In a note written to Admiral Poindexter on 24 September 1986, North gave free rein to the high hopes that had taken possession of him:

We appear to be in contact with the highest levels of the Iranian Government. It is possible that the Iranian Government may well be amenable to a United States role in ending the Iran–Iraq war. This, in and of itself, would be a major foreign policy success for the President.

Charles Allen of the CIA, who was closely involved in the operation, reported that the new contact had informed the Americans that Khomeini's son had briefed his father in great detail and that the Iranians had decided that it was worth talking to the Americans 'not just for arms, but, I think, for broader reasons'. Allen, in particular, was conscious of the broader strategic aims which had guided McFarlane, Ledeen and the Israeli team at the outset of the operation.

In a memorandum dated 13 October 1986, Allen spelt out what he considered to be those original objectives of the initiative – 'to open up a long-term geo-strategic relationship with Iran, to get the hostage situation out of the way because it was an obstacle to improved relations, and to discourage Iran from terrorist operations'. Allen recommended the setting up of a planning cell in the National Security Council – headed by someone like Henry Kissinger, Harold Saunders or Richard Helms (the former head of the CIA and former Ambassador in Tehran) – to make a hard programme review of this whole initiative. 'What are we trying to achieve? What are our short-term objectives? What are our long-term objectives? What are our options? A critical review of everything.'

But it was not to be. Allen's proposals came too late. Even as his memorandum was being discussed in Washington, the opponents to the operation in Tehran were preparing their counter-offensive that was to end the entire initiative – arms, hostages and, above all, the renewal of relations between the United States and Iran. The American team had, in the meantime, met once more with their Iranian counterpart at the beginning of October. This was followed by more consignments of TOW missiles sent via Israel to Iran. Hopes were high that two more hostages would now be released and, on 2 November, David Jacobsen was set free in Beirut.

A day later, on 3 November, the Lebanese *ash-Shiraa* published full details of the story that the United States had been supplying arms to Iran and that McFarlane had visited Tehran to meet Iranian officials. The curtain had been effectively brought down on the Iranian operation. There was no shortage of helping hands in Tehran willing to throw a spanner into the attempted rapprochement with the United States.

The disclosure had been inevitable. The only cause for wonder was that it had come so long after the Tehran visit of May 1986. The Iranians are as prone to rumour and gossip as any other people – maybe more so. There was no way of keeping that four-day visit from the rumour-mongers. Whether it was the Russians who caused the story to be published in the obscure Lebanese journal or whether the leak was initiated by Iranian radicals for domestic political reasons, one does not know.

The internal power struggle between the three rival factions, which Ghorbanifar had so graphically described to us at our meeting in Hamburg in July 1985, had meanwhile grown in intensity; shortly before the *ash-Shiraa* leak, Rafsanjani had one of the leading hardliners, Mehdi Hashemi, arrested together with some of his supporters. This radical faction was bitterly opposed to Rafsanjani's contacts with the United States through his relative and, after Hashemi's arrest, had an added incentive to strike back.

The tidal wave of indignation and distorted information unleashed in the United States in the wake of the publication of the *ash-Shiraa* story falls outside the scope of this book. Most of the accusations and recriminations were directed more to the Nicaraguan sub-plot in the later revelations than to the original Iranian context. Criticism of the Iranian operation centred almost entirely on the arms-for-hostages aspect, with critics paying little attention to and showing even less understanding for its broader, strategic aims. The meshing by Poindexter and North of the two sensitive clandestine operations of Iran and the Contras was a cardinal operational mistake, contravening one of the elementary rules in clandestine activity.

The failure to maintain relations with representatives of the pro-western political faction in Iran and to concentrate instead almost entirely on the hostage question was another serious error. As Ledeen so aptly put it, the operation itself became hostage to the hostages. I am still convinced that we had a duty to embark on the Iranian operation when the opportunity presented itself to bring Iran out of her isolation halting her support for terrorism, bringing her back into the geopolitical association with the West, and so tilting the balance of power in the Gulf against aggressive Iraq.

17
Gulf: Peace with Problems
1986–90

AT THE END OF 1986, when the Iranian operation came to its inglorious end, the Iran–Iraq war was still in full swing. But by then Iranian victory was no longer on the agenda. The ayatollahs had, at first, pinned their hopes on an uprising of the Shia tribes of the south – Iraq's poor and downtrodden – against the Sunni Arab minority which ruled in Baghdad. The Iranian leaders convinced themselves, if no one else, that it was only a matter of time before Saddam Hussein's regime in Baghdad would be overthrown by the Shia-dominated Iraqi army, which had suffered such heavy casualties because of Saddam's tragic decision to invade Iran. But by 1987, it had become evident to the Iranians that the Shia Arabs identified themselves more with their nation and their people – the Arabs – than with their religion. And by then it was clear, too, that Saddam's grip over the country was stronger than ever and no one had dared challenge him.

The Iranians could have ended the war victoriously in 1982, when their armies swept the Iraqis from nearly all the territory they had conquered and laid siege to Basrah. But they missed that opportunity and, by 1987, the Iranian war machine was palpably incapable of mounting another successful offensive to threaten Iraq. Seven years of war had taken their toll. Difficulties in obtaining the enormous quantities of arms needed, spiralling casualties, shortages of virtually everything, continuing Iraqi missile attacks against civilian centres and rocketing inflation all combined to create diminishing enthusiasm for a war with no end in sight.

With the military situation deadlocked on land, the focus of the war moved to the Gulf. Iraq's air superiority was increasingly disrupting Iran's oil industry and depriving her of the means to pay for the war. But while Iraq dominated the skies, Iran ruled the waves. Iran's navy had the means to retaliate against Iraq's air strikes by making the Gulf unsafe for any ships carrying Arab oil. The Iraqis, however, were not deterred. They had found the chink in Iran's armour and were determined to prevent the export of oil from Iran, whatever the consequences and whoever might be hurt. The Iraqis, moreover, had long sought to internationalize the war as a means of bringing additional pressure on Iran to end the fighting. Finally, the Iraqis succeeded in doing so beyond all expectations.

As the Iran–Contra scandal burst on the American scene, the policies of the administration turned full circle. The National Security Council and the CIA, which had initiated the approach to Iran, were now out in the cold. The Pentagon, which had all along favoured a moderately pro-Iraqi policy, was now able to dictate decisions.

Conveniently for Defense Secretary Weinberger, this change coincided with mounting tension in the Gulf. The Iraqis had increased their air attacks against Iranian oil installations and also bombed, for the first time, Iran's southern oil ports at Sirri Lavan and Larak in the lower reaches of the Gulf. The Iranians, for good measure, had escalated their threat against ships supplying Iraq and her Arab backers by acquiring the land-to-sea 'Silkworm' missiles from China. In view of this increasing violence, Kuwait, by far the most exposed of the Gulf states, made a dramatic appeal to the Great Powers for renewed protection for her tankers.

For the men of the Pentagon the Kuwaiti appeal was the opportunity for which they had been looking to redress the political damage, as they saw it, caused by the Irangate revelations. They now had an opportunity to reassure their friends in the Arab world, and particularly in the Gulf states, that America had not forsaken them for the Iranians. The swift positive response given to Kuwait's request for naval protection was justified by the need to keep open the sea-lanes of the Gulf, and by the fear that the Soviet Union might step in and provide this service if the United States failed to do so.

By mid-1987, the United States had reflagged a dozen Kuwaiti tankers and had despatched more than thirty ships of the American navy to patrol the Gulf, thus cancelling out Iran's advantage at sea. This also enabled the Iraqis to continue their air attacks against neutral tankers plying Iranian oil and against Iranian oil ports and installations. In effect, the United States had almost openly joined the war on the side of Iraq, after having given constant, but surreptitious support to Iraq beforehand. But the real gain for Saddam Hussein was that the United States' presence in the Gulf, backed by mine-sweepers from Great Britain, France, Italy, Holland and Belgium, had at last internationalized the Gulf conflict. The Iraqis had been seeking this desperately so as to increase pressure on Iran to end the war, and so it did. The UN Security Council passed Resolution 598 on 20 July 1987. This called for a cease-fire and a withdrawal of Iranian and Iraqi forces from occupied territory.

The Resolution was backed by the Russians, who, parallel to the Americans, had been following a zig-zag policy between Iraq and Iran. Neither of the Great Powers could afford to jeopardize its position with either of the protagonists. The Soviet Union dealt with that problem by alternately blowing hot and cold on both parties. It remained the principal supplier of arms for Iraq, which had signed a Treaty of Friendship with the Soviet Union in 1972; yet, at the same time, Eastern Bloc countries were the largest suppliers of military material to Iran.

The Soviet Union, at first, supported the UN Resolution, which was seen as a victory for Iraq; but soon afterwards she supported the Iranian demand that a commission be set up to establish who had been responsible for starting the war, Iran or Iraq. The Soviet Union responded positively to Kuwait's request for protection and then condemned the presence of foreign warships in the Gulf. Both Iraqi and Iranian leaders visited Moscow; both sought to proscribe the aid given by the Soviet Union to the other.

Meanwhile, the Soviet Union was endeavouring to protect her own interests, which were basically self-contradictory. Iran, with her long common frontier with the Soviet Union, was of vital importance, but the Russians could not afford to estrange the Arab world by exclusively supporting Iran. They were also fully aware of the extent of Iran's helping hand for the Afghan Mujahadeen against the Soviet-backed Afghan regime.

Beyond these considerations there was a change in Soviet foreign-policy attitudes. The extent of the economic malaise in the Soviet Union was becoming evident by 1987. Soon after the Geneva Gorbachev–Reagan summit of November 1986, it became apparent that a new chapter in Soviet–US relations had begun. The overriding Soviet need was for retrenchment, for a period of grace to enable her to put her own house in order. The resulting new face of the Soviet Union was to have important consequences in our region. Already in 1987 it led to increasing American–Soviet co-operation to end the Iran–Iraq war.

The Iranians, however, were holding out against this international pressure. They insisted that the Iraqi 'aggressor' be named and punished. At the end of 1987, Khomeini was speaking of a new military strategy which would bring ever-increasing pressure on Iraq. Rafsanjani was calling for a 'financial *jihad*' to mobilize all the country's resources in order to pursue the war until victory. However, while exhorting their people to make ever-bigger efforts and sacrifices, the Iranians were extending discreet feelers about ending the Gulf War without losing face. These peace moves were not made through the United Nations, nor through friendly or neutral governments.

The Iranians made their soundings through European businessmen who had business ties with the Government in Tehran. Iran, they were told, would be willing to terminate hostilities if Iraq were to admit her guilt of aggression and would agree to pay the sum of a $100 billion in indemnity for the loss of life and destruction of property that her aggression had caused. An agreement to pay the sum would be sufficient, the businessmen were told; there was no need actually to pay it. The Iranians knew that Iraq was not in a position to pay anything like that figure; the actual amount would be a much more modest one, which could be settled in quiet negotiations once the war had ended.

But the Iranians were too late. By 1988, the military tide was turning in Iraq's favour. In a successful surprise offensive, the Iraqi army succeeded in retaking the Faw Peninsula, inflicting heavy losses on the Iranian forces. Iraqi troops, their confidence restored, were once again advancing while the Iranians were suffering from a severe shortage of every kind of war material and from a war fatigue accentuated by their heavy loss of life, which could no longer be ignored. It was these factors, together with the renewed Iraqi successes at the front, which convinced the Iranians in 1988 that they would have to end the war on the best terms possible.

In the event, it was the American presence in the Gulf, and in particular the inadvertent shooting down of an Iranian civilian airliner, which provided the Iranian leadership with an honourable way out. It would not have been possible for Khomeini to admit to his people that he intended to sue for peace without achieving Iran's objectives because the Iraqi adversary had been too strong for him. It was a different matter, however, for him to tell the Iranian people that he was stopping the war because the United States was fighting alongside Iraq against Iran. That was more than they could manage. But even more telling was the emergence of Rafsanjani as the strong man of Iran under Khomeini.

In the internal power struggle which reached a climax after the publication of the Iran–Contra Affair, the Speaker of the Majlis had gained the upper hand. In contrast to his radical opponent, Prime Minister Mussavi, Rafsanjani's approach to Iran's problems was pragmatic. He realized that the war had long outlived its usefulness. It had served to drum up enthusiasm for the Revolution during its first year or so, but those days had gone. The war had long since become an unbearable burden, causing heavy loss of life, despair and discontent. Rafsanjani understood that the only way to rescue the country was by renewing contacts with western states and by diverting Iran's oil wealth away from military waste so as to finance her economic recovery.

Under Rafsanjani's direction, some of the largest commercial and industrial companies of Britain, Germany and France were invited to Tehran and offered attractive terms to resume active trading relations. At the same time, Rafsanjani persuaded the ageing Ayatollah Khomeini to accept the United Nations Resolution terms for a cease-fire. On 20 August 1988, all hostilities ceased. The eight-year Iran–Iraqi War, which Iraqi intelligence had estimated would last at the most for three weeks, had, at long last, ground to a halt.

Neither side had achieved its objectives. Saddam Hussein had not wiped out the 'shame of 1975', nor had he regained the entire Shatt-el-Arab and placed it once more under Iraqi sovereignty. The Iraqi dream of annexing the oil-rich, largely Arabic-speaking province of Khuzistan remained an unfulfilled dream. Just as the Shia of southern Iraq had remained loyal to the Iraqi state, so had the Arabs of Khuzistan proved to be more loyal to their country, Iran, than to their Arab identity. They had refused to join up with the invading Iraqis at the outset of the war. Saddam's third objective, the removal of the threat to Iraq which Khomeini's regime presented, had been equally unattained, for even after the guns had fallen silent, the strident voices exhorting the Iraqis to overthrow the 'atheist' regime of Saddam Hussein and to join the 'Islamic nation' continued unabated from Tehran.

The Iranians fared no better. They had succeeded in repelling the Iraqi invader, but for eight years virtually every mullah in every mosque had been repeating, time and again, the Imam's vow to overthrow the atheist Baathi regime of the infidel Saddam, to bring the light of the Islamic Revolution to the darkness of Iraq and to restore the Iraqi people to true Islam. After eight years of terrible suffering and sacrifices, the Iranians had achieved none of their goals: they had failed to export their Muslim Revolution to Iraq; Saddam was still firmly entrenched on their doorstep, at the helm of the Baghdad Government; the international community refused to brand Saddam as the aggressor; and, to cap it all, Iran in the end was forced to agree to a cease-fire with no prior agreement, indemnity or admission of Iraqi guilt.

There were no victors; only the vanquished: the people of Iran and of Iraq with their two million dead and maimed, or was it three million? No one would ever know the true cost of this senseless, cruel war.

But the causes of the war had not been removed. Iraq still coveted the Shatt-el-Arab, now firmly in Iranian hands, and was still determined to win it back. Iran still vowed to 'Islamize' Iraq. And, above all, the antipathy between Arab and Persian, Iraqi and Iranian, was stronger than ever: it had grown into an active deeply rooted hate. A balance of weakness brought about the end of the war; now an uneasy lull has taken its place – until one side or the other believes it is strong enough to start again. Therefore, neither Iran nor Iraq can drastically relax military preparedness, and the two armies remain poised on their common frontier, wary and fearful, unable in effect to look beyond their immediate horizon.

The end of the fighting brought new problems. Iraqis and Iranians released from the constraints of the emergency could become a potential danger to their respective rulers. Saddam did not wait for it. Within months after the war had ended, hundreds of officers and government officials were purged; many were executed without trial on suspicion or because of denunciation. Ministers, even family members such as the Minister of Defence, were reshuffled or relieved of their posts or of their lives. Saddam's regime became more autocratic than ever. There were few states in the world in 1989 which were more repressive, more addicted to arbitrary arrest, imprisonment, torture and execution than Iraq; more so in many respects than the blood-soaked Islamic rule of her neighbour and adversary, Iran.

In Iran, in the months following the end of the war, thousands of opponents, generally accused of supporting the outlawed Mujahadeen el-Haq, were summarily executed in Tehran and elsewhere in the country. Fear that enthusiasm for the Revolution might be waning was probably almost as great a driving force as anger and indignation at the insult to Islam by author Salman Rushdie and the edict to kill him. The ensuing world outcry and diplomatic isolation of Iran may have been bad for her economic recovery, but it served to demonstrate once more to the people of Iran that their duty was to suffer and to sacrifice for the sake of the true faith against which there existed a world conspiracy backing Rushdie. The spirit of unity, of solidarity and of identification with the Revolution was largely restored by the Rushdie affair, at the expense of Iran's good name in the world.

As Iran and Iraq prepared to face their post-war world, there were strikingly similar problems facing these two destitute, unsavoury and unlikeable regimes, destined to exist side by side in mortal enmity and terrorized by their respective rulers. Both feared the consequences peace might have on their respective regimes, and both were eager to repair the economic and social consequences of the war – the shambles that was left for them. They looked to their still substantial oil wealth to redress the adverse balance of the war.

The capture of Iran's oil-rich Khuzistan had been a central feature of Iraq's war aims. She had failed to do so, but it was symbolic for the future. For the production and distribution of oil as the only means of repairing the damage caused by the war, both countries would need to maximize their output on the world market if they were to meet the most pressing demands of their people. But in doing so, they were bound to destabilize the carefully balanced pattern of OPEC price control and plunge the world oil industry into disarray.

The price of peace in the Gulf War was the transfer of hostilities to the OPEC countries. Control over the Khuzistan oilfield had started the Gulf War; the battle for control of the world oil market had been waiting in the wings for the Gulf War to finish. Now the OPEC oil producers, especially in the Middle East, and their multinational allies had to pick up the pieces. This convoluted and manipulated oil operation had been a constant – and very silent – partner of the events in our region during these last two critical decades. We shall therefore take a closer look at the way in which Iraq in particular sought to use her oil not only as a valuable commodity but also as a lethal political weapon.

Peace without victory over Iran had left Saddam Hussein in a critical situation. He had totally miscalculated the economic and political cost and consequences of ending the war with Iran. He had evidently failed to see that the war and its concomitant weakening of Tehran would remove the Iranian threat to the Gulf rulers and to their vulnerable oil economies. In doing so, Iraq had negated the single most powerful motive for the Arab Gulf states, and also Egypt and Jordan, to provide substantial financial, economic and military aid, without which Iraq's war effort would have collapsed. When it was all over, the Gulf states no longer had the incentive to rescue Saddam from the consequences of the war. On the contrary, they were now more concerned to recoup some of the huge resources they had spent on Iraq's wartime needs. Since there was not much chance of getting back any of the money advanced to Iraq, the Gulf creditors directed their attention to ways of increasing their own oil revenues, their own major source of income.

Thus at the end of the war, with little to show for his 'victory', Saddam found himself deprived of the economic, political and ideological basis on which his regime had flourished during the eight years of war with Iran. The war was now over, but there was no peace dividend. Saddam had to find an alternative source of revenue to shore up his floundering economy and a new cause to assuage the post-war restlessness of the Iraqi people; and he had to produce results quickly.

His difficulties were further exacerbated by the steep decline in OPEC oil prices and sales, accentuated by the shrinking value of the US dollar, and in 1990 by a huge lake of unsold OPEC oil, which filled worldwide all available storage on land and at sea and acted as a constant depressant on the actual market price. During the winter 1989/90, conditions in Iraq became critical and there was no solution in sight. Iraq had difficulty selling her oil even to her traditional customers in France, Germany and Japan. All OPEC producers were exceeding their allocated quotas and offering their oil at almost any price. The so-called 'spot price' for oil in Rotterdam, London and New York was little more than a convenient figleaf for the cut-throat reality of the 'free' oil market. There was no joy there for Iraq's problems.

By February 1990, Saddam had decided that he needed to do something drastic to loosen the economic stranglehold which had gripped Iraq. In terms of Iraq's economic viability, his massive military profile with a million men unproductively under arms with some 5,000 tanks and 500 aircraft had become a liability: they were sapping the economic virility of the nation; so was the huge expenditure on sophisticated weapons, which only added to the overall insecurity of the region and not least to that of Iraq. Before he embarked on the Kuwaiti adventure, Saddam had estimated that he would have to spend $14 billion on defence in 1990, almost three-quarters of Iraq's total revenue, and he was no longer getting the friendly loans from the Gulf states, or from anyone else, to bridge the gap. The support of the PLO, the Yemen and Cuba were of little use when it came to providing the billions of dollars Saddam needed. It was therefore a much-chastened Saddam who flew into Amman on 24 February 1990 for a meeting of the leaders of the Arab Co-operation Council. It was the fourth summit of this rather pointless and ineffective institution and was attended by the four 'heads' of its strange mix of members: Egypt's Mubarak, Iraq's Saddam Hussein, Jordan's King Hussein and the Yemen's Ali Abdullah Salih.

At the summit Saddam spoke first for about an hour. He suggested that the relative intimacy and smallness of their meeting provided a better opportunity for serious analysis and discussion than the customary Arab summits; and he proceeded to discuss in thoughtful manner the changed superpower balance in the Middle East and the general transformation since the Second World War. He noted that British and French influence had become marginal and that Soviet power, on which the Arab leaders and especially the Palestinians had depended, could no longer be relied upon as a makeweight against the growing influence of the United States. He asked some pertinent questions about US policy in relation to the Gulf

War and the protection of Gulf shipping. He also said some predictably silly things about the United States and Israel.

However, it was essentially a thoughtful and self-critical speech of a kind rarely heard at an Arab assembly. It was clearly the speech of a desperate leader looking for answers and not getting any. He tried to impress on Mubarak and Hussein that the core of the Arab problem was not in Palestine but in Iraq. It was Iraq, not the PLO, that had to be helped. 'The Arabs have to be realistic to the new posture and power of the United States that has led the Soviet Union to abandon its erstwhile position of influence.'

There were new priorities to be considered as conditions in the world had changed. The eastern European alliance with the Arabs, and particularly with the Palestinians, had disintegrated. He implied that the Palestinian question had become marginal. In a memorable passage winding up his speech, which had only a passing reference to the 'Zionists' and none at all to Kuwait, he concluded that

The Gulf has become the most important spot in the region and perhaps in the whole world due to the changed international alignments and their effect on the international oil market. ... The country that will have the greatest influence in the region of the Arab Gulf and its oil will maintain its supremacy as a superpower without an equal to compete with it.

He called on the Arabs to be alert to this. He urged them to overcome their weakness and mutual distrust, and volunteered to lead them in preventing the Americans from assuming absolute control of the Gulf region.

For all the impact Saddam's plea made on his fellow 'heads', he might have been spitting into the wind. They could not have misunderstood the message, but Hussein and Mubarak pretended otherwise. They discussed everything except Saddam's central theme. He had wanted their public underwriting of his urgent request to the Gulf oil states to provide the massive financial aid which he had requested. Instead, Hussein ranted against the Jewish emigration from the Soviet Union, which was 'organized hostile action against the entire Palestinian Arab territory and threatening us in this part of the Arab homeland'. Mubarak, likewise, lamely followed Hussein's denunciation of Soviet Jewish emigration and studiously ignored Saddam's call for urgent economic help.

This Amman summit attracted little public attention at the time and had no immediate political significance. There had been no joy for Saddam in the response from Hussein and Mubarak; in any case, neither of them had the kind of financial clout that Iraq required most. For that he would need the Saudi ruler and the Emirs from the Gulf states, who were all due in Baghdad for a meeting of the Arab heads of state at the end of May.

While preparing for this crucial meeting, Saddam conferred, as was his wont, with his oil industry gurus – his expatriate 'consultants'. They were a mixed lot: former American and British senior diplomats who had served in Iraq and the Gulf states; former senior officials in the US State Department and the British Foreign Office; and important personalities from the multi-national oil companies and their lobbies. Over the years, in 1973, in 1979 and now again in 1990, they all sang the same song: they urged him to create conditions that would ensure much higher oil prices for the OPEC producers and their international distributors.

Impressive reinforcement for Saddam came within weeks from an unexpected and influential source, illustrating once again the importance of discreet consultations away from the limelight. In what could be described as his inaugural address, the newly appointed energetic chairman of British Petroleum, Robert Horton, gave voice to conclusions drawn from these discreet preliminary consultations. These had a curious, but evidently meaningful, similarity to the views being advanced by the Iraqi leader. In a keynote speech reported in the London *Times* on 22 March 1990, Horton noted that oil market conditions were such that oil companies should be giving financial aid to countries such as Iraq so that they could expand output to meet the rising demand which Horton anticipated in the near future along with a substantial increase in price, with $40 a barrel as the norm. He had earlier quoted sums in excess of $50 billion, which the western oil industry would have to provide to Iraq and the Gulf states.

All this was most encouraging for Saddam Hussein, but there was one snag: he could not afford to wait on Horton's pleasure. He needed money immediately. The only possible instant providers were his Arab neighbours – the Saudis and the Gulf states – who were coming to Baghdad on 28 May for the summit conference. Saddam decided on a low-key strategy. He made only a passing reference to the problem of oil pricing in his long opening speech devoted almost entirely to the recounting of Israel's sins. Then he sounded out the rulers of Saudi Arabia, Kuwait and the Emirates in private. They were not in favour of artificially forcing up the price of oil. They argued that the oil glut around the world was so great that this could not work.

Forty-eight hours later, Saddam called a closed session of the summit and made a very different kind of speech, details of which were not made public until they were released by Saddam himself seven weeks later on 18 July. The speech was short, frank and to the point, and it was obviously made under conditions of great personal tension and disillusionment, without the customary preliminary blessings and courtesies. 'I personally have learnt many lessons from this conference,' he began unceremoniously and meaningfully. He emphasized that oil was at the core of Arab well-being and its role was an essentially pan-Arab question. Individual Arab oil producers could not ignore this. They had to abide by their OPEC quota and drive the price of a barrel of oil from its then current $16 to at least $25. He was, in fact, closely following the Horton–BP scenario, which had also been advocated by his American oil consultants.

However, it was to no avail. The conference ended, the Arab rulers dispersed and Saddam was no better off. He had received a lot of advice, but no money. The lesson he had learned at the Arab summit was that he himself would have to take the necessary measures to ensure the higher oil price in order to get the kind of money he needed. No one else would help.

By forcing up the price of crude oil from its existing low level of around $16 or under per barrel to $25 or over, he could add anything up to $10 billion to Iraq's current annual revenue of some $30 billion. It would not be enough to meet all the demands on Iraq's economy, but it would ease the immediate pressure. However, the Gulf oil producers – Saudi Arabia, Kuwait and the Emirates especially – remained unimpressed and unhelpful. They left the Baghdad summit with Iraq's economic problems unresolved and with Saddam very much on his own. However, they did not understand the compulsive pressures at work in Iraq and they failed to comprehend the cataclysmic change that had overtaken Saddam's calculations, which, by mid-July, had transformed his planned intentions.

18
The Kuwaiti 'Lorelei'
1990

EVER SINCE THE FORMAL END of the Gulf War with the Iran–Iraq cease-fire – and even before that – there had been intense public discussion in the specialist circles of the Israel Defence Forces about Saddam Hussein's further intentions. The private unpublicized debate in Israel was even more intense. In short, it centred on the argument that Saddam had undergone an important change in his attitude towards Israel; that he had to be counted henceforth among the Arab 'moderates' who preferred a political settlement with Israel, if only as reinsurance against a potentially resurgent Iran. It was argued, therefore, that Israel needed to reassess her posture towards Iran and Iraq and to seek a rapprochement with Iraq, if only on the basis of their common opposition to the threat of Iranian expansionism and Islamic fundamentalism.

An influential pro-Iraqi lobby had, in fact, come into being, which was carefully researched by Laurie Mylroie, a professor at Harvard University, immediately after the end of the Gulf War in July 1988. Her conclusions were published in Washington's Middle East Institute's *Journal* in winter 1989. Mylroie's enquiries were not confined to Israel, but ranged over our entire region. From these, she had concluded that, with the end of the war, Iraq had fundamentally moderated her previous position. 'It had strengthened its ties with its friends, Egypt and Jordan,' and had moved to weaken Syria by her support of the anti-Syrian Christian groups in Lebanon. This weakening of Syria 'and the promotion of an Egyptian–Jordanian–Iraqi triangle enhanced the prospects for Arab–Israeli nego-tiations'.

Mylroie's documented account of the discussion about Iraq's future, and the position taken by opinion-shapers in this field in the United States, in Europe and even to a certain extent in Israel, clearly resulted in a pre-set evaluation of Iraq's future role among the Arab moderates with whom Israel could come to terms. I mention it here because this fallacy contributed greatly to the general misreading of Saddam's intentions and provided a kind of intellectual justification for the military and economic aid that the western world was giving Iraq. Saddam managed to bamboozle not only the Americans and Europeans, but also his fellow-Arab rulers who had come to Baghdad for the May 1990 summit. They were reassured by

Saddam – even when he raised the question of the oil price during the last hours of the summit. He had done it in a manner that was attractive to all oil producers and he had not singled out any country, not even Kuwait, for special mention.

In a manner of speaking, this was Saddam's sedative for Washington and the Gulf states. It worked. The participants and the outside observers departed when the summit ended on 30 May. No one was upset, no one made any fuss. The official summit had been a Roman holiday for denouncing Soviet Jewish emigration to Israel, on which all agreed. The closed session on the last day with Saddam's desperate appeal for economic help was conveniently kept a close secret by the participants. Iraq's new moderate orientation was not considered to be a threat to anyone.

The immediate aftermath, June 1990, would be remembered only for its unbearable soaring temperatures everywhere. It was too hot for crises. The people who mattered had taken off to the hills or, preferably, the Swiss mountains. Only the British Foreign Secretary, Douglas Hurd, chose to be in the Saudi capital on 3 June for a meeting with King Fahd. Iraq was not on the agenda; in fact, it was not on anyone's agenda. Neither was the price of oil, according to Hurd's regulation press conference that followed; only, as always, Israel and the PLO. The British had followed the Americans in breaking off their informal discussions because of the PLO's malpractice. However, Hurd reassured the eager pressmen in Riyadh that this had not made his feelings towards Israel 'any warmer'. It would have been difficult, in any case, in that June heat in Riyadh. But for the rest, it seemed as if the politicians and propagandists had wisely gone to ground – except for 700 Islamic enthusiasts from seventy Islamic countries who assembled in Baghdad on 16 June 1990 to express their solidarity with Saddam 'in the face of the Zionist–American conspiracy against Iraq'.

One further piquant encounter in that eventful June came to Israel's attention. The PLO leader, Yasser Arafat, sent a personal message to the Emir of Kuwait, Sheikh Jabr el-Ahmad, with his personal aide, Hani el-Hassan. Arafat praised 'Kuwait's major role in confronting the barbarian Shamir's campaign against Jordan and against Israel's plans to reoccupy the Sinai Peninsula and cross the Suez Canal into Egypt'. He warned the Emir to beware Israel's claim that she wanted to make peace with the Palestinians. 'The PLO', Arafat assured him, 'is planning how best to defeat Israel in the coming war. We shall continue our armed struggle against this dirty enemy.' The poor Emir, probably the world's richest if not its wisest man that day, did not realize that only seven weeks later it would be he and his country, Kuwait, who would be Arafat's 'dirty enemy' at the receiving end of the 'armed struggle'. However, Arafat had played his assigned part in helping to disarm Kuwait before Iraq struck on 2 August.

Saddam Hussein was evidently anxious not to alarm either his Iranian or his Arab neighbours. He was preparing various pressures in readiness for the day – it was to be the 18th of July – when he would uncover his hand

and demand that Kuwait should agree to terms which he communicated, not to Kuwait, but to the Arab League Secretary. At the same time, Iraq began to move troops and tanks demonstrably to the Kuwaiti border to impress on the Kuwaiti ruler that she meant business. Saddam had to move in a hurry; he could not afford to wait any longer, for the Kuwaitis had been alerted by the well-informed Iranians, whose intelligence in Iraq was of the best. They had warned the Kuwaiti rulers of Saddam's intentions and initiated talks to counter his plans.

The Americans and the Kuwaitis had, indeed, known that Iraq wanted to force up the price of oil, to reduce Kuwait's output and to negotiate on the remaining difference with Kuwait concerning the boundary with Iraq, the disputed small islands in the Gulf and outstanding debts estimated at $10 billion. Kuwait was prepared to negotiate the oil price and output, and to listen to what Iraq had to say on the territorial question. It was a manageable situation and, therefore, there was no cause for the Americans to worry unduly. That was the situation at the beginning of July.

But then the unexpected happened, which sounded the alarm bells in Baghdad. The Americans and also Israel had been aware for some time that Saddam had been playing a double game with his fellow Arabs. His mercurial Foreign Minister, Tariq Aziz, had been quietly – and, he believed, secretly – negotiating with the Iranian Foreign Ministry. However, these talks had been effectively monitored – and not only in Washington. It was fascinating to observe Iran's agile and sophisticated Foreign Minister, Ali Akhbar Veliyati, play with Aziz like an experienced fisherman accustomed to netting the Caspian sturgeon. Aziz was no match for the Iranian, and the terms offered by Iraq were unacceptable to Iran. But Veliyati did not say so. He kept the diplomatic ball in play and the Iraqis quiet while he was preparing an altogether different game. On 9 July 1990, while Saddam and Aziz were still maintaining their low profile, talking only of the need for upping the oil price and alarming no one except consuming motorists, Veliyati went public with what he believed would be Iran's masterstroke and Kuwait's lifeline.

On the morning of 9 July, the Foreign Affairs Ministry in Tehran dropped its diplomatic bombshell into Saddam's lap. It announced that Veliyati, who was leading a high-ranking political delegation to Kuwait at the invitation of Kuwait's Deputy Prime Minister, had begun his first round of talks in Kuwait that morning: 'Veliyati has been assured by the Kuwaiti leader that Kuwait will take any action necessary to secure a lasting peace and tranquillity in the region.'

On the following day, the Iranian Foreign Minister and his formidable team of soldiers, diplomats and expert economists met the ruler of Kuwait, his Prime Minister, the Crown Prince and leading officials. Most of the preparatory work for far-reaching agreements had been done in advance. As a token of goodwill, the Kuwaitis released a number of Shi'i prisoners held for terrorist activity against the Government. Veliyati welcomed the agreements with Kuwait as 'very productive for the new relationship between Iran and Kuwait'. It was the beginning of a new course which would ensure a bright future for the area 'on the basis of co-operation, good neighbourliness and Islamic brotherhood between the countries in the Gulf region'.

It was not what Saddam had visualized. It might even have been intended as a warning to Iraq. The entire timescale and scope of Saddam's planned operation was thrown into disarray. He could no longer afford to proceed as he had intended, as he was to explain later that month to April Glaspie, the US Ambassador in Baghdad.

He was still unsure of the turn which events would take when, on 25 July, he discussed these with Glaspie, an Arabist with some thirty years' experience in the Middle East. In a lengthy résumé of Iraq's position, Saddam's words sharply reflected his uncertainties only a week before he ordered his troops into Kuwait. According to the stenogram, he told Glaspie:

I beg you clearly to take note of Iraq's rights which are mentioned in the memorandum we sent to the Arab League on 18 July. We will take these rights one by one. That might happen now or after one month or after one year, but we will take them all. We are not the kind of people to relinquish our rights.

Kuwait and the United Emirates had no historic right to deprive Iraq of her legitimate claim, Saddam insisted.

The only thing Saddam did not spell out to the US Ambassador was the fact that he had abandoned his step-by-step tactic and was preparing to take all of Kuwait, all of Iraq's 'rights', within a matter of days. The Americans did not believe the threatening signals, nor did the Kuwaitis and nor did President Mubarak. In fact, Mubarak described the situation as no more than a 'passing cloud'. He accepted Saddam's assurance that Iraq was not going to invade Kuwait so long as the Kuwaitis were prepared to negotiate. Neither Mubarak nor the Americans seemed to appreciate that Saddam was no fool and would understand the implications of the Kuwaiti agreement with Iran, which had pre-empted any negotiation between Kuwait and Iraq.

Iran's agreement with Kuwait had been made public by Tehran on 10 July. It was the watershed for Saddam and the hoped-for reinsurance for Kuwait. It decided Saddam to jettison his timetable and to stake all before the Americans, the Iranians and the Kuwaitis realized what was happening. Kuwait's Iranian deal caused Saddam to act without due preparation. However, as so often happens, he had not calculated the consequences of his intended move any more than had Kuwait and Iran when they concluded their agreement to pre-empt Iraq.

In a different class, but belonging to the same family, were the consequences for Israel of President Bush's instant reaction to the Iraqi occupation and sacking of Kuwait on 2 August 1990. With UN approval and Saudi consent, the United States put together an American–Arab–European expeditionary force based in Saudi Arabia to interdict Iraqi plans.

Israel was to be excluded so as not to offend Arab susceptibilities.

It was to be a fateful decision for us, whether good or bad only time would show. However, we had some early indications of what we could expect in the wake of the Kuwaiti crisis however it would be resolved. First came a confidential message – soon made public across the world – from the Bush administration to Israel's Prime Minister Shamir. It expressed the President's wish for Israel to maintain what the message euphemistically called 'a low profile' in the current Kuwaiti crisis. Less diplomatically phrased, it was a request for Israel to be neither seen nor heard, nor to participate in the unfolding international campaign against Saddam's aggression in Kuwait. Reluctantly, and with justifiable misgivings, Shamir complied with Bush's urgent plea to keep the international alliance against Iraq strictly *Judenrein*. We were told that without the international community's acceptance of this policy of Arab apartheid concerning Israel, the anti-Saddam coalition at the United Nations and in the field in Saudi Arabia would disintegrate. The American request for an Israeli 'low profile' and Israel's acceptance, since we really had no choice in the matter, was understandably not publicly discussed or fully considered in Israel at the time.

The first short-sighted and partisan reaction to our new 'low profile' came from the British Foreign Office spokesman in an early debate on the Gulf crisis for which Parliament had been recalled from its long summer recess. The Foreign Office's exploitation of Israel's gesture to help Bush came as no surprise to me. As Director-General of Israel's Foreign Ministry, I had first stormily encountered Britain's future Foreign Secretary, Douglas Hurd, when he was still a junior minister at the Foreign Office in the early 1980s. But, in the event, it was the British Minister of State at the Foreign Office, William Waldegrave, who gave vent to Foreign Office feelings on the first day of the parliamentary debate on 6 September. It was an opportunity not to be missed.

As Hurd's principal minister responsible for Middle East affairs, his comments on the changing face of Middle Eastern alliances following the UN call for sanctions against Iraq received and deserved special attention. Waldegrave did not disappoint the expectations of Israel's critics and adversaries; all the more so, since his comments appeared to be impromptu in response to another member's question and, therefore, in rather less guarded language than the customary, bland set-piece brief provided for such occasions.

Waldegrave had been interrupted by an opposition member and asked whether he would care to make his own comments on the implications for the situation in the Gulf of the strategic alliance between Israel and the United States. The Minister was only too willing to oblige. The interesting point, he told the House, was that this strategic alliance had no relevance to the Gulf situation. Indeed, he added, it was noteworthy 'what a small part Israel is playing in any of these events'. He conveyed his firm conviction that in this new order in the Middle East, Israel had ceased to matter.

That might lead certain people in the US Congress, Waldegrave mused hopefully, 'to learn a lesson': that an American strategic alliance with Israel 'was not particularly useful if it cannot be used in a crisis such as this'. The United States would now be looking for 'invitations from the Arab nations to seek allies in the wider Arab world. The dog that has not barked in the night is interesting.'

So was Waldegrave. We listened with fascination to his further revelations of the Foreign Office's new concept for American–Israeli relations 'after Kuwait'. It would be necessary, in the first place, to ensure that 'Israel was kept out' of the new American–Arab association that would be handling the Middle East, because were Israel to be involved, Waldegrave warned, the resulting consequences and instabilities would be difficult to handle. The 'low profile' which had been imposed on Israel had also, in the Foreign Office estimate, largely marginalized Israel as a strategic or political factor in the region. Thus, in this new situation, when Kuwait and Iraq had 'returned to their own countries', we could then negotiate 'about the far more complex and deeper issues of the Palestinians in relation to Israel'. He had been particularly saddened 'by the way the PLO had missed a wonderful opportunity' by choosing to support Saddam. They would have done so much better if only they had listened to their friends in the Foreign Office. However, there was still time for them to correct their tragic mistake. 'I hope and pray that they will do so,' the Foreign Office Minister concluded with evident feeling.

Four weeks later, on 2 October, Bush addressed the UN General Assembly. He also believed that in the aftermath of Iraq's unconditional departure from Kuwait, there would be new opportunities for Iraq and Kuwait to settle their difficulties, for the states of the Gulf themselves to build a new arrangement for stability and 'for all the states and peoples of the region to settle the conflict that divides the Arabs from Israel'. It was a nice thought, but the supporting evidence was thin. In the years I have surveyed in this book, I have seen seven hopeful US Presidents promising a new order of peace and any number of British Foreign Secretaries and Foreign Office ministers telling us what we should do for our own good. We would then have peace.

However, even without Saddam Hussein's Kuwaiti 'Lorelei', we had to concern ourselves with the 'peace problem' on our doorstep, the supposed key to all else – the Palestinian denouement which I now propose to consider.

PART 4
The Denouement: Israel and the Palestinian Arabs

19
There Could Have Been Peace in Palestine
1967

THERE WAS A MOMENT of hope, a fleeting opportunity, when we occupied Judea, Samaria and the Gaza Strip in June 1967. In those heady days, in the wake of our incredible success, Israelis – and many Palestinians – believed we were on the threshold of peace. It did not need all that much to bring about the transformation of our military triumph into political achievement. All it required was some imagination, some magnanimity and a lot of understanding.

It was not to be. In the event, neither side rose to the occasion. It could have been otherwise. There were voices on both sides beckoning, pointing the way. Instead, we had a continuation of our war waged by the blind against the deaf. Israelis and Palestinian Arabs have since co-existed in mutual hostility without at any time accepting or even understanding the realities which have produced it. All they can see is the deep gulf which separates them, two people fighting for the same land in the certainty that Justice and Right are on their side.

The dividing line between the two peoples had been sharpened in 1948, when the Arab League states tightened their hold on Palestinian affairs and rejected the UN partition plan which would have created an independent Arab state and an independent Israeli state in Palestine. Instead, Egypt, Syria, Saudi Arabia, Jordan and the other Arab League states sought to undo the UN decision by force when they launched their armies against Israel on the day she had been established in accordance with that decision. The Arab League states half succeeded in their mission. They failed to bring about the elimination of Israel, but they managed to prevent the establishment of a State of Palestine alongside the newly created Israel, which had been an integral part of the UN plan.

In doing so, they set in train a spiral of violence and frustration, followed by the occupation of what was left of Palestine by Egypt and Jordan. These territories had been allocated by the United Nations to the Palestinian Arab state, which had been aborted by the political rejection and military action of the Arab states without any real consultation with the Palestinian Arab population. The new occupiers of the rump of Palestine made certain that there would be no resurgence towards an accommodation between Israel and the Palestinian Arabs after the West Bank and the Gaza Strip had come under Jordanian and Egyptian control.

However, the Gazans and the West Bank population were compensated by Egypt and Jordan for the Draconian administration which they imposed on the local population. For the next nineteen years, the Palestinian subjects of the Hashemite Kingdom of Jordan and of Egypt were provided with an unmitigated hate-campaign directed at Israel. This successfully implanted in the Palestinians a perversely distorted image of Israel and of the Israelis. We were turned into monsters depicted in Streicher-type caricatures. We were hated and feared.

Then, suddenly, in six fateful days in June 1967, the Israeli 'monsters' – as they had perceived them – were in their midst. King Hussein had been guilty of a mixture of monumental wishful thinking and miscalculation when he believed President Nasser's assurances on the first day of the war that the Egyptian armies were marching victoriously on Tel Aviv.* His mistake was to cost him the West Bank of his kingdom and was to change the history of the Middle East.

Hussein had chosen to ignore and reject the personal message brought to Amman by a UN emissary, which urged him, for his own sake and that of his people, to stay out of the war. Israel had no quarrel with him that warranted going to war. The message from Prime Minister Eshkol, which General Odd Bull, commander of the UN Truce Supervision Organization, brought personally to Hussein on the morning of 5 June, said: 'We are engaged in a defensive battle on the Egyptian front, and we shall not engage in any action against Jordan unless Jordan attacks us first. Should Jordan attack Israel, we shall respond with all our strength.'

It seemed to us at the time that we were offering the King a straight-forward alternative to war and disaster. It was self-evident to us, as it was to General Bull and to an American envoy who took a similar message to Amman. They were shocked and we were surprised by Hussein's almost off-hand rejection of an opportunity to save his army and the integrity of his kingdom. We had believed that he was a man of sound judgement, and this reckless action on his part appeared to be wholly out of character. What we did not realize then was the extent to which he was determined to go to war against us.

It was not merely a question of military planning, but more one of general policy of inculcating hatred of Israel and fostering the belief, among Palestinians especially, that Israel's days were numbered as the prospect of war and an Arab victory drew near. On the West Bank, especially in the towns, there were noisy and enthusiastic demonstrations calling for war; it was the same in Gaza, where thousands of members of the PLO had been armed and were demonstrating wildly with chants of '*Itbah, Itbah, Itbah*' (Kill, Kill, Kill) and calls for 'Tomorrow in Tel Aviv', and hailing Nasser

---

* The telephone conversation between Nasser and Hussein was conducted on an open line and was overheard and recorded by Israel. The cassette is kept in our Foreign Ministry in Jerusalem.

as the new liberator of all Palestine. The euphoria, and the hatred of Israel which Nasser and Hussein had encouraged over the years, was now bearing fruit.

Hussein was later to use this popular enthusiasm among the Palestinians as his alibi and excuse for so recklessly going to war against us. But he also had other reasons: he saw himself again as a popular partner of Nasser, a war hero among his usually disaffected Palestinian subjects, and he credulously accepted the estimates of his senior officers that together with Egypt and with the promised support units from Syria, Saudi Arabia and Iraq, Jordan's armed forces would master the Israelis this time.

Perhaps it is idle now to speculate on the course Middle Eastern history – and particularly that of Israel and Jordan – would have taken had Hussein shown some of that personal courage for which he has become justly famed when he spoke to Nasser on that fateful morning of 5 June; instead, Hussein seemed at pains to show that he accepted Nasser's version of events. But even without Nasser's call, there was no going back for Hussein: he had conditioned his armed forces and his civilian subjects for just this situation. And now that the moment of truth had come, he could not back down. He claimed afterwards that, even if he had not joined in the war, Israel would have invaded Jordan if only to wrest the West Bank from his rule. He must have known that this was not true. We had always respected Jordanian military intelligence and they were completely aware that we had no intention of attacking Jordan; we were, moreover, fully occupied on the Egyptian and Syrian fronts.

When Jordanian artillery began shelling Jerusalem and other Israeli centres, the Israeli command diverted units sparingly and reluctantly to the central front. But once battle was joined, there was no turning the clock back. Once the first shots are fired, war has a logic all of its own. The consequences of those first ill-conceived shots by the Arab Legion were devastating for the Palestinians and the Jordanians, while the bemused Israelis, who only a week previously had felt that their very existence as a state hung in the balance, now suddenly found themselves in the role of conquerors, masters of all the land of Palestine to the west of the River Jordan to which the Zionist movement had originally laid claim.

At the time, I was a reserve officer in the Israeli army. My duties were to establish links with leading Palestinian Arab residents on the West Bank. Dan Bawli and I were ordered to engage in a fact-finding expedition to determine who were the Palestinians who could be considered to be part of the political elite in their respective communities, and what were their political opinions. For the next three weeks we scoured the West Bank and, within the framework of our reserve duty, conducted what was in effect an ad hoc opinion poll of representative Palestinians. We were subsequently appointed by Prime Minister Eshkol to a 'special inter-ministerial committee responsible for political contacts in the occupied territories'. Bawli and I must have visited virtually every village and town on the West Bank and spoken with innumerable politically inclined Palestinians.

With some, such as Aziz Shehadeh, we became close friends. Shehadeh was a prominent lawyer and a forceful protagonist for the establishment of an independent Palestinian state comprising the West Bank and Gaza. He was a long-time opponent and critic of Hashemite rule over the Palestinians and had defended many nationalists brought to trial by the Hashemite regime. We met with prominent supporters of Hussein and Jordan such as Anwar el-Khatib and Anwar Nusseibeh (who only two years previously had refused to speak at the annual conference of London's Institute of Strategic Studies because there was an Israeli in the audience); with traditionalist leaders, such as Hikmat el-Masri and Sheikh Ja'bari; and – not least – with the revolutionaries, some of whom would later be expelled and become leaders of the PLO. Among them were Ibrahim Bakr, Kamal Nasser and Mohammed Abu Meizar (Abu Hatem).

We experienced also the hatred against Israel which had been instilled over the years by Jordanian propaganda. One example was sharply etched in our memory. We met a Palestinian Arab teacher in one of the larger villages. Bawli and I had already noted that there were hardly any women or children in the village. We asked the teacher what had happened to them. At first, he seemed too embarrassed to reply, but eventually he told us the reason for their absence: shortly before Israeli units reached the village, a Palestinian Arab from a neighbouring village had come to them and told them that Israeli soldiers were killing all the children and raping the women. 'So we quickly assembled as many women and children as we could find and took them across the river to Jordan before the soldiers arrived,' the teacher explained. We then asked what had happened to those women and children who had been left behind. 'We could not understand it,' the teacher replied in evident bewilderment; 'the soldiers gave candy to the children and were polite to our women.' It was just one example among many. The people we talked to were in varying degrees of shock from the sudden and dramatic change that had transformed their lives and their surroundings and particularly had brought them into direct contact with the Israeli 'monsters'. But they recovered quickly when they discovered the Israeli reality; their relief to be rid of Jordanian rule was genuine, not simply a way to find favour with the new occupier.

There could be no doubt about this. A clear picture emerged from our many conversations across the political and social spectrum. The Palestinian Arabs – except for a minority with special interests – did not want to return to Jordanian rule. Most of them distrusted and hated King Hussein. They despised the Bedouin of the East Bank, Hussein's pillar of strength, and feared the heavy-handed Bedouin soldiers of Hussein's Arab Legion. They suffered from economic discrimination designed to favour the East Bank Jordanians against the West Bank Palestinians. More than anything, the West Bank Palestinian Arabs wanted to be free to shape their own future. They were therefore prepared to strike a deal with their latest masters – one they could never have contemplated under the previous Turkish, British or Jordanian overlordship: in return for an independent state or entity on the West Bank and in Gaza, they were willing to sign a formal peace treaty with Israel and co-operate and co-exist with us in every way. This was in stark contrast to the conventional position of the Arab states.

Forty leading Palestinian Arabs, organized by a small group of activists led by Shehadeh, proposed holding an assembly in Jericho to set in motion this encouraging development towards a peace agreement and to some form of Palestinian independence. Those of us who had been in daily touch with this Palestinian group felt that we had before us an opportunity to reach an agreement with representative Palestinians which should not be missed, even if it meant giving up some of the land which we considered to be ours. We were convinced that such a Palestinian entity, closely linked to Israel, would not pose a security risk to the existence of Israel. The details concerning borders, security measures, economic co-operation and many other matters would have to be negotiated. Shehadeh and his activists were prepared and willing to go ahead. We recommended that Israel should enter into these negotiations forthwith.

In the event, neither the Palestinian Arabs nor the Israelis were politically or psychologically ready to contemplate such an eventuality. Hussein, the PLO and Israel joined forces in their separate ways and for their separate reasons to prevent this revolutionary idea of an Israeli-Palestinian peace taking root.

Most alarmed by this turn of events had been the activist factions of the PLO. As yet, these had still not attained the leadership role among the Palestinians which they were to achieve in later years. The Fatah organization, which was to become the largest and most influential in the PLO, had been in existence for less than three years and had not yet become the predominant factor in Gaza, Judea and Samaria. Even so, the independent action taken by Shehadeh and his associates was viewed with alarm by the PLO leadership in Beirut.

Arafat and his colleagues among the PLO leaders singled out Shehadeh's objective of an independent Palestinian state in territories evacuated by Israel for vitriolic condemnation. The historian of the PLO, Alain Gresh, has vividly recalled the tenor of Arafat's denunciation of Shehadeh, which he first made in 1967 and repeated again and again, not least after the PLO's 'Black September' in Jordan in 1970.

Arafat told Shehadeh and his associates that he could not accept their proposal to establish a Palestinian state. This was part of an American–Israeli plot to establish a Palestinian state linked to Israel. He accused the Palestinians of not wanting to continue to fight, of having had enough of war and seeking a peaceful way out by agreeing to establish a Palestinian state on the West Bank and in Gaza. Then followed Arafat's classic denunciation of the idea of a Palestinian state alongside the continued existence of Israel. Gresh quotes Arafat's actual words:

This is the most dangerous proposal that could be made. In the name of the

Palestine Revolution I hereby declare that we shall oppose the establishment of this state to the last member of the Palestinian people, for if ever such a state is established it will spell the end of the whole Palestinian cause.

Shehadeh was not intimidated by Arafat's fury. He was aware of the extent of the support of informed Palestinian opinion on the West Bank and in Gaza. He now reached out also to the Palestinians in exile, especially to the students in Beirut, Cairo and Kuwait. It took a little while, but by November 1968 he had made up his mind and drafted a public appeal to the Arab Governments and the Government of Israel. It was published a month later in the London *New Middle East*, which had a considerable circulation in Beirut and in other Arab capitals as well as in Israel. The impact was 'electric', especially among the Palestinian students at the American University in Beirut. Shehadeh had concluded his appeal with a message to the Arab world and to Israel:

Do not ignore the Palestinians as a party capable, morally and physically, of taking a leading role in any peace offensive ... to make possible such a move, such a settlement, such co-existence and genuine peace between the peoples who inhabit this country, and who must do so in peace and understanding.

The response to this simple appeal, he told me soon afterwards, was unbelievable. He realized that he had struck a cord, especially among the younger Palestinian generation at universities abroad. He decided that, if he had meant what he had said, he would have to take the bull by the horns and confront Arafat himself. He felt encouraged and justified by the support he was receiving from Palestinians of every class.

Once again, he chose the *New Middle East* as his medium to reach as wide an audience as possible. Although the political climate had become tense, following an Israeli commando attack on the airport at Beirut, he decided to go ahead for the moment seemed propitious. It was a challenging pronouncement addressed to the new leader of the PLO, Arafat, who had been 'elected' chairman of the executive after a political coup at the 5th Palestine National Council in Cairo on 4 February 1969 and had proclaimed the objective of a Palestinian democratic state in all Palestine. Shahadeh finished his policy statement early in February 1969, and it was published in London a month later under the title, 'Our way to Palestinian Nationhood – a reply to Yasir Arafat'.

Shehadeh proceeded to explain 'why Fatah did not speak for democratic Palestine', despite its pretension to do so. He charged Arafat, in effect, with double-talk designed to mislead the Palestinians with his call for a Palestinian state. 'What the Fatah leaders are asking for', wrote Shehadeh, 'is not the establishment of two states in Palestine, one Israeli and the other Palestinian: they are calling for one state for the whole area of Palestine. They aim therefore at the elimination of the state of Israel and the final solution of Zionist ambitions.'

In a staged interview in the official Fatah publication *Free Palestine*, in August 1969, Arafat confirmed the accuracy of Shehadeh's accusation.

Asked how he reconciled his objective of a 'democratic state' in all Palestine with Fatah's call for 'Palestine, Arab and Free', he replied:

We have offered our solution: a democratic Palestinian state; such a state can only acquire viability by forming a part of the surrounding Arab area. ... The word Arab implies a common culture and a common language and a common background. The majority of the future State of Palestine will be Arab. For there are at present 2,500,000 Palestinian Arabs of the Moslem and Christian faiths and another 1,250,000 Arabs of the Jewish faith who live in what is now the State of Israel. ... The immediate objective of el-Fatah is the total liberation of Palestine from Zionism.

As for the 1.25 million Jews in Israel who were not 'Arabs' in Arafat's eyes, they would be repatriated 'to their former homes' in Germany, Central Europe and the Soviet Union, in accordance with official PLO policy.

Shehadeh's stand did not endear him to the PLO leadership. It spared no effort and no expense to discredit the idea of an independent Palestinian state on the West Bank and in Gaza. Shehadeh was threatened with physical violence if he did not desist. But the PLO was not alone in its condemnation of the Palestinians who had supported Shehadeh. The Jordanian authorities launched a co-ordinated campaign directed at the notion of a separate Palestinian entity as advocated by Shehadeh and his friends.

Hussein himself opened the attack and set the tone. 'As far as we are concerned,' he insisted, 'the two banks of the Jordan form one homeland and will continue to do so.' The Jordanian Government-sponsored broadcasts sought to outdo the PLO in verbal violence when they denounced the Palestinian 'separatists' as traitors and warned all Palestinians who were thus, in effect, 'collaborating' with the Israelis that they would be punished by death, by summary execution. Jordan called on all Palestinians to remain loyal to king, country and the Arab homeland. This was the stick.

The much more effective carrot was the promise by Hussein that all government employees, judges, teachers, nurses, postal workers and street cleaners who remained loyal to the King would continue to receive their salaries from Amman (in addition to their normal salaries paid to them by the Israelis) unless they were 'collaborating' with Israel.

This Jordanian campaign against the Palestinian 'separatists' had a much greater impact among Palestinians than the PLO's attempt at intimidation. Nineteen years of harsh Jordanian rule had left its mark. The Palestinians may not have liked the King's Bedawi establishment on the East Bank, but they respected its authoritarianism and feared its clout, which the Jordanians knew how to use with great expertise and effect. Even so, it is questionable whether Hussein's policy to thwart the incipient Palestinian attempt at independence would have been so effective had it not received support from a most unlikely quarter – from the Eshkol Government in Israel.

Flushed by the amazing victory of the Six Day War, Israel's leaders had convinced themselves that at last, nineteen years after the establishment of the state, peace was at hand. Israel's partners at the peace table were to be the Arab states which had waged war against her. They would sit together and negotiate; Israel and each of her neighbours would talk to each other directly and without intermediaries. That was the generally held belief.

Two days after the fighting had stopped, Israel's Prime Minister set out the new ground rules for the negotiation of the coming peace in a speech to the Knesset. It was a tough speech, which reflected the feeling of confidence – and relief – of the people of Israel. Eshkol addressed himself more to the world leaders than to the Israeli members of the Knesset:

Do not be under any illusion that the State of Israel is prepared to return to the conditions which prevailed until a week ago. ... Now a new situation has been created which should become the basis for direct negotiations for a peace settlement with the Arab countries.

A month later, the Cabinet decided unanimously that Israel would not withdraw from the cease-fire line until agreement had been reached as a result of direct negotiations with the Arab country concerned. The following day, all major parties in the Knesset formally endorsed this Cabinet decision. 'Until peace is achieved,' read the Knesset resolution, 'Israel will continue to maintain the present situation as established by the cease-fire which was brought about by the successful action of the Israel Defence Forces.'

In those heady days it seemed to us that at last there was a real opportunity to bring about a state of peaceful co-existence with our Arab neighbours. 'We ask world opinion, which rallied to us in our plight, to accompany us faithfully in our new opportunity,' pleaded Foreign Minister Eban at the UN General Assembly on 19 June 1967, less than ten days after the end of the war. And he added Israel's undertaking that, 'in free negotiations with each of our neighbours, we shall offer durable and just solutions redounding to our mutual advantage and honour'. Israel hoped to replace the armistice agreements negotiated with Egypt, Jordan, Syria and Lebanon in 1949, which, in Eban's words, 'had been shattered', with a durable peace.

The Palestinians did not figure in this rosy scenario. Shehadeh's proposals for a separate Palestinian entity in return for a formal Israeli–Palestinian peace agreement were considered by the Israeli Government to be in conflict with the concept of peace negotiations with the sovereign states which had waged war against Israel. The Palestinian–Arab status was in a legal limbo.

As the Hashemite Kingdom of Jordan and not the Palestinian Arabs had made war against Israel, it was with Jordan and not with the Palestinian Arabs that Israel would have to reach a peace settlement. Eshkol, Golda Meir and Eban set their sights on the ever-beckoning and ever-elusive King Hussein, not on the forty Palestinian notables who proposed to meet in Jericho in order to negotiate a peace with Israel.

The Israeli Defence Minister, Moshe Dayan, did not share in this preference for Hussein and the Jordanian option. In an interview with CBS before the end of the war, he had warned that, in his opinion, the West

Bank would not wish to return to Jordanian rule. As a result, he was later accused by his fellow ministers of conducting pro-Palestinian policies to the detriment of Hussein and contrary to Israeli Government policy. Dayan, however, as with many other critical issues, was not decisive. He was not willing to make an issue of his opposition to the prevailing Hashemite orientation in the Eshkol Government; he did not consider that the circumstances justified him openly opposing the then dominant figures in the Government, Prime Minister Eshkol and Foreign Minister Meir.

Dayan explained to friends that he believed he could do more good by remaining in his position of Defence Minister, even with the restricted authority imposed by the Government, than by going into the political wilderness, where he would have no influence comparable to his ministerial position at a time when there were still high hopes of an early peace settlement. The optimistic, almost naïve expectations of Israel's leaders that peace was around the corner were cogently couched in Dayan's often quoted and now notorious comment that he was waiting for a telephone call from King Hussein. Dayan's quip reflected the passive attitude of Israel's policy-makers immediately after the war, who were waiting for that figurative telephone call. The Israeli establishment felt it had won a glorious war, but it had no idea how to translate this unique military victory into political gain. All it could offer was to hold on to the territories which had so unexpectedly come into its possession.

The policy laid down first by Eshkol and later by Mrs Meir was to hold fast, not to budge an inch and not to agree to anything less than direct negotiations for a permanent settlement. It may have been a theoretically logical approach, but under the prevailing conditions it was politically unsound, for it imposed a political freeze at a time when some movement might have been possible. As a result, nothing was done, no 'facts' to facilitate movements towards a peace settlement were created, and the opportunity of reaching out to the Palestinian Arab residents of the West Bank and Gaza was rejected. The period of real opportunity immediately after the war of June 1967 was frittered away.

There were no telephone calls. Instead, the euphoria in Jerusalem was rudely shaken by the meeting of Arab heads of state summoned by President Nasser. They met on 1 September 1967 in Khartoum and succeeded in imposing Arab immobility on Israel in a way that effectively stifled all hopes and efforts of achieving any kind of peaceful co-existence between Israel and her Arab neighbours. We have already referred to the Khartoum decisions in an earlier context, but they deserve to be repeated as a kind of full stop to the Six Day War. They offered no option other than yet another war.

The Arab states declared their determination 'to eliminate the effects of Israel's aggression and to ensure the withdrawal of the aggressive Israeli forces from the Arab lands which have been occupied since the 5 June aggression'. They would do this within a framework of principles to which the Arab states would adhere: 'Namely, no peace with Israel; no recognition of Israel; no negotiations with Israel and adherence to the rights of the Palestinian people in their country.' These Khartoum decisions were to become one of the most negative turning-points in the recent history of the Middle East. They legitimized the diplomatic immobility on the part of Israel and of the Arabs. They emphasized and justified in the eyes of the Israeli Government its policy of not moving and of not making, or for that matter having, any coherent peace proposals. Israel could argue with some considerable justification that the Khartoum 'Noes' on which the Arab heads of state had decided made any such Israeli initiative wholly academic. They would be right. But that did not bring peace any nearer.

On the Arab side, there were half-hearted but altogether unrealistic attempts to find a political formula that would bring about an Israeli withdrawal from the territories occupied during the 1967 war in line with the Khartoum resolutions. But this was never a practical proposition. For the Arabs were interested only in an Israeli withdrawal and not at all in the achievement of a genuine peace settlement.

By the end of the year, barely six months after the end of the war, Nasser's much quoted spokesman, Hassanein Heikal, was again writing about the inevitability of another war and of the Arab determination never to make peace with Israel, while Nasser himself had proclaimed the axiom by which he proposed to abide that 'whatever is taken by force can be restored only by force. That is the rule.' Professor Malcolm Kerr, one of the shrewdest observers of the Arab scene at this time, described coming to terms with Nasserism to be 'like changing the tyres of a moving automobile'.

By then, the massive airlift of Soviet arms, equipment and ammunition, which we have described in Part 1, had so replenished the stocks of the Egyptian and Syrian armed forces that a renewal of the war had become a possibility. Thus, by the end of 1967, the flicker of hope for peace had been all but extinguished. There was still a possibility, however, for Israel effectively to bypass the Arab rejection of peace by the Arab states by reaching Palestinian Arabs who had sought to establish a normalized and peaceful co-existence with Israel. Shehadeh and the Palestinians who had met in Jericho were still waiting in the wings. But the Hussein–Jordan lobby in our Government was too strong and convinced that they could make a deal with the King. It was a pipe-dream then and it has been one ever since. It was, moreover, an expensive illusion, for it cost us probably the best opportunity which Israel has had to bring about a settlement of the Palestinian problem in a manner acceptable to Israel and beneficial to the Palestinians. It might not have pleased King Hussein or the Egyptians and the Syrians at that time, but we could have lived with that.

20
Hussein Fails to Deliver
1968–74

ISRAEL NOW HAD to confront new and less promising realities. She had to adjust for a long stay in the territories, while the Arab states had taken the first steps that would eventually lead to the War of Attrition along the Suez Canal. The UN's Jarring Mission* did nothing to dispel the gloom.

The principal losers of the war in 1967 were the Egyptians and, even more so, the Palestinians. In a personal letter to me, Shehadeh wrote, on 8 April 1968, that he considered 'the prospect of peace now more remote than ever. It seems that 1967 is no better than 1949 or any other year. ...' Shehadeh and his colleagues had been convinced that despite the negative decisions of the Arab leaders at the Khartoum summit, as many as three-quarters of the Palestinian Arab population in the territories would have supported the plea for peace in exchange for some sort of independent entity; but our Government preferred to place its hopes on a deal with King Hussein, who claimed to be the legitimate representative of the Palestinian Arabs. By 1968, disillusionment had replaced hope.

The direct result of Israel opting for a solution with Jordan was to impel the Palestinians into the wide-open arms of the PLO. Our Government had not accepted the conclusions Bawli and I had reached after our fact-finding mission, that the Palestinians were no longer willing to be represented by Amman. With Israel refusing to deal with them directly, the Palestinians turned to the PLO as the only alternative to Jordanian or Israeli overlordship.

From then, we were on an increasingly steep and slippery slope. PLO violence begat reprisals, terrorism gave rise to repressive measures. Every act of terror swelled the ranks of those Israelis who considered the Palestinians to be a mortal threat to their peaceful and stable existence. Every counter-measure taken by the Israelis brought new recruits to the PLO. What had been misconception, lack of understanding and absence of communication was transformed into a chasm of hatred separating the two peoples as never before.

---

* Security Council resolution 242 of 22 November 1967 is best known for its formula of withdrawal from territories in exchange for peace. The Resolution also called for a special representative to promote the agreement. The Swedish Ambassador, Gunnar Jarring, was appointed.

The PLO, whose leaders had so feared the reconciliation that had appeared possible in 1967, proceeded to exploit this new situation. The refugee camps in Jordan were transformed into armed barracks; PLO bases were established along the east bank of the River Jordan, and almost nightly incursions were made into the territories and into Israel in an effort to sow terror and to destabilize the Israeli regime. From 1968 until September 1970, when the Arab Legion destroyed the PLO military infrastructure in Jordan, more than 5,000 incursions and cross-border shellings took place, in conformity with the Palestine National Charter, which declared that 'armed struggle is the only way to liberate Palestine'.

Yet the attempts of the PLO to establish bases on the West Bank, in the Israeli-administered territories, were singularly unsuccessful; even the optimists in the PLO leadership must have realized that their 'armed struggle' was making very little impact on their Israeli enemy. At the same time, Israel's reprisal attacks on the PLO bases in Jordan were creating an increasingly untenable situation for the PLO inside the Hashemite Kingdom.

This Israeli retaliation, however, could not be compared to the ferocity and violence of the final showdown in September 1970 between Hussein's Hashemite army and the Palestinians who challenged the King's control of his kingdom. Conservative estimates have put the number of Palestinian dead at 4,000. Arafat claimed that as many as 20,000 were killed by Jordan's Arab Legion, when its tanks and artillery savaged the Palestinian refugee camps.

'Black September', as it became known, had a traumatic effect on the Palestinians. It intensified the ideological differences between the factions of the PLO. Many Palestinians, especially the radical supporters of George Habash's Popular Front for the Liberation of Palestine, considered Jordan to be an artificial product of Britain's colonial machinations. Her territory had been an integral part of the original Palestine which had been mandated to Great Britain after the First World War. Great Britain had decided to dismember the Palestine mandate in 1921 in order to establish Arab Trans-Jordan on the east bank of the river, from which Jews and Zionist institutions were to be excluded. Therefore, it was argued, Palestinians and Jordanians were no different; they were one and the same people.

This argument, however, was used by different groups for different purposes: the radical factions of the PLO have called for the liquidation of the Hashemite regime as a prerequisite to the reuniting of the Palestinian Arab people on both banks of the Jordan and to the 'elimination of Zionist Israel': 'The road to Jerusalem leads through Amman.' In one of the most important documents signed shortly before the Arab Legion attack on the Palestinian camps on 6 May 1970, the PLO's leadership called for 'the unity of the people in the Jordanian-Palestinian theatre'.

This summons became a central theme at the 1970 and 1971 sessions of the Palestine National Council. The Jordanian regime, however, used this new PLO policy to discredit the Palestinian 'separatists', who wanted a

Palestinian state with no ties to Jordan. Jordan's Foreign Minister, for example, stated categorically in 1972 that 'Jordan is Palestine and Palestine is Jordan and Jordan hails every Palestinian who seeks to do his duty to his cause and his country.'

This same call was taken up in later years by no less a person than General Sharon, who, in words similar to those used by Habash and Naif Hawatmeh (head of the Marxist Popular Democratic Liberation Front of Palestine, one of the factions of the PLO), spoke of Jordan as being a child of colonialism. Jordan, in Sharon's thinking, should rightfully be Palestine. He has said, albeit unofficially, that he would rather see Arafat ruling in Amman than King Hussein, whom he considers to be an obstacle to any true peace in the region. With Jordan reverting to her true Palestinian self, there would be no justification for a second Palestinian state to the west of the River Jordan, or for self-determination, as a Palestinian state would already be in existence.

Sharon's attitude to Hussein was not, however, typical of the Israeli leadership, which, throughout the 1970s sought to reach agreement with the King. It is no longer a secret that numerous meetings were held between the King and the Israeli leaders. Nothing came of them. Hussein insisted that all the territory he lost in 1967, including East Jerusalem, be restored to him as a precondition for entering peace talks; the Israelis demanded that negotiations begin without preconditions, avowing that everything was negotiable at the talks themselves. The claim of the Arabists in Europe that the settlements Israel established were a hindrance to the peace talks was without foundation; the contacts with Hussein had, in fact, begun before a single settlement was established in Judea or Samaria, though much to Hussein's chagrin, Israel's Prime Minister at that time, Levi Eshkol, never agreed to meet him.

When Dayan became Foreign Minister in the Begin Government in 1977, he asked to meet the King in order to find out for himself whether any form of territorial compromise could provide a possible solution. He met Hussein in two lengthy, secret meetings in London in the house of one of the King's friends. Dayan repeatedly urged the King to depart from his 'all or nothing' attitude so that they could explore a formula for beginning the peace talks. It was to no avail.

When Dayan reported to the Cabinet, he stated flatly that 'territorial compromise', which Israel's Labour Paty had been proposing along the lines of the Allon Plan*, as the means to reach a peaceful solution with Jordan, was a non-starter; Israel had no partner for such negotiations. For Begin and his Herut Party** colleagues, who had from the start opposed the idea of giving up any territory of *Eretz Israel*, Dayan's report gave

---

* Yigal Allon, who served as Foreign Minister in Rabin's cabinet in 1974–6, proposed a partition of the West Bank which would leave the Jordan Valley in Israeli hands.

** The Herut Party was one of the two parties that formed the right-wing Likud Party, and was successor to the Irgun Zvai Leumi, the underground movement which had fought the British during the mandate.

added impetus to the formation of an alternative solution which Begin had in mind: 'home rule' or autonomy for the Palestinian Arabs of Judea, Samaria and Gaza, without actually annexing those territories to Israel. Begin envisaged an eventual confederation between Jordan and Israel, in which the Palestinian Arabs would find a 'natural' solution for their national aspirations.

In the meantime, however, the PLO had consolidated its position as the political representative of the Palestinian Arabs. In 1974, the Arab heads of state and a summit meeting of the non-aligned governments recognized the PLO as sole representative of the Palestinians; the Soviet Union took a similar position. Arafat was received in Moscow with all the pomp afforded a head of state.

The PLO's success climaxed soon afterwards, in November 1974, when the UN General Assembly recognized the 'rights of the Palestinian people to sovereignty and national independence'. The United Nations afforded 'observer status' to the PLO and invited Arafat to address its General Assembly. Despite King Hussein's rather muted objections, it was evident that a transfer of power had taken place, even though Israel, backed by Kissinger and the US Government, maintained their position that Jordan would still have to be the chosen partner in a Palestinian settlement.

21
The PLO's Folies de Grandeur
1974–80

THE EXTRAORDINARY SPECTACLE of the leader of a de facto terrorist organization addressing the World Assembly while toting a pistol at his hip came as a climacteric to efforts spearheaded by the Soviet Union to unite the 'progressive' and Third World countries into a massive anti-colonialist and anti-imperialist camp, with strident anti-western overtones. Vietnam had been the principal banner under which this great army of voices opposed to the West had initially been mobilized. It had been the catalyst which brought them together to point their collective accusing finger at the United States. However, once the Vietnam War was over, a new whipping boy had to be found and a new hero elevated in place of Vietnam. Israel and the PLO were the obvious choices.

The word went out from Moscow through the myriad channels the Soviet Union has used to fashion and mould public opinion the world over: from peace movements to trade union activists, from the Afro-Asian Peoples' Solidarity Organization to the anti-nuclear movements, and to countless other often seemingly innocent groupings of parties, movements and organizations. The key arena, however, was the United Nations itself, where the overlapping layers of the Arab League, the Organization of Islamic Countries, the Non-Aligned Movement and the Communist Bloc created an automatic majority which could pass any resolution it wished, including the one which brought Arafat to the UN General Assembly podium in New York in 1974.

An Israeli delegate present remarked bitterly that if an Arab delegate had proposed a resolution stating that the world was flat and not round, it would have obtained a large majority. Conversely, Israel was the country in the United Nations that was not admitted to any international grouping – not NATO, not Europe, not any Asian conglomeration, nor any of the UN policy-making committees. Israel was the pariah, and the PLO was the brave 'David' striking the Israeli Goliath.

This bias against Israel was further emphasized when the Soviet Union supported a UN General Assembly resolution stating that the use of force in a struggle for national liberation was legitimate, and therefore the violent terrorist actions of the PLO against Israelis were not to be considered as a violation of the UN Charter. And every year – until 1988 – the Soviet

Union joined with Arab member states who challenged the legitimacy of Israel's membership of the United Nations.

The PLO was thus backed by the Soviet propaganda machine and supported by the Arab League, the Organization of Islamic Countries and the Non-Aligned Movement. Not surprisingly, the PLO had succeeded far better in its international and diplomatic propaganda than in the real world of the 'armed struggle' against Israel.

Yet public relations, important as they may be, could neither win the war for the Arab countries nor replace Israel with a PLO state. This was made evident by the political and military consequences of the Six Day War in 1967 and, six years later, by the Arab failure in 1973, in the Yom Kippur War, to rectify them. On the contrary, the ensuing non-belligerency talks between Egypt and Israel, initiated by Kissinger, and preparations for a peace conference in Geneva, compelled the PLO leadership to reassess its policy and reconsider its strategy in the light of these changed conditions.

The PLO's policy since the war of 1967 had been simple and uncomplicated. The PLO – as was made plain by the resolutions of its policy-making National Council – was not interested in a political peace settlement, or in any partial agreement with Israel; its only objective was the total elimination of Israel as a state and its replacement by a 'democratic' Palestinian Arab-dominated state in which only relatively few and imprecisely defined Jews would be permitted to remain. The Israeli capture of the West Bank and of Gaza in 1967, and the Arab defeat in the Yom Kippur War six years later, while more than a million Palestinian Arabs on the West Bank and in Jordan had remained completely passive, had revealed the total unreality of the PLO's strategic aims and political programme.

The Yom Kippur War, in particular, underlined the futility of the PLO policy. And with Egypt edging towards a disengagement agreement in 1974, the PLO felt constrained to make a major policy move. The Palestine National Council meeting in Cairo in June 1974 reversed its former opposition to an independent Palestinian state on the West Bank and in Gaza, and now called for the establishment of such a state in any part of 'Palestinian land' that could be 'liberated'.

Yet this change, which was heralded by the Arabists of Europe as a major concession on the part of the PLO for the sake of peace, did not in fact alter in any manner the corner-stone of PLO policy, which was the absolute rejection of Israel's right to exist. The PLO continued to negate any political solution which would, of necessity, entail dealing with Israel and thus implicitly recognizing her existence.

The Palestine National Council's decision in 1974 to favour a state in part of Palestine was tempered by a resolution which declared that

the PLO will oppose any plan for the establishing of a Palestinian state which would require the PLO's recognition of Israel, peace with Israel, acceptance of secure borders for Israel, and renunciation of Palestinian Arab rights to return to their former homes, and to full self-determination 'in all Palestine'.

It then elaborated on the decisions previously taken that the PLO objective remained 'the establishment of a democratic Palestinian Arab state which would embrace all the territory of historic Palestine', which, of course, would include all the territory of Israel.

The PLO was not prepared to pay any price in return for its demands. It certainly was not prepared to offer peace in exchange for any concessions on Israel's part. PLO leaders never tired of pointing out – in Arabic to their people, but never in any European language – that the establishment of an independent state in the territories would be only a stage towards the 'liberation' of the entire country.

In this strategy of stages promulgated by the PLO in the 1970s, the final stage would be the elimination of Israel. This aim was barely concealed in the preamble to the ten-point 'political programme' of the 1974 meeting in Cairo. Basing itself on the Palestinian National Charter, it expressed the PLO's position that a permanent and just peace was impossible unless 'our Palestinian people first recover all their national rights'. These comprised the right of all Palestinians to return to their former homes on the West Bank and Gaza – and in Israel; and the right of Palestinian Arab self-determination 'on the whole of the soil of their homeland', which included the State of Israel. It then rejected in cavalier manner any association with UN Resolution 242 or with the planned international peace conference at Geneva.

Point Five of the PLO statement was aimed at King Hussein's Hashemite rule in Jordan. The PLO would 'struggle along with the Jordanian national forces' – a euphemism for the opposition to Hussein – to establish a Jordanian–Palestinian national front, whose aim would be 'the setting up in Jordan of a democratic national authority in place of the Hashemite regime, in close contact with the Palestinian state to be established'. Finally, the PLO-controlled state in part of Palestine (which would not recognize the existence of Israel) 'would endeavour to unite the Arab confrontation states with the object of completing the liberation of all Palestinian territory from Israeli rule as a step towards the attainment of comprehensive Arab unity'.

It was all pure fantasy when set against the realities of the American rescue of the Egyptian and Syrian armed forces, only eight months earlier, from total military disaster at the hands of the Israel Defence Forces.

Two wars which resulted in the occupation by Israel of the West Bank, the Gaza Strip and the Golan Heights in 1967, and which failed to dislodge Israel in 1973, appeared to make no impact on the PLO leadership. A few brave PLO activists openly questioned the wisdom and the realism of Arafat's official policy, but they were denied a hearing at the Council session; when Issam Sartawi, a much respected surgeon and associate of Arafat, persisted throughout the 1970s in his unpopular, embarrassing and often sarcastic questioning, he was 'liquidated'.

The brutal killing of Dr Sartawi not only silenced a perceptive critic inside the PLO establishment, but also sent warning signals to others who shared his critical sentiments. The murder – like that of other colleagues who had become bothersome to Arafat – was conveniently attributed to the shadowy Abu Nidal group, which seemed to serve as a ready-made executioner and lightning conductor for the PLO leadership.* It did the job, and it accepted the opprobium. An inconvenient voice in PLO councils was thus stilled, and Arafat could carry on as if nothing had happened. Sartawi – like the murdered PLO representative in London, Said Hamami, before him – became a non-person in the annals of the PLO.

Undaunted by the Yom Kippur War setback, and encouraged by the support it was receiving internationally, in particular in the United Nations, the PLO continued playing the part of vanguard in the struggle against Israel. Its objective was to sap Israel's inherent strength and undermine her national cohesion with acts of terror and by the disruption of normal daily life. At the same time, the PLO sought to promote conflict between Israel and her Arab neighbours designed to lead to one war after another, which would necessarily wear down Israeli resistance until she was compelled to submit to Arab pressure. The only dialogue with Israel, in Arafat's words, would be conducted through the barrel of a gun.

This was no idle boast. Throughout the 1970s, the PLO sought to put Arafat's precept of gun-law against Israel into practice, primarily from illicit bases it had occupied for this purpose in southern Lebanon. This policy was expanded after 1975 with the outbreak of the civil war in Lebanon, in the igniting of which the military wing of the PLO had played a significant role.

It was a policy which left no room for any political manoeuvring, a policy of implacable hostility and violence, which could only be met with violence, for there was no political answer to it other than the complete capitulation of Israel to PLO demands, a political suicide which no one in Israel was willing to envisage. The result of this policy of violence was the Lebanese War of 1982, which was waged against the PLO and which, as we shall see, created the conditions for a basic change in the relationship between Israelis and Palestinians.

However, in the meantime momentous events were taking place on what should have been the PLO's principal front-line: the West Bank and Gaza. Presidents Carter and Sadat, and especially their expert advisers, were engaged in preparing for peace negotiations between Egypt and Israel. They were particularly concerned at this stage with the Palestinian Arab connection to the overall peace negotiation, but there appeared to be no interest in this by a PLO leadership whose fixation was evidently pre-empted by the conflict in Lebanon.

As we have shown in our account of the Camp David negotiations, this remoteness from reality left the PLO isolated and bewildered by events. When Sadat told Egypt's National Assembly of his proposed journey to

---

* According to the former head of the Romanian intelligence service, who defected to the West, Arafat had told Ceauşescu that the Abu Nidal assassinations were, in fact, co-ordinated with him.

Jerusalem, Arafat was in the audience sitting next to Jehan, Sadat's wife. She has recalled Arafat's stunned reaction. He did not walk out, nor make any demonstrative protest; he just sat and applauded without evident enthusiasm. Similarly, when Egypt and Israel signed the Camp David Accords in September 1978, the PLO was left ineffectually on the sidelines, muzzled by its own policy decisions, which had been taken at its 15th National Council meeting in Cairo during March 1977 and were altogether irrelevant to the events unfolding at Camp David.

The real significance of this 15th National Council meeting became evident only some time later. It had made no noticeable impact on Israel other than to confirm the already widely held belief that the avowed intention of the PLO was to bring about, by whatever means, the liquidation of Israel as a Jewish state. In fact, this 15th Palestine National Council made no attempt during its Cairo sessions, from 12 to 20 March 1977, to disavow this objective; on the contrary, the fifteen Articles approved by it, which comprised the political programme of the PLO for the coming year, made no bones about the planned 'elimination' of Israel. Peace with Israel was neither mentioned nor considered. It was this fact that soon became evident to Sadat and changed his negotiating stance in his encounter with Carter in Washington. More than anything, this PLO position caused Sadat to revise his policy and to bring about a dramatic change in Washington's plans for a peace settlement and, not least, in Carter's personal position.

While Carter and Sadat had been probing ways to a peace settlement with Israel, the PLO had closed all roads involving its participation after first leading its western friends into the confident belief that it had undergone a profound policy change to facilitate a 'full state of peace' with Israel. Acting on Arafat's behalf, Sartawi had written to the Austrian Chancellor, Bruno Kreisky, on 27 January 1977 along these lines. On 13 February, three weeks later, Kreisky told the world's press in Vienna that he had been assured that the PLO had carried out a total change of policy and that the way was open for a state of co-existence between Israel and the Palestinian Arabs.

However, when the National Council met just four weeks later, on 12 March, it decided instead, in response to the urging of the spokesman of the Popular Front, Bassam Abu Sharif, to escalate the military struggle, to reject any negotiations based on Security Council Resolution 242, and to refuse to consider attendance at the proposed international peace conference in Geneva. It also reiterated its policy that the PLO would never recognize Israel's existence, would never make peace with Israel and would never accept the concept of secure borders for Israel. Furthermore, the National Council decided that the PLO would seek 'the liberation of the entire national soil'. The PLO would establish an independent state and would ensure that all Palestinians would be able to return to their former homes in the historic Palestine, which included Israel. And that was not all.

The Council then proceeded to vote for two Articles – Numbers 5 and 9 – which were given special attention but not unduly advertised abroad.

Article 5 called on Morocco, Iraq, the Yemen, Libya and Egypt 'to agree to the repatriation of their Jewish citizens who have emigrated to occupied Palestine, and to support all Arab activities directed to this end'. Article 9 reaffirmed 'the Arab character of all Palestine and particularly of Jerusalem'. There was thus no evidence of any 'profound change' that could have encouraged Israel to 'find a way of co-existence' with this PLO policy, as Kreisky had somewhat credulously described the situation barely a month before.

Instead, these decisions finally convinced Sadat that he would not recover the Sinai Peninsula if Egypt were to continue to seek a comprehensive peace in harness with the PLO. It is not too much to say that the 15th Palestine National Council, at which Sadat had delivered the opening speech, was the occasion which sowed the seed of Egypt's separate peace with Israel. Arafat had been the sower, Sadat the reaper.

More than anything else, the extravagant and unrealistic demands of the PLO gave substance to the alternative of a separate peace between Egypt and Israel as the only way forwards towards a peace agreement. Without the PLO's *folies de grandeur* in the 1970s, the Palestinian Arabs might have also been beneficiaries of the accords which Egypt and Israel were about to reach at Camp David in September 1978.

Israel, for her part, had no difficulty in deciding how to respond to these PLO demands. Throughout this period Israel's position remained as it had been defined immediately after the Six Day War: she was prepared to enter immediately into direct negotiations for peace with the Arab states that had fought her. There would be no preconditions to such talks, and both sides would be free to bring any subject to the negotiating table. However, until negotiations got under way and brought results, Israel would remain in firm control of all territories she had taken in 1967.

It says much for the Soviet-led campaign to discredit Israel – plus the power of Arab oil money – that, despite these policy positions of the PLO on the one hand and of Israel on the other, the European Community saw fit at its summit in Venice in June 1980 to recognize the PLO as the rightful spokesman for the Palestinian cause, notwithstanding the hard-line attitude it was taking, while, at the same time, it completely ignored Israel's call for negotiations.

Small wonder we felt that Europe had forsaken justice for expediency; in the years following the Venice declaration, we paid scant attention to what the Europeans had to offer to further the peace process. We received visiting Europeans courteously, but their impact – after Venice – was next to nil. Venice, for us, marked the nadir of Europe's Middle Eastern policy. We have, therefore, to look more closely at the events that led to the Venice summit declaration in June 1980.

22

Venice 1980: Europe Joins the PLO

IT HAD BEEN a turbulent spring for the western community – for the Europeans and for the Americans. The Shah had been toppled. The American Embassy in Tehran had been occupied by revolutionary student demonstrators and fifty American diplomats and staff were held hostage under conditions of maximum indignity. A rescue mission mounted by the Carter administration failed and, on 28 May 1980, the US Secretary of State, Cyrus Vance, who had been one of the principal architects of the Camp David agreements, resigned because he disagreed with the President.

American policy in the Middle East was in disarray. The President was clearly at a loss about his next move in Iran and on the best way of responding to the Soviet occupation of Afghanistan, which had taken his administration, the NATO allies and their Arab friends by surprise. The only NATO counter-action considered adequate or possible was the boycott of the summer Olympic games, which were about to open in Moscow – and even on that there was no solidarity among the NATO allies.

By now, the hard-pressed Carter administration must have felt itself entitled to a demonstrative show of support from its European friends, who, as luck would have it, were about to assemble in Venice for a nine-nation European heads-of-state summit. Carter had proposed to attend the closing session as an example of American solidarity with the Europeans, who were planning their first major initiative in the Middle East to bring the Arab states, Israel and especially the Palestinians to an acceptable solution.

However, the primary concern of the nine members of the European Community, led by Britain, France, Germany and Italy, was not the current difficulties of the United States; nor were they unduly concerned with achieving an unattainable regional comprehensive peace in the Middle East. The real problem facing the Europeans at Venice was how best to ensure conditions that would safeguard their special interests and those of their allies, including Israel, in the region.

We understood and sympathized with the formulation of the problem, but we had our doubts about the means by which the Europeans proposed to achieve their purpose. Our reservations were shown to be fully justified by the outcome of the Venice summit and its aftermath. What we did not know at the time, we came to understand only weeks later when, on 5 August 1980, the Foreign Affairs Select Committee of the British House of Commons published its fifth report for 1979/80.

It was a remarkably revealing document, unique among British parliamentary publications both for the extent and the frankness of the information it provided concerning the intentions and objectives of the Venice summit. It described in great detail the evidence presented in support of this European, PLO-sponsored initiative.

Foremost among the witnesses were Lord Carrington, then British Foreign Secretary and later Secretary-General of NATO; Douglas Hurd, then Carrington's principal assistant and Minister of State at the Foreign Office; Edward Heath, the former Conservative Prime Minister; and a number of other notable spokesmen from the British Middle Eastern establishment, among them the former Middle East editor of the *Financial Times*, Edward Mortimer. He presented a memorandum to the Committee on the 'Effects of the Palestinian Problem on Instability in the Arab World', with which the PLO would have been hard put to find fault.

After considering the evidence and listening to the eminent politicians, the Committee concluded that 'there was widespread support from witnesses for a European initiative to solve the Palestinian problem'. It would enable the European countries, the report emphasized with unaccustomed frankness, '*to distance themselves from United States diplomacy* [author's italics]'.

Evidently and indiscreetly thinking about what was clearly uppermost in the mind of the Anglo-European establishment, the report mused that the United States alone would be unable to satisfy Palestinian and Arab demands 'since domestic political constraints limited the amount of pressure the United States could put on Israel'. Such consideration would not hamper the proposed European initiative. However, the Committee added with engaging frankness, that they had been advised by expert witnesses on these matters that the Europeans would also have to support the Arab position on the future status of Jerusalem if they wanted to be fully assured of a welcome from the Arab states – and of continuing uninterrupted oil supplies.

Lord Carrington gave evidence to the Committee two weeks after the Venice summit had launched its European initiative, symbolically, perhaps, on Friday 13 June. He told the Committee, on 2 July, 'that in his opinion the Palestinian problem represented the biggest threat to the stability of the area' and that its solution was of primary importance, both from the point of view of future stability in the Gulf and also for the protection of western interests in that region. Surely this was a remarkable assessment of the relative importance of Palestine and the Gulf by so eminent an authority just nine weeks before the outbreak of the Gulf War between Iraq and Iran, which was to cost nearly a million lives, continue for eight years and threaten at one time the stability and security of the Arabian Peninsula.

It had not been just a casual aside by the Foreign Secretary. The Committee noted in its report (in paragraph 89) that representative diplomats from British missions in the Middle East, and other witnesses, had told it repeatedly that 'the Arab identification of the West with Israel exposed Saudi Arabia to political risks involving internal instability and criticism and hostility from other Arab states'.

It did not strike the Select Committee as strange that the British Foreign Secretary's preoccupation with the Palestinian problem should be grounded altogether on the stability of the Gulf and on western interests in the region; the merely local interests of the Palestinian Arabs and Israelis hardly figured. In Carrington's opinion, the threat to the security of the Gulf and to the Gulf states did not come from the Soviet Union but from within; presumably the half-million Palestinian Arabs who had settled in the Gulf states. 'This threat is met only by taking due note of the Palestinian factor,' Carrington told his constant travel companion, John Dickie, the veteran diplomatic correspondent of the London *Daily Mail*. One aspect of this 'Palestinian factor', according to Carrington, was that Europeans must not be seen to be in the same boat as the United States, and not only in the Middle East: the United Kingdom therefore did not wish to be associated with the then planned enlarged United States' presence in the Indian Ocean because of the adverse impact this would make on the Arab world.

That was in 1980. Carrington and Hurd were under great pressure at the time. They had to assimilate a number of pressing international situations, of which the Middle East was only one of many. It would be doing no injustice to either of them to say that at that time concern for the Palestinian Arabs or a deep insight into Arab politics was not their first priority, probably not even their second.

The European initiative was not of their making. It had been received by the Foreign Office as a tailor-made policy package from the well-connected and highly experienced European Arab lobby. In the United Kingdom, it was represented by a mixture of powerful commercial and banking interests with a protective covering of able former British diplomats who had served in Arab countries and had become business and media consultants for multi-national oil companies, for defence and building contractors and for the proliferating Arab financial services. They were supported by a younger group of politicians and newspapermen with considerable experience and connections in the Arab world.

But in may ways, the ablest member of this group, and intellectually in a class of his own in his partisanship to advance the PLO cause, was the former owner and editor of the weekly *Spectator* and, at this critical moment, Lord Carrington's deputy and spokesman for the Foreign Office in the House of Commons, the Lord Privy Seal, Sir Ian Gilmour, the most eminent British critic of the 'Zionist settlers' in Palestine. The British Arab lobby was by far the most sophisticated in Europe – and the most influential with the strategically placed Lord Privy Seal at the heart of the policy-making process in the Foreign Office.

Moreover, the timing could not be bettered. Europe's dependence on Arab oil had never been more basic – or so it was made to look at the time. The United States had need of friends in Arabia, if only to sustain the oil requirements of her NATO allies. All through the spring and early summer of 1980, the British Foreign Office, encouraged by the French, argued for a European Middle East initiative with the reluctant Dutch and Germans.

However, the German and Dutch leaders found that their resistance to the British Foreign Office scenario was strongly supported by the British Prime Minister, Margaret Thatcher, who ploughed a lonely furrow on this issue in her Cabinet, which, on the Palestinian initiative, uniquely dared to overrule the Prime Minister. The final version of the European initiative was approved by the European Foreign Ministers meeting in Naples on 14 May 1980. The British and French Foreign Ministers were in an extraordinarily confident mood, convinced that they had made a striking breakthrough in asserting an independent European position in any planned Middle Eastern settlement.

A 'senior British foreign official', subsequently identified as Carrington himself, briefed British correspondents on the outcome of the conference and concluded with this undiplomatically tart footnote: 'President Carter and Mr Muskie [the new Secretary of State who had replaced Cyrus Vance] will be left in no doubt that the Common Market countries will not be talked out of their planned initiative even if Washington regards it as unfriendly.' Following their presumed success at Venice, the European heads of state prepared to meet Carter. But, even while the formal publication of the European initiative was being prepared, those on the inside were becoming aware that all was not going well. Just at the moment when so much preparation was to be rewarded, it all began to look like a hollow victory.

The main unspoken objective of the sponsors of the Venice formula was to set aside the terms of the Camp David Accords concerning the Palestinian Arab areas occupied by Israel in 1967 and to replace them with the Venice formula favouring the PLO. It had been concluded by leading supporters of the anti-Camp David European initiative at the Foreign Office and in the Quai d'Orsay that a most effective way of undermining American and Israeli opposition to the European initiative was to obtain Sadat's tacit approval for the Venice formula. It was decided at the Foreign Office that, under prevailing circumstances, the approach to Sadat should be unorthodox and that the best man for the job was the Lord Privy Seal, whose Arab credentials were impeccable.

Under conditions of semi-secrecy, Sir Ian Gilmour arrived in Cairo on 10 May, four days before the European Foreign Ministers were to meet in Naples to finalize the text for the Venice declaration, for which Gilmour wanted Sadat's blessing. It was an unprepared, ill-informed and foolish mission, quite unlike the customary meticulously prepared visits of this kind. Like so many before him, Gilmour had underestimated Sadat's grasp of semi-clandestine diplomacy.

For three days the Egyptians listened politely and curiously to Gilmour's confidential briefings, but they made no comments. Sadat himself was 'not available' for a meeting with Gilmour. Then, on his last day in Cairo, Gilmour called a press conference. Sadat, however, wanted 'no surprises' and ordered his Minister of State for Foreign Affairs to join Gilmour at this meeting with the media and to make sure that there was no 'misunderstanding' about Egypt's continued support for the Camp David agreements.

The Egyptian Minister, Butros Ghali, explained to the press conference that Egypt welcomed European help in the shaping of a Middle East peace so long as it followed the current policy pursued by the United States and Egypt. This meant support for the UN Security Council Resolution 242. It also meant backing the Camp David agreements, not writing them off as Gilmour had proposed.

Ghali's supporting statement at the press conference must have sounded to Gilmour like a funeral service for the coming Venice summit. When Gilmour returned to London on 13 May, without the eagerly desired 'piece of paper' from Sadat which would have overcome the growing resistance and sceptism to the proposed European formula for peace in the Middle East, not only from the United States but also from the Germans and the Dutch, it was evident that the Venice peace formula would be still-born. Only a word from Sadat could have saved it, but Gilmour brought no such word from Cairo. Worse was yet to come.

Even while the draft summit declaration was in transit from the Foreign Ministers' meeting in Naples to the heads of state summit in Venice, the Fatah Congress representing the PLO majority had met in Damascus at the end of May and had made a nonsense of the Europeans' good intentions and of the PLO's claim to be a serious partner in the search for peace in the Middle East. The Fatah policy statement was made public on 1 June 1980, by its chairman, Arafat, twelve days before the Europeans' Venice declaration, though I wonder whether any of the European heads of state at Venice had been informed by their expert advisers of the decisions just taken by the Fatah Congress, which were of fundamental relevance to the Venice deliberations.

The Fatah Congress had declared in public, 'in the name of its 600 delegates', that it stood for the armed liberation of the whole of Palestine and for the liquidation of the 'Zionist state' in every way. It declared that it was in a de facto state of war with the United States and her allies in the Arab world. It called for a 'strengthening [of the] strategic alliance with [Brezhnev's] Soviet Union and the world's liberation movements', and singled out the Islamic Revolution in Iran for special support.

On the following day, 2 June, an editorial in the Soviet Communist Party newspaper, *Pravda*, urged the Europeans to go ahead with their initiative, which should aim at the restoration of the legitimate rights of the 'Palestinians' which had just been itemized by the Fatah Congress in Damascus. The inclusion of the PLO in the negotiations was 'an imperative of our time' *Pravda* concluded with understandable enthusiasm for the European initiative.

Even if the Venice declaration did not go quite as far as the contemporary Fatah Congress in Damascus, it did travel a good distance along the same road. PLO demands were approved in general terms; Israel was admonished in specific terms. She was told to get out of all territories occupied in 1967, including Jerusalem; to evacuate Jewish settlements on the West Bank; and to accept the PLO as a negotiating partner.

Israel received the message from Venice with jaundiced cynicism. But for the PLO leadership this European intervention was heady stuff, because it ostentatiously aimed at undermining American support for Israel while backing the PLO position. The leading European countries had publicly cocked a snook at the Americans and had proclaimed that the Palestinian Arabs, as presented and represented by the PLO, were at the centre of Middle East affairs; everything stemmed from them – especially the pending crisis in the Gulf. Palestinians were important to the Europeans. Israel had best understand this fact of Middle East life. That, in short, was the seemingly unmistakeable message from Venice.

The Venice declaration fed on the confidence felt by the PLO leaders in the early 1980s. Arafat and his colleagues were so sure of themselves after they had received the European endorsement from Venice. They were convinced that the PLO now had the active support of the Soviet Union, of the Non-Aligned countries and of the United Nations; it had military help from Syria and Iraq; it had the financial backing of Saudi Arabia and the Gulf states; and now it also had the significant political and diplomatic approval of the nine leading members of the European Community. The PLO even had friends in the State Department in Washington. What then could go wrong?

Despite its many influential connections and more than adequate financial resources, good and accurate political intelligence has never been the PLO's strong card, be it intelligence about Israelis or about Europeans and Americans. This was particularly true of the PLO's assessment of the value of the Venice declaration. Arafat and his colleagues appeared to be unaware that, almost immediately after the Venice summit, European enthusiasm for the initiative began to wane.

Pressures from inside the British Cabinet, especially from Prime Minister Thatcher, from Bonn and other Europeans, from Sadat and, not least, from the Israelis, had forced the Foreign Office to rethink its European initiative. The first European leader to visit Israel after Venice, Luxembourg's Foreign Minister, was left in no doubt about Israel's reaction to the European declaration after hearing some very plain talk from Yitzhak Shamir, the then Foreign Minister. Anger in Jerusalem over Venice had been so great that many voices had advocated cancelling the proposed visit of the

Luxembourg Minister. It was made clear to him that Israel would have nothing to do with the European initiative.

But, in the event, it was the PLO itself that was the prime factor that undermined the European initiative. The European leaders must have considered the Palestinians to be their own worst enemy. The Fatah policy statement had been a public relations disaster. But there was worse to come. It was followed by the fifteenth session of the Palestine National Council, which convened in Damascus on 11 April 1981. Its chairman, Khaled el-Fahoum, minced no words. He told the 300 delegates, Arafat's de facto 'masters', that the PLO's official and parliamentary dialogue with the Europeans had produced no results. He protested against the European invitation to Sadat to address the European parliament; it was 'an interference in Palestinian affairs'. The European initiative which they had been discussing was, in effect, 'a disavowal of friendship and a disregard for the Arab people'.

Before that smack in the face for the Europeans, and even more so for Carrington's personal British initiative, the conference heard a renewed avowal of the PLO's total alignment with the Soviet Union and total denunciation of the United States. A special announcement from the chairman, clearly aimed at Israel, confirmed that there would be no amendment of the controversial Article 6 of the PLO's Palestine Charter, which calls for the total obliteration of the 'Zionist state'.

We had received reports that Carrington, on becoming President of the European Community on 1 July 1981, intended to mount a concerted peace initiative aimed at bringing Israel and the PLO to the negotiating table. He had sent one of his ablest diplomats, Sir John Graham, to the Middle East in February 1981 to prepare the ground for a political settlement of the Palestinian problem. Graham met Arafat in Beirut and came away from the meeting with a promise of co-operation.

Yet barely two months later, the PLO National Council was sending an altogether different message to the Europeans. But even more telling than the words of the Council were the deeds of unrelenting terrorism and continuing attacks on the civilian population in northern Israel and the consequential depopulation of Israel's northern towns. Arafat's assurances were meaningless against the background of the reality on the ground; however, they served to illustrate the difficulties which the British 'peace initiative' encountered.

Carrington had been assuring his friends before these developments that there would be a change of climate in the Middle East when he took charge of European affairs. But when the critical day dawned and he assumed the presidency of the European Council of Ministers, Arafat's credibility and assurances lay in tatters – and so did the European initiative: it had been lost without a trace in the rough borderlands of northern Israel and southern Lebanon; in synagogues and civilian airports attacked by the PLO; and – not least – in the determined counter-measures Israel had taken against the PLO bases in Lebanon.

It was the end of Arafat's attempt to enlist the European Community in support of his campaign against Israel. It was also the end of the European attempt to enlist Arafat as an instrument to help them distance themselves from United States policy in the Middle East – and from Israel – and to enjoy the rich pickings of Middle East commerce without the handicap of such association. It did not work.

23

'Heartland Israel'

WHEN I BECAME Director-General of Israel's Foreign Ministry in 1980, I found that a PLO offensive to isolate Israel and to delegitimize her was in full swing. Black Africa, which had shown particular sympathy towards Israel in the 1960s, had broken off diplomatic relations with us after coming under intense pressure from Arab and so-called progressive countries. Other states in Asia, Latin America and even in Europe were careful not to inject too much substance into their relations with us so as not to offend their oil-rich Arab customers. Mighty Japan, which certainly had nothing to fear from Arab countries, begged me at the time not to publicize my visit to their Foreign Minister in Tokyo. Israel, the supposed Goliath, was confronted by the twenty-one member nations of the Arab League, who together commanded an awesome concentration of wealth and enjoyed the automatic and enthusiastic backing of most countries in the world. We did not feel a bit like Goliath.

This was particularly so in Europe, where we were waging a losing battle for sympathy and understanding. The Europeans could not comprehend that we did not like the term 'occupied territories' because it implied that we were taking possession, by force, of land which was not ours. But no Jew who knows his Bible and his heritage would consider Judea and Samaria – the West Bank – as foreign land. The Jewish religion, perhaps more than others, is not so much an expression of the relationship between the individual and God; it is, rather, a national religion in the sense that it deals with the covenant between a people – the Jewish people – and God; moreover, it is national because it applies to a people and its land – the Land of Israel, including, of course, Judea and Samaria. There is hardly a page in the Jewish prayer book without some reference to the Land of Israel. A Jew in London, New York or wherever he has been allowed to live has over the centuries prayed for rain every October during the Feast of Tabernacles – rain in *Eretz Israel* – and when he prays he turns automatically towards Jerusalem, a city mentioned more than 600 times in the Old Testament. By no stretch of the imagination can a Jew consider any part of *Eretz Israel* as foreign land.

Yet, despite this innate attachment to all of the land, we agreed in 1947 to the UN partition plan and gave up part of our land as the price for having our own state. When, twenty years later in 1967, that part which we had reluctantly surrendered in 1947 came into our possession as a result of King Hussein's imprudent aggression, it was hardly surprising that the temptation to keep what we considered to be ours was very great.

We believed our position was fully legitimized by the negative attitude of the Arab leaders at the Khartoum summit in September 1967 and by the PLO's 'strategy of stages', which would enable it to use any territory given up by Israel as a springboard for it to 'liberate' all of Palestine from 'Zionist rule'. Thus, our attachment to the land became interlocked with our basic security considerations; this strengthened our determination not to return to the untenable pre-1967 borders – the 'Auschwitz boundaries', as former Foreign Minister Eban had branded them.

Unfortunately, the problem was not just one of land. There were people on the land, more than a million of them, for whom Israel was very much the occupying power, however distasteful this description was to us. Our policy was designed to interfere as little as possible in the daily lives of the Palestinians and to keep a minimal number of soldiers and Israeli officials in the territories, while the 'open bridges' policy enabled the Palestinian Arabs to visit and conduct trade with Jordan and the rest of the Arab world.

For twenty years an uneasy but nevertheless workable arrangement existed in the territories. Tens of thousands of Palestinians came daily to Israel to work in our fields and factories. Over the years, since 1967, the economies of Israel and the territories had become increasingly enmeshed. On the surface it appeared – certainly to most Israelis – as if the fusion between Israel and the territories had succeeded, and the 'facts' on the ground lent credence to this belief.

Without any formal act of annexation, the West Bank and Gaza were becoming by deed and fact an integral part of the State of Israel. The old 'Green Line', which had divided the pre-1967 Israel from the territories, had disappeared; the Jewish settlements which had been established throughout the territories, and the new roads that criss-crossed Judea and Samaria, effectively changed not only their physical geography but also the economic and social geopolitics of the West Bank and Gaza.

Under such circumstances, it was hardly surprising that the Likud leaders wanted the status quo to continue, even for a hundred years if possible. For with each year Israel's grip on the territories tightened. So, at least, it appeared to her leaders throughout the 1970s and the 1980s – up to December 1987.

But appearances can deceive and below the surface, even during those years of relative quiet, the situation was very different to that perceived in Israel. For there is no such thing as a benign occupation. It does not exist. The fact that the Palestinians had never in their history led an independent existence made no difference: they had been part of the Syrian *Sanjak* under Turkish occupation until the end of the First World War; they had then come under British rule until they were taken over by the Jordanians and Egyptians in 1949. The irony of the Palestinian saga is that it was only with the Israeli 'occupation' in 1967 that Palestinian nationalism was galvanized into a living, vibrant force. It had, of course, existed long before, but it was largely passive and the British, Jordanians and Egyptians contained it without undue difficulty. It was only after Israel had taken charge of the territories that it crystallized into a dynamic nationalist movement, which inevitably clashed with the occupying power. This clash grew in intensity as the PLO consolidated its power and influence over the Palestinian population. Below the surface Palestinian nationalism, which had come of age in 1967, grew in strength and stature with each year that passed, and the Israel administration was forced to take ever more stringent measures to preserve basic security and to prevent open expressions of defiance.

We have been much criticized about the hardships and humiliation with which we have subjected the Palestinians. I believe we made many mistakes in the territories because overriding considerations to maintain security at all costs blinded us to the psychological consequences of some of our actions; security needs took priority over any political moves that might have been taken in order to find a way towards real co-existence between Israeli and Palestinian. Given the clash of nationalisms, there was no way that we could have remained in the territories without exerting pressures, without using force, without creating hardships for the local population. It could have been otherwise, if the Arab states had been willing to negotiate with us as Egypt had done. But they refused – and the Palestinian Arabs had to pay the price. For us, 'Heartland Israel' was a negotiable option, but not on PLO conditions. We were prepared to negotiate this supreme concession for the sake of co-existence, for a genuine and viable peace settlement with our Arab neighbours, Palestinian, Jordanian and Syrian. But there were no takers – no Arab negotiators.

24
Palestinians in Search of a Saviour
1981-7

IN JULY 1981 – just when Lord Carrington had assumed the presidency of the European Community, bent on pursuing the European initiative in the Middle East – Arafat and the PLO turned their backs on the Europeans. Europe was of no use to the PLO in Lebanon, where it was in dire need of a breathing-space – a cease-fire; only the United States could deliver this. On 24 July 1981, Philip Habib, President Reagan's personal envoy, provided the PLO with its much needed year of grace, a cease-fire which effectively shackled the IDF on the Lebanese border. What Arafat and the PLO leaders did with it belongs primarily to the record of events in Lebanon rather than to those in Palestine (which have been fully recounted in Part 2 of this book). But the consequences of these PLO decisions were to shape the fate of the Palestinian Arabs during the 1980s – especially in Judea, Samaria, Gaza and, not least, in Lebanon.

By the beginning of the decade, the Palestinians stood poised in southern Lebanon ready for their showdown with Israel, protected from Israeli military counter-action by the cease-fire negotiated by the Americans. However, the PLO now suffered from the side-effects of its split personality: it was preparing to launch a military terrorist challenge against northern Israel, while at the same time it was engaged, incongruously, with the Saudi Crown Prince Fahd in a 'peace initiative'. Arafat had planned to use Fahd as a stalking-horse lending Saudi respectability to the peculiarly PLO version of the proposed 'peace plan' designed to convince the Americans and Europeans of the PLO's pacific intentions.

Unfortunately for Arafat, in this high summer of 1981, Fahd was not in his customary pliant mood, prepared to go along with anything Arafat proposed concerning Palestine. Fahd had his own objective, which was very different from Arafat's. He felt uncomfortable without Egypt's presence in the Arab League. He believed that, in order to counter Sadat's unilateral peace, a comprehensive Arab attitude towards the Palestinian question should be hammered out which would enable Egypt to support it and thus bring her back into the Arab fold. The result was the Fahd Plan, based on the lowest common denominator which he believed could be acceptable to all the Arab states as well as to the PLO. Fahd made no secret of his upstaging of Arafat in an evidently prepared interview with his own Saudi

News Agency on 3 November 1981. This was three weeks before the Arab heads of state met in conference in Fez ostensibly to discuss the Lebanese situation and to provide Arab back-up for the PLO.

Fahd explained in his carefully staged interview that the Saudis were thinking of an 'alternative to Camp David', which would not mean confrontation with Egypt and which would also emphasize the Arab desire for peace. He explained that, in pursuance of this objective, the Saudis had added two extra clauses to the draft resolution which the PLO had circulated to the heads of state. The PLO's original draft had six clauses; Fahd had added an important seventh clause, which declared that all states in the area had the right 'to live in peace'. Moreover, his overall comments in the November interview were also much more moderate than they had been in the summer, for the Saudi stake in peace had become significant. Saudi oil revenues that year reached an unbelievable $280 million per day, every day: £102,000 million for 1981. With Iran and Iraq at war on the Saudi doorstep in the Gulf, the Saudi rulers wanted no further complications from the Palestinian Arabs.

Arafat and his colleagues did not seem to be aware of the warning signals coming from the Saudi camp. In what seemed to be an indication of the PLO megalomania evident at that time, they denounced this Fahd addition to the PLO formula, conditionally 'permitting' Israel to 'live in peace', as constituting 'implicit' recognition of Israel. This addition was, therefore, firmly rejected as unacceptable by Arafat (in secret session at the summit) and by the PLO's 'foreign minister', Faruk Qaddumi, in a widely publicized statement issued in Beirut ten days before the summit. Qaddumi said: 'It should be clear to everyone that we, as Palestinians, object to Clause 7 and reject it categorically. This position is not open to discussion.' The PLO's opposition to Fahd's revised text was supported by Syria and other 'rejectionist' Arab states. Fahd did not put his resolution to the vote and the summit of Arab heads of state, who had assembled in Fez on 25 November 1981, ended abruptly and inconclusively – a non-event.

The PLO must have bitterly regretted Arafat's cavalier treatment of Prince Fahd, when some six months later they were pleading – in vain – for urgent help from the Saudi rulers against the Israel Defence Forces advancing against them in Lebanon. Meanwhile, the Arab rulers had allowed – mainly by default – the PLO to present itself as the undisputed spokesman for the Palestinians, and to be accepted as such. King Hussein was no longer a realistic alternative – if he had ever been one. The pro-Jordanians on the West Bank had shrunk to a small uninfluential faction. Yet many West Bank Arabs were disturbed by and disapproved of the growing PLO violence, which was directed as much against Palestinian 'dissidents' as against Israelis; but, understandably, there were few who had the courage to protest. Some who had done so paid dearly for it.

Critics of the PLO leadership were prime targets for PLO terror. The killing of the Mayor of Nablus and the gunning down of prominent PLO officials, such as Said Hamami and Dr Sartawi – who believed they were acting on Arafat's behalf when they established contact with Israelis and criticized official PLO policy – had a chilling effect on Palestinian Arabs who favoured peaceful co-existence with Israel and had dared to question the negative policies of the PLO leadership.

All the same, the West Bank and Gaza Arab population was united in their opposition to the Israeli 'occupation'. They were convinced by every new Jewish settlement that was established in the territories that the Israelis were there to stay.

They were suspicious of Israeli intentions; however, they were hardly less suspicious of Jordanian and Syrian intentions. Despite the lip-service of Arab leaders to the 'sacred' Palestinian cause, dealings with the Palestinians often verged on the brutal. Kamal Jumblatt, the late Druze leader, quoted a revealing statement by President Assad to Arafat, which goes a long way towards explaining the peculiar relationship existing between Syria and the PLO. Jumblatt recalled in his memoirs* that they were discussing the future of a Palestinian state when Assad referred to a meeting he had had with Arafat in April 1976 during the civil war in Lebanon. According to Assad, he reminded Arafat of Syria's special relationship with the Palestinian Arabs and told him:

You do not represent the Palestinians as much as we do. Never forget that there is no such thing as a Palestinian people; there is no Palestinian entity; there is only Syria. You are part of the Syrian people. Palestine is a part of Syria. It is we, the Syrian authorities, who are the true representatives of the Palestinian people.

It was a reminder which the Palestinian Arabs can forget only at their peril.

Altogether it was not a reassuring situation for the Palestinian Arabs. Their leaders, however, did not reflect their justified concern at the state of political isolation into which the PLO had led them.

The tale of the two Fez summits of Arab heads of state vividly illustrated the vagaries of Arafat's PLO policy-making. The first – abortive – summit met in Fez in November 1981, as we have described above, with Arafat and the PLO, arrogant and over-confident, dictating policy to the Arab rulers in a long, private session at which the summit broke up without decisions or resolutions. The PLO, supported by Syria, Libya and the Yemen, had rejected the peace plan submitted by Prince Fahd. They did so because the Fahd Plan envisaged, without saying so explicitly, that Israel should be allowed to live in peace once she had conceded all Arab territorial demands.

It was a concept which Arafat and Qaddumi, riding high and preparing for their showdown with Israel in Lebanon, rejected 'for ever'. That was nine months before 'the battle for Beirut'. To underline the point made in Fez in November 1981, Arafat's deputy, Salah Khalaf (Abu Iyad), addressed a huge rally of Palestinians in Beirut in December. At its conclusion, he solemnly affirmed 'that the PLO will never approve a

---

* Kamal Jumblatt, *I Speak for Lebanon* (London, 1981), p. 78.

solution that involves negotiations with, or recognition of, Israel. We will never agree to any initiative which includes the recognition of Israel.'

The awakening, when it came in June 1982 with the Israeli assault on the PLO positions in Lebanon, was swift and rude. The resulting transformation was reflected by the second Fez summit, ten months after the first. The Saudi Crown Prince had meanwhile become King Fahd and he again submitted his amended peace plan to his fellow rulers. It was the same plan which the PLO and the Syrians had rejected out of hand less than a year previously, but it now had support from Arafat, who pleaded with 'their majesties and honourable presidents' to come to the aid of the hard-pressed Palestinians in Lebanon. It was an appeal which the Arab heads of state studiously ignored.

When the crunch came, the Palestinians were left on their own. They looked in vain for a saviour. There was none: not the European Community, not the American mediator, not the Islamic states and, finally, not even Brezhnev's Soviet Union. All that was left for Arafat was the second Fez summit and the despised Fahd Plan, which the PLO had so energetically rejected. It now became Arafat's life-line. It was elevated into the Fez Charter, the holy writ of PLO policy.

But, once again, Arafat's reputation, if not the Palestinian cause, was saved by the simplistic response in Europe and the United States to his political somersault at Fez. Encouraged by PLO propaganda, Arafat's newly discovered enthusiasm for the Fahd Plan, which still included the previously detested Clause 7, was hyped into a major political breakthrough. It represented the 'implied' recognition of Israel by the Arab world and, particularly, by the PLO. Therefore, it was argued by European and American Fahd Plan enthusiasts, there was no longer any reason for Israel's refusal to accept and fully implement the other seven clauses of the Plan.

Clause 7, it is true, asserted that 'all states in the region should be able to live in peace', but there was no mention of either negotiations or a formal peace between the parties. Yet in return for this phantom 'implied' recognition, which did not even mention Israel by name, Israel was called upon to withdraw from all territories 'occupied in 1967 including Arab Jerusalem'; to 'remove' all Jewish settlements from the West Bank and Gaza; to agree to an independent Palestinian state 'under the leadership of the PLO' with Jerusalem as its capital; and to the United Nations guaranteeing 'peace' for all states in the region and the implementation of these measures. It was hardly a tempting offer for Israel. This anodyne plan, which Begin had branded as 'a formula for Israel's liquidation' and which had been rejected by Syria, Libya and the PLO in 1981 because it might have been construed as accepting Israel's existence, was transformed miraculously into a basic tenet of PLO policy when Israeli troops crossed the frontier on 6 June 1982 and drove out the PLO forces entrenched in Lebanon.

The war in Lebanon changed all existing alignments. When the PLO was down and almost out, the Arab leaders looked the other way, even when the Syrians and Arafat's PLO critics launched a savage attack on Arafat's forces in northern Lebanon and compelled them to evacuate their remaining troops from Lebanon. The PLO was now split into warring factions. Arafat had been evicted from his last territorial base adjacent to Israel and his men had been scattered throughout the Arab world. The PLO was in deep crisis.

It was this situation that brought about the second extraordinary paradox in recent Palestinian history: the first had been Israel's entry into the territories in 1967, which had revived and stimulated Palestinian nationalism. The second was the product of Israel's entry into Lebanon in 1982. It led to the near-demise of the Palestinian national movement in the diaspora. But, at the same time, it reactivated Palestinian national consciousness on the West Bank and in Gaza. For years, Lebanon had been turned by the PLO into a surrogate *ersatz* national home for the Palestinians – without, of course, Lebanese consent. But all that came to an end with the expulsion of the PLO from Beirut. The Palestinian national idea had nowhere to go – except home, to the West Bank and Gaza: the territories. The countdown to the *intifada* had begun: the objective factors were moving into position without the PLO leadership being aware of it. However, the political manipulation of the Palestinian Arabs was to continue until the politicians themselves – Palestinian and Israeli – were overtaken seven years later by the consequences of the *intifada*. But first came the fateful aftermath of the PLO's war in Lebanon.

The Palestinian leaders did not know what to do next. They were defeated, discredited and isolated in the Arab world. They survived because the Israelis also failed at this critical moment in history to present a viable alternative policy for a Palestinian settlement. Instead, Israel withdrew from Lebanon and engaged in ill-informed domestic recrimination. Meanwhile, the Palestinians clung desperately to the myth that the PLO's expulsion from Beirut had been a great political success for Arafat, a triumph over the retreating Israelis.

This was the central theme of the 16th Palestine National Council when it met in Algiers in February 1983. The PLO's expulsion from Lebanon might never have happened judging by the policy decisions taken and the lessons learned in Algiers by its leadership. The Council restated the Palestinian attitude towards Israel and the United States. It was to be confrontational; the armed struggle 'against the Zionist enemy' was to be escalated; Israeli and American peace initiatives were denounced; the Reagan Plan was rejected; and the Egyptian people were urged to overthrow the Camp David Accords and the Peace Treaty with Israel – and, by clear implication, the Mubarak regime. It was an inauspicious beginning for the PLO's return to realism. The only reference to the Fahd Plan, which Arafat had supported at the Fez summit five months previously, was to say that 'it should be complemented by military action in order to alter the balance of power in favour of the Palestinians'. Clearly, it would take a long haul before the PLO leadership was psychologically and politically able to confront the reality of the Palestinian situation.

In any democratic movement, however flawed, the consequences would have been instant and radical: the failed leaders would have been sent packing. Moreover, the Palestinian Arabs were more accustomed by now to democratic thinking and practice than any other Arab group; the fifteen years' co-existence alongside democratic Israel since 1967 had left its mark: on the intellectual and educational level, the Palestinian Arabs had no peers in the Arab world. Yet the PLO leaders were able to act as they wished largely because of the internal ruthless terror apparatus at their disposal. PLO dissidents and critics were dealt with peremptorily. The PLO leadership was constrained and repeatedly forced to rethink its position only because of the pressures brought to bear on it by Israel's policies, which were designed to compel Palestinian Arab acceptance of an equitable peace and co-existence.

The PLO leadership's determination to resist and prevent such an outcome becomes evident and documented when we consider its policy and practice during the seven lean years that followed its fall in Beirut in 1982. Seen in this longer perspective, Arafat's diplomatic twists and turns assume a recognizable pattern. Therefore, we have found it most instructive to treat this period as a composite whole which carried a message Israel could not afford to ignore. However, it was the PLO that had most to learn during these seven difficult years. It failed to do so. It refused to face reality and, instead, engaged at each of the four policy-making National Council conferences during this period in futile shadow-boxing.

Thus, at the meeting in Algiers in February 1983, the first since the Lebanon débâcle, Arafat boasted of the great political victory the PLO had won in Lebanon. They only had to read and listen to the plaudits of the world media and of friendly western politicians to appreciate the triumph of the PLO; it had all but defeated and routed the IDF in Lebanon, Arafat claimed. It had been a remarkable achievement that they could now be meeting in Algiers. This was too much for Dr Sartawi. Speaking with biting sarcasm, he said that they were meeting almost a thousand miles from their homeland; it was the nearest they could get to Palestine. Next year, Sartawi mused, after our next encounter with Israel, we shall be forced to meet in Fiji, from where our leaders will be able to proclaim yet another great political victory for the PLO. Six weeks later, on 10 April, he was assassinated in the lounge of his hotel while attending, on behalf of the PLO, the 16th Congress of the Socialist International in Portugal.

As I have mentioned, the murder of one of the brighter lights of the PLO, an independent-minded surgeon of considerable reputation, who had dared in the National Council to question Arafat's leadership, was conveniently attributed to the Abu Nidal group. But murder of this kind was not the only hallmark of PLO policy-making.

Another feature of this 16th Palestine National Council was the familiar Arafat duet with his PLO executive. These performances were a recurring by-play in the making – and unmaking – of PLO policy. As a follow-up to this Council meeting in Algiers, Arafat hastened to Amman. There he issued a statement on 30 March 1983 that he had agreed with King Hussein to pursue 'a special and distinguished relationship' to build a confederal union between the two peoples on the basis of the Fez summit resolutions and of the Reagan peace plan. Arafat – though not Hussein – must have known that the PLO executive would in all probability reject the joint statement when, five days later, on 5 April, he flew to Kuwait to seek the executive's approval of his agreement with Hussein.

It was not forthcoming. Instead, the PLO executive made radical changes in Hussein's text, to which Arafat agreed, and altered the whole thrust of the agreement; it was now totally unacceptable to Hussein. Arafat decided that, under these new circumstances, discretion might be the better part of valour: he did not return to Amman 'within forty-eight hours' as he had promised the King. Instead, he sent a junior member of the PLO executive to inform Hussein of the proposed changes to their agreement. Understandably, Hussein was angry. He waited until 10 April and then brusquely rejected the changes proposed by the PLO executive: they ruled out any prospect of a peace settlement.

However, this Jordanian interlude had served Arafat's purpose. It had demonstrated – above all to the Americans and Europeans – that he was a moderate leader shackled by a recalcitrant and extremist executive. It was to be his favourite card during his long retreat as he pondered his next move. The Jordanian option had, however, become essential to the PLO after it had lost its Lebanese bastion as a convenient bridge to the Palestinian Arabs on the West Bank and in Gaza. Arafat needed this connection more than anything. Moreover, the Saudi rulers and the Egyptian Government were keen on a rapprochement between Jordan and the PLO as a counterweight to the activities of the Arab radicals led by Syria and Libya. Accordingly, after a short interval, Arafat resumed his courtship of Hussein. It was, however, only with great difficulty that the Saudi rulers and Egypt's presidential adviser, Osama el-Baz, managed to persuaded Hussein to overcome his profound personal aversion for Arafat and to resume negotiations for an agreement with the PLO. Moreover, he felt deeply insulted by the PLO's handling of the 1983 agreement and by Arafat's subsequent rudeness.

The opportunity presented itself when Hussein agreed, in response to a forthright demand from King Fahd, to host the PLO's 17th National Council meeting in Amman in November 1984. It was a desperate situation for Arafat. The PLO as a corporate body was breaking up; only three of its nine constituent factions – the Arafat loyalists – came to Amman; the others, backed by Syria and Libya, boycotted the National Council meeting and opposed any deal with Hussein. In many ways, this rump National Council in Amman in 1984 was the least important of any of the nineteen National Council conferences at which PLO policy was decided between 1964 and 1988.

It turned out, however, to be in many ways the most revealing: Arafat bared his innermost thoughts for this Council meeting, which, more than any other, was all his own work. He alone had decided its time and place. He had not sought the customary consensus with his colleagues in the leadership or with the constituent factions of the PLO. He achieved the necessary quorum through the manipulated attendance of so-called 'independents' – virtually all Arafat appointees.

But then came the revealing feature of this unusual gathering. Arafat was his own man there. He made the decisions. He was not under pressure. His critics, his rivals and his adversaries inside the Palestinian movement were absent. He could say what he wanted, and he did. He dictated the contents of the 'political report', which he presented to the National Council. This was, in effect, his conception of the Palestinian Arab situation two years after his expulsion from Beirut. It failed completely to comprehend Israel's aims in the Lebanon War and ignored its adverse consequences for the PLO. These were described correctly and very differently in the official journal of the PLO by Arafat's respected colleague, Ibrahim Abu Lughod, who summed up the consequences of the Lebanese defeat as 'having effected the forced exodus of the PLO, the destruction of its civil infrastructure in Lebanon, and causing the most significant political crisis the Palestinian movement has ever faced'.

There was no evidence of Arafat having any such thoughts in his 'political report', nor did he tolerate any kind of critical assessment of the PLO's Lebanese experience. As a result, discussion at the Amman Council meeting was muted, ill-informed and sycophantic.

The contents of Arafat's 'political report' constituted a singular record of doctrinaire make-believe. Thus, the delegates were asked to believe that the PLO executive had incontrovertible evidence that Peres and Shamir, with the Labour and Likud Parties, had the identical objective 'to destroy the Palestinian people, obliterate its identity, and end its existence'; that, basically, there was no difference between Peres and Labour or Shamir and Likud; and that it was simply a question of which one of them could do the job better and quicker. The 'report' claimed that the PLO leadership wanted to restore relations with King Hussein, but he had refused. It called on Egypt to denounce her peace treaty with Israel and asserted the PLO's refusal to have any dealings with the Mubarak regime; and, finally, it rejected President Reagan's peace plan as an instrument for destroying the Palestinian people.

If Arafat led the way into this fantasy world, King Hussein was not far behind. The King, usually so suave and sophisticated, so reasonable when speaking in Washington or London, was another persona in front of these Palestinian Arab representatives who were his guests in Amman. His address to them, on 22 November 1984, was a demagogue's dream. He told them that 'Jerusalem groaned under the weight of Jewish impositions', and that two of the holiest sites of Islam, 'the el-Aqsa Mosque and the Dome of the Rock, are threatened by the Jewish enemy with demolition and

obliteration'. He then asked this supposedly 'moderate' rump of the Palestinian parliament, 'How much longer can we allow this greedy enemy to
eat up our land while we argue and recriminate?' And he warned them that
'history will record your answer because in it lies the last feasible chance
to save the land, the people and Holy Places'. History, alas, did not pay
undue attention to these flights into unreality by the King and his PLO
guests. Nor did anyone else.

Despite opposition from the PLO leadership, which rejected every one
of Hussein's proposals and backed those of the PLO radicals opposed to
Arafat, the PLO chief would this time not be put off. He had the strong
support of the Saudis, who were convinced that Arafat had first to come to
terms with Hussein if he wanted to recruit the Americans to his side, as
Sadat had done. Thus sponsored by the Egyptians and the Saudis, Hussein
and Arafat tried again to cobble together yet another version of the Jordanian option. On 11 February 1985, Hussein made public details of his
agreement with Arafat.

However, we were aware that this was not simply yet another rehash of
Arafat's Jordanian option. It was now a means to a much more ambitious
objective – to Arafat's American option. The Saudis, in particular, had
been convinced that the PLO by itself, and Arafat on his own, would get
nowhere, with or without Hussein, in compelling Israel to withdraw from
the territories she had occupied in 1967 – including Jerusalem; only the
Americans could make this happen.

The tortuous dealing and double-dealing between Arafat and Hussein
that followed on their agreement of 11 February 1985 was, in reality, quite
irrelevant. All that mattered was whether the PLO would accept the formula
which Hussein had provisionally agreed with the US State Department as
the next step forward. Yet, despite Hussein's further concessions (at Israel's
expense) about which he did not consult the Americans, the PLO executive
rejected the Hussein–Arafat agreement in forthright and brutal terms.

Its spokesman, Arafat's diplomatic Number Two, Faruq Qaddumi,
described the agreement as being based on 'capitulationist projects and
unilateral deals such as the autonomy project, the Camp David Accords,
the Reagan initiative and on the UN Security Council Resolution 242, all
of which were totally unacceptable to the PLO executive'. They could not
be even a subject for discussion, any more than the American proposal that
Palestinian delegates should be part of a Jordanian delegation which would
conduct direct negotiations with Israel. 'It would be better for all of us',
Qaddumi concluded, 'if we were to forget about these proposals – for
ever.' Other PLO factions joined in the chorus of denunciation, which was
directed exclusively at Hussein. Arafat said nothing either in defence of the
agreement he had signed, or in defence of the King who had treated with
him and who now felt he had been tricked by the PLO.

Hussein waited awhile. On 19 February 1986 – one year and eight days
after concluding the agreement with Arafat – Hussein spoke about it. He
did so for over three hours in an emotional, pre-recorded televised broadcast

from Amman, in which he realistically assessed the contemporary Arab condition – so different from the anti-Israel diatribe which he had made just a year previously to the Palestine National Council in Amman. Hussein now recalled the many Arab 'initiatives' in which he had participated except, of course, the Camp David agreements, but he had been unable to reach any understanding with Arafat and the PLO despite their agreement of 11 February 1985 to collaborate in solving the Palestinian problem.

He recounted, step by step, his attempts to come to terms with the PLO and with Arafat, and how they had ended in complete failure. As a result, 'after two long attempts, I and the Government of the Hashemite Kingdom hereby announce that we are unable to continue to co-ordinate politically with the PLO leadership until such a time as their word becomes their bond, characterized by commitment, credibility and constancy'. Arafat had shown himself to be a liar and a cheat. These were strong words; Hussein had been deeply offended by Arafat's conduct. Except in times of war, there had been few more damning indictments of an adversary's probity – and in this instance Arafat was rated as an ally, not as an enemy. Apart, however, from the self-evident clash of personalities and policies between these two men, the experience of it, be it only as involved observers, was an eye-opener for those Israelis seeking a negotiating position with Jordan and with the Palestinian Arabs. It coloured all our preconceived notions.

Much to our astonishment, high Jordanian officials were making angry and sarcastic comments that we were being too soft on PLO supporters in the West Bank; that we were far too tolerant with the Palestinian Arab institutions; that we should have closed down their newspapers and schools, arrested editors and teachers and all known PLO activists. All this advice was given to us while the Jordanians – and especially the King – were making strenuous efforts to win over the Palestinian Arabs. But the heavy-handed, unimaginative Jordanian tactics offered no inducement to the Palestinians to side with Hussein against Arafat. In any case, Hussein had waited too long; he had actually believed that Arafat would bail him out.

By the end of 1986, he knew better. Hussein was in a black mood and gave voice to his despair, when he addressed the graduation ceremony at the Command and Staff College of the Jordan Defence Forces on 13 December 1986. He warned the Arab world that its internal feuding was tearing itself apart and was leading them into violence and war. Even worse, he told the passing-out parade, the condition of the Arab world had made it irrelevant in global affairs. 'What has happened to the Arab League?' he demanded. 'Who ever thinks of it in connection with NATO and other international organizations?' He urged the Staff College graduates 'to open their eyes to these bitter and painful facts. The United States no longer considers the Arab states a strategically important region because of our divisions, disputes and fragmentation which produce contempt, not respect or concern for our region.' And Hussein added for the benefit of his wider audience that, in his opinion, 'the Arab system under which we live is in danger of collapse and, when that happens, no Arab state will be safe however great its military or financial power'. This was just three years before eastern Europe confirmed what can happen to totalitarian monoliths – and how swiftly and suddenly it can happen.

Hussein's failure to win the backing of the West Bank Arabs had many reasons; among the least important were the activities of the PLO. Far more significant was the profound antipathy felt by the Arab population of the West Bank for Hashemite rule and rulers. The Jordanians had done everything possible to earn this Palestinian dislike. Their rule had been harsh and at times brutal; and economic matters had always been so managed as to favour Jordanians at the expense of Palestinians, who had no democratic redress; consequently, they voted with their feet. It is generally forgotten that during Jordanian rule of the West Bank – from 1948 to 1966 – some 400,000 Palestinians left the West Bank, according to Jim Lederman's perceptive study in *Foreign Policy/72*. They emigrated to escape conditions brought about by Jordan's policy of economic discrimination; another 147,000 Palestinians emigrated voluntarily between 1967 and 1983 in response to the tempting job markets in the Gulf states.

This came to an abrupt half with the collapse of worldwide oil prices. Skilled and educated Palestinians were no longer in demand in the Gulf, and the outlook at home on the West Bank was grim. More than 2,500 West Bank Palestinians graduated from universities every year, but there were only some 400 new jobs annually requiring their qualifications. The situation was much worse in Gaza.

The consequences were evidently apparent to King Hussein when he made his gloomy prediction in December 1986. That year there had been a sudden and dramatic spurt in Palestinian Arab emigration. Average emigration between 1983 and 1985 had been less than 8,000 a year, but in 1986, it leapt to 23,000 and preliminary figures show that emigration for 1988 and 1989, the years following the *intifada*, reached flight proportions.

It was the combination of the explosive and self-destructive political condition outlined by Hussein at the end of 1986, and the social and demographic upheaval in the territories in the run-up to the *intifada*, which provided the background to the Palestinian National Council meeting in Algiers on 20 April 1987. It marked, so it seemed, the final liquidation of Arafat's Jordanian option. Every aspect of it was to be eradicated from PLO policy. The search for a compromise acceptable to the Americans, who would then compel Israel to accept it, was abandoned by Arafat. Instead, he turned to the PLO radicals – extremists and self-proclaimed terrorists – for succour. Under this radical banner, he proposed to re-establish the unity of the PLO. The way he planned to do this provided us with a unique insight into the unbounded opportunism with which he operated. It had taken him just two years from his agreement with Hussein in Amman in February 1985 and his resultant breach with the PLO's radical factions to arrive at exactly the opposite stance – in harness with every radical Palestinian enemy of Hussein – at the Palestine National Council in Algiers in April 1987.

Officially, this was the great reunion of all the factions of the PLO, moderate and extreme, united behind Arafat's charismatic leadership. There was an infectious carnival atmosphere among the 319 delegates and the more than 600 genuine and not so genuine reporters, who attended the opening session at the elegant Club des Pines securely situated some twenty miles outside Algiers.

However, by the time Arafat made his belligerent opening speech to this 18th Palestine National Council, the serious internal divisions and disputes which had preceded it had been settled. Decisions to be made by the Council had been agreed. The secret conclave of PLO faction leaders which met before the formal opening of the conference had arranged the public agenda for what was to be a euphoric demonstration of PLO unity. It was made possible by the political price Arafat was prepared to pay and the concessions he was willing to make to the 'radicals and terrorists' of the PLO. The Algiers Palestine National Council was their show.

By now, Arafat had realized that actually his leadership was at stake. The showdown had come not at the official Palestine National Council conference, which opened on 20 April, but at the secret pre-conference which met in Algiers during the week preceding the formal opening. This was essentially a conference of leaders. All the different PLO shades were present: Arafat and his Fatah colleagues; Habash and Hawatmeh, Ahmed Jibril, Abu Nidal and many of the lesser-known 'radicals and terrorists'. Arafat was very confident that his proposed compromise would find general acceptance. Before the critical session of this pre-conference, he had a meeting in Algiers with the Egyptian special envoy, Taha el-Farnawassi, who brought him a message of support and encouragement from President Mubarak. Arafat did not tell the Egyptians that he had made a political U-turn and had joined his former critics in condemning not only Jordan and Hussein but also Egypt and Mubarak, and the UN Security Council Resolution 242.

When the 18th Palestine National Council was opened after this secret preliminary conference, Arafat's keynote speech said it all. Political solutions had been abandoned. He made his pledge to the assembled PLO delegations and wanted their united support for his new policy: no more deals with Jordan, no more embraces for Egypt's President. 'This is my pledge,' he told the 319 delegates, 'the Palestinian rifle shall not be put down until we reach Palestine – all Palestine.' There would be no compromise, not with anyone – not Egypt, not Jordan, not Syria; Israel was not even mentioned except as an enemy to be destroyed.

He was asked about this at the press conference at the Aures Hotel in Algiers immediately after the conference had ended on 26 April by the knowledgeable and perceptive correspondent of Radio Monte Carlo's excellent Arabic Service, Nabil Darwish. His shrewd and loaded questions forced answers from Arafat which he had evaded during the formal sessions of the Council. At the outset, Darwish wanted Arafat to explain how he had overcome the 'internecine fighting, the many differences and disputes' which had been a feature of the preparations for the Council meeting and particularly of the proceedings at the secret pre-conference. Arafat's reply was angry and aggressive. They had no differences within the PLO; all the trouble stemmed from interference in the PLO's internal affairs by the Arab countries. Darwish was not easily put down. He reminded Arafat that he had demonstrably distanced himself from the positions taken by Egypt, Jordan, Syria and Saudi Arabia. 'Frankly, Abu Ammar,' asked Darwish, 'how can you go to an international conference with such a confused and confusing Arab situation?' Arafat's inconsequential reply was to assure Darwish that he was used to walking in minefields. With his customary tact, Darwish did not remind Arafat that people who wander into minefields usually get blown up.

There was another question-and-answer which was of particular interest to us and which deserves to stay on the record. Darwish wanted to know Arafat's answer to the offer Ezer Weizman had made to sit down with Arafat and talk about establishing an Israeli–Palestinian confederation. Arafat's reply – let us recall the date, 26 April 1987 – was illuminating and instructive. 'My answer is to ask, "Why talk about confederation? Why not return to a democratic state in Palestine?" If you are prepared to come to an international conference, then come to the conference.' Darwish pressed his question: did the Palestine National Council not permit his meeting with Weizman? Arafat hedged. He would meet Weizman 'within the United Nations', but he would not elaborate.

The most telling comments on Arafat's politicking at the Council and on his policies came from Egypt and from representative Palestinian Arab notables, the Mayors of Bethlehem and Gaza. The leading Egyptian commentator broadcast the Egyptian view on the Algiers proceedings. They were 'a foolish game and a losing gamble'. Arafat had accepted 'bizarre conditions' for the restoration of PLO unity with the radical and extremist factions. No one in Egypt or Jordan would seriously consider this PLO game. Palestinian Arab comment was pithy and pointed. Bethlehem's respected Mayor, Ilyas Freij, considered the Algiers decisions a prescription for 'regional paralysis'. Gaza's influential Myor and elder statesman, Rashad el-Shawwa, said simply that it was 'a joke', which had been perpetrated 'by the minority dictatorship' within the PLO. Next day, Egypt closed all PLO offices and institutions in the country and expelled the principal officials. So did Jordan.

As if to underline the political somersault he had executed, the breach with Egypt and Jordan and the contemptuous refusal to take note of Palestinian Arab opinion in the territories, Arafat announced immediately after the end of the Council meeting that the PLO executive had decided to establish contacts with the extremist Syrian-backed groups based in Damascus which had boycotted the Algiers meeting. The political programme published at the same time – 26 April 1987 – was based in its

preamble 'on the Palestinian National Charter', which called for the elimination of the State of Israel and reiterated its total rejection of any political
settlement. Arafat's final message to the delegates left no room for doubt
that he had crossed the Rubicon and finally abandoned the Jordanian option
in favour of the PLO's new radicalism. His message was symptomatic of this
new radical PLO which Arafat had launched at Algiers. It was addressed, in
particular, 'to the Zionist braggarts' who thought they had a claim to the
Land of Israel.

In his closing words, Arafat cried:

I tell them that this Arab nation was created to stay in this Arab land which will
continue to speak Arabic; our forebears' bones are buried in it, and our children's
bones will be buried there. This land – including Jerusalem – headed by Jerusalem –
will remain Arab, Arab, Arab. . . . We are the will of this Arab nation in our occupied
land. Fire and destruction on the occupiers until we regain Palestine, until the
Palestinian flag is raised and we build the Palestinian state on these Palestinian
territories, on Palestinian national soil. Together and side by side until victory.

In the entire history of the Palestinian Arab movement for recognition,
there had never been a position so extreme, so negative and so provocative
to Israel as that at the conclusion of the 18th Palestine National Council in
Algiers on 26 April 1987. It marked another stage in the PLO's long retreat
since Beirut 1982 – the question was, retreat to what? Peace or to more
evasion and manipulation? The PLO had saved the formal unity of its
organization at Algiers, but it had at the same time blocked out all lights at
the end of the tunnel for the Palestinian Arabs living under Israeli rule on
the West Bank and in Gaza. Any hope these might have had for a peaceful
settlement of their problems had been effectively extinguished by the tone
and substance of the decisions of the Algiers 'unity' conference of the
Palestine National Council.

With this Algiers meeting the PLO had reached the pinnacle of extremism. Arafat had succeeded in bringing the radicals back into his fold.
Judging by the praise showered on him by the western governments and
media, it had been a remarkable achievement, a display of his statesmanship.
However, the reality was very different. Arafat had lost control over the
PLO in Algiers in April 1987. In order to retain his claim to be the
spokesman for the Palestinian Arabs, he had to accept the demands of the
radical factions and of his own more principled colleagues led by Khalil el-
Wazir (code-named Abu Jihad). At Algiers, Arafat lost his aura of authority
and leadership. His former political friends and allies on the National
Council felt betrayed by his surrender to the extremist demands of
Qaddumi, Habash, Hawatmeh and even of Abu Nidal, with whom Arafat
had negotiated terms during the secret pre-conference before the formal
opening of the Council.

All this had not taken place in a political vacuum. Across the line, in
Israel, ever since 1984, when Shimon Peres had become Prime Minister of
the National Unity Government, his overriding purpose had been to lift

the dormant peace process out of its inertia and to fire it with a new dynamism. His ardour in pursuit of peace was matched only by his frustration as month after month slipped by without producing any tangible results, for Peres was working with a stop-watch in his hand. According to the coalition agreement, his term of office as Prime Minister was only for a period of two years, after which Shamir would automatically succeed him. Shamir and his Likud Party would then be in the driving seat and they would not share Peres's zeal targeted on King Hussein as the logical partner who would continue the peace process which had been set in train with the Camp David Accords and with President Sadat's initiative.

Hussein, however, was no Sadat. He was temperamentally incapable of defying the Arab world as Sadat had done. He was unwilling to enter into peace talks with Israel without first being assured of support from the Arab world, which was a political *non sequitur*. He initially – and over-optimistically – pinned his hopes on the alliance with Arafat, while Peres helplessly watched Hussein wasting time on this sterile love affair. When, predictably, that came to nothing, for the support he believed he needed was not forthcoming, he turned to Syria instead. President Assad, unlike Arafat, was master of his own house and was not averse to a harmless flirtation with King Hussein, whose courting of the PLO he had not liked. The Syrian President was prepared to go along with the idea of an international peace conference so long as Hussein agreed not to conduct direct peace negotiations with Israel.

Hussein's permutations with Arafat and then with Assad consumed almost the whole of Peres's two-year term as Prime Minister. It was, moreover, only during his last days of office that Peres succeeded in meeting Egypt's President Mubarak, and then only after Peres had agreed to take the Taba boundary dispute to international arbitration. Most of the two-day Mubarak–Peres summit at the Ras el-Tin Palace in Alexandria was taken up with formula-hunting that would make an international peace conference acceptable to all parties – a Utopian ambition at that time. Mubarak and Peres were primarily concerned to find a way of overcoming Hussein's resistance to direct negotiations with Israel.

They took account of his insistent demand for Arab reinforcement for Jordan's position when they concocted a formula that would restrict the international conference to acting as an 'umbrella' for direct talks. It was, however, not a very realistic solution to Hussein's worries and fear of Arab retribution for, at the end of the day, the Arab states, the United States, the Soviet Union, the PLO and the Israelis had their own interpretation of the functions and objectives of the proposed international conference. There was no meeting of minds.

Within a week of the Alexandria summit, Shamir had taken over as Prime Minister and Peres had taken charge of the Foreign Ministry under the terms of the coalition agreement. Shamir's attitude to an international conference was totally different from that of Peres. Shamir was convinced that any such international conference, whatever its terms of reference, would become a public relations platform for basically unfriendly Arab delegations. Shamir did not believe that the Arabs – and particularly the PLO – wanted to reach a peace settlement with Israel. If they could not destroy Israel, then they preferred to do nothing and to make life for Israel as difficult as possible. Shamir and Peres were agreed on the desirability of direct negotiations between Israel and each Arab party, but they differed on the ways to bring them about.

Then suddenly, in almost total secrecy, nine days before the Palestine National Council was about to meet in Algiers, on 11 April 1987, there appeared to be a significant breakthrough in this deadlocked situation. After they had met twice secretly in London, King Hussein and Foreign Minister Peres agreed on the form of the proposed international peace conference. The details were set out in a paper described as the London Document. These were its salient points:

* The UN Secretary-General will invite the five permanent members of the Security Council and the parties involved in the Arab–Israeli conflict;
* Regional bilateral committees will conduct independent negotiations;
* The international conference will not impose solutions and will not veto agreements reached by the independent sides;
* Representatives of the Palestinian Arabs will be included in the Jordanian–Palestinian delegation.

The document was approved by the United States administration but not by Israel's coalition Government. For reasons of his own, Peres had failed to inform his Prime Minister of his negotiations with Hussein. Shamir did not know about the Document until the American Ambassador, Thomas Pickering, referred to it in conversation with him. Peres's unfortunate deliberate oversight turned out to be a costly political blunder which Shamir did not forget or forgive. He accused Peres of disloyal conduct and vowed that the London Document would remain a dead letter. He feared he had been set up by Peres in collusion with Hussein and the Americans. He saw the London Document as a trap designed to induce Israel to agree to an international conference, but he was convinced that no good for Israel could come from it. Fully supported by his Likud ministers, Shamir refused to endorse the Hussein–Peres agreement.

The long-expected confrontation between Shamir and Peres seemed at last to be about to materialize. Peres had threatened that if the National Unity Government failed to approve the London Document, he would withdraw the Labour ministers from the coalition Government. His failure to do so greatly damaged his political credibility among his own supporters and, even more so, in his international standing. But for Hussein, for the Egyptians and for the Americans, this saga of the London Document carried an unmistakeable message: the person to deal with in Israel was Shamir, not Peres, who had failed to deliver. Good intentions were not enough. However, the real reason for the collapse of the idea of an international conference was neither Shamir's nor Peres's position. The concept of an international peace conference had been sunk by the position taken by the PLO leadership. It had stipulated terms for such a conference which no Israeli party would find acceptable, and which confirmed Prime Minister Shamir's adamant refusal to have anything to do with the idea that realistic negotiations could take place under such conditions.

The breaking point for Israel came in November 1987, when the Arab heads of state met in a summit conference in Amman. What they did there was to demonstrate that all the Arab countries shared in the concept of an international peace conference which would meet only after the preconditions demanded by the PLO had been conceded by Israel. Thus, before there were any negotiations, Israel would have to accept that the outcome of the international conference, according to the resolution passed by the Arab heads of state in Amman, including the PLO, 'would guarantee the regaining of the occupied Arab and Palestinian territories, the resolution of the Palestine question in all its aspects and the attainment of the legitimate rights of the Palestinian Arab people'.

It was an Alice-in-Wonderland formula that was not likely to inspire enthusiasm for an international conference in any political quarter in Israel. Just in case any Israeli politician had thought that this had been a temporary aberration by the Arab heads of state, the PLO executive committee, meeting in Tunis on the 22 August 1987, had already stipulated these preconditions for any international conference and, for good measure, added constraints on any suggestion that there could be any kind of negotiation with Israel, for such a conference would have the power to impose a settlement on a presumably unwilling Israel. All that would be left for Israel to discuss, according to the spokesman of the PLO, was how she would comply with the decisions of the international peace conference. No one could complain that there was any imprecision about its position: the PLO would take part in an international peace conference only if all its basic demands were accepted by all parties before the conference was convened; there were to be no bilateral negotiations. There was only one slight omission from these preliminary discussions: 'peace' was not mentioned and did not rank in the PLO's catalogue of demands.

Thus, 1987 drew to a close in a state of disarray. At their Alexandria 'summit', Mubarek and Peres had proclaimed it a year of negotiation for peace, but the entire train of events which had been set in motion by Hussein and Peres and backed by Mubarak and the Americans had become derailed. The prospect of an international peace conference evaporated into unreality under the impact of the preconditions set by the PLO and confirmed by the Arab heads of state. Peres was discredited and Hussein was left suspended in the limbo that filled the space between Israel's Labour Party and the Likud Party. Israel's Jordanian option, which successive governments had so assiduously pursued, was dead. So was the PLO's Jordanian option. Now, Israel had only the Palestinians as partners for peace and the Palestinians had only Israel: both had exhausted all other alternatives – or so it seemed. But we were not there yet.

25
Intifada
1987–91

WE HAD TURNED a full circle. After twenty-five years, we seemed to be back where we had been in 1967, face to face with the Palestinians. It had taken three wars and much sorrow for us – the Palestinians and the Israelis — to realize that we alone could settle this conflict. We had to do it; we could not farm it out to the Great Powers or to the Arab rulers or to an international conference. We had to decide our own future, difficult and painful as this might be.

Compared with the threat to Israel's existence – real and not hypothetical – of the armed might on our eastern front, the Palestinians, including all the militant factions inside and outside the PLO, were the least dangerous militarily. In the spring of 1990, while we were considering a Palestinian solution, we had to go to sleep every night knowing that Syria, still in a state of war with Israel, had 500,000 men with 4,000 tanks under arms only hours from our northern frontier and 500 combat aircraft only minutes from our major civilian centres, while sophisticated Soviet-supplied missiles were trained on Haifa and Tel Aviv. Beyond Damascus there was the ever-hostile Iraq – Jordan's ally – which had rejected even an armistice agreement with Israel. In 1989, it had a defence budget of $13 billion. It had more than a million men under arms with 5,500 tanks, over 500 combat aircraft and a sophisticated armoury which included long-range missiles and chemical weapons. Iraq, moreover, had demonstrated only too effectively – first in Iran and then in Kuwait, and against Israel and Saudi Arabia – that she had no compunction in using this armoury.

These weapons, and not the rocks and fire-bombs of the Palestinian *intifada*, provided the constant threat with which the Jewish state has had to contend. Small wonder that Prime Minister Shamir would have preferred to keep the Palestinian settlement on a back-burner while he concentrated on reaching an agreement with Syria and Jordan and, in due course, also with post-Saddam Iraq, or, for that matter, that Ariel Sharon considered the most pressing problem for the Middle East to be a comprehensive disarmament programme. But the Palestinian problem could not be shunted into a convenient lay-by. While the Palestinians were the least dangerous militarily for Israel, they were, however, politically the most sensitive and complicated problem confronting the Government. The Palestinians had become the major issue of Israel's foreign and domestic policies and a critical element in our international relations, especially with the United States. They were thrust into the centre of our affairs by a combination of circumstances neither foreseen by any of Israel's civilian or military authorities, nor planned by the PLO. The *intifada* had caught Israel unprepared and – at first – lacking in understanding.

For the first time since Israel had taken charge of the West Bank and Gaza in 1967 the Palestinians rose against her in open defiance. But, instead of the swift and savage retribution which the Palestinian Arabs had expected and feared, the Israelis were hesitant, surprised and ineffective in their response to the initial disorders. We could have mastered them easily had we allowed the army to use its fire-power as was customary in our neighbouring Arab countries, in Syria, Jordan and Iraq; or in India, Pakistan and Algeria; or even in Panama and in Baku in the Soviet Union. The *intifada* would have been stopped in its tracks. However, Israeli soldiers were justly and expressly forbidden from opening fire on rioters except in cases where their own lives were evidently at risk. Moreover, the IDF had not been trained or equipped to deal adequately with massed and organized civilian violence, and they were additionally handicapped by their flawed assessment of Arab capability and individual Arab courage, especially when fuelled by fanaticism.

The demonstrations spread rapidly and soon all of Judea, Samaria and Gaza were aflame. What had begun as an outburst of anger at an isolated incident – an accident involving a military truck in which several Palestinians were killed – was rapidly transformed into a full-blown uprising, the *intifada*.

Its early manifestation in Gaza was notable for the incitement by Islamic fundamentalist agitators rather than by concerted action from PLO activists. The Gaza Strip had been an ideal breeding-ground for religious fundamentalism. More than 650,000 Palestinians crowded into this bleak and poverty-stricken strip of 360 square kilometres. Their natural growth rate was such that by the end of the century they would number nearly a million, mostly unemployed Palestinian Arabs, crammed into squalid refugee camps which should have been resettled during the twenty years when Egypt was master of the Gaza Strip. The PLO, the Arab states and the United Nations had combined to prevent any real social alleviation – especially better housing – which had been proposed by Israel and the United States. The camps, as well as the crowded back alleys of Gaza, Rafah and Khan Yunis, became strongholds of Hamas, the Islamic fundamentalists who reject Israel's right to exist and are also committed opponents of every political or cultural expression of western values in Arab society. The wretched conditions of daily life drew old and young alike towards the mosque – towards Islam's offer of a better life in the next world and an overpowering sense of solidarity and of belonging. The frenzied exhortations of the fundamentalist preachers inflamed passions and ignited the *intifada*.

The pent-up frustrations and humiliation, held back for so long, were now given free rein. They burst forth with the force of an erupting volcano. They were galvanized by the hatred felt for the Israeli overlords and by the still smouldering anger directed at the Arab states for their callous indifference and lack of help during the Lebanese War. Moreover, many Palestinians felt that they had been betrayed by the PLO leaders in Tunis; they had led the Palestinians from one calamity to another until their followers were dispersed throughout the Arab world and elsewhere as a result of the climactic débâcle in Lebanon. The Lebanese War had become a crucial turning-point, for the Palestinians in the territories had been passive before this war, accepting without question the centrality of the PLO leadership in Lebanon, and its axiom that the armed struggle against Israel could only be won with the support of the Arab countries.

The war in Lebanon made nonsense of both these assumptions. With the PLO rank and file dispersed and in crisis, and with the total absence of the anticipated help from Arab countries cruelly demonstrated in Lebanon, the local Palestinians on the West Bank began to assert themselves. New leaders emerged and self-reliance became the essence of their thinking.

One man in the PLO leadership stood out from the others at this critical juncture: Khalil el-Wazir, known best by his code-name Abu Jihad, one of the founders of the Fatah, and Arafat's principal deputy. Arafat was the politician; Abu Jihad was the military commander, master-minding many of the major PLO terrorist strikes until a commando unit, purported to be Israeli, ambushed and killed him in his home in Tunis in 1988.

At the height of the PLO's disarray after the Lebanese War, Abu Jihad established a PLO office in the Jordanian capital, Amman, almost next door to Israeli territory. This had much more resemblance to an advanced military headquarters than to a diplomatic mission. From this base, Abu Jihad set about organizing the Palestinians in the territories, transforming the PLO there into a mass movement, with its own highly disciplined youth movement, the Shabiba. It was a movement that owed allegiance to the PLO leadership in Tunis, that held the PLO as a symbol of its national aspirations, but which had a mind of its own. For these Palestinians, the centre of political gravity had moved back from the diaspora to their home ground. The new mood inevitably led to the demonstrations of December 1987, which became the *intifada*.

The resulting explosion of violent demonstrations had a profound effect on Israeli thinking. But it made an even deeper impact on the Palestinians living in the territories. It took time, but not too much, for them to understand – for the Palestinian Arabs were by common consent among the politically best-educated and informed political community in the Arab world – that throwing rocks and Molotov cocktails at Israelis would not produce the kind of political dividends they wanted: the Israelis were not likely, as a result, to pack up and leave the territories. It was politically naïve to believe that. And the Palestinians in the territories were anything but that: it was thus only a matter of time before they grasped the actual nature of the political opportunity presented by the *intifada*.

Its initial driving power had been protest: protest against the Israeli occupation; but protest also against the PLO's flawed leadership and policies, which had closed all doors that could lead to a political settlement and the attainment of acceptable conditions of self-determination for the Palestinian Arab people. If the *intifada* was to achieve its purpose, then it would have to make possible the reopening of these closed doors to a political settlement with Israel; it would have to compel the absentee PLO leaders in Tunis and Damascus to accept their Palestinian initiative on its own terms and not on the bases of the impossible preconditions set by the PLO diaspora at its National Council and by the Arab heads of state at their 'emergency' summits. These ignored, or did not comprehend, the message signalled to them by the *intifada*.

There were many on our side of the 'Green Line' who were also oblivious to the opportunities. Yet, despite the rhetoric and posturing of Israeli 'hawks', there was a de facto near consensus in Israel, as there was among the Palestinians in the territories, that the only acceptable answer to the *intifada* was a mutually agreed political settlement acceptable to a majority of Israelis and Palestinian Arabs. It would take time; however, it was the only realistic prescription for peace and the only alternative to the violence of the *intifada*; what the *intifada* had achieved and changed was that it had broken the seemingly unbreakable Arab and Israeli political moulds that kept the Israeli–Palestinian conflict in a frozen political and psychological condition. All this had been transformed by the *intifada* and by the Israeli responses to it, often in chaotic and messy ways which were not always 'nice'.

The dialectic of these events produced, in turn, their own wider repercussions which, again, were not all that Palestinians and Israelis would have expected. The Arab rulers made sympathetic noises but were clearly scared, lest the example of direct action by the Palestinians might be catching and that their own 'subjects' in the Gulf states, Syria, Jordan and Egypt might be encouraged to take similar steps against their own unpopular 'establishments'.

Meanwhile, Israeli military and civilian authorities absorbed the lessons of their initial failures to contain the uprising and began to deal with the orchestrated violence with increased effectiveness. As this became evident, Palestinian Arab concern in the territories turned on the PLO leadership, which had continued to proclaim its impractical and unrealizable objectives. The course of the *intifada* had underlined the unreality of the PLO's stand and made a mockery of the policies which Arafat and his colleagues had advocated. But it also did something much more positive than that; it sent a clear message: either a political solution is found or the spiral of violence will continue, deepening the ravines of hatred dividing the two peoples. It was a message we could not evade, or so the Palestinians in the territories believed.

However, at that point, political conditions in Israel had become more than usually complex. The divisions in the country were genuine; they touched the raw nerve of survival, Israel's security as an independent state. They cut across all customary and traditional political – and personal – loyalties. At issue was nothing less than the price which Israel was asked to pay for the sake of 'peace'; and how much 'security' she was prepared to sacrifice for this 'peace', which, at best, was still an uncertain promise without real guarantees and with many potential pitfalls. Israel was fairly evenly divided between those who believed that the seeming certainty of 'security' was preferable to the dubious uncertainties of 'peace', and those who were willing to risk possibly hidden dangers for the sake of 'peace'. It was therefore inevitable that we could not reply unequivocally to the Palestinian 'signals'. All the same, most Israelis were prepared to make a positive response to the Palestinians in the territories, to further the mutual desire for peaceful co-existence under mutually acceptable conditions.

But the real problem for both of us – Israelis and Palestinian Arabs – remained, as before, the intractable hostility to Israel of the PLO and its leader, Arafat. His 'Arab peace' was like a desert mirage: shimmeringly beckoning from a distance, but ever elusive and unsubstantive when approached. His equivocal stance seemingly justified the fears of those Israeli leaders, with Shamir at their head, who refused to deal with the PLO. This was the real problem for the Palestinians – and for Israel.

26
Arafat: False Prophet of Peace

WE COME NOW TO the heart of the matter. Sooner or later we have to face it – realistically, explicitly and without preconceptions. What are we to make of the PLO, its leaders and its policies? Will it continue to be the sole expression of Palestinian national aspirations? Can the Palestinians find an alternative leadership to lead them to peace in view of the shattering loss of credibility sustained by the PLO – not least among Israel's doves – after the downfall of Saddam Hussein?

Before examining the effects of the Iraqi débâcle on Palestinian politics, we have to reassess the essentials of the PLO's track record during the seminal years of the *intifida* – a crucial period in Israeli–Palestinian relations. To begin with, then, we had better look at Arafat's and the PLO's response to the uprising. Organizationally, it was, to say the least, traditional. Comments from Arafat himself and the other better-known faction leaders were at first muted. The PLO central committee met in Baghdad on 9 January 1988, a month after the outbreak of violence in Gaza; the executive met some time later in Tunis. They produced no new thoughts, no guidance and no inspiration for the Palestinians engaging the Israelis in the territories; and no recognition of the ultimate need for genuine and realistic co-existence with Israel.

Instead, the central committee, the executive and the PLO loyalists in the territories repeated the familiar dreary rhetoric without an original thought or any realistic understanding of Israel – every tired cliché, as Churchill once said, from 'God is love' to 'Please adjust your dress before leaving'. That was the true level of the PLO leadership at a time of real opportunity for the Palestinians. Arafat and his men continued to sulk for the best part of six months. It was as if they resented the self-assertion of the Palestinians in the territories and their temerity of taking action without Arafat's permission. It took Arafat and the PLO leadership all the time from the outbreak of the uprising in December 1987 to the emergency summit of the Arab heads of state in June 1988 to get their act together – and even then it was not much of an act.

When the summit of Arab heads of state assembled in Algiers in 8 June 1988 to celebrate the Palestinian uprising, it was soon evident that the real issue before the Arab rulers was the credibility or trustworthiness of the

PLO and particularly that of its chairman Arafat. The Kings of Saudi Arabia, Morocco and Jordan were particularly incensed with Arafat and the PLO; they felt that the PLO was playing games and acting with an unforgivable lack of responsibility.

Arafat's speech to the Arab rulers reflected neither the lessons nor the hopes of the *intifada*. It was simply an extension of the hard-line irres-ponsibility of the 18th Palestine National Council decisions of April 1987. Arafat called on the Arab heads of state to support the PLO 'to impose the Arab will' on Israel and on the international community; there was no hint of any desire for a political settlement. This was familiar stuff coming from Arafat. In the wake of the winds of change coming from the *intifada*, Arafat's rhetoric sounded even more than usually unrealistic, *'caduc'*, as the French would say. There was, however, more to it this time than just a dreary repetition of past clichés: Arafat had another card to play at the conference.

Just before he made his tough, unyielding speech to the Arab Kings and Presidents, the PLO circulated a document to all delegations and the assembled media. It purported to set out the PLO's 'consistent' position concerning talks with Israel. The author of the document, Bassam Abu Sharif, was described as 'Arafat's political adviser'.

Two things were particularly instructive about the Abu Sharif document. Firstly, it was the exact opposite to the harsh speech Arafat had just delivered. The document explained PLO policy towards Israel in terms of sweetness and light; it advocated direct negotiations between equals while recognizing Israel's legitimate security preoccupations. There was no hint in the Abu Sharif document of the denunciation of and pejorative references to Israel which had been the centre-piece of Arafat's address to the summit. The second significant feature of this affair was the way in which the Abu Sharif document was ignored by the participants of the summit and by the Arab and international media at the conference. All had received an advance copy together with a specially packaged PLO dossier. But none of the recipients had thought it worth a mention, let alone serious attention. That was on 9 July 1988 – the date has some significance.

Eight days later, the document reappeared, this time as a sensational article in the Arab-language newspaper, *al-Fajr*, in East Jerusalem. It was then picked up and quoted by the international news agencies and reproduced by the *Washington Post* and, not least, by Israeli newspapers and television as marking a major breakthrough – Arafat's peace option. Arafat's political adviser was now identified as a genuine moderate, reaching out for an understanding with the Israelis on behalf of his master. What did it mean? What did it portend? We were excited; we were intrigued; and we were seriously interested. The answer, when it came, was a revelation – and also the clue to Arafat, the man and the PLO politician – the com-bination that was to produce the Geneva 'peace' declaration six months later and its strange aftermath.

However, before we take a closer look at this curious association of Arafat and his newly appointed political adviser, we must pause a while longer with the Arab heads of state at Algiers to witness an event unique at these periodic gatherings – King Hussein speaking his mind with no holds barred. He had been outraged by the policy advocated by Arafat without consideration for the interests of the Palestinians in the territories. He was even more infuriated by the meek acceptance of Arafat's 'conditions' by the Arab Kings and Presidents. It was one of those rare occasions when Hussein abandoned his bland balancing act. In terms of barely disguised and rare sarcasm, he told his regal audience that 'if they find it necessary and useful to approve of the PLO demand that there should be an independent Palestinian Arab state as a precondition to the convening of an international conference, and, further, if they insist on the participation of the PLO as a separate delegation even if this were to lead to the cancellation of such a "conference",' he would go along with them.

With heavy irony, Hussein explained that such an outcome was preferable to the absurd and self-defeating policies which had been proposed by the PLO and approved by the heads of state. He would not be associated with such folly. The PLO could not be trusted and his fellow Arab League members had defaulted on their commitments to the Palestinians. 'What worth, then, can be placed on the new assurances given at this summit?' Hussein did not bother to answer his own questions. There was no need. His tough intervention had, at last, alerted Arafat and the PLO leadership to their loss of credibility among the Arab heads of state and even more so in the territories. They had to begin making their U-turn.

It was not easy. There was confusion and division among the PLO leaders and their advisers. Some wanted Arafat to play his much-debated 'American card' and for Abu Sharif to deal it. But Arafat, as always, could not make a decision. He wanted the best of both worlds: the support of the radicals inside the PLO and the support of the Americans outside it. After the failure of the Abu Sharif document to make any impact at the Algiers summit, Arafat decided to test it directly on the Israelis and the Americans. At the same time, he wanted to protect himself in case the Abu Sharif ploy backfired.

Accordingly, timed to coincide with the publication of Abu Sharif's moderate appeal to Israel on 17 June, Arafat launched his own most extreme declarations of total war against Israel. He boasted that 'the uprising had succeeded last month [May 1988] in setting fire to 80,000 dunam [20,000 acres] of forests and agricultural land in the occupied territories. These were incinerated with the help of "Molotov cocktails" by the vanguard of the Palestinian Popular Army.' This message threatening Israel with fire and sword was broadcast by Arafat from Baghdad barely an hour after Abu Sharif in Jerusalem had published the Algiers summit document, Arafat's message of peace and goodwill towards Israel. Which then was the genuine message? Which was the real Arafat?

We can now attempt to answer this double-barrelled question in conjunction with those we posed at the beginning of this chapter. Moreover, we can do so now with the added advantage of hindsight – a facility never to be underestimated in politics. These questions become all the more relevant when considered against the backdrop of the 'peace offensive' unleashed by the PLO in November 1988. Fortunately, we have enough information of every kind to map the PLO's journey from the extremes of the 18th Palestine National Congress in Algiers in 1987, which proclaimed total and merciless war against Israel, to the much-publicized moderation of the 19th Congress, also in Algiers, in November 1988 – from tiger to pussycat in just eighteen months. What had wrought this metamorphosis in the PLO and its leader? More to the point, perhaps, would be to ask why had they changed?

The explanation has to be sought in the territories, with the *intifada*. The PLO had been carried on the backs of the Palestinian demonstrators to a position of unprecedented world prominence and popularity. Within months of the outbreak of the *intifada*, the drooping fortunes of the PLO were fortuitously resuscitated; Arafat was again riding high. However, he was now aware that his new-found position of strength was dependent on the support of the Palestinians in the territories. For the first time he was accountable to them.

Previously his constituents had been the Palestinians who had left Israel before and during the wars of 1948 and 1967. The PLO had flourished on the advocacy of the right of return of this Palestinian diaspora to their former homes in what had become Israel – and it continued to do so throughout the 1980s. It was a policy that could be fulfilled only after the effective elimination of the State of Israel. For these hard-core constituents of the PLO Arafat brandished the sword.

However, this was not the objective of the Palestinians of the West Bank. Their interests and their aims were different. They wanted to come to terms with their Jewish neighbour so as to end the Israeli occupation. They knew that the apocalyptical dreams of the PLO – however dressed up – had no basis in reality. Israel was not going to be wiped off the face of the map by the PLO's rhetoric nor the *intifada*'s stones. The Palestinians in the territories wanted a political solution. They made this clear to Arafat and they expected him to act accordingly. It was to satisfy them that Arafat had floated the Abu Sharif formula and had launched the new seemingly moderate PLO policy. For them he waved the olive branch.

Arafat, the supreme dissimulator, the man of many faces who had been over the years consistent only in his continuing and repeated inconsistencies, was left with no choice. The hard reality of the *intifada* had made a mockery of the ne/er-never world which found expression in the policy resolutions passed by the Palestine National Council in 1987 only seven months before the outbreak of the uprising in Gaza and the West Bank. These had negated everything the *intifada* sought to achieve. Arafat had no other option but to abandon the stand he had taken in Algiers at the National Council in April 1987, which had blocked every path to a political settlement. There was nothing for it but to execute a political about-turn with as much grace as he could muster.

Not only had he been pressed to do so by the leaders of the *intifada*, but he had also to contend with growing international pressure, not least by the Soviet Union. According to Khaled el-Hassan, who had accompanied Arafat on a visit to Moscow in the spring of 1988, Gorbachev had urged Arafat to recognize Israel and to discuss with Soviet Foreign Minister Shevardnadze a formula for a 'phased policy' leading to 'two states in Palestine'. Arafat had been under similar pressure from influential European leaders with friendly relations – especially the French and Italian – who urged the PLO leaders to abandon the self-destructive extremism agreed by the PLO National Council in April 1987.

Accordingly, when the PLO appeared to sing a new tune with the Abu Sharif initiative in June 1988, the Americans, Europeans, West Bank Arabs and many Israelis (though not Prime Minister Shamir) responded hopefully to this apparent evidence of Arafat's switch to moderation, without troubling to inspect its credentials. The fact that Arafat ostensibly denied paternity did not discourage those who saw it as the dawn of a new 'moderate' PLO. This euphoria increased as some 2,000 media representatives made their way to Algiers in November 1988 for the meeting of the 19th Palestine National Council. It was going to be the grand turning-point of Palestinian Arab relations with Israel – Arafat's definitive peace gesture for which, at last, he would accept personal responsibility.

The advance publicity left nothing to chance. An eager world was waiting. It was told that the 19th National Council of the PLO would proclaim the establishment of an independent Palestinian state; it would accept the existence of Israel; it would agree to the formula of 'two states in Palestine'; and it would accept Security Council Resolutions 242 and 338 as requested by the Americans and by the Soviet Union. It sounded like Arafat's grand concession to bring about a peace settlement with Israel and it was this propagandist preview of the Algiers National Council which has found ready acceptance in the history books of our time.

This reversal of policy from the Algiers decisions of 1987 to those of Algiers in 1988 appeared to be so remarkable that it calls for closer examination. The records of the discussions and decisions of this seminal Council meeting of the PLO are now available for all to see who really want to know what did happen in Algiers, what Arafat really said and what decisions were actually taken.

A reading of these records revealed so many ifs and buts as to make the so-called concessions virtually meaningless. Nowhere in the political statement was there any explicit recognition of the State of Israel, let alone of Israel's right to exist. UN Resolution 242 was accepted only as a basis for an international conference, and on condition that the Palestinians' right to self-determination and all other UN resolutions concerning 'the Palestinian cause' would also form part of that basis together with Resolution 242. The fact that many of the General Assembly resolutions –

passed by the automatic majority of the Communist Bloc, the Non-Aligned and the Muslim groups – flatly contradicted 242 was not addressed. Moreover, it was hardly surprising that the format of the international conference demanded by the PLO bore no relation to the conference which Israel's Foreign Minister, Shimon Peres, and King Hussein had agreed as practicable in their London Document, which had the support of the Americans. The London version favoured a conference which would act as an 'umbrella' for direct bilateral negotiations between the various Arab parties and the Israelis. The PLO brand was something different altogether: in its conference 'the Security Council will draw up and guarantee the arrangements for security and peace among all the affected states in the region, including the Palestinian state'. The parties concerned would have no say in the matter. There would be no direct negotiations, and the establishment of an independent Arab Palestinian state was a precondition before an international peace conference could be convened.

Everything else was fudged in some way – implied, implicit or inferred – except when it came to defining the characteristics of the Jewish state. Thus, in its message to the Council, the PLO's political statement declared that it was 'not alone in confronting Israel's racist, fascist onslaught and foiling the Israeli aggressors'. Or, by way of variation: 'The true image of Israel is that of a racist, fascist settler state intent on the usurpation of Palestinian territory and the extermination of the Palestinian people. ...' It did not sound much like the language of conciliation and intended coexistence, but it was typical of the general run of references to Israel at this Council meeting, which, it was claimed, marked the turning-point in the PLO's attitude to Israel, the expression of the outstretched hand seeking peace and friendship. It was not very reassuring for Israelis.

What then – precisely – was this new-look policy of the PLO? Experience had taught Israeli negotiators that explanations by intermediaries, however friendly, were rarely reliable – even when they came from the Swedish Foreign Ministry or from the Brookings Institute or from British ministers and parliamentarians with an inside track to the PLO chairman in Tunis. There was only one reliable guide: the actual records of the proceedings, official and informal, at the 19th National Council meeting. These constituted a veritable Baedecker to the art of double-speak.

As we worked our way through these voluminous records, it became evident that the actual proceedings at the Algiers meeting of the Palestine National Council bore little – if any – resemblance to either the advance publicity or the post-conference hype. No decisions were taken that could be seen to further the peace process specifically between the Palestinians and Israel. On the contrary, every step taken by this PLO National Council was wrapped in a cocoon of reservations and qualifications. There was only one clear message from this policy-making Council: that even before any of its 'peace proposals' could be discussed in an 'effective international peace conference under UN auspices', Israel would have to meet all PLO demands as set out in the decisions of the National Council. She would have to agree to withdraw from 'all' Arab territories occupied in 1967; to accept Palestinian self-determination; to agree to the establishment of an independent Palestinian state and to the repatriation of all Palestinians to their former homes 'in Palestine' if they wished to return or compensate them if they did not. Only when Israel had met all these conditions would the PLO enter into negotiations – not with Israel, but with an international peace conference convened by the five permanent members of the UN Security Council, who would then be authorized to impose a so-called peace settlement. Israel was not impressed.

However, Israel was about to be taught a lesson in the power of make-believe diplomacy and news-management. What had actually transpired at this 19th PLO Council meeting, and what decisions had been taken or not taken, became quite irrelevant in its aftermath. What seemed to matter were the altogether unjustified claims of the PLO lobby that the supreme policy-making body of the PLO had agreed to 'recognize' Israel, to approve a 'two-state' solution and to accept UN Resolutions 242 and 338 as the basis for a peace settlement with Israel.

In fact, none of this was true. The 19th PLO National Council had taken no such decisions. It wanted western governments and the Third World countries to believe it had done so – and they did. Only George Shultz, the US Secretary of State, remained unconvinced; but he could do little to prevent the PLO bandwagon from merrily rolling along to nowhere, with the Europeans, the Africans and the Arabs on board – and, for good measure, some well-intentioned but equally ill-informed American Jews and Israelis along with them.

The ambiguous language of Algiers was not good or clear enough for the Americans and did not meet United States' terms for lifting her ban on negotiations with the PLO: recognition of Israel's right to exist, acceptance of the UN Security Council Resolutions 242 and 338, and renunciation of terrorism. The PLO had to do better than its performance in Algiers, and the opportunity lay conveniently at hand – at the UN General Assembly in Geneva, convened expressly to provide a forum for Arafat after he had been denied a visa to attend the General Assembly in New York. It was a perfect setting for him and he made the most of it.

The assembled Foreign Ministers and Ambassadors gave a standing ovation to his emotion-laden speech, in which he summoned Israel to make peace – on PLO terms; this was described by an Israeli as the peace of a graveyard. Yet, once more, the substance for which the Americans had been looking was not there. Arafat had not been able to persuade his colleagues in the PLO leadership – and himself – to utter, clearly and unequivocally, the statement of policy that the Americans had stipulated as the minimum necessary to start a diplomatic dialogue with the PLO. Despairing American well-wishers of the PLO sat through the night with Arafat, imploring him to try again, spelling out word for word what he should say.

Arafat's third attempt was successful. On 14 December 1988, he convened a press conference in Geneva and, evidently well coaxed, read out the magic formula which contained the three concessions that the Americans had demanded. He spoke of his reference in his speech 'to our acceptance of Resolutions 242 and 338 as the basis for negotiations with Israel within the framework of an international conference', and of 'the right of all parties concerned in the Middle East conflict to exist in peace and security, and – as I have mentioned – including the State of Palestine, Israel and other neighbours, according to Resolution 242 and 338'. As for terrorism, 'I renounced it yesterday in no uncertain terms and yet, I repeat for the record, I repeat for the record that we totally and absolutely renounce all forms of terrorism, including individual, group and state terrorism.' Arafat ended his statement with an emotional, 'We want peace. We want peace. We are committed to peace. We want to live in our Palestinian state, and let live. Thank you.'

On the face of it, nothing could be clearer. The Americans announced forthwith that Arafat's declaration had removed the obstacles to a dialogue between them, and shortly afterwards, a jubilant PLO delegation met the US Ambassador in Tunis, Robert Pelletreau. Yet the meeting in Tunis had hardly dispersed when the back-tracking began. Only five days after the Geneva press conference, Arafat was saying to Austrian television: 'I did not mean to renounce terrorism.' All he wanted to do, he said, was to repeat what the Palestine National Council had accepted. The Council had linked its condemnation of terrorism to several previous formulations, which, in effect, severely qualified it.

That was only the beginning. It was soon evident that in the eyes of the more prominent leaders the only decision binding on all PLO factions were those of the Palestine National Council. This should not have been a matter for surprise to the Americans. Arafat's Geneva declaration had been preceded by indignant pronouncements from Palestinian leaders distancing themselves from any concessions on this score. The Palestine National Council had taken a firm stand on this issue, and no one – not even Arafat – was authorized to change it.

On Thursday, 15 November 1988, the day that the political statement was accepted in Algiers, and on which the National Council approved the PLO statement, Arafat's deputy, Salah Khalaf, better known as Abu Iyad, told a Kuwaiti newspaper: 'Acceptance of 242 and 338 does not mean recognition of Israel.' A day later, George Habash, leader of the Popular Front faction of the PLO, made the same point to the *New York Times*: 'I do not regard that the Palestine National Council recognized Israel'. The PLO's 'Foreign Minister', Faruk Qaddumi, went further: 'The entire Palestine National Council is opposed to 242,' he told the Kuwaiti *al-Siyassa* on 19 November 1988. A senior PLO leader emphasized that the PLO covenant, which calls for the destruction of Israel, was still 'the foundation of the PLO's political and militant action', while the Speaker of the Council, Abd el-Hamid el-Sa'ih, declared: 'If you read the political statement carefully, you will find that what some term recognition of the

Security Council's resolutions and consequently recognition of the Zionist entity is untrue.'

Arafat himself never repeated the explicit recognition of Israel he had made at his Geneva press conference, which had brought him a ticket to a dialogue with the United States. It had been a one-night stand. Less than two weeks after Geneva, Arafat was again holding a press conference, but this time under rather different auspices. The PLO executive committee had met in Baghdad on 29 December 1988 to review the political situation after Algiers and Geneva. This time there was no ode to peace; it received no mention in Arafat's statement nor in the decisions taken by the PLO leaders. Israel was mentioned only as the enemy that had to be overcome. There was no hint of the conciliatory assurances Arafat had given in Geneva.

But there was even worse to come. In August 1989, Fatah – Arafat's own mainstream faction in the PLO – held its fifth General Congress in Tunis. The 1,200 delegates approved with acclamation Fatah's 'political programme'. It was vintage PLO of the classic, terrorist period: no mention of 242; no acceptance of Israel alongside a Palestinian state; and no call for peace. Instead, Article 5 of the Fatah Programme called on Palestinians to 'intensify and escalate armed action and all forms of struggle to liquidate the Israeli–Zionist occupation of our occupied Palestinian land'. In Article 4 the Palestinians' inalienable rights were spelt out: 'The right to repatriation, self-determination and the establishment of the state of Palestine on Palestinian soil with Holy Jerusalem as its capital.' Article 13 called for the setting up of a special committee 'to oppose Zionist immigration to our homeland and to assume all cultural, information and political tasks to prevent the arrival of Jewish immigrants into our occupied homeland'. The old anti-Israeli invective, the statements denying Israel's right to exist, the denigrating phrases were back in all their dubious splendour. The PLO leaders were back to square one.

American protests and criticism led Arafat and the Fatah leadership to issue a hasty, revised 'final political statement' aimed at appeasing the Americans: Article 13 on Jewish immigration was omitted; commitment to Arafat's UN speech in Geneva was added; some of the more offensive language was changed. But the original programme was not cancelled or repudiated, and there was no doubt in the minds of anyone that it, and not the sanitized revised version, reflected Fatah policy.

The leaders of the *intifada* understood that this sort of thinking would only strengthen Israel's determination not to withdraw. They may have subscribed to the Fatah resolutions in their hearts, and would doubtless have liked to see Israel disappear, but they were realists. Therefore, they continued to advocate their desire to live in peace with Israel, as a separate, independent Palestinian state on the West Bank and in Gaza.

One of the more prominent of the new leaders in the territories was Feisal el-Husseini. He had all the credentials needed for leadership: he was the scion of the powerful el-Husseini family, whose best-known member in

recent times had been Haj Amin el-Husseini, the notorious Mufti of Jerusalem. Feisal's father, Abd el-Kader el-Husseini, had been one of the
Palestinian commanders in the 1948 war. Feisal himself had spent two years
in administrative detention, a respected school for any would-be leader.
While completely loyal to Arafat and the PLO, he developed his own
outlook which some Israelis found acceptable, despite his insistence on an
independent Palestinian state. 'Our message to the Israelis', I once heard
him say, 'is that we are struggling not to enslave others; our struggle is to
build a state not to destroy other states, our struggle is for the security of
our grandchildren, not to endanger the security of anyone else.'

He gave me his own version of events leading up to the *intifada*:

We were waiting in the territories for the PLO to come to liberate us. Then, in
1982, in the Lebanese War, the PLO leadership was again dispersed. In the
territories we started to ask not why the PLO didn't do this or that, but why are
we not doing this or that. We saw how the PLO was abandoned by the Arab
regimes, we also saw how the PLO succeeded in reuniting itself, and its heroic fight
for eighty-eight days in Beirut. All these things led to the *intifada*.

And, he added, 'the only way to enter the twenty-first century is through
regional co-operation. But first the Palestinian problem must be defused.'
For him the way to do that was to set up a Palestinian state, and the way
to go about it was to convene an international conference. Both the ideas
of a Palestinian state and an international conference in place of direct
negotiations was anathema to the majority of Israelis. Yet it was felt in
Israel that Husseini and other leaders in the territories could become
partners for negotiations, while the diaspora PLO, with its unrealistic
dreams and its avowed aim of bringing about the destruction of Israel,
could not. But before this could happen, Palestinian 'notables', such as
Husseini, would have to learn to say the same things – and mean the same
things – when they spoke to their fellow Palestinians as when they spoke
to their Israeli friends. It was a fundamental matter that could not be
fudged by Husseini. Yet, at the height of Saddam's Gulf offensive in
January 1991, Husseini publicly declared his – and the Palestinians – full
support for Saddam in statements made to British television.

This dichotomy between the local and the diaspora Palestinians persisted
even after the PLO leadership adopted the same public attitude as that of
Husseini and of other Palestinian leaders in the territories. For Shamir,
Rabin and most of the Israeli Government, the distinction was crucial.
Shamir once told me:

If we enter into negotiations with the PLO, the subject of the negotiations will
automatically become the establishment of a Palestinian state in Judea, Samaria
and Gaza. This could be mortally dangerous for Israel. We will be put on the
defensive on a demand that could threaten our very existence. I will never agree to
negotiations with the PLO.

The local Palestinians might be asking for the same thing, but it was
believed in Jerusalem that they, as opposed to the diaspora PLO, would

accept less than their maximalist demands and would agree to a mutually acceptable settlement that would ensure the peaceful co-existence of Israelis and Palestinian Arabs in the territories.

It was this reasoning that led Shamir to make his own peace proposals, directed at the Palestinians in the territories, for a curious consequence of Arafat's 'peace offensive' in Geneva was to pressurize the Government of Israel to meet this seeming challenge with its own precise proposals for peace. The Americans called for it and, more to the point, the Israeli public demanded it. The two streams of thought which dominated Israel's attitude to the Palestinian question in those days, as we have noted, was the yearning for peace even at the price of giving up territory, and the deep-rooted fear that concessions, especially in the form of territory, would weaken Israel and endanger her security.

Most Israelis had long ceased to visit the territories in the way they used to. They were tired of their problems and they would be glad to be rid of them. However, many Israelis feared the consequences of abandoning control over the territories and allowing a Palestinian state to be established. In an opinion poll conducted in 1988, seventy per cent of Israelis questioned believed Jews in Israel would face another holocaust if Israel ever lost a war. There was in Israel a genuine 'angst' regarding security, which was understandable considering the hostility and numerical superiority of the Arab world surrounding it, the number of wars Israel has had to fight, and the hostile world from which so many Jews had fled in order to find security in Israel. The fears, especially regarding the Palestinians, contain psychological undertones, left-overs of a diaspora attitude of the 'we' against the hostile outside world which had been so prevalent among the Jewish people.

Superimposed on these fears exists the ideology of holding on to all of *Eretz Israel*. The fears and ideology feed on each other, creating a formidable obstacle in the path of those many Israelis who wish to come to terms with the Palestinians and are willing to pay a territorial price in order to have peace. These contrasting attitudes were reflected in the National Unity Government; the whole gamut of views was represented, from Ezer Weizman's secret contacts with the PLO to Ariel Sharon's demands that no peace initiative at all be taken before the *intifada* be crushed. Whereas Peres's Labour Party was willing to accept the formula of territories for peace, Shamir's Likud was resolutely opposed to the idea of giving up any part of *Eretz Israel*.

These pressures from within and others from Washington left Shamir with no choice. In April 1989, he was scheduled to meet President Bush and Secretary of State James Baker in Washington and he knew that he could not come empty-handed. His own party stalwarts – Moshe Arens, Dan Meridor, Ehud Olmert, Ronni Milo – were urging him to adopt a plan which the Defence Minister, Labour's Yitzhak Rabin, had proposed for elections in the territories. Shamir agreed after some hesitation and his initiative was adopted by the Cabinet on 14 May 1989. It called for free elections of Palestinian Arabs living in the territories. It was a move frankly designed to separate the Palestinian electorate from the diaspora PLO leadership. Those elected would represent the local Palestinians during an intermediate period of autonomy, after which they would participate in negotiations for a final, political settlement of the Palestinian problem.

Shamir's initiative put new life into the sagging peace process. It was welcomed by the Americans as 'the only game in town'. Peres's Labour Party and Israeli public opinion endorsed it wholeheartedly, while in the territories Husseini and other Palestinian leaders were known to favour the idea. It was left to the extremists in both camps – the diaspora PLO and right-wing Israelis headed by three Likud ministers, Sharon, David Levy and Modai – to do their utmost to undermine Shamir's effort.

The plan for elections had been thrust on a reluctant Shamir. He may have shared the doubt of some of his right-wing Likud ministers who did not believe that this plan could be implemented.

Yet there was an innate logic in the idea of a gradual evolution towards a final settlement; even the more thoughtful Palestinians realized that they could not jump straight from the *intifada* to a Palestinian state. Shamir's plan had, in fact, left all options open, including that of a Palestinian state. This had been the reason why Sharon and his right-wing colleagues had been so opposed to it. But, in the event, Shamir's plan was hamstrung by amendments and constraints that were heaped upon it by all sides.

Shamir himself, uncompromising in his fierce belief that the Jewish people has to stand firm, make no concessions and show no signs of weakness, was not prepared to accept a compromise formula which Secretary of State Baker had proposed by way of elaborating on Shamir's own proposals. Baker wanted to bring together Israelis and Palestinians at a meeting in Cairo to discuss Shamir's ideas for Palestinian elections in the territories. Shamir, however, had reservations about the implications for Israel of Baker's terms of reference for the meeting. In his eyes, these posed serious potential dangers for Israel, and he was prepared to sacrifice the friendship with the United States and his own position as Prime Minister for this conviction that Israel should not risk making concessions to the PLO.

His refusal to accept the American proposals brought to a head the clash of Israel's increasingly polarized political forces. It was, ironically, on the anniversary of the Ides of March – 15 March 1990 – that Shamir's Government was defeated in a vote of confidence in the Knesset after he had dismissed Shimon Peres, the vice-Premier and Finance Minister, from the coalition Cabinet, from which the remaining Labour ministers had then resigned.

The ensuing crisis and confusion emphasized again the stark realities of Israeli politics, the already existing divisions which we have described at the end of the last chapter. However, the two opposing camps overlapped in the centre in their common conviction that there would have to be peace without the PLO. The PLO had totally failed to win Israeli trust and credibility as a partner in the making of a genuine peace; its practice of double-talk, with the simultaneous brandishing of the sword and olive-branch as its symbol, had become the characteristic hallmark of the PLO in Israeli eyes. Even those Israelis who were prepared to talk to the PLO had no illusions about the PLO's peace credentials.

Thus, the hopes for a political breakthrough, which had been engendered by the *intifada*, were fading by mid-1990; the desultory violence of the *intifada* seemed set to continue indefinitely, even if on a reduced level. The Palestinians were unwilling to enter into talks with Israel without the participation of the PLO. However, the PLO remained suspect in Israeli eyes, and when, in May 1990, one of the PLO factions launched an abortive attack from the sea on crowded holiday beaches aimed at taking a maximum number of lives, the PLO also lost its credibility with the Americans; all official contacts between the US administration and the PLO were broken off.

However, before long, more dramatic events were preoccupying our attention and that of the entire region – and beyond: Iraq's invasion of Kuwait on 2 August 1990 and the arrival of tens of thousands of Soviet Jewish immigrants in Israel, which was assuming unimagined proportions. Saddam Hussein's aggressive acts and threats had a profound impact on the Israeli–Palestinian conflict. For a majority of Palestinians in the territories and in Jordan, Saddam was the new – and effective – champion of the downtrodden and the oppressed: the fabled Salah ad-Din (Saladin) and the revered Nasser rolled into one. Scant attention, if any, was paid to the brutal and tyrannical character of Saddam's regime in Iraq, or to the manner of his sacking of Kuwait. His blood-curdling threats against Israel, followed by the launching of Scud missiles on Tel Aviv, breathed new life into the flagging *intifada* and brought lyrical support from Arafat and the PLO leadership for the Iraqi aggressor.

The devastating defeat of the Iraqi forces and the untold misery that the war wreaked upon the Arab populace of Iraq and Kuwait brought home to the Palestinians the awful realization that their hero, Saddam Hussein, was a false prophet, one more would-be saviour unable to deliver. The more ignorant in the territories and in Jordan might still believe the stories of victory emanating from Radio Baghdad, but there was no way of keeping out the truth. The destruction of the Iraqi army jolted the Palestinians into a rude awakening from their dreams.

Meanwhile, the Palestinian economy was seriously damaged by the crisis and by its political fall-out; Saudi Arabia and the Emirates were incensed by Arafat's – and the Palestinians' – support for Saddam. They halted their massive financial backing for the PLO. Kuwait, with her large and well-to-do Palestinian population, had been one of the principal sources of finance for the Palestinians. More than half a million Palestinians had lived in the Gulf countries, almost more than those crowding into the Gaza Strip. Most of them had sent regular remittances to their families in the territories and in Jordan. Tens of thousands of these Palestinian expatriates were sent packing from the Arabian Peninsula, swelling the ranks of unemployed in Jordan and in the territories, and heightening the undercurrent of frustration and despair which had overtaken many Palestinians as a result of the failure of the *intifada* to produce worthwhile results.

The situation in Jordan was, in some respects, even worse than that in the territories. The Hashemite Kingdom had become the 'Sick Man' of the Middle East. Its economy had been in a shambles even before the Gulf crisis and the UN's embargo on trading with Iraq. Jordan's fragile economy had been held together by massive financial aid from Saudi Arabia and the Emirates. However, when King Hussein, the Jordanian Government and the large Palestinian population in the Kingdom aligned themselves demonstrably with Saddam Hussein's aggression, all this massive financial support came to an abrupt end at the same time as the UN blockade effectively shut down the Jordanian port of Akaba, which had been the principal gateway for seaborne supplies to Iraq. The blow to Jordan's economy was further intensified by the compulsory return of the thousands of Jordanians and Palestinians who had been expelled from Saudi Arabia and the other Gulf countries because of Hussein's and Arafat's alignment with Saddam.

As a result, Jordan was treated as a pariah by many Arabs; her King was reviled in Egypt and in Saudi Arabia, Jordan's former principal benefactors. Hussein fared little better in the international community. In vain he sought to explain that he had no alternative, that if he wanted to keep his head on his shoulders he had to be sycophantic to the Iraqi ruler. A combination of Islamic fundamentalists and Palestinian nationalists had hijacked the Jordanian state and its ruler. Hussein could no longer, as was his wont, straddle the fence. Both his Islamic fundamentalist and Palestinian radical constituencies had converged in massive support for Saddam.

It seemed to many of us that we were witness to a replay of events before the Six Day War in 1967. Then, Hussein sailed along with the tide of Nasserist passions which had engulfed his country; as a result, he lost the West Bank of his Kingdom. Once again, in 1990, he felt compelled to gamble, this time to risk his friendship with the United States and his ties with the conservative regimes of Arabia, in order to ride out the swelling pro-Saddam emotions which had swept through his country and which threatened to unseat him.

This danger of a possible collapse of the Hashemite regime was not lost on Israel. Either Iraqi or Syrian intervention on the east bank of the River Jordan would sound the alarm in Jerusalem; so would a Lebanese-like situation with rival factions of Palestinians and Bedouin fighting each other for ascendancy. For many Israelis, the possible 'Palestinization' of Jordan – the Palestinian majority in the country taking over control of the Jordanian Government – was becoming an increasingly attractive solution to their problems with the Palestinians. It was a policy which had been for long strongly advocated by Sharon, and which was becoming all the more appealing as the violence of the continuing *intifada* demonstrated the seeming and growing incompatibility of Israelis and Palestinians living together in mixed co-existence.

A vivid example could be seen in the changing attitude of the leading moderates of the 'Peace Now' movement, who had been urging the Israeli Government to talk with the PLO and to make far-reaching concessions to meet the PLO-sponsored demands of the Palestinians. The wholehearted support of Saddam Hussein by the PLO caused great disappointment in the Israeli peace camp. Following the violent incidents after the riot on the Temple Mount on 8 October 1990 and the indiscriminate individual attacks which followed, the leaders of 'Peace Now' moved into the forefront of a forceful demand for a complete separation of the two peoples in place of the hitherto much-favoured policy of 'meshing' Israelis and Palestinian Arabs. When Israel's Defence Minister, Moshe Arens, temporarily barred the entry of Palestinians from the territories into Israel following a particularly nasty spate of arbitrary killings of individual Jews in October 1990, the move was welcomed by almost the entire Jewish population of Israel. It underlined the increasingly popular desire of most Israelis to be rid of responsibility for the Palestinians and of the territories. It was an elemental reaction to events rather than a calculated policy carefully considered.

However, this very real and growing desire for separation from the Palestinian Arabs was also a mirror reflection of the attitude of the Palestinians. Even so, it might not have taken root in Israel the way it did had it not coincided with a remarkable metamorphosis that was taking place in the Jewish state as the exodus of Jews from the Soviet Union gathered momentum. The handful of Israeli diplomats who were allowed by the Soviets to operate in Moscow in 1990 were working feverishly, seven days a week, issuing visas to the huge numbers of Jews who daily filled Bolshaya Ordinka Street outside the Israeli offices. From every part of the USSR, from even the most remote areas, Jews, who for seventy years had been insulated from any contact with other Jewish communities and whose ties to Judaism were often rudimentary to say the least, were now setting course for the Promised Land.

I visited an area in Uzbekistan less than 100 miles from the Chinese frontier and met a delegation from the 500 Jews in that district. In the presence of the district secretary of the Communist Party, they told me, proudly and defiantly, that within a year almost the entire Jewish community would have left for Israel.

And so it was throughout the Soviet Union and eastern Europe. In the wake of the reawakened traditional nationalist and populist sentiments asserting their influence, Jews found themselves yet again threatened by the insidious anti-semitism which had been latent in, but never eradicated from the lands of eastern Europe, the graveyards of Jews during the Second World War.

The survivors and their children had not forgotten; how could they? They did not need to be clairvoyant to recognize the symptoms and sense the dangers of the revival of what was so delicately described as 'the new populism'. There was nothing for it then, in 1939: Jews had no choice; they had nowhere to go. Now they had a choice. In the winter of 1989 and in the spring of 1990, as the Soviet Union opened her gates, tens of thousands of Jews in the Soviet Union and in eastern Europe began to pack their bags; their destination, Israel.

It had been a largely unanticipated development. It had an explosive impact on Israel, where the whole country geared herself to absorb this demographic revolution of Israeli society. It marked a new phase in the development and evolution of the Jewish state. It overshadowed the political haggling and petty manoeuvring of politicians and confronted them with the necessity of finding work and homes for something like a million newcomers from the Soviet Union. It was the much-needed injection of new blood which Israel had need. Nearly half the total of adult arrivals were university educated or trained.

In a sense this was highlighted by the PLO's and the Arabs' response. For years, Palestinian Arab leaders had pinned their hopes on the seemingly immutable demographic imbalance that was inexorably tilting the population scales in favour of the Palestinian Arabs. It was only a question of time – and not a very long time – so they thought, before the Jewish majority in Israel would be whittled away by the much higher Arab birthrate. Then, suddenly, these hopeful Arab anticipations evaporated as Soviet Jews in their tens of thousands made their way to Israel and transformed not only the demographic imbalance but also the strategic balance in Israel's favour. We had seen it before. In the 1930s the Arab world mobilized worldwide agitation to halt the immigration of Jews seeking refuge in Palestine from Hitler's rule in Germany and Austria. It was the same again in the 1940s, when the Jews escaping from the ultimate consequences of Hitler's 'Final Solution' in Europe, and the remnant who survived it, encountered the sustained hostility of the Arab world in their desperate attempts to find safety in Palestine.

Now, once more, Jews in large numbers were on the move to Israel. The countries of eastern Europe, which had distanced themselves from any association with Israel for so many years, demonstrably resumed diplomatic relations and facilitated the transit of Soviet Jews to Israel, ignoring Arab threats of terror and retribution. This new buoyancy in Israel, as the country braced herself to receive and absorb the newcomers, was not lost on the Palestinians.

However, the need to absorb new immigrants on this scale placed unanticipated demands on Israel's hard-pressed economy. The challenge to find housing and work, and to provide education and acceptable social integration for such numbers – more than 20,000 newcomers every month in the autumn of 1990 – transformed our society. Our perspective was focused not on a speculative distant future but on present pressing realities. It was the equivalent of some three million new immigrants arriving in the United Kingdom in 1991, or fifteen million in the United States. For

Israelis, however, this incredible homecoming of entire communities from eastern Europe and the Soviet Union demonstrated once more the justification of the existence of the Jewish state. The need to provide a home for the newcomers dwarfed all other considerations. Beleaguered by constant Palestinian violence and threats from her Arab neighbours, Israel yearned more than ever for peaceful co-existence with them. We all needed peace if we wanted to master our difficulties and overcome our economic and social problems. And now we had an additional reason for wanting peace; we needed it in order to overcome the problems of absorbing the influx of Soviet Jews.

But peace evaded us, enticing like a mirage, ever far away. There seemed to be no effective way of ending the spiral of violence. Every killing deepened the gulf of hatred dividing Jew from Arab. Yet, as the intermittent and changing violence of the *intifada* dragged on, it must have become evident to the Palestinians that Israel had learnt to live with their uprising. They must have realized how much the *intifada*'s success was, in effect, dependent on its television projection in the world media; but the *intifada* had become stale news, overtaken by more dramatic events in the world.

The violence – and the effective Israeli counter-measures – merged into a routine pattern of stone-throwing Palestinian youngsters and Israeli troops dispersing them with tear-gas. Palestinian casualties dwindled as the Israeli troops made great efforts to avoid provocations and clashes. By the end of 1990, more Palestinians were being killed by Palestinian nationalist and Islamic 'death squads' than by Israelis. Masked gangs were 'executing' so-called 'collaborators', who generally were, at most, Palestinians holding moderate views or critical of the excesses and brutalities of the Palestinian activists. It was evident that the *intifada* could continue indefinitely, causing ever more suffering and hardship to the Palestinians in the territories.

There was, however, no magic formula for the Palestinians to free themselves from Israeli occupation and for the establishment of a Palestinian state. As one of their leading intellectuals put it, 'A Palestinian state will not arrive by registered post; we shall have to work for it and seek to reach it in stages.' It was not, as yet, a popular realism, but there was no other way for the Palestinians. Similarly, there was no way back for the Israelis to the relative tranquillity of the pre-*intifada* status quo so beloved by the Likud. For both of us, Israelis and Palestinians, there remained only the last option – the political process leading to peace.

For the Palestinians this fact was underlined by the defeat of Saddam Hussein. They opted for what they conceived as the ultimate challenge to Israel: Saddam's policy which offered Israel no accommodation, only annihilation – 'incineration'. The Palestinians went along with Saddam, mistaken in the assumption that he was their best hope of ensuring the humiliation and final destruction of Israel. The PLO's President, Yasser Arafat, had encapsulated this policy only days before the crushing defeat of Iraq's armed forces when he proclaimed that he would 'stand with Saddam in the same trench – until victory'. We had assumed that such claims would be disowned by the Palestinian Arabs – our neighbours in the territories whom we had known and respected, men such as Feisal el-Husseini, Sari Nusseibeh and others; they at least would reject Arafat's disastrous leadership along with those Palestinians who had assured us and their friends in the West time and again that they stood for a policy of peaceful co-existence with Israel. However, it was not like that. The Palestinian leaders in the territories seemed to close ranks in their support of Saddam, the PLO and Arafat, and emphasized this when they met Secretary of State Baker in Jerusalem on 14 March, after Baker had urged them to 'dump the PLO'. However, we were aware that there was a groundswell among Palestinians in the territories to have done with the catastrophic leadership of Arafat and the PLO.

For the downfall of Saddam Hussein jolted the Palestinians out of their dreams of Israel's destruction. The basic condition of distrust and hostility of the Palestinian Arabs towards Israel had not changed. The war had, in fact, served only to emphasize this confrontation in the territories. But the Iraqi defeat closed yet another of the options left open to the Palestinians. Out of the wasted extravaganza of Iraq's challenge to the world emerged Baker's 'window of opportunity' to bring peace to our strife-torn region.

But we were not there yet. The spectre of Saddam Hussein still hung over the region long after his defeat. For the Palestinians the lesson of his downfall was plain, though it was difficult for them to absorb. But what was the lesson for us in Israel?

27
Account Rendered: Must Israel Pay?

We entered the Kuwaiti war as non-participating, but involved, spectators, with few illusions about our exposure. We had been told in the politest possible way by the Americans not to intervene or interfere in UN and American plans, and to take no hostile measures against Iraq, lest association with Israel would disrupt the American–Arab UN alliance against Saddam Hussein. We were repeatedly and forcefully reassured by President Bush and Secretary of State Baker, by the British Prime Minister, John Major, and Foreign Secretary Hurd, and by France's President, François Mitterrand, that Israel's security and interests would not be jeopardized by her de facto exclusion from the anti-Saddam alliance. We were not happy with this arrangement because we had never before handed over responsibility for the defence of Israel to another power, not even one so unquestionably supportive as the United States. Even more, we disliked the underlying reasons for this request for demonstrative Israeli restraint. For all the pleasing noises which accompanied our acquiescence, we did not doubt that once Saddam had been expelled from Kuwait, Israel would in no time receive an account for payment due; we did.

Saddam had failed to exact from the United States a policy of linkage with the Palestine question as the price of his withdrawal from Kuwait, but it took no time for the victorious UN allies – Bush, Major, Mitterand and the 'Damascus Eight' (the Foreign Ministers representing Egypt, Syria, Kuwait, Saudi Arabia, Qatar, Bahrein, the United Arab Emirates and Oman) – to promote as a priority the policy of linking the 'settling' of the Palestine question and of the Arab–Israeli conflict with the successful expulsion of Iraq from Kuwait on 3 March 1991, when formal hostilities ceased. Seven days later, Baker was in Saudi Arabia meeting King Fahd, the Emir of Kuwait and the 'Damascus Eight' Foreign Ministers. They all approved the American thesis that peace and regional security were a necessary and good thing. On 11 March, Baker was in Cairo before coming to see us for the first time in Jerusalem. Clearly the Americans were intent on demonstrating to Israelis and Palestinians that they were in earnest and meant business without undue delay, though in the event, when Baker came to Jerusalem on the 11th, he unexpectedly left us with the impression of being a firm, warm and understanding friend.

Baker evidently understood our concern that, if Saddam had succeeded in his intended take-over of Gulf oil and wealth, Israel would have been the ultimate target for his weapons of mass destruction. The major flaw in Saddam's grand design had been the destruction by the Israeli air force in June 1981 of his treasured nuclear plant at Osirak. Had that plant become active, his threat to Iran during the eight-year war, to the Gulf oil states and to Israel would have been such that it would have required counter-measures of a kind that were considered 'unthinkable'.

I was present when the Israeli Cabinet debated whether to authorize the Israeli air force to attack and destroy the Iraqi nuclear plant. It was an agonizing decision. We knew that the plant was about to become active, and to delay action would entail risks of a kind difficult to imagine. Prime Minister Begin had no illusions about the way the world would judge our pre-emptive security measure, but he felt that he could not accept the moral responsibility of allowing the Iraqi regime to obtain the nuclear means that could enable it to fulfil its avowed aim of destroying the Jewish state. Our action was condemned by the UN Security Council and by the US State Department. Iraq was assured that there must be no interference in her nuclear programme. The French Government volunteered to rebuild the sector and the Saudi King offered to pay.

After our bombing of the nuclear reactor, I appeared before a Select Committee of the European Parliament in an effort to explain and justify what we had done and why we had needed to do it. It was to no avail.

Now, in hindsight, we can see that the destruction of the Osirak nuclear plant paved the way for the blocking of Saddam Hussein's effort to dominate Gulf oil and thus blackmail the world. One of the more frightening lessons to be learnt from the rise and fall of Saddam Hussein is the terrible danger of dictators obtaining weapons of mass destruction – biological, chemical or nuclear – and dictating terms for not using them. This potential danger, compounded by the fact that it is becoming progressively easier and less expensive to manufacture these weapons, was one of the prime reasons for the determination of the coalition countries to challenge Saddam's aggression.

But Saddam himself was oblivious to the world's reaction to his deeds. His knowledge of international relations was rudimentary; his experience of the world outside the Middle East was next to nil. He held President Bush and the American people in utter contempt. He interpreted the public debates in the United States on whether to go to war or not as signs of weakness, and believed that the need for the President to obtain Congress's approval showed that he was not master in his own house. He saw the anti-war demonstrations on the CNN news channel, listened to endless debates by pro- and anti-war factions, and became convinced that the Americans were 'soft' and that he had nothing to fear from them. His lack of understanding of democratic procedures was compounded by his own flawed intelligence apparatus, which only fed him with information he wanted to hear. Even after the air strikes against Iraqi military installations began on

17 January 1991, he still believed that the Americans would have no stomach for a ground offensive. If only he could hold out against the aerial attacks, he would be hailed as a hero by the Muslim world and by Third World countries – the underdog who had dared to stand up against the might of the white, infidel oppressors. But it was not to be. His consistent miscalculations led him to his doom.

Ten years after the attack on the Osirak nuclear plant, we were again assessing our security situation. Saddam was no longer the prime threat to our security, but we were still unsure about the Syrians. Secretary of State Baker understood this.

Syria's President Assad with his customary skill had manoeuvred his country into a central position in the Arab anti-Saddam alliance. Egypt needed the Syrian diplomatic figleaf for domestic reasons – and so did the Saudis. Syria's presence in the coalition would help diffuse radical opposition. Assad understood this only too well and was fully prepared to quote his terms and state his price for providing these benefits. He let it be known that one of his conditions for participating in any regional or international conference would be that Lebanon would not appear on the agenda. Bush had on several occasions declared that Lebanon would form part of his all-embracing Middle Eastern peace package. However, Assad was not going to allow anyone to interfere in Lebanon, which had virtually been transformed into a Syrian 'colony', and he made that plain as the post-war offensive gathered steam.

The Syrians had been loath to enter the US-led coalition wholeheartedly. It had not been easy for them to shed their radical clothes and to don the uniform of an ally of the United States. From the onset of the crisis, the Syrians blew hot and cold on the coalition's aims. On 11 November 1990, after a meeting in Cairo of the Egyptian, Saudi and Syrian Foreign Ministers, the Egyptian Foreign Ministry spokesman remarked: 'Syria believes that the Arab forces of the Gulf alliance must act independently and that co-ordination with the United States and other international forces should be confined to a minimum.'

Syria's attitude to the crisis – and to the coalition – was further elaborated on five days later at a festive gathering at Damascus University. A close confidant of the President, the assistant Secretary-General of the Baath Party, Abdullah el-Ahmar, explained that the Kuwaiti affair was only a diversion from Syria's principal preoccupation: the Arab conflict with the Zionists, 'our nation's foremost struggle'. The reason for Syria's intervention in the Gulf alongside the Americans 'was inspired by a desire to mobilize Arab forces against the Zionist danger'. Iraq's withdrawal from Kuwait 'will help us to re-establish Arab solidarity against the Zionist enemy. It will help us also to end the pretext for the presence of American and other foreign forces in the Gulf and to ensure their early departure.'

Syria's Foreign Minister, General Talas, recalled that since the outbreak of the Kuwaiti crisis, Syria had sought 'to confine it within the Arab family and prevent its internationalization'. It was in this context, he said, that

President Assad had met President Bush in Geneva, and that Syria had resumed diplomatic ties with Britain. 'These were important and positive steps by Syria as part of the Arab conflict with the Zionists. Both were taken to serve the interest and cause of the Arab nation,' Talas concluded.

These were no temporary aberrations under the special conditions of war against Saddam. The same attitudes were evident in the wake of the military defeat of Iraq and of Saddam Hussein. The ambivalent position of the Arab members of the anti-Saddam alliance was formalized at the meeting of its eight Arab Foreign Ministers in Damascus on 6 March and incorporated in the 'Damascus Declaration'. Its tone and substance were in stark contrast to what the same Foreign Ministers had told Secretary of State Baker at their meeting in Riyadh a few days earlier about their willingness to support his search for a peaceful settlement which would bring about peace between the Arab states and Israel.

Yet the Syrians were careful to remain within acceptable bounds. They were in dire need of massive aid from the Saudis and they wanted to improve their relations with the United States, for they could no longer rely on automatic support and help from their erstwhile big friend, the Soviet Union. Thus, they received Baker in a warm and friendly manner when he arrived in Damascus on 13 March. In a four-hour session Assad did not close any doors, nor did he reject the notion of a regional conference in which Israel would participate, an idea which had first been floated in 1990 by Prince Hassan of Jordan.

Therefore, despite innate Syrian hostility, Assad listened but did not react to the offer we made to him – a mutually accepted peace settlement within the framework of a regional conference, with no preconditions.

Israelis have never forgotten the formula propounded by Jordan's King Abdullah, who was assassinated in Jerusalem in 1951 by his Arab associates. He had warned Israel and the Palestinians to remember that the Arabs could not make war without Egypt and could not make peace without Syria. It was timely for us to recall that wise old man's advice.

Prospects for an Israeli–Syrian settlement, however, still appeared remote in the spring of 1991. While Baker was in Damascus, Assad let it be known that Syria had forthright opinions concerning the solution of the Palestine question. He did not accept the PLO as a legitimate representative of the Palestinians; if anything, he said, Syria alone was the rightful spokesman for the Palestinians since Palestine was historically part of Syria (see also chapter 24). Assad's statement served to deepen the Palestinians' state of shock caused by the sudden and disastrous ending of the war. The complete collapse of Saddam's much-vaunted war machine, the mass surrender of his troops to the advancing allied forces, together with the stories of torture, execution, pillage and destruction emanating from liberated Kuwait, all had the effect of de-idolizing Saddam Hussein among those who had previously placed him on a pedestal; this was particularly true of the Palestinians.

We could understand that this was not an easy or happy situation for the

Palestinian Arabs. However much their friends, members and supporters tried to rationalize the situation, the PLO had been discredited by its own actions as never before. The Arab leaders of the anti-Saddam coalition were dismissive of Arafat and spoke publicly of encouraging an alternative leadership for the Palestinians in the territories. Saudi Arabia and the other Gulf states had halted their massive financial aid to the PLO, which in 1991 – for the first time in its history – was short of funds, as were the many front and satellite organizations which the PLO had spawned and financed. European politicians who had sought in the past – before Kuwait – to share the limelight with Arafat now stayed in the shadows.

It was particularly difficult for the Palestinians in the territories. Only a small number of the 100,000 who worked in Israel before the *intifada* and the war were still able to find work when the war ended. Heightened security and the great migration of Soviet Jews into Israel had closed the doors to many Palestinian Arabs who had daily crossed into Israel and had no problem finding work. Added to the burden of unemployment were the swelling number of Palestinian Arab refugees driven from Kuwait and from other Gulf countries where they were no longer wanted. Thus, with the *intifada* no longer effective – not even as propaganda – with their leadership discredited and their cause suspected by many Arabs and Israelis, the Palestinian Arabs found themselves in an increasingly desperate situation with no way to turn other than towards a political settlement with Israel.

But the second Gulf war had also taught the Israelis a lesson: that there was no prospect of promoting peace with the Palestinians as long as her Arab neighbours remained hostile and in a state of war with her. The Iraqi Scud missiles which landed in Tel Aviv and Haifa had made this point in an unmistakeable manner. The guns had hardly stopped firing in the Gulf when Israeli intelligence learned that a consignment of improved Scud missiles, with a longer range and greater accuracy than the Iraqi models, was on its way to Syria from North Korea. Moreover, the brutal and ruthless conduct of the Iraqi military in Kuwait – Iraq's friendly Arab neighbour until 2 August 1990 – had not gone unnoticed in Israel. We had no need of undue imagination to conjure up the fate of Israel if she were ever to be overrun by Arab armies.

The sudden end of the war and the dramatic reassessment of the Saddam–Iraqi factor galvanized those most concerned with the war into recognition that there could be an opportunity for a forward move to peace in the Arab–Israeli conflict. In Israel, however, this hopeful outlook was qualified by the well-grounded distrust that, in their haste for a cosmetic solution, the Great Powers and the Europeans might sell Israel short and expose her to dangers which, whatever the circumstances, she was not prepared to accept.

Despite the war-weary Israelis' yearning for peace, Israeli leaders remained cautious. Basically, very little had changed in the Arab world around us; there was still the same hostility, and the same refusal formally to accept Israel and treat with us. Even as Israel considered the American-brokered Arab 'peace overtures', we received reports of fresh Saudi financing of the Palestinian Arab *Hamas* organisation, the most extreme Islamic fundamentalist group in the territories, more so even than the PLO, which rejected reconciliation with Israel on any terms and which spurned every expression of western culture.

Thus, there was no explosion of Israeli euphoria when the war ended. There was plenty of wishful-thinking and of yearning for a peaceful future, but there was no feeling that we were on the brink of peace. In the final analysis and after much hype, the visit to the region by Secretary of State Baker had not yet produced any basic change in Arab attitudes. The Arab demands – their so-called 'peace' – remained unchanged: complete Israeli withdrawal from territories occupied in 1967, including Jerusalem; self-determination for the Palestinian Arabs leading to an independent Palestinian state; and a UN-sponsored international peace conference to formalize these demands and to ensure their implementation.

Against these Arab demands Israel had set out her options for a peace settlement based on direct negotiations with each of the Arab Governments or within the framework of a regional conference, along with free elections for a representative Palestinian authority in the territories. The elections would bring to the fore a new Palestinian leadership with which Israel would negotiate terms for a political settlement between Israelis and Palestinians. This two-track policy became the accepted formula of the United States and of Israel after Baker's visit to Jerusalem in March 1991. But these were starting positions – Arab demands and Israeli options. It was not the first time we had experienced the seemingly impossible gap that divided us. We managed the transition from total deadlock to peace in the case of Egypt – with American help. The circumstances in 1991 were very different, but the need for all parties was just as great – and the American mediator more powerful – than in 1979, and this time there was Soviet support for the peace effort. We need to look ahead, but we also need to remember the past. It is an essential part of our future.

I began this tale of twenty-four years of unrelenting effort to destroy the Jewish state with Brezhnev's war against Israel in 1967, and I have concluded with Saddam's failed war in 1991. During these years we had to overcome seven major wars – attacks designed to bring about our destruction as an independent nation and to eliminate our status as a people in our own state – Israel. In overcoming these assaults, we had to learn – and unlearn – a great deal. It was an education we had to put to the supreme test in the spring of 1991: we had mastered the repeated challenge of war and now had to face the uncharted future of our quest for peace.

Out of violence and hatred, of Jew pitted against Arab, of moderate Israelis and Palestinians in confrontation with their own fanatics and fundamentalists, the one ray of hope was that more Israelis and Arabs were beginning to understand that the road to peace was the only way to avert the certainty of disaster. We had come dangerously close to the brink in January and February 1991.

Like our Arab neighbours, we had to find the answer to the unsolved

315

enigma of history: whether, if you want peace, you have always to prepare for war, or whether in our time, if we really want peace, we must prepare for peace. I believe that it can be achieved, always providing that we can avoid falling victim to false prophets or doctrinaire demagogues, be they Arab or Israel. It is our last option.

A Comment on the Sources

I HAVE HAD FULL ACCESS to the files of my brother Jon, a former correspondent on Middle Eastern affairs for some of the leading international journals and press agencies, accumulated during the period covered by this book. These comprise notes and texts of private interviews, discussions and correspondence with American, Arab, British, Israeli, Soviet, Swiss, United Nations and miscellaneous other politicians, soldiers, government officials and with specialists on the Middle East.

Naturally, I have also drawn on my own experience of some thirty years in government service in Israel and abroad. I have done so within the limits of my obligation as a senior civil servant, to which I have strictly adhered. I am as firm a believer in the necessity of confidentiality in certain aspects of government as I am of the importance of openness where the national interest is not jeopardized. I found that there was no lack of hitherto uncharted material from public and non-governmental private sources to allow me to take a fresh look at our own and other Governments' policies during this period.

In this connection, I found particularly helpful my brother's archive of annotated American, Arab, British and Israeli documents, including texts of the very long but often very revealing Arabic speeches of Arab leaders, and in particular those of Sadat and of the various PLO factions; and texts, speeches, resolutions and decisions at conferences, and confidential background papers prepared by defence establishments and foreign ministries. Of outstanding significance were the annotated monitoring reports of Arab, Israeli and Soviet broadcasts issued daily by the BBC, which, sadly, are no longer as comprehensive and as invaluable as they used to be for most of this period. Even so they remain indispensable.

In addition, there were those memoirs, diaries and informed assessments which were relevant or noteworthy for other reasons, frequently as examples of disinformation or of special pleading.

In fact, during a long life in government service I have not come across another experience quite like the selective presentation of the pre-history of the Yom Kippur War in general and of Soviet–Egyptian relations in particular. There have been other exercises in disinformation in our time, but there have been none that found such widespread acceptance by friend and foe as has the Sadat version of the Yom Kippur War, especially of its preparation and aftermath.

The principal conduit Sadat used as a start for the dissemination of his version of events were two remarkably highly respected journalists, one Egyptian and the other American – Hassanein Heikal, Sadat's Minister of National Guidance and the Editor of *al-Ahram*, the leading Cairo newspaper, and Arnaud de Borchgrave, then Foreign Editor of the American magazine, *Newsweek*. Later, Sadat made use of his major speeches and press conferences to popularize his version of the planning of the war and of his relations and alleged breach with the Soviet Union; many historians of the war accepted Sadat's seemingly authoritative account as self-evident gospel. All the more so, when it was reinforced and elaborated by Heikal's presumed independent and more colourful descriptions. Finally, came the book that told all: Sadat's own memoirs, *In Search of Identity* (London, 1978), so evidently frank and engaging and so totally misleading on major issues, but all the more convincing for the reader because it was quite evident that Sadat had also convinced himself of its accuracy.

Heikal's case was more complicated. He had been Nasser's authoritative spokesman, so much so that some believed that, in effect, Nasser was on many occasions actually giving expression to Heikal's ideas. However, his relations with Sadat were different and more troubled. Sadat resented Heikal's posture of the elder statesman who was the true repository of the Nasser legacy. All the same, on the question of the Yom Kippur War, Heikal toed the Sadat line, sometimes even more effectively than the master himself. His three books about this period span the whole gamut of this relationship. Heikal is always interesting and readable, but he is not always accurate. For one so well-informed about Egyptian affairs, Heikal must have been aware that Sadat was 'shooting a line' in his version of his relations with the Soviet leaders and on other matters concerned with the Yom Kippur War. Yet, since Heikal repeats them uncritically, one must presume that this was in the service of Sadat's disinformation campaign.

Along with Sadat's memoirs, Heikal's writings have become for many the principal source for the diplomatic and military history of the events leading to the Yom Kippur War, and its aftermath. *Sphinx and Commissar* (London, 1978) described the rise of Soviet influence during Nasser's rule and its decline under Sadat, though Heikal believed that the Soviet Union would soon have another chance to restore her Middle East fortunes. Heikal's previous book, *The Road to Ramadan* (London, 1975), had purported to tell 'the inside story of how the Arabs prepared for and almost won the October War'. The book is full of interesting gossip, the accuracy of which has to be taken on trust. But, on a more substantive level, Heikal's account is seriously flawed. The most important shortcoming in all his writing is that he does not understand Israel or the Israelis, and does not want to know. This emerges clearly from the last of his Sadat trilogy, *Autumn of Fury: The Assassination of Sadat* (London, 1983). All pretence of appreciation of Sadat's role in 1973 is abandoned; he had reduced Egypt, the former centre of the Arab world, into 'a centre of nowhere'. And as for Israel, now at peace with Egypt, 'it was a state which came into being on the back of terror' and had started to expand her power into an empire based on blackmail and terror.

Sadly, therefore, I had to exclude Sadat and Heikal as credible sources except where other independent confirmation was available. The same is not true of the memoirs of other Egyptians involved in policy-making at this time, even though every one of them had fallen out with Sadat and was understandably concerned to grind a personal axe. Yet, their memoirs and diaries provide a wealth of important factual source material. In a class by itself is the book by General Saad esh-Shazli, Egypt's Chief of Staff for the two years of preparation for the Suez crossing. He was Sadat's golden boy until he was dismissed after the Israelis had themselves crossed the Canal and turned the scales on the Egyptians.

Shazli's book and diaries are, therefore, suspect as a possible self-serving exercise. However, close examination of the diary, especially for the pre-paratory period from 1971 to 1973, has confirmed at least its accuracy concerning negotiations with the Soviet Union. Shazli's *The Crossing of Suez* (London, 1980), in his words, 'is to the best of my knowledge unique, being the only memoir of its kind by an Arab commander of our generation'. (Since the publication of Shazli's book, two other Egyptian commanders, General Abden Ghani el-Gamasi and Kamal Hassan Ali, have published their memoirs.)

Three other memoirs are by Sadat's Foreign Ministers. The most valu-able of these is Mahmoud Riad's *The Struggle for Peace in the Middle East* (London, 1981). Riad was Foreign Minister from 1964, first under Nasser and then under Sadat, until 1971, when Sadat replaced him with Ismail Fahmy. This book is important because Riad was a good and accurate reporter. When he attended conferences and discussions – especially in Moscow – he more often listened and recorded than talked, something which his successor, Ismail Fahmy, found difficult to accomplish. Despite this shortcoming and his uninhibited and sustained self-justification against Sadat, Fahmy finds it necessary in his memoirs, *Negotiations for Peace* (London, 1983), to quote from documents and confidential discussions to support his theses – and these are often most revealing. When Fahmy refused to accompany Sadat to Jerusalem in November 1977, Sadat appointed Mohammed Ibrahim Kamel, Egypt's Ambassador in Bonn and an associate from Sadat's early terrorist days, as his new Foreign Minister. Kamel was overwhelmed by the unexpected appointment and found refuge and consolation in profuse note-taking. *The Camp David Accords* (London, 1986), his documented account of the activities of the Egyptian Foreign Ministry's intent on undermining Sadat's peace-making attempts before and during the Camp David negotiations, is a unique record, all the more so because of its wholly uninhibited detestation of Sadat, his President and former friend.

The details of the actual negotiations in Moscow are recorded by Riad and Shazli, and reinforced by Egyptian naval records based on research done by the then head of the Egyptian Department of Naval History, Commodore Mohrez Mahmoud el-Hussini. His book, *Soviet–Egyptian Relations, 1945–85* (London, 1987), is a mine of information and rightly commended by the then Egyptian Minister of Defence, Field Marshal Mohammed Abd el-Halim Abou Gazala, for its meticulous attention to accuracy.

The prelude to the Yom Kippur War, the 'War of Attrition' between Egypt and Israel, was no less fortunate in its historians. Lawrence L. Whetten's writings on the War of Attrition during Nasser's last years have not been bettered: *The Canal War: Four-Power Conflict in the Middle East* (Cambridge, Massachusetts, 1974), and more searchingly in the *Adelphi Paper* (No. 128, 1976) published by the International Institute for Strategic Studies on the Great Powers' behaviour in the Arab–Israeli dispute. Indispensable for this period are the volumes for 1968 and 1969/70 of the *Middle East Record*, published by the Shiloah Centre, Tel Aviv University (Jerusalem, 1977); as is Yaacov Bar-Simon Tov's *Myth of Strategic Bombing* (London, 1984).

Two other unusually instructive studies of the Brezhnev years, which do not subscribe to the now fashionable denigration of Brezhnev when he was at the height of his power, are Robin Edmonds's *Soviet Policy: The Brezhnev Years* (London, 1983) and Anatole Shub's *An Empire Loses Hope: The Return of Stalin's Ghost* (London, 1971).

The negotiations for a peace settlement between Egypt and Israel under President Carter's aegis have been massively and contradictorally documented by all the principal participants. Careful analysis of the different emphases has been instructive, especially when set against my private information and interviews to complement the published versions. However, an essential prelude to the Carter period was that initiated by Henry Kissinger. He can rightly claim to have fathered the post-Yom Kippur War developments which led to Carter's peace initiatives. These are fully and fascinatingly described with not too much hindsight by Kissinger himself in his massive two volumes of memoirs, *The White House Years* (London and Boston, 1979) and *Years of Upheaval* (London and Boston, 1982).

Gaps in Kissinger's version of the United States' attitudes to Israel at times of crisis are ably filled by the Kalb brothers' *Kissinger* (Boston, 1974), and by Edward R. F. Sheehan's much neglected account of American policy during these years, *The Arabs, Israelis and Kissinger* (New York, 1976). An indispensable adjunct to these were the contemporary records of Kissinger's public and private pronouncements in my brother's archive, which were particularly noteworthy for their range and frankness, not experienced before – or since – in ministerial briefings; they were often like seminars in depth. Yitzhak Rabin's *Memoirs* (London, 1979) provide a useful and not too discreet Israeli supplement to the Kissinger version.

The contrast with the accounts of the Carter years which followed was striking. Carter himself (*Keeping Faith*, New York, 1984), his National Security Adviser, Zbigniew Brzezinski (*Power and Principle*, London, 1985), his Secretary of State, Cyrus Vance (*Hard Choices*, New York, 1985) and the National Security Adviser for Middle East Affairs, William Quandt (*Camp David – Peacemaking and Politics*, Washington, 1986), tell essentially the same factual story. But the interest lies in their often contradictory emphases and revealing omissions. These are particularly exposed by the Egyptian partner, Sadat's Foreign Minister, Kamel, in the planned American–Egyptian collusion, which is described in our Chapter 7. An even more noteworthy contribution to the role of Carter's advisers at Camp David is the essay by Zahid Mahmood, *Sadat and Camp David Reappraised*, in the *Journal of Palestine Studies*, no. 57, Autumn 1985 (Kuwait and Washington). This essay is based on 200 taped interviews with Egyptians and Americans involved in the peace-making and, sometimes, in the unmaking of the peace process.

The Israeli side of these negotiations is best told by Moshe Dayan's *Breakthrough* (London, 1981) and by Sasson Sofer's *Begin* (Oxford, 1988). Two books of outstanding and lasting value about the Yom Kipper War are Avraham (Bren) Adan's *On the Banks of Suez* (London, 1980), a carefully balanced but not uncritical account of the Israeli conduct of the war on all levels, a model military history; and T. N. Dupuy's *Elusive Victory: The Arab–Israeli Wars, 1947–74* (Fairfax, 1982), a remarkably informative *tour de force*, combining detail and objectivity, which is quite indispensable as a military guide.

Regarding Part 2, Israel's relations with Lebanon, my own intimate association naturally provided many insights, but I am also indebted to my many Lebanese friends who have since kept in touch with me, and have apprised me of events in that troubled country. I have also benefited from my brother's massive documentary records of the Syrian and PLO involvement in Lebanon before the war in 1982, most of which were derived from original PLO and Syrian sources.

Essential background to the conflicting interests is provided by Walid Khalidi's *Conflict and Violence in Lebanon* (Harvard, 1979), which published for the first time the full text of the secret Cairo Agreement of 1969, one of the sources of Lebanon's misfortunes, which virtually gave the PLO a free hand in Lebanon. A more objective assessment is that by David C. Gordan, *Lebanon: The Fragmented Nation* (London and Stanford, 1980). An original and stimulating assessment is Yair Evron's *War and Intervention in the Lebanon: The Israeli–Syrian Deterrence Dialogue* (London and Baltimore, 1987), while Rashid Khalidi's *Under Siege: PLO Decision-making during the 1982 War* (New York, 1986) provides a factual account based on the PLO documents to which he was given access. The special Lebanon issue of the *Middle East Journal*, vol. 38/2, spring 1984 (Washington, DC), gives useful insights into American and Syrian thinking by Jim Muir, Adeed Dawisha and William Quandt. This insight is singularly absent when Israel's case is considered. For a more balanced general background, Kamal S. Salibi's *Cross-roads to Civil War: Lebanon 1958–76* (London, 1976) is informative and perceptive. *Syrian Intervention in the Lebanon* by Naomi Joy Weinberger (New York, 1986) traces Syria's involvement in Lebanon and with the PLO by focusing on the beginning of the civil war in 1975/6 and on the Syrian President's resulting mis-calculation. The story is carried further in books of outstanding quality by three Israeli scholars: Moshe Maoz's *Assad, the Sphinx of Damascus* (London, 1988), Avner Yaniv's *Dilemmas of Security: Politics, Strategy and the Israeli Experience in the Lebanon* (Oxford, 1987), and in Ittamar Rabbinovich's numerous publications on Lebanon and on Syria. Reuven Avi-Ran's *Syrian Involvement in Lebanon 1975–85* (Jerusalem, 1990) gives an excellent insight into Syrian attitudes to Lebanon in the period under review.

For the Iran–Iraq section, I have been able to draw extensively on my personal experience in that region. Here, too, I have to thank many col-leagues in Washington, Paris and London – American, Israeli and Iranians with whom I have consulted. My meeting with Amir Taheeri was as fruitful as reading his books, especially *The Spirit of Allah* (London, 1985), *Holy Terror* (London, 1987) and *Nest of Spies* (London, 1988). The American experience in Iran has been best described by Gary Sick in *All Fall Down – America's Fateful Encounter with Iran* (London, 1985) with a wealth of first-hand knowledge. William Shawcross gives a grim and authentic picture of the mighty fallen in *The Shah's Last Ride* (London, 1989). *The Gulf War* (London, 1989) is authoritatively assessed by Sharam Chubin and Charles Tripp in their invaluable book and in their ongoing separate articles in *Survival*, the bi-monthly magazine of the International Institute for Stra-tegic Studies. A book which sheds more light on the arcane world of Shi'ism in Iran and Iraq and on the emergence of Shi'i fundamentalism in Syrian and Lebanon is *Shi'ism: Resistance and Revolution*, edited by Martin Kamel, with important contributions from Bernard Lewis, Shaul Bakhash, Elie Kedourie, Clinton Bailey and other leading authorities. However, the voluminous literary contribution to the so-called Irangate is surprisingly flawed on detail and frequently distorts facts of which I have first-hand knowledge.

My principal source for the section on our relations with the Palestinians was my personal experience, private and official, with the problems of our relationship over something like twenty-five years. There is no book I know that provides the kind of knowledge acquired from this personal experience and from the benefits of the many contacts and friendships which helped me to understand our basic difficulties. There is, of course, a great mass of custom-tailored published information in books, newspapers and magazine articles. Unfortunately, with some rare exceptions, most of these fall into the categories of pro-Israeli or pro-Palestinian propaganda or dis-information and have had, understandably, only a brief if often much publicized shelf-life. The worst examples of this genre are those written or produced by non-Palestinians and non-Israelis. The exceptions, however, deserve the highest praise; whatever their stance or political orientation, their concern was primarily with information and understanding. Outstanding in this league is *The PLO: The Struggle Within* by Alain Gresh (London and Paris, 1988). The book is appropriately dedicated to Issam Sartawi and Henry Curiel, who were assassinated by their Palestinian 'friends'. They died, says Gresh's dedication, so 'that the Palestinian and Israeli peoples might live in peace'.

The other rarity among publications is the *Journal of Palestine Studies*, published and edited by Hisham Sharabi since 1971, a quarterly magazine that is critically pro-PLO, but invaluable in its documentary presentation of the PLO position. Unfortunately, no comparable journal exists yet in Israel.

I have not dwelt on the numerous, and often extremely valuable, publications in Hebrew that have helped me understand the exigencies of Middle Eastern politics. Israel is a major listening post for events in the Middle East. Her radio, television and press maintain a constant coverage of the region, accompanied by expert commentaries. Sovietologists such as Galia Golan, Middle East scholars such as Shimon Shamir, Moshe Maoz, Ittamar Rabbinovich, Ehud Yaari, Avner Yaniv, Meron Benvenisti and many others provide a wealth of material and comment that enriches anyone in pursuit of knowledge and understanding of the Middle East. I feel indebted to them all, but none more so than to my brother Jon, without whose constant aid, encouragement and guidance this book would never have been written.

Index

This index primarily consists of the main names mentioned in the text. For subjects, please refer to the contents list.